AUGUSTINE AND THE DIALOGUE

Augustine and the Dialogue argues that, contrary to the scholarly consensus, Augustine's dialogues, with their inconclusive debates and dramatic shifts in focus, betray a sophisticated pedagogical method that combines strategies for "un-learning" and self-reflection with a willingness to proceed via provisional answers. By shifting the focus from doctrinal content to questions of method, Erik Kenyon seeks to reframe scholarly discussions of Augustine's earliest surviving body of works. This approach shows the young Augustine not refuting so much as appropriating Academic skeptical practices. It also shows that the dialogues' few scriptural references, e.g. Wisdom 11:20's "measure, number, weight," come at key structural points. This helps articulate the dialogues' larger project of cultivating virtue and their approach to philosophy as a form of purification. Augustine is shown to be at home with pluralistic approaches, and Kenyon holds up the dialogues' methodology as an attractive model for thinking through problems of the liberal academy today.

ERIK KENYON holds a PhD in Classics from Cornell University and since 2012 has taught courses in Philosophy, Classics and Humanities at Rollins College, Florida.

AUGUSTINE AND THE DIALOGUE

ERIK KENYON

Rollins College

CAMBRIDGE UNIVERSITY PRESS

CAMBRIDGE
UNIVERSITY PRESS

University Printing House, Cambridge CB2 8BS, United Kingdom

One Liberty Plaza, 20th Floor, New York, NY 10006, USA

477 Williamstown Road, Port Melbourne, VIC 3207, Australia

314–321, 3rd Floor, Plot 3, Splendor Forum, Jasola District Centre, New Delhi – 110025, India

79 Anson Road, #06–04/06, Singapore 079906

Cambridge University Press is part of the University of Cambridge.

It furthers the University's mission by disseminating knowledge in the pursuit of education, learning, and research at the highest international levels of excellence.

www.cambridge.org
Information on this title: www.cambridge.org/9781108422901
DOI: 10.1017/9781108525558

First published 2018

Printed in the United Kingdom by Clays, St Ives plc

A catalogue record for this publication is available from the British Library.

Library of Congress Cataloging-in-Publication Data
NAMES: Kenyon, Erik, 1980– author.
TITLE: Augustine and the dialogue / Erik Kenyon, Rollins College, Florida.
DESCRIPTION: 1 [edition]. | New York : Cambridge University Press, 2017. |
Includes bibliographical references and index.
IDENTIFIERS: LCCN 2017049387 | ISBN 9781108422901 (Hardback) |
ISBN 9781108435932 (pbk.)
SUBJECTS: LCSH: Augustine, of Hippo, Saint, 354-430. Dialogues. | Dialogue. |
Theology–Early works to 1800. | Philosophy–Early works to 1800.
CLASSIFICATION: LCC BR65.A9 K3955 2017 | DDC 270.2092–DC23
LC record available at https://lccn.loc.gov/2017049387

ISBN 978-1-108-42290-1 Hardback

*For my parents
and grandparents*

Contents

Acknowledgments

I began this book as a doctoral student at Cornell University and finished it at Rollins College as a teacher of the liberal arts. It is the result of much dialogue. I would like to thank first of all my adviser, Charles Brittain, for many hours of close reading and rich conversation. I am also grateful for active committee members, Scott MacDonald and Eric Rebillard, as well as Tad Brennan, who came to Cornell after the project was underway. Aaron Pelttari, Zachary Yuzwa and Jeff Leon joined me in a dissertation writing group. Our lunchtime discussions remain some of my fondest memories of Ithaca. I was fortunate to be teaching assistant to Gail Fine and Fred Ahl, whose quite different approaches helped me become a teacher.

I am thankful for many excellent colleagues at Rollins, especially Lisa "Ryan" Musgrave, Margaret McLaren, Tom Cook, Scott Rubarth and Hoyt Edge. I have also had the rare opportunity to design courses for three different General Education programs. Conversations with Jennifer Cavenaugh, Claire Strom, Meribeth Huebner and Gabriel Berreneche have helped me develop my thinking about education, as has reflection on my own undergraduate teachers at the University of Vermont, particularly Jacques Bailly, Barbara and Robert Rogers, Z. Philip Ambrose, William Mann and Derk Pereboom. I myself have taught all eight of Augustine's dialogues at the undergraduate level. Students of Intro Ethical Theory and Advanced Latin, and seminars on Evil, Skepticism, and Medieval Dialogue have helped me refine my views and answer the toughest question: So what? Many thanks to all of them, in particular Mollie Jones, Alex Earl and Kolten Ellis.

Portions of this work have been presented at the American Philological Association, American Philosophical Association and Oxford Patristics Conference, and I have presented related material at a three-year *De Trinitate* reading group, hosted by Cornell University and the University of Bonn. I am grateful for my "conference friends" Christina Van

Dyke, Emmanuel Bermon, James Patterson, Michael Siebert and Theo Harwood. Particular thanks go to Karin Schlapbach, Isabelle Bochet, Moshe Dahaman, Christian Tornau and Thomas Williams for commenting on drafts of individual chapters and to Peter Osorio for looking over my translations. My dissertation explored only Augustine's earliest dialogues, written at Cassiciacum in 386 CE. This book has doubled both the length and the scope of the original project. My thanks go to Michael Sharp of Cambridge University Press for guiding me through this process and to three anonymous readers for their insightful, rigorous and supportive comments. Beyond my corner of the field, Jessica Evans, Antonia Ruppel and Leigh Harrison have been wonderful companions as we all make our way in the Academic world. And, above all, my thanks go to my partner, Jack Austin, for so many years of loving support, solid hymn playing and ruthless proofreading.

The original impetus for this study stretches back to an Augustine *lectio*, which I participated in from 2003 to 2010. This reading group brought together philosophers, classicists and their graduate students, moving annually between Cornell University, the University of Vermont and the University of Massachusetts at Amherst. Under the kind eye of the late Gary Matthews, we spent a day each year working through a single book, a few pages at a time, before descending on a Chinese restaurant for dinner. The *lectio*'s winding discussions and dozens upon dozens of handouts taught me what it means to love a text. At the end of the day, though, I felt myself lacking a sense of what all the details added up to. This book raises and attempts to answer the basic question: What is Augustine's project in the dialogues? With Augustine studies growing rapidly in several fields, my greatest hope is that the present work will be useful for framing questions and setting details in context. As the readers from Cambridge have demonstrated, portions of my argument will strike some as controversial. I look forward to continuing the discussion.

Abbreviations

Aristotle
EN   *Ethica Nicomachea*

Augustine
C. Acad.   *Contra Academicos*
Conf.   *Confessiones*
De beata v.   *De beata vita*
De imm. an.   *De immortalitate animae*
De lib. arbit.   *De libero arbitrio*
De Mag.   *De Magistro*
De Mus.   *De Musica*
De ord.   *De ordine*
De quant. an.   *De quantitate animae*
De Trin.   *De Trinitate*
Retract.   *Retractationes*
Sol.   *Soliloquia*

Cicero
Acad.   *Academica*
N.D.   *De natura deorum*
Hort.   *Hortensius*
Tusc.   *Tusculanae Disputationes*

Plato
Ap.   *Apologia*
Grg.   *Gorgias*
Men.   *Meno*
Phd.   *Phaedo*

Phdr.	*Phaedrus*
R.	*Respublica*
Smp.	*Symposium*
Ti.	*Timaeus*

Plotinus
| *Enn.* | *Enneades* |

Introduction
Back to the Drawing Board

Come to think of it, I should have mentioned this much earlier: even his ideas and arguments are just like those hollow statues of Silenus. If you were to listen to his arguments, at first they'd strike you as totally ridiculous; they're clothed in words as coarse as hides worn by the most vulgar satyrs. He's always going on about pack asses, or blacksmiths, or cobblers, or tanners; he's always making the same tired old points in the same tired old words. If you are foolish, or simply unfamiliar with him, you'd find it impossible not to laugh at his arguments. But if you see them when they open up like the statue, if you go behind their surface, you'll realize that no other arguments make any sense. They're truly worthy of a god, bursting with figures of virtue inside. They're of great – no, of the greatest – importance for anyone who wants to become a truly good man.

Alcibiades' Praise of Socrates (Plato, *Symposium* 221d–222a)[1]

Augustine's dialogues confront basic questions about the nature and purpose of philosophy. In the process, they develop an approach to philosophical inquiry that is centrally concerned with pedagogy. Their habits of self-reflection advance a project of thinking about thinking, which should resonate with twenty-first-century audiences (Augustine coined the term "*soliloquium*" to describe a dialogue between himself and "Reason"),[2] while their embrace of ambiguity and perplexity is a breath of fresh air for those suspicious of religious and philosophical claims to sure knowledge. Their casts of characters include men and women, children and adults, elites and illiterates, while the works themselves are page-turners akin to a good mystery novel. One of the few times my students have knowingly read

---

[1] Translation from Alexander Nehamas & Paul Woodruff, *Plato: Symposium* (Indianapolis: Hackett Publishing Company, 1989). Unless otherwise noted, all translations are my own.

[2] See *Soliloquia* 2.14 and C.T. Lewis & C. Short, *A Latin Dictionary* (Oxford: Oxford University Press, 1963), *ad loc*. In what follows, references to Augustine's work include book and paragraph numbers but omit the somewhat extraneous chapter numbers. The one exception is *Retractationes*, for which I present all three, given that this work restarts its paragraph numbering each chapter.

beyond a night's assignment was to find out how *Contra Academicos* was
going to end. Ideally, we could simply read these texts, let ourselves get
caught up in them and apply their insights to our world today.

Unfortunately, the last 120 years of scholarship have reduced the dialogues
to a bewildering mess of fragmented ideas. Philosophers, theologians, historians and literary scholars have all engaged in extreme cherry picking: focusing
on individual passages, sentences or even words, while passing over the main
bulk of each text. Nor do specialists from these various fields talk much with
each other. As a result, the scholarly community has come to view Augustine's
dialogues as juvenilia, which rehash the same tired old points, engage in
extraneous exercises, wander off topic, advance flawed arguments, misunder-
stand Christian doctrine and in general fail to attain any substantial literary or
philosophical coherence. If we were somehow to lose all eight dialogues and
had only the scholarship to go on, few would likely mourn the loss. The
picture is particularly bleak for Augustine's earliest dialogues. In the months
following his conversion (386CE), Augustine gathered a community of
family and friends at a villa in Cassiciacum (outside Milan) to pursue
philosophy. The works depicting this community – *C. Acad.*, *De beata vita*
and *De ordine* – have struck scholars as so badly composed that many have
preferred to see them as transcripts of real conversations rather than literary
works of a single hand. Opinions of Augustine's later works such as *De libero
arbitrio* (388–395/6CE) are generally higher, although, to judge by the
scholarship, even that work degenerates from a philosophically rigorous
discussion of the problem of evil to a dogmatic exercise in scriptural exegesis,
with the end having little to do with the beginning. What we lack is a sense of
how each of Augustine's dialogues functions as a unified whole.[3]

It is the contention of this study that, appearances to the contrary,
Augustine's dialogues are literary triumphs of sophisticated philosophy,
truly worthy of a god and bursting with figures of virtue inside. They
engage basic questions about philosophy, education and human life. To
see this, we must go beneath their surface and articulate the philosophical
method and rhetorical strategies that drive each work. By addressing these
basic questions of how the dialogues work and what they are trying to
accomplish, I hope to bring scholarly discussions of them back to the
drawing board. Doing so will help us recognize that Augustine's dialogues,
even the earliest of them, are Platonic in both their outlook and their

---

[3] We may, of course, assume that these works simply do not add up to anything very unified. Against
this assumption, however, I would point out Augustine's advice at *De ord.* 1.2, that if a mosaic looks
unorderly to someone standing too close, then the viewer should take a step back and look again.

caliber. It will also help us recognize the rich resources they provide for contemporary debates on pedagogy, virtue theory, skepticism as a way of life and rational approaches to religion. The dialogues have useful things to say to the liberal academy at large, not just its religious institutions.[4]

Obstacles to a Holistic Reading: Twentieth-Century Scholarship

In one sense, Augustine himself is the source of the obstacles to reviving a holistic approach to his dialogues today. The Cassiciacum dialogues are presented as conversations with the friends, family and students who accompanied Augustine on his philosophical retreat. The works proceed with an extreme realism, to the point of breaking off discussions because the notetaker (*notarius*) is running out of writing space. In 1895 Rudolf Hirzel questioned the dialogues' self-presentation as basically transcripts of actual conversations.[5] Ohlmann replied two years later by defending the works' historicity.[6] With this, the historicity debate was born. In the decades that followed, Ohlmann's arguments were improved by Van Haeringen, while Meulenbroek defended the claim that a *notarius* actually could accomplish the task of recording philosophical conversations as they unfold.[7] The debate reached something of a stalemate with O'Meara, who argued that the claim to historicity was itself a trope of the dialogue genre, and Madec, who argued that generic conventions found in the dialogues reflect the fact that the discussions that actually occurred at Cassiciacum were modeled after the dialogues of Cicero.[8] Along the way, opponents of

---

[4] In focusing on questions of pedagogy, I build and expand upon the work of Ryan Topping, *St. Augustine* (New York: Continuum International Publishing Group, 2010), and *Happiness and Wisdom: Augustine's Early Theology of Education* (Washington DC: Catholic University of America Press, 2012).

[5] Rudolf Hirzel, *Der Dialog, ein literarhistorischer Versuch* (Leipzig: S. Hirzel, 1895), II, 377.

[6] Desiderius Ohlmann, *De Sancti Augustini dialogis in Cassiciaco scriptis* (Strassburg: Argentorati, 1897).

[7] Johann Hendrik Van Haeringen, *De Augustini ante baptismum rusticantis operibus* (Groningen: M. de Waal, 1917); B. L. Meulenbroek, "The Historical Character of Augustine's Cassiciacum Dialogues," *Mnemosyne* 13 (1947): 203–229.

[8] John O'Meara, "The Historicity of the Early Dialogues of Saint Augustine," *Vigiliae Christianae* 5 (1957): 150–178; Goulven Madec, "L'historicité des Dialogues de Cassiciacum," *Revue des Études Augustiniennes* 32 (1986): 207–231. The current scholarly consensus prefers treating the works as basically literary. Foley is a notable exception, although the only grounds he offers for this is "Augustine wouldn't lie" about the works' being records of actual conversations. Michael Foley, *The De Ordine of St. Augustine* (PhD diss., Boston College, 1999). Whatever the status of the future saint's moral character, it seems implausible to me that Augustine himself would have seen engaging in generic practices as lying in the first place. Cf. *De mendacio* 2, where Augustine affirms as obvious that jokes do not count as lies, because no one expects them to be true.

the historicity thesis pointed out that cross-references internal to the dialogues, when combined with later sources' accounts of the dialogues' composition, create problems for situating the works into a single historical progression. In response, defenders of the works' historicity attempted to reconstruct the order of the initial conversations by rearranging the individual books (*libri*) that make up the longer works.[9] The practice became entrenched. Today even scholars who reject the historicity thesis still argue for arranging individual books in a philosophical or pedagogical order other than the one in which Augustine left them.[10] In treating this as an intellectually defensible project, the scholarly community has effectively given up on the idea that each of the longer dialogues might already have some robust structure binding its individual books into a whole.[11]

The scholarly search for points of doctrinal detail in the early dialogues has produced a second obstacle to holistic readings. Augustine is the ultimate source of this problem as well. In composing *Confessiones* (401CE) he takes steps to distance Christianity and Platonism on various points. The dialogues, by contrast, are happy to treat the two worldviews as compatible. These differing attitudes led Prosper Alfaric in 1918 to claim that Augustine's famous conversion was to Neo-Platonism rather than Catholic Christianity.[12] Since then, the period between Cassiciacum

---

[9] *Sol.*, also written at Cassiciacum, presents a conversation between Augustine and Reason, which seems to happen within Augustine's head and is thus left out of this discussion. The question is what to do with *C. Acad.*'s three books, *De beata v.*'s one and *De ord.*'s two. *C. Acad.* 2.1 refers to a "seven-day break from debate" (*septem fere diebus a disputando fuimus otiosi*), which provides enough time for all of *De beata v.* and *De ord.*, while at *Retract.* 1.2, Augustine reports that he wrote *De beata v.* "not after but between the books of *C. Acad.*" (*non post libros de Academicis, sed inter illos*); likewise at *Retr.* 1.3.1, he reports that *De ord.* was written "*inter illos qui Academicis scripti sunt.*" Internal cross-references are provided at *De beata v.* 13, which clearly refers to the debate of *C. Acad.* 1, and at *De ord.* 2.1, which refers to the birthday feast recounted in *De beata v.* Ohlmann gives the order *C. Acad.* 1, *De beata v.*, *De ord.* 1, *C. Acad.* 2–3, *De ord.* 2; Van Haeringen distinguishes between the order in which the conversations occurred, viz. *C. Acad.* 1–3, *De ord.* 1, *De beata v.*, *De ord.* 2, and the order in which their literary accounts were composed, viz. *C. Acad.* 1, *De beata v.*, *De ord.* 1–2, *C. Acad.* 2–3.

[10] Phillip S. Cary, "What Licentius Learned," *Augustinian Studies* 29/1 (1998): 141–163, argues that we should "read Augustine's dialogues the way we read anyone else's," but proceeds to argue for the order *C. Acad.* 1, *De beata v.*, *De ord.*, *C. Acad.* 2–3. Joanne McWilliam, "The Cassiciacum Autobiography," *Studia Patristica* 17 (1990): 14–43, leaves the three dialogues whole but situates them between the two books of *Soliloquia*, which never figured in the historicity debate in the first place.

[11] I take this project, which has no parallel in the works of any other author, to be an artifact of the scholarship that has done more harm than good. I argue in "The Order of Augustine's Cassiciacum Dialogues," *Augustinian Studies* 42/2 (2011): 173–188, for a cross-reference that has gone unnoticed between *C. Acad.* 2.27–28 and *De beata v.* 13–16. The result is that the only viable ordering is the one that does not split up individual works and follows Augustine's review of the set at *Retract.* 1.1–3, i.e. *C. Acad.*, *De beata v.*, *De ord.*

[12] Prosper Alfaric, *L'évolution intellectuelle de saint Augustin* (Paris: Émile Nourry, 1918).

and the writing of *Conf.* has been minutely scrutinized, as scholars attempted to reconstruct Augustine's development or lack of development over the first few decades of his literary career.[13] Peter Brown's biography of Augustine, first published in 1967, has been the most influential statement of the developmentalist reading. According to Brown, Augustine moved from an early "classical optimism" about the capacities of unaided human reason to a "Christian pessimism" about the extent of human sin and the need for God's grace.[14] The most recent round has come with Carol Harrison, who defends a Unitarian reading, arguing that all the elements of Augustine's mature theology are to be found within the early works,[15] and Brian Dobell, who defends Developmentalism, arguing that it was only over the course of several years that Augustine came to appreciate the implications of his own early ideas about Christ, ideas that he would later identify with the Photian heresy.[16] While the dialogues make significant forays into Christian theology, the issues that Augustine would later use to divide Christians from non-Christian Platonists simply do not arise in these works.[17] The end result is a series of somewhat procrustean readings as one of the most active scholarly debates over the

---

[13] On Augustine's sources for Platonism and an attempt to gauge his debt to them, see Charles Boyer, *Christianisme et néo-platonisme dans la formation de saint Augustin* (Paris: G. Beauchesne, 1920); Willy Theiler, *Porphyrios und Augustin* (Halle: Niemeyer, 1933); John O'Meara, "Neo-Platonism in the Conversion of Saint Augustine," *Dominican Studies* 3 (1950): 334–343, and "Porphyry's *Philosophy from Oracles* in Eusebius' *Praeparatio Evangelica* and Augustine's Dialogues of Cassiciacum," *Recherches Augustiniennes* 6 (1969): 107–138; Pierre Courcelle, *Recherches sur les Confessions de saint Augustin* (Paris: de Boccard, 1968); Robert O'Connell, *St. Augustine's Early Theory of Man* (Cambridge, MA: Harvard University Press, 1968); Michele Cutino, "I Dialogi di Agostino dinanzi al *De regressu animae* di Porfirio," *Recherches Augustiniennes* 27 (1994): 41–74. In a related vein, Solignac goes so far as to critique the accuracy of Augustine's knowledge of the pre-Socratics. Aimé Solignac, "Doxographies et manuels dans la formation philosophique de saint Augustin," *Recherches Augustiniennes* 1 (1958): 8–148. For more theologically oriented attempts to critique the state of Augustine's orthodoxy in the dialogues, see Ragnar Holte, *Béatitude et Sagesse: Saint Augustin et le problème de la fin de l'homme dans la philosophie ancienne* (Paris: Études augustiniennes, 1962); Eugene TeSelle, *Augustine the Theologian* (New York: Herder and Herder, 1970).

[14] Peter Brown, *Augustine of Hippo: A Biography* (Berkeley: University of California Press, 2000). See also Robert Markus, *Conversion and Disenchantment in Augustine's Spiritual Career* (Villanova, PA: Villanova University Press, 1989).

[15] Carol Harrison, *Rethinking Augustine's Early Theology* (Oxford: Oxford University Press, 2006).

[16] Brian Dobell, *Augustine's Intellectual Conversion* (Cambridge: Cambridge University Press, 2009).

[17] Explicitly Christian language is almost entirely absent from the early dialogues. At *Conf.* 9.7 Augustine attributes this to his companion Alypius, who saw such language as inappropriate for their philosophical context. Be that as it may, the Incarnation features prominently at *C. Acad.* 3.42. *De beata v.* culminates in an account of the Holy Trinity at 34–35. *De ord.* is centrally concerned with questions of providence, but it is unclear what if anything is specifically Christian about its discussion. *Conf.*, by contrast, revolves around issues of humanity's fallen nature, our need for grace and Christ's role as Mediator.

early dialogues sets them within the preoccupations of a work written over a decade later.[18]

The final obstacle to a holistic reading of the dialogues is that parts of them are simply so interesting in their own right that they distract readers from the larger structures to which they belong. *C. Acad.*, for instance, presents antiskeptical arguments that are regarded as milestones in the history of philosophy.[19] Philosophers thus assume that the goal of the part is the goal of the whole, while those portions of text that do not contribute to this goal – which end up constituting most of the work – are dismissed as so many warm ups and spiritual exercises. Thanks to accidents of history, *De lib. arbit.* has encountered its own special version of this problem. John Mackie's 1955 article, "Evil and Omnipotence," sparked a vigorous debate among a circle of Anglo-analytic philosophers over the problem of evil, which set the agenda for readings of *De lib. arbit.* for the next fifty years. Alvin Plantinga presents the most influential reading of the work's "free-will defense," which he reconstructs using the full resources of contemporary modal logic.[20] Given these philosophers' preoccupations with questions of logical consistency, the more philosophical arguments of books 1 and 2 have been given pride of place, particularly those bits that lend themselves to formal reconstruction, while the scriptural explorations of book 3 are glossed over or ignored. As with the Cassiciacum works, there is no generally accepted sense of how, or even whether, *De lib. arbit.* functions as a unified whole.

This kind of philosophical attention, together with the debates over the Cassiciacum dialogues' historicity and the status of Augustine's conversion, has occupied the bulk of twentieth-century scholarship on the dialogues. Together, these scholarly preoccupations have conspired, however unintentionally, to reinforce an increasingly fragmented view of the works. While Augustine's antiskeptical arguments and theological reflections might be more worthwhile subjects of our attention than Socrates'

[18] It is also worth mentioning Jason BeDuhn, *Augustine's Manichaean Dilemma 1: Conversion and Apostasy, 373–388 C.E.* (Philadelphia: University of Pennsylvania Press, 2010) who shifts the focus of this debate by approaching Augustine not so much as a convert to Platonism or catholicism as an apostate from the Manichees. While BeDuhn provides a useful new perspective on Augustine's biography, he is not interested in making sense of the dialogues on their own terms. From the standpoint of finding a holistic reading of these texts, he merely offers a variant on the standard problem.

[19] For an excellent discussion, see Blake Dutton, *Augustine and Academic Skepticism: A Philosophical Study* (Ithaca: Cornell University Press, 2016).

[20] Alvin Plantinga, "God, Evil, and the Metaphysics of Freedom." In *The Problem of Evil*, ed. Marilyn McCord Adams & Robert Merrihew Adams (Oxford: Oxford University Press, 1990), 83–110.

musings about pack asses and blacksmiths, the same basic point stands: By focusing on what sits on the surface of the text, scholars have stopped asking what bigger project might be at play beneath.

The Way Forward: Recent Scholarship and a Revised Methodology

Over the last ten years, scholars have started turning toward more holistic readings of the dialogues. Catherine Conybeare takes a literary approach, addressing the Cassiciacum dialogues' seeming lack of order by looking to the role of "irrationality" within them.[21] Finding a tension between rational argument and emotional outburst, Conybeare sets concerns for argument to the side and seeks an "emotional logic" as what ultimately gives the texts their unity. In effect, Conybeare simply accepts that these dialogues are bad philosophy and works from there. While this approach has various uses, identifying the holistic structure of a philosophical dialogue is not among them. Simon Goldhill approaches the matter at a more fundamental level by calling into question the modern assumption that dialogue is an open, democratic process carried out between equals.[22] By building on Goldhill's suggestion and holding Augustine's dialogues up to a different set of expectations, we could start working toward a fresh, holistic reading of them. Unfortunately, Goldhill calls modern assumptions into question but offers no clear alternatives to work from.[23] Brian Stock does better on this score.[24] Like Conybeare, Stock sees emotion as the key to understanding

---

[21] Catherine Conybeare, *Irrational Augustine* (Oxford: Oxford University Press, 2006). Her approach is new, in that it is primarily concerned with these texts as texts, and she approaches them in primarily literary ways. TeSelle, *Augustine the Theologian*, while primarily concerned with reconstructing Augustine's theological perspectives and practices, also offers numerous insights into how these texts work as texts. Michael Foley, De Ordine, presents various literary motifs and features running through *De ord.*, although when it comes to explaining how the three dialogues work as a set, he looks beyond the texts themselves, invoking Cicero's dialogues as providing the pre-Christian model to which Augustine gives a Christian reply through a series of "antiphonal-referents."

[22] Simon Goldhill, ed. *The End of Dialogue in Antiquity* (Oxford: Oxford University Press, 2008), 4 and Alex Long, "Plato's Dialogues and a Common Rationale for Dialogue Form," 45–59, in the same volume.

[23] While two essays in Goldhill, *The End of Dialogue*, deal centrally with Augustine, they treat dialogue as a kind of cultural practice and focus on those instances when Augustine did not write literary dialogues, e.g. the Pelagian controversy, rather than those times when he did. See Gillian Clark, "Can we talk? Augustine and the possibility of dialogue," 117–134 and Richard Miles, "'Let's (not) talk about it' Augustine and the control of epistolary dialogue," 135–148. In discussing "Why Christians don't do dialogue," Goldhill himself, 5, acknowledges that Augustine did write dialogues, yet he claims that Augustine "explicitly rejected the form for serious theological undertaking."

[24] Brian Stock, *Augustine's Inner Dialogue: The Philosophical Soliloquy in Late Antiquity* (Cambridge: Cambridge University Press, 2010).

Augustine's works, in particular the petty rivalries that may arise during discussions with others. Stock argues that Augustine's habit of ending dialogues via an uninterrupted speech (*oratio perpetua*) dramatizes the short-comings of "open dialogue" between multiple human individuals and demonstrates the need for "inner dialogue" or soliloquy, which Stock finds in the *orationes* that conclude six of Augustine's eight dialogues. In this, Stock is one of the few scholars to offer a holistic reading of the dialogues that finds a clear motivation for the entirety of each text. Yet, so far as I can tell, Stock's characterization of the works' discussions and concluding speeches simply does not fit the texts very well. For reasons that will become clear in the chapters to follow, I take Stock to be asking the right question but giving the wrong answer.[25] Ryan Topping has made further headway, using the dialogues to reconstruct Augustine's pedagogical theory.[26] While Topping's interest is in pedagogy, he raises issues at the heart of what the dialogues are up to. Yet Topping follows a certain scholarly narrative, grounded in a certain reading of *Conf.*, that pits Christianity and Academic skepticism against each other in ways that sit ill with key portions of the dialogues, especially *C. Acad.*'s closing suggestion that the Academics weren't really skeptics but dogmatic Platonists in disguise (see later in this chapter).[27] Joseph Pucci likewise looks to the pedagogical project of the Cassiciacum dialogues, focusing on characters' attempts to "recuperate" classical authors such as Virgil for philosophical uses. While this approach provides useful context for *Conf.*, it merely scratches the surface of Augustine's project at Cassiciacum.[28] Simon Harrison, finally, presents *De lib. arbit.*'s three books as pursuing a single, graded course, intended to lead readers gradually into Augustine's ideas about the human will.[29] In terms of holistic readings, this is a great improvement on existing scholarship, as it uncovers a single overarching project for this work. His analysis is, however, tied up in the details of this particular text. It is thus unclear what bearing Harrison's reading of *De lib. arbit.* has on Augustine's other dialogues or, for that

---

[25] See Chapter 5.

[26] Ryan Topping, *Happiness and Wisdom: Augustine's Early Theology of Education* (Washington DC: Catholic University of America Press, 2012).

[27] For a focused example, see Ryan Topping, "The Perils of Skepticism: The Moral and Educational Argument of *Contra* Academicos," *International Philosophical Quarterly* 49/3 (2009): 333–350.

[28] Joseph Pucci, *Augustine's Virgilian Retreat: Reading the* Auctores *at Cassiciacum* (Toronto: Pontifical Institute of Medieval Studies, 2014). See my review in *Augustinian Studies* (forthcoming).

[29] Simon Harrison, *Augustine's Way into the Will: The Theological and Philosophical Significance of* De Libero Arbitrio (Oxford: Oxford University Press, 2006).

matter, what bearing Augustine's other dialogues have on Harrison's reading of this one.

There is much more that could be said about all of these studies. Yet if we limit our scope to the problem of providing holistic readings of the dialogues, then Conybeare sidesteps the problem; Goldhill asks the right questions but without answering them; Stock, Topping and Pucci provide answers, just not the right ones; Simon Harrison makes progress but does not engage with the entire corpus. This is the current state of the scholarship.[30] In order to make real progress toward a holistic reading, we must first move out of the corner that twentieth-century debates have backed us into. This study's methodology is designed to pursue this end. In what follows, I respond to the existing debates and propose ways around the obstacles they pose for a holistic reading.

The debate over Augustine's conversion and to a lesser extent the historicity debate are both concerned with recovering "Augustine's view" on various matters. My considered response to both debates is that I simply don't care what the man himself thought. In one sense, that is merely to say that I am not writing an intellectual biography after the manner of Brown's. Still, in making their primary object of interpretation "Augustine," the historical individual, whether at a certain point or over the whole of his career, historians and theologians have managed to avoid making sense of difficult passages within their immediate contexts. My focus, thus, will not be on what Augustine *thinks* as a historical individual, but on what he *does* as an author: how he arranges the various components of his works to pursue greater ends. To avoid the pitfalls of existing scholarship, I will be studiously ignoring *Conf.* and what it has to say about Augustine's early life. I will begin by attempting to make sense of the Cassiciacum dialogues on their own terms.[31] This, in turn, provides a

---

[30] If this seems somewhat bleak, I should stress that the present survey is focused on obstacles to holistic readings. That is not to say that good work is not being done on other questions. For an overview, see the commentaries of Fuhrer, Simon Harrison, Schlapbach and Trelenberg listed in the bibliography.

[31] It is, of course, impossible to compartmentalize one's thinking completely: In all likelihood, my reading of the dialogues is in various ways colored by my understanding of *Conf.* Yet my argument at no point depends on evidence from *Conf.*, and I do not treat agreement with *Conf.* as a *desideratum*. The connections between *Conf.* and the dialogues are, of course, numerous: If anything, my focus on method shows more connections than the normal focus on points of doctrine does. While I do not explore those connections here, I hope that readers of *Conf.* will find the present study useful for approaching that later work in new ways. In a similar vein, I make use of *Retract.* in the process of reconstructing the never-written third book of *Sol.* from its sketch, now known as *De immortalitate animae*. While my reconstruction is in accordance with *Retract.*, it does not depend on it.

context for approaching Augustine's later dialogue, *De libero arbitrio*, though here too my reading should be judged primarily by how well it makes sense of that text in its own terms.

When it comes to philosophical cherry picking, we need not replace current discussions of specific passages, so much as set them within broader questions of philosophical method and the overarching argument of each work. Following the example of Vlastos' work on Socratic elenchus and Benson on Plato's method of hypothesis,[32] I will focus on these broader questions and engage individual arguments only insofar as doing so helps us address these broader questions. The philosophical payoff of setting the part within the whole, in some cases, is a fresh perspective on what individual arguments are meant to accomplish. This is particularly true for *De lib. arbit.* The work's free will defense has been carefully scrutinized during the debate sparked by Mackie in 1955. Yet at the turn of the twenty-first century, Marilyn Adams declared the "generic theism" of the twentieth-century debate a dead end and called for a turn to the particulars of lived religious traditions for conceptual enrichments.[33] In this, she sets a new agenda, one as concerned with explanatory power and flexible resources as with formal rigor and airtight proofs. Accepting this new agenda, I suggest that *De lib. arbit.*'s combination of philosophical argument and scriptural exegesis is ripe for reconsideration.

In keeping with both this approach to broad argument and the literary turn of the last ten years, I prefer readings of the dialogues that can attribute a clear motivation to *every* part of a text. When it comes to works such as *De ord.*, which starts with a discussion of providence and ends with Augustine laying out a curriculum of liberal arts study, we must move beyond questions of particular content to find the single thread running through a work. Malcolm Heath's discussion of textual unity in classical Greek literary theory provides a useful point of departure.[34] Drawing on ancient literary criticism and works such as Plato's *Phaedrus*, which yokes discussions of love and rhetoric, Heath contrasts modern assumptions about literary unity, which tend to focus on thematic content, and ancient conceptions of a text as an organic whole whose various parts serve some

---

[32] Gregory Vlastos, "Socrates' Disavowal of knowledge," *Philosophical Quarterly* 35 (1985): 1–31. Hugh Benson, *Clitophon's Challenge: Dialectic in Plato's* Meno, Phaedo, *and* Republic (Oxford: Oxford University Press, 2015). I discuss these works in Chapter 2.

[33] Marilyn McCord Adams, *Horrendous Evils and the Goodness of God* (Ithaca: Cornell University Press, 1999).

[34] Malcolm Heath, *Unity in Greek Poetics* (Oxford: Oxford University Press, 1989), especially chapters 1, 2 and 9.

common *telos*. While these two conceptions of literary unity overlap to a degree, applying modern assumptions to ancient works can lead to rather superficial readings. Current scholars, for instance, usually connect *De ord.*'s two halves insofar as one explores the "order" of providence and the other explores the "order" of study. This is not, however, very useful for making sense of the text, and most scholars conclude that *De ord.* is simply not very well unified. To go deeper we must reframe our questions. As Heath concludes:

> On this account there is no reason at all to expect a dialogue like *Phaedrus* to have a single theme. For Plato's conception of philosophical discourse is not dominated by the idea of exploring a given theme but (as we have seen) by that of achieving through a broader discussion which may range widely over different themes a certain end – instilling virtue or promoting philosophical understanding ... The appropriate structure of philosophical discussion is: whatever an ideally skilled teacher (Socrates) would say to such-and-such a person in order to instill virtue or promote understanding.[35]

In this spirit, I would ask: What is the *telos* of each of Augustine's dialogues?

Finally, I insist that we must stop assuming, as nearly everyone does, that Augustine saw the Academic skeptics as the enemy. The standard narrative, which is loosely based on *Conf.*, is that Augustine started out with the Manichees, left them for skepticism, got depressed and eventually came around to Platonism and/or catholic Christianity. While many scholars would see this as an oversimplification, nearly everyone who discusses Augustine's encounter with Academic skepticism treats it as an obstacle, whether to faith in Christian Scripture, fruitful philosophical inquiry or even a course of liberal arts study.[36] While details vary, all present skepticism as something to be refuted, overcome and set aside as quickly as possible. For understanding the early dialogues' stance on Academic skepticism, I maintain that we need to take seriously what the early dialogues have to say about it. The picture that emerges from *C. Acad.* bears little resemblance to the standard narrative. In particular, Augustine's closing suggestion that the Academic skeptics were really dogmatic Platonists in disguise needs to be revisited. Judging simply by what the text says, Augustine does not refute so much as appropriate the Academics' skeptical practices for his own purposes. I take this passage to be Augustine's way of articulating his own philosophical method, which he has pieced together out of Platonist and Academic sources, while situating

---

[35] Heath, *Unity*, 26.   [36] See Chapter 1 for my review and response to each position.

his own project within the tradition of Plato as a philosopher and author of dialogues.

In sum, this study will:

(1)   Seek to understand the dialogues themselves not their author's views
(2)   Focus on overarching argument and rhetorical strategy instead of individual passages, while treating explanatory power and intellectual flexibility as valuable philosophical contributions on par with formal proof
(3)   Prefer interpretations that make sense of a text as a whole, recognizing that identifying a common goal, rather than mere thematic unity, may best serve this end
(4)   Ignore later accounts of Augustine's attitude toward skepticism, including *Conf.*'s

By invoking these four methodological strategies, I will attempt to approach the dialogues with fresh eyes. Doing so will help us articulate the philosophical method and rhetorical strategy that provide the basic shape of each work.

The picture that emerges is of works centrally concerned with the practice of inquiry. When it comes to finding guidance, the dialogues look foremost to the act of inquiry itself: The fact that we can inquire at all tells us various things about ourselves. By reflecting on our own act of inquiry, we are put in a position to improve how we go about inquiring. From this basic idea, Augustine works out a method consisting of three main stages. An initial impasse gives rise to debates that fail to reach any definitive conclusion; these failures, in turn, expose the shortcomings of debaters' various assumptions and modes of thought. Yet each work moves beyond perplexity (*aporia*),[37] as Augustine reflects on these debates as instances of rational activity. From these reflections, he draws various conclusions about human nature as a way of expanding his interlocutors' stock of self-knowledge. On the basis of such perplexity and self-discovery, he then takes a great leap to various "big picture" theories that he presents as plausible (*probabile*), i.e. richly explanatory without being proven true. These conclusions explain what came before by exposing the problematic assumptions that led to *aporia* and by integrating self-reflective discoveries within larger theoretical frameworks. Each work thus moves through three

---

[37]   While Augustine does not use the Greek term, *aporia*, I have adopted it as a term of art from the Socratic tradition that Augustine claims to be operating in. Chapter 2 explores this somewhat convoluted pedigree.

stages: (A) aporetic debate, (R) reflection on the act of debating and (P) the revelation of a final plausible conclusion. By applying this basic framework, ARP, we may see how the flawed arguments and shifts in topic that have so frustrated scholars actually contribute to the broader project of each work. Augustine himself presents ARP as a pedagogical method pursued by the Academic skeptics: The teacher conceals his own views and "un-teaches" (*dedocere*) his students' assumptions to prepare them for initiation into the philosophical "mysteries" (*mysteria*) of Platonic Intellectualism.[38] The shift from aporetic debate to reflection on debate, finally, is marked in each work by the shift from dialogue between characters to *oratio perpetua*. In this way, the dialogues' basic philosophical method explains the characteristic shape of Augustine's dialogues, and provides a clear purpose to their closing *orationes*.[39]

The Cassiciacum Dialogues and *De libero arbitrio*

So far, I have talked about the unity only of individual dialogues. It is my considered opinion that the three "scenic dialogues"[40] from Cassiciacum – *C. Acad., De beata v., De ord.* – as well as Augustine's inner dialogue, *Sol.*, are meant to form a unified set. By approaching each work as an application of ARP, we may articulate the two schemes that Augustine used to bind this set. The plausible accounts that conclude the first three are built around a set of key phrases: *C. Acad.* addresses the question of whether wisdom can be found, and concludes that it can be, provided one is guided by the "dual weight of reason and authority" (*gemino pondere ... auctoritatis atque rationis*);[41] *De beata v.* asks what it takes for a human being to attain happiness and concludes that the human mind must conform itself to Christ as the "Measure of the Soul" (*modus animi*);[42] *De ord.* addresses issues of providence, asking what makes the world good for human beings, and concludes that the apparent disorder of everyday experience invites human beings to seek the underlying unity of things, as a first step in turning toward "Unity" as the first cause of everything.[43] These phrases

[38] *C. Acad.* 3.38.
[39] I defend this reconstruction of Augustine's method in Chapter 1 and apply it to the dialogues throughout.
[40] Which is to say that the conversations presented in these works are set in particular places at particular times. Bernd Reiner Voss, *Der Dialog in der frühchristlichen Literatur* (Munich: W. Fink, 1970), 197, coins the term "*szenisch Dialog*" to differentiate *C. Acad., De beata v.* and *De ord.* from the rest of Augustine's works in this genre. See Chapter 4 for discussion.
[41] *C. Acad.* 3.43. [42] *De beata v.* 30–35. [43] *De ord.* 2.47–48.

bring together the various threads running through their respective works, thus binding each dialogue into a unified whole. They also neatly correspond to Wisdom 11:20, "You [God] have ordered all things in measure, number, weight." Since explicitly scriptural language tends to be reserved for these final conclusions, the overall effect is that Christian Scripture, which Augustine presents as being in accordance with Platonist philosophy,[44] provides solutions to Hellenistic problems drawn from Cicero. Reading Augustine's dialogues as applications of ARP reveals how these three works form a set devoted to protracted reflection on the scriptural triad: measure, number, weight. At the same time, this reading underscores the centrality of the classical virtues to these works: *C. Acad.* is ultimately a study of wisdom; *De beata v.*'s discussion of happiness turns on questions of moderation; *De ord.*'s inquiry into providence exposes assumptions that are basic to any account of justice.

These two schemes, founded in Scripture and virtue theory, in turn, provide a framework for situating *Sol.* within the Cassiciacum set. While written at the same time and within the same general intellectual horizons, this final work sets aside the villa setting of the other three as well as Augustine's role as teacher of his family and friends. Here, Augustine takes a position as student at the feet of Reason, whom he engages through inner dialogue. *Sol.*'s position as similar yet different to the other dialogues – something akin to John's relation to the synoptic gospels – is mirrored in the mismatch between Cassiciacum's two organizing schemes: On the one hand, *Sol.* completes the set by turning to the last of the classical virtues, courage, which it approaches by asking whether the soul survives death. Yet rather than looking to Wisdom 11:20, which Augustine has already worked through, *Sol.* takes the Pauline virtues of 1 Corinthians 13:13 as its scriptural point of departure and constructs complete "rounds" of ARP around the theological virtues of Faith and Love. The sketch for its incomplete third book, now known as *De immortalitate animae* (387CE), finished the project by devoting multiple rounds, or perhaps "sub-rounds" to Hope. By approaching the combination of *Sol.* + *De imm. an.* as an application of ARP, I argue that we can carve the text at joints that both reflect Cassiciacum's broader explorations of Scripture and virtue theory, while providing a framework for seeing how *Sol.* and *De imm. an.* advance a single overarching project.[45]

---

[44] *C. Acad.* 3.43.
[45] In terms of uncovering the basic argument of each work, the application of ARP to *Sol.* + *De imm. an.* is the most ambitious step in my reading of the Cassiciacum works. I argue for it at length in Chapter 5.

The reading I sketch here brings us back to the drawing board. With this accomplished, we may turn with fresh eyes to the question of how each work builds upon the last. In terms of content, the dialogues' plausible conclusions provide a series of sketches, each filling out details of the last: *C. Acad.* suggests that wisdom can be found by using intellectual, as opposed to empirical, means; *De beata v.* spells out the implications of this for the pursuit of happiness; *De ord.* explains that the world is good for humans insofar as it invites us to engage in inquiries that will advance that pursuit. *Sol.* then dramatizes what happens when one accepts such an invitation in the right way. The cumulative result of all this is a progressively more detailed outline of a Christian-cum-Platonist worldview.

The dialogues' originality sits not so much in the content of the worldview they propose as in the pedagogical program through which students are drawn into it.[46] We can judge the progress of this pedagogical program by watching Augustine's teenaged students, Licentius and Trygetius. The first three works present them gradually putting aside immature desires to win debates as they come to embrace perplexity and follow arguments wherever they lead. In the process, they take on habits of self-reflection, allowing them to think about themselves and their place in the world in progressively more sophisticated ways. That is to say, they get better at thinking via ARP. *Sol.*, in turn, presents an advanced student in the figure of Augustine himself. This difference in pedagogical level is reflected in a structural progression across works: while *C. Acad.*, *De beata v.* and *De ord.* pursue one round each, *Sol.* pursues multiple rounds or even rounds within rounds. Because of this, the works plot a trajectory of sorts, as the processes that constitute ARP are internalized, expanded and adapted in an ever-more advanced approach to inquiry.

I suggest that *De libero arbitrio* operates at a level of sophistication that is comparable to the Cassiciacum set in its entirety. Presenting a discussion of evil with Augustine's friend, Evodius, each of its three books presents a full round of ARP, though book 2 varies the method by presenting three little *orationes*, each of which presents a different element of the book's plausible conclusion. Unlike the Cassiciacum works, scriptural language is brought to the fore. The clearest example is book 3's protracted discussion of Genesis, which Augustine uses to construct a plausible Christian account of why God

---

[46] The rhetoric of the dialogues presents this worldview as something Augustine reveals rather than creates. Given his early project of finding commonalities between Platonism and Christianity, he may, however, be inventing more than he cares to admit. For questions of Augustine's doctrinal accuracy, see the studies cited earlier.

permits evil to exist in our world. In terms of method, *C. Acad.* looks to
Hellenistic philosophy and the Platonist tradition; *De lib. arbit.* looks to Isaiah
7:9, which in the translation Augustine had available read, "Unless you
believe, you will not understand," to present its conversation as an exercise
in "faith seeking understanding."[47] These scriptural preoccupations may
appear to represent a break from the more philosophical orientation of the
Cassiciacum dialogues. I resist this appearance by tracing the use of ARP in
both and arguing that *De lib. arbit.* provides a natural next step along the
methodological trajectory set by the Cassiciacum works. If we move beyond
superficial differences between the works' scriptural and philosophical language, we find that Augustine's Isaiah actually outdoes the Academics at their
own game, as his contrast between "faith" (i.e. in something we take to be true
while lacking certainty of it) and "understanding" (i.e. something that has rich
explanatory power) pulls apart two different meanings that were fused in the
Academics' single term "plausible" (*probabile*).

While each of the Cassiciacum dialogues is built around a classical
virtue, *De lib. arbit.* continues the project by incorporating a new theological virtue: piety. As with the earlier works, I argue that *De lib. arbit.*'s
concern for this particular virtue provides the key for identifying the single
project binding the work's three books into a single whole. According to
De lib. arbit., piety is a reality check, calling individuals to be thankful for
what they have been given while not shirking responsibility for their own
shortcomings. Augustine presents piety as the correct attitude for anyone
looking to Scripture for answers about life's big questions. I argue that the
"philosophical" discussions of books 1 and 2 offer a preparation for the
"scriptural" exegesis of 3, by refining the set of questions on the table, by
enriching the conceptual vocabulary with which Evodius thinks about evil
and, just as importantly, by instilling in Evodius (and by extension the
works' readers) a pious outlook with which to approach Genesis.

In what follows, I focus not so much on the dialogues' conclusions as on
how each work gets to them. With the back and forth of the Develop-
mentalist/Unitarian debate, scholars lost track of the fact that even those
who reject some or all of Augustine's conclusions can draw much of value
from the methods he uses to present them. That said, certain details of the
dialogues may present stumbling blocks for readers who do not keep
Augustine's broader doctrinal context in mind. Like Plato, Augustine sets
his works in a world of fallen souls. In Plato, the soul's preexistence

---

[47] *De lib. arbit.* 1.4. Augustine takes this from the phrase, "*Nisi credideritis, non intellegetis*," which is,
in fact, a mistranslation of the Hebrew. The original says something closer to "Unless you believe,
you will not stand firm." The Vulgate gives, "*si non credideritis non permanebitis*."

underpins its ability to recollect knowledge from former lives.[48] This process begins with perplexity[49] and leads to recollection of forms.[50] In some cases, this perplexity is tied to erotic love (*eros*) and it is through experience of beauty of bodies, character and knowledge[51] that the soul "heals its wings" and rises again to take its place among the gods feasting on Truth.[52] While that may be a lot of metaphysics to bite off, the basic Platonist commitment here is the idea defended by Cicero in *Tusculanae Disputationes* 5 that the individual already has everything he needs to be happy.[53] To this extent, Augustine is fully in line with Plato: The Cassiciacum dialogues sketch an account of the world and the soul's place within it that lays bare the way back to happiness through knowledge of Truth/God. The details of this account might be a bit less pagan: *Smp.*'s pederasty with its focus on beautiful bodies (i.e. of young men) gives way to *De Musica*'s exploration of poetic meter culminating in an account of *caritas* as the lynch pin of all Creation; *Phaedo*'s gods who feast on the Truth give way to *De beata v.*'s Christ who is the Truth; and *Meno*'s recollection of already learned truths gives way to *De Magistro*'s account of the Inner Teacher, Christ, who illuminates the mind, thus sidestepping the need to claim the soul's preexistence, which is something Augustine had trouble deciding on;[54] even *Tusc.* 5's basic claim is challenged, or at least historicized, as Augustine suggests that human individuals need Christ to heal their souls of the ignorance and trouble that resulted from Adam's sin. Given these changes, should we consider Augustine a Platonist? A Christian Platonist? A Christian rather than a Platonist? I suggest that it doesn't much matter. In approaching Platonism more as a set of moves, as captured by Augustine's ARP, rather than a body of doctrine, I hope to have captured an element of Platonism that is directly applicable today: its teaching methods. If, while working through Augustine's works, we find that Augustine uses Platonic methods to draw conclusions that depart from orthodox Platonic doctrine, then why should we not engage in the same intellectual dance, engaging in Augustinian *aporia* and self-reflection as a way of reaching whatever conclusions strike us as most plausible today? To my thinking, the flexibility and

---

[48] Plato, *Men.* 81.   [49] Plato, *Men.* 82a–86c and *R.* 523c.

[50] Plato, *R.* 502c–518d and *Phd.* 72e–77a.   [51] Plato, *Smp.* 203b–212c.

[52] Plato, *Phdr.* 246a–257a. Questions of how, if at all, accounts from these different dialogues of Plato may be combined can and have filled several books. Matters are further complicated by the fact that Augustine's access to Plato's thought was likely mediated via works of later figures such as Cicero and Plotinus. Chapter 2 looks in detail at how Platonic method may have made its way to Augustine via these authors. Chapter 4, in turn, discusses Augustine's account of beauty against the backdrop of Platonic theory.

[53] My thanks to anonymous Reader A for suggesting this neat summary.

[54] See *De lib. arbit.* 3.70.

wide-ranging resilience of this method, rather than the doctrinal unity of its proponents, is the lasting value of the Platonist tradition.

Overview of Study/How to Use This Work

I have taught all the dialogues discussed here at the undergraduate level. In my experience, students find the dialogues' combination of philosophical sophistication and literary flare to be immediately engaging and consistently rewarding objects of critical scrutiny. At a time when online courses, "practical majors" and standardized tests threaten to overwhelm today's Academy, the dialogues' reflections on the purpose and nature of education provide college students useful food for thought. In short, the dialogues should be more widely read and taught. To this end, the present study is designed to be used in two ways. On the one hand, each chapter builds on the last, tracing Augustine's use of a certain method for writing dialogues, as it developed from *C. Acad.* to *De lib. arbit.* At the same time, each chapter can be read as a standalone piece accompanying a particular dialogue. By giving each dialogue's overarching project and setting that project within current discussions on a range of issues, I hope to provide a useful companion to the dialogues for first-time readers and seasoned scholars alike.

Chapters 1–6 are dedicated to giving a holistic reading of the Cassiciacum dialogues, both individually and as a set. This is by nature a somewhat circular undertaking, as our understanding of a whole rests on our understanding of its parts, while we cannot help but understand those parts in light of our understanding of the whole. That said, not all circles are vicious, and while it might be inappropriate to expect deductive clarity from a project such as this, we may still judge interpretations based on their ability to explain how a wide range of parts create a whole.

When it comes to questions of method, *C. Acad.* is rich enough to warrant two chapters. Chapter 1 looks to this first work of Augustine's extant corpus to establish ARP as the method Augustine himself pursues in writing dialogues. This chapter is central to my project. I suggest that Augustine advocates a kind of Christian skepticism, which is attractive in itself and a milestone in the history of philosophy as a way of life. In the revisionist history that closes *C. Acad.*, Augustine claims a Platonic pedigree for his method. Scholars have mostly ignored this claim for the simple reason that Augustine likely never read much Plato firsthand. Be that as it may, Augustine's dialogues bear striking similarities to works such as *Men., Phd.* and *Smp.* In Chapter 2, I explore the Platonic pedigree of Augustine's method by focusing on works of Cicero and Plotinus that we can be confident he did read. Both figures drew key, albeit different, methodological and rhetorical elements from Plato. I argue that Augustine, a rhetorician turned philosopher, was able to reassemble these pieces into something close to their original whole. The preoccupations of these intermediaries and their developments on their Platonic model help explain the peculiarities of Augustine's approach, such as his concluding *orationes*. Chapter 2 contributes to the larger study by setting out a methodological history of the ancient dialogue and situating Augustine within it.

While *De beata v.* lacks the explicitly Academic skeptical terms of *C. Acad.*, I argue that the work's opening "philosophical" discussion of desire satisfaction and closing "theological" account of the Trinity's role in human psychology advance a single round of ARP. The cumulative effect is that Christian theology provides a plausible explanation for various easily observed features of human moral psychology. Chapter 3 thus looks to *De beata v.* for a compatibilist position, bridging the gap between rational and religious approaches to ethics. While this position is similar to the one more famously advanced by Aquinas, Augustine's skeptic-cum-Platonist approach lacks Aquinas' Aristotelian epistemology, which contrasts reason and religion as alternative sources of first principles. In my eyes, this makes Augustine's version more attractive, while the dialogue's short length and mostly nontechnical writing make it a more practical option than Aquinas for entry-level courses in ethics.

Chapter 4 traces a single thread through *De ord.*'s opening discussion of providence and its concluding *oratio* on liberal study. In attempting to connect the two halves of this work, scholars typically construe Augustine's suggestion in terms of the *content* of study (viz. knowledge of geometry, rhetoric, etc.) as necessary for understanding the providential structure of the world. Against this, I argue that what Augustine finds useful here is the *act* of study. The liberal arts are formalized versions of natural human activities; by engaging in liberal study and then reflecting on the process, we may come to a greater degree of self-knowledge, which, in turn, will help move the project of understanding providence forward. On my reading, the world is good for human beings insofar as experiences of apparent disorder move us to look for deeper unity, thus setting us on a road that may bring us to the characteristically human good of knowing Unity itself, which Scripture identifies as God. The world, in effect, is God's classroom. The dedications of the scenic dialogues are centrally concerned with questions of providence. Having set out *De ord.*'s account of providence, I suggest how each dedication situates its work within the bigger picture of providence, education and happiness.

De ord. presents the earliest extant statement of the medieval *trivum* (grammar, dialectic, rhetoric) and *quadrivum* (music, geometry, astronomy, arithmetic). Scholars typically see this as setting out Augustine's program to write dialogues on each of the seven liberal arts. In the remainder of Chapter 4, I use the one surviving work, *De Mus.* (387CE), as a model for this subgenre of the "disciplinary dialogue."[55] While this is the only one of Augustine's dialogues to lack a concluding *oratio*, I argue that the shift from *De Mus.* 1–5's thinking about poetic meter to book 6's inquiry into the elements of human psychology that allow us to think about poetic meter betrays a single course of ARP. I argue that *De Mus.* shows us Augustine engaging most fully with the theoretical underpinnings of Platonic approaches to education. In *Phdr.* and *Smp.*, it is the experience of beauty that rouses the fallen soul, through *eros*, to recollect the Forms. The purpose of *De Mus.* 1–5, I propose, is to rouse similar delight: first at the actual sound of poetry, then at intellectually understanding what makes these sounds delight the ear. This delight, in turn, anchors the more theoretical discussions of book 6, and its culminating account of *caritas*' role in Creation. To judge from this one example, the disciplinary dialogues pursue a project of thinking about thinking. This emphasis on self-knowledge and metacognition provides a fresh perspective on the value of the liberal arts, while sidestepping the conflicts between content and marketable skills that dominate current discussions of curricula.

Chapter 5 takes up the task of reconstructing the overarching argument that binds *Sol.* and *De imm. an.* into a single whole. My reading depends on treating the combined work, *Sol.* + *De imm. an.*, as part of the Cassiciacum set. As a working hypothesis, I assume that this last dialogue from Cassiciacum employs ARP in an exploration of the last of the classical virtues, courage, which Augustine structures around scriptural cues. The fit is imperfect. So far as I can tell, *Sol.* + *De imm. an.* moves through three rounds of ARP, not one, and structures them around 1 Corinthians 13:13's "faith, hope, love" rather than Wisdom 11:20's "measure, number and weight." Nevertheless, the work's concern with death is clearly relevant for questions of courage, while the differences between this and Augustine's other Cassiciacum works may be explained by looking to the particular cast of characters, Augustine and Reason, who are operating at a more advanced level than Augustine's human companions. Its intricate reflections on the soul, truth and purification provide a kind of sequel to Plato's *Phd.* and will be of use to more advanced readers and those interested in Augustine's dialogues as a corpus.

[55] Augustine abandoned the project after completing only two works and proceeded to lose one of them. A text survives that some have identified as Augustine's original sketch for *De Dialectica*. Evidence for this attribution is, however, slight. For discussion see Belford Darrell Jackson, *Augustine: De Dialectica* (Dordrecht: D. Reidel, 1975).

Having worked through the four Cassiciacum works individually, in Chapter 6 I use Augustine's slightly later dialogue, "On the Soul's Greatness" (*De Quantitate Animae*; 388CE), to frame the set's distinctive approach to cultivating virtue. Arguably the most obscure of Augustine's dialogues, this short work starts with the question of soul's spatial extension (*magnitudo*), proceeds through heavily aporetic debate to conclude that the question was ill-formed, restates the main question in terms of the soul's power (*vis*) and concludes with an *oratio* spelling out the soul's seven grades of activity. This betrays the Platonist idea, most clearly articulated by Plotinus and Porphyry, that virtues come in grades:

(1) Civic Virtue = living well in the world on the world's terms
(2) Kathartic/Purifying Virtue = turning from embodied life to something higher
(3) Contemplative Virtue = intellectual contemplation of God/Truth

Philosophy occupies a middle position in this scheme, as a form of purification, an exercise in kathartic virtue meant to turn individuals from everyday perspectives to a more sophisticated way of looking at things. This process is grounded in critical scrutiny and self-reflection, and its ultimate end is the vision of God, i.e. contemplative virtue. Language drawn from mystery cult is scattered throughout the Cassiciacum dialogues, beginning with *C. Acad.*'s presentation of aporetic debate and self-reflection as types of "purification." In terms of reconstructing the dialogues' central project, I argue that *De quant. an.* provides a kind of capstone to the set, as Augustine makes explicit the mode of kathartic philosophy he has pursued throughout these earlier works.[56] What's more, I suggest that the fusion of Classical and Christian virtue presented here and in the Cassiciacum set goes beyond the Aristotelian preoccupations that tend to dominate current discussions of virtue theory and deserves attention in its own right.

Having argued that Augustine's earliest dialogues pursue a kind of Christian Platonism devoted to developing kathartic virtue, I turn to the worry that in *De lib. arbit.* Augustine is engaged in a fundamentally different project. In Chapter 7, I argue that piety provides the key to understanding both how *De lib. arbit.* functions as a unified whole – though many scholars doubt that it does – and how it develops the methodology set out years

---

[56] As a capstone, *De quant. an.* both rests upon and links together what came before. While I have attempted to make each chapter of this work stand on its own, Chapter 6 is best suited to pairings with chapters preceding it. The argument is, to some extent, cumulative, and in the notes of Chapters 1–5, I point out threads that are taken up again in Chapter 6.

before in *C. Acad.* Augustine presents piety as an attitude, in which individuals think of God in the highest terms possible, thank God as the source of all goods and take responsibility for their own shortcomings. According to Augustine, this is the necessary attitude for anyone looking to Scripture for answers to life's big questions. I argue that the discussions presented in *De lib. arbit.* 1 and 2 contribute to the larger whole by instilling a pious attitude in Augustine's companion, Evodius, in preparation for book 3's attempt to reconstruct a scriptural response to the problem of why a just God would permit the evil in the world around us. Each book, meanwhile, advances its own course of ARP as Evodius' questions about evil are progressively sharpened and his self-knowledge refined. While the work is more overtly scriptural in its language, I suggest that its method of "faith seeking understanding" is an outgrowth of, rather than a break from, *C. Acad.*'s Platonic method, ARP. *De lib. arbit.* has much to recommend it. Book 1's account of temporal and eternal law gives a powerful tool for thinking about a wide range of moral questions and deserves a place in our ethical toolkits alongside the categorical imperative and the greatest happiness principle. Book 2's proof of God's existence is equally powerful, though on my reading it is intended to prove the existence of only a generic highest being and, in turn, to make plausible the existence of the God described in Scripture. Its exploration of piety brings philosophical depth to a virtue seldom considered in contemporary philosophical discussions. Its emphasis on explanatory power over certainty, finally, and its use of rational scrutiny and self-reflection to guide one's reading of Scripture provide an attractive model for how to adhere to a religious tradition within our own pluralistic society.[57]

At the end of the day, ARP is not a rubric that Augustine rigidly adheres to, but a characteristic way of approaching problems that he adapts and

---

[57] The one notable exception from this study is *De Magistro* (389CE). This dialogue between Augustine and his son, Adeodatus, is massively important when it comes to content. Its debate presents an extended treatment of semiotics, which builds on and preserves aspects of Stoic theory, and its *oratio* presents a theory of Christ as the Inner Teacher, which was of central importance throughout the Medieval period. *De Mag.* is not terribly noteworthy, however, when it comes to philosophical method or literary form. A discussion of signs raises an *aporia* about how learning is possible; reflection on that discussion shows that learning is possible; an account of Christ as the Inner Teacher provides a plausible resolution to what came before. If anything, the work's one round of ARP represents a methodological step backward from the innovations of *Sol. + De imm. an.* and *De Mus.* Given that *De Mag.*'s epistemological themes pair nicely with *C. Acad.*'s, I suggest that anyone interested in my take on *De Mag.* should read Chapter 1. The application to *De mag.* should be clear enough. See also Herman J. Cloeren, "St. Augustine's *De Magistro*, a Transcendental Investigation," *Augustinian Studies* 16 (1985): 21–27, whose analysis of *De Mag.*'s "transcendental argument" focuses on what I am referring to as the work's self-reflective turning point.

expands as his works take up new challenges. By tracing the dialogues' progressively more sophisticated approach to method, we may enrich our own understanding of their genre's characteristic approach to teaching and take away habits of thought. My Conclusion suggests ways that the dialogues may prove useful for thinking about twenty-first-century problems, particularly those involving the purposes and nature of higher education.

As a final note, Gary Matthews once told me not to be one of those people who says everything there is to say about a subject and leaves nothing for other people to do. In attempting to read each dialogue as a whole, my goal is to spark discussion, not to bring it to a close. My attempt to bring things back to the drawing board takes issue with basically all existing scholarship. Yet my real goal is simply to bring about a shift in perspective, to free new and useful work from the brambles and preoccupations of last century's debates. The ultimate contribution of this study is to get a handle on how Augustine uses the dialogue as a vehicle for philosophical inquiry and the cultivation of virtue. There is much more to be said about the rich and varied material that Augustine uses to pursue this basic project. Through numerous seminars, conferences and reading groups – many with Gary himself – I have found Augustine's philosophical works to be of a caliber that, the harder you press them, the more they give you in return. If there is a final word on any of the dialogues, it lies beyond my intellectual horizons.

CHAPTER I

The Pursuit of Wisdom
Contra Academicos

Augustine begins the first work of his new career by letting his students do the talking. Following the model of Cicero some four centuries earlier, he had left the city for the suburbs and a period of philosophical "leisure" (*otium*), in this case at a friend's villa at Cassiciacum outside Milan. While Cicero's dialogues present such periods of villa-bound *otium* as a break from the "business" (*negotium*) of running the state, Augustine takes on the pursuit of wisdom as a full-time calling and has assembled a ragtag community including his young son, elderly mother, illiterate cousin, friend Alypius and two teenaged students. It is these last two who are given the floor for all of *C. Acad.* 1. The topic under discussion, as befits this new beginning, is the pursuit of wisdom, in particular the Academic skeptical claim that one may be happy in searching for the truth without ever finding it.[1] Trygetius, a budding poet just returned from military service, argues that this is impossible; Licentius, the bright yet headstrong son of Augustine's patron, Romanianus, defends the skeptical position.[2] Once their debate takes off, Augustine and Alypius, who is also present, step back to let the young men hash it out. While Augustine presents himself as opposing the skeptics, he seems more pleased with Licentius' performance than Trygetius'. In the work's dedication to Romanianus, Augustine goes so far as to hold up the son for his father to imitate.[3] While Augustine and Alypius take a more active role in the work's later books, Augustine's choice, as author, to devote all of book 1 to his students' conversation speaks volumes about him as a teacher and the kind of philosophy he is engaged in at Cassiciacum. Today, professors' lectures often provide material for later discussion sections. Augustine starts by figuring out his students' perspectives and works from there. We should

---

[1] For discussion, see Karin Schlapbach, *Augustin* Contra Academicos (vel De Academicis) *Buch 1: Einleitung und Kommentar* (Berlin: De Gruyter, 2003), 67–116.
[2] *C. Acad.* 1.4. [3] *C. Acad.* 1.4.

not, however, infer from his hands-off approach that he lacks a plan. He has a quite elaborate plan for this "lesson," one which provides for the various moves his students might make as they explore a problem. The trick is that he does not reveal this plan until the very end. To do so earlier would have overwhelmed his students, who were not ready for the big picture. What's more, it would have spoiled all the fun.

Surprisingly, scholars have failed to recognize the good pedagogy on display in *C. Acad.* 1. This is largely due to the preoccupations of twentieth-century scholarship. Historians and theologians have been interested in determining *what* Augustine thinks, not *how* he presents those thoughts.[4] Philosophers are somewhat better in this respect, yet in approaching this work as Augustine's refutation of skepticism, they tend to focus on "arguments" in the sense of premises leading to a conclusion, rather than the broad strategies that bind all those individual collections of premises and conclusions into a single overarching project. As a result, book 1 is most often passed by as a mere "exercise," a perhaps helpful but unnecessary "warm up," to the real discussion that follows.[5] Meanwhile, the century of scholars who have taken *C. Acad.* to be the transcript of a real conversation have kept anyone from worrying about this lack of a holistic reading. This problem is self-perpetuating: the failure to find any robust structure to the work supports the historicity thesis, while the historicity thesis, in turn, undermines any impetus to find a robust structure. What's worse, this line of thought simply assumes that conversations between real people cannot be structured in robust philosophical ways. This is simply a failure of imagination. Not all teaching proceeds by lecture, and it is perfectly possible for a teacher who knows both his subject matter and his students to create situations where students drive the discussion yet arrive at a place the teacher foresaw but the students didn't.[6]

In what follows, I argue that standard readings of *C. Acad.*, which see refuting Academic skepticism to be the work's ultimate goal, fail to produce a

[4] See Introduction for discussion.
[5] For *C. Acad.* 1 as a "school exercise," see Joanne McWilliam, "The Cassiciacum Autobiography," *Studia Patristica* 17 (1990): 14–43; Carol Harrison, *Rethinking Augustine's Early Theology.* For *C. Acad.* 1 as "protreptic" in a way that the rest of the work is not, see Cary, "What Licentius Learned"; Pierre Valentin, "Un Protreptique Conservé de l'Antiquité: Le '*Contra Academicos*' de Saint Augustin," *Revue des Sciences Religieuses* 43/1 (1969): 1–26. Topping, "Perils of Skepticism," and Cary, "What Licentius Learned," have called attention to the work's argument in the broader sense and recognized it as a pedagogical project. Yet their readings invoke assumptions about Augustine's attitude toward the Academic skeptics that, at best, fit only portions of the text. As a result, no scholar has told a coherent story about how *C. Acad.* works as a single, unified whole.
[6] For instance, the most effective way I've found to teach Plotinus' idea of the One as cause of all things is to challenge students to think of something that is not somehow "one."

viable reading of the text as a whole. Instead, I suggest reading *C. Acad.* as a study of pedagogical method, one whose relationship to Academic skepticism is more complicated than existing scholarship admits. Approaching the work this way will allow us to articulate the single project running through the whole of the text and to show the contribution made by book 1's young debaters to that project. To this end, I begin with a review of existing scholarship. From here, I set out *C. Acad.*'s overarching project and then situate the work's various parts within it. Given that *C. Acad.* reads a bit like a mystery novel, what follows is effectively a series of "spoilers." To anyone who has not yet read *C. Acad.* from cover to cover, I suggest thinking twice about the experience you would cheat yourself of by first reading what I have to say.

The Standard View: *C. Acad.* as a Refutation of Academic Skepticism

Book 1 of *C. Acad.* opens with a dedication to Romanianus and proceeds to Licentius' and Trygetius' debate over the skeptical thesis that one can be happy in seeking the truth without actually finding it. It is unclear who wins. Book 2 opens with a second dedication to Romanianus and moves forward as Licentius asks for more information about the Academic skeptics. Augustine and Alypius respond by presenting a conventional history of the Academy, which I will refer to as the work's "public history." This sets the stage for Augustine's argument against the Academic practice of following "plausible" (*probabile*) or "truthlike" (*ueri simile*) impressions without prior knowledge of any "true" (*uerum*) ones. All four characters debate this thesis for the rest of the book, yet they still reach little consensus. Licentius and Trygetius step back in book 3, leaving Alypius to defend the Academics against Augustine, though Alypius eventually bows out as well, leaving Augustine to complete the work via an "uninterrupted speech" (*oratio perpetua*). He starts this speech by attempting to capture the Academics in a dilemma, proceeds to offer numerous counterexamples to the Academics' claim that knowledge is impossible and takes a second pass at the Academics' use of plausible impressions. Yet, having refuted the Academics' skepticism on two fronts, Augustine ends with a "secret history" of the Academy, suggesting that the Academics were not really skeptics but dogmatic Platonists in disguise. Philosophical studies of *C. Acad.* typically assume the work to be a refutation of Academic skepticism and then set out to identify which part of the work's three books accomplishes this task. Given that no scholars look to book 1 for *C. Acad.*'s central argument, let us turn to book 2's conventional history of the Academy, which provides context for the antiskeptical arguments that follow.

Book 2's debate opens as Licentius asks for "the entire view of the Academy" (*totam Academicorum sententiam*) so that he can better defend their cause.[7] Augustine complies by presenting the Academic skeptics as engaging in four basic practices,[8] and Alypius sets these practices within a broader falling out between Plato's Academy and the first Stoics.[9] The combined narrative provides the basic content for standard readings of the work's main argument. According to their joint presentation, the Academics begin by adopting Zeno's Stoic definition of the cognitive impression[10] as one which, (a) is true, (b) is impressed from what is the case and (c) could not have been impressed from what is not the case (*...id uerum percipi posse, quod ita esset in animo inpressum ex eo, unde esset, ut esse non posset ex eo, unde non esset*).[11] According to this third criterion, (c), an impression fails to be cognitive if there is even the possibility that a state of affairs other than the one portrayed may have brought about an impression with the same content.[12] The Academics use this criterion to argue that cognition is impossible, since for any impression, even if that impression is true, it is always possible that an impression with the same content could be produced by an optical illusion, divine possession, madness, dreaming, etc.[13] The Academics use the impossibility of cognition, in conjunction

---

[7] *C. Acad.* 2.10.

[8] *C. Acad.* 2.11–12. The term "skeptical" is used by neither the New Academics nor Augustine. Sextus Empiricus is our first attested source. He uses the term *"skeptikos"* to denote a seeker after truth in opposition to a "dogmatist," who considers himself to have found the truth, and what we might call a "negative-dogmatist," who holds that the truth cannot be found (*Outlines of Skepticism* 1.33). Sextus claims that followers of his own Pyrrhonean school *are* skeptics, while the New Academics are negative-dogmatists. See Gisela Striker, "On the Difference between the Pyrrhonists and the Academics." In *Essays on Hellenistic Epistemology and Ethics* (Cambridge: Cambridge University Press, 1996): 135–149. I will use the term "skeptic" merely to denote those who argue that knowledge has not been (or perhaps cannot be) found by current means and therefore recommend that one refrain from holding any belief.

[9] *C. Acad.* 2.14–15.

[10] Zeno uses variations of the Greek verb "to grasp" (*katalambanō*) to refer to this idea. Augustine uses Latin equivalents coined by Cicero: *percipio, comprehendo*. In the absence of a good English equivalent, I will follow Anthony Long & David Sedley, *Hellenistic Philosophers* (Cambridge: Cambridge University Press, 1987) in reserving "cognition" and its cognates for this technical sense, i.e. a "cognitive impression" as one that can be grasped and "cognition" as the epistemic state that results from assenting to such an impression. Since the verb "cognize" makes for cumbersome prose, I will reserve "grasp" for the act of assenting to a cognitive impression.

[11] *C. Acad.* 2.11.

[12] For discussion of Augustine's use of Zeno's criterion, see Therese Fuhrer, "Das Kriterium der Wahrheit in Augustins *Contra Academicos*," *Vigiliae Christianae* 46 (1992): 257–275.

[13] Augustine lists these scenarios within a general list of the kinds of examples the Academics would use to challenge claims to knowledge: "Thus disagreements between philosophers, errors of the senses, dreams and fury, fallacies and sophisms all flourished in service of this cause." (*Inde dissensiones philosophorum, inde sensuum fallaciae, inde somnia furoresque, inde pseudomenoe et soritae in illius causae patrocinio uiguerunt*). *C. Acad.* 2.11.

with the Stoic definition of error as assent to the incognitive, to argue that it is irrational ever to assent to any impression. And in reply to the Stoic "inactivity" (*apraxia*) argument that a person who never assents to anything would be rendered completely inactive, the Academics argue that one may perform actions by approving impressions as "plausible" (*probabile*) or "truthlike" (*veri simile*) without assenting to them as true (*verum*).[14] To put it briefly, the Academics:

(1)   Adopt Zeno's definition of the cognitive impression
(2)   Argue that cognition is impossible
(3)   Argue that assent is always irrational
(4)   Approve *probabilia* as a means of performing actions.

Each of these four practices is discussed at length within *C. Acad.*[15] As a result, the work presents several different discussions of Academic skepticism, each of which has been held up by scholars as presenting *C. Acad.*'s "definitive refutation." Therese Fuhrer focuses on Augustine's argument at *C. Acad.* 2.16 that the Academics could not identify *veri similia* without prior acquaintance with *vera*.[16] Blake Dutton focuses on a series of dilemmas at *C. Acad.* 3.18–21, which Augustine bases on the supposedly cognitive status of Zeno's definition itself.[17] Gareth Matthews looks to *C. Acad.* 3.21–29 for Augustine's list of candidate cognitive impressions

---

[14] The English term "probable," the French "*probable*" and their cognates prove to be false friends: the Stoic/Academic notion of *probabile* is closer captured by "plausible," i.e. something worthy of belief. Any sense of likelihood is an artifact of translation. See Miles Burnyeat, "Carneades Was No Probablist," (unpublished); Richard Bett, "Carneades' Distinction between Assent and Approval," *Monist* 73/1 (1990): 3–20; James Allen, "Academic Probabilism and Stoic Epistemology," *Classical Quarterly* 44 (1994): 85–113. Failure to make such distinctions has led to great confusion in studies of *C. Acad.* See most especially Bernard J. Diggs, "St. Augustine against the Academicians," *Traditio* 7 (1951): 73–93.

[15] I have formulated this list in terms of practices in order to avoid complexities that are not relevant for the present undertaking. It is unclear whether the Academics themselves endorsed Zeno's certainty criterion or the impossibility of cognition and irrationality of assent, which, they argue, follows from it, or simply presented all of this material dialectically in an *ad hominem* attack against Stoic theory. Either way, the Academics do *use* this criterion and they do *argue* for these conclusions. By approaching Academic skepticism in terms of *practices*, we capture what it is about Academic philosophy that is most relevant to the big project of *C. Acad.*, viz. their way of going about philosophical inquiry and their characteristic method, which, in turn, employs various assumptions, arguments and commitments. This is clearest when it comes to the Academics' use of *probabile* impressions: There is no particular set of impressions that the Academics identified as *probabile*; it is rather the practice of using such impressions, whatever they may be, that is characteristic of their school.

[16] Therese Fuhrer, "Der Begriff *veri simile* bei Cicero und Augustin," *Museum Helveticum* 50/2 (1993): 107–125.

[17] Blake Dutton, "Augustine, Academic Skepticism, and Zeno's Definition," *Augustiniana* 53 (2003): 7–30.

taking the form of logical necessities, mathematical truths and first-person statements of subjective states.[18] Christopher Kirwan presents a critical appraisal of all these passages and finds each lacking.[19] John Heil, David Mosher and Brian Harding share in this general appraisal of what they have dubbed *C. Acad.*'s "epistemological arguments," and they proceed to argue that the work's real refutation of the Academics comes in what they see as the "moral argument" of *C. Acad.* 3.34–36.[20] John O'Meara, Ragnar Holte and Matthias Smalbrugge go further. Declaring all such arguments failures, they conclude that Augustine's refutation of the Academics rests on the authority of the Incarnate Christ, as expressed at *C. Acad.* 3.42–43.[21] While these interpreters disagree about which passage is most important to the work, each of them focuses on relatively small passages of text and passes over what remains as so many warm ups, afterthoughts and digressions.

Just as scholars cannot agree on what *C. Acad.*'s refutation of Academic skepticism is, there is also little agreement as to what this refutation is for. Heil, Mosher and Harding see skepticism as a corrupting influence on moral behavior, while Curley sees it as undermining civic society. Foley presents skepticism as an obstacle that must be overcome before one may take up faith in revealed doctrine.[22] Cary and Topping present it as an

---

[18] Gareth Matthews, *Augustine* (Oxford: Oxford University Press, 2005): 15–22. For the first-person statements of subjective states, see also Therese Fuhrer, "Skeptizismus und Subjektivität: Augustins antiskeptische Argumentation und das Konzept der Verinnerlichung," in *Geschichte und Vorgeschichte der modernen Subjektivität*, ed. Reto Luzius Fetz, Roland Hagenbüchle & Peter Schulz (Berlin: Walter de Gruyter, 1998), 319–339.

[19] Christopher Kirwan, "Against the Skeptics." In *Augustine* (London: Routledge, 1989), 15–34.

[20] On this reading, Augustine counters the Academics' prohibition against assent, on the grounds that such a prohibition undermines morality. John Heil, "Augustine's Attack on Skepticism: The *Contra Academicos*," *Harvard Theological Review* 65/1 (1972): 99–116; David Mosher, "The Argument of St. Augustine's *Contra Academicos*," *Augustinian Studies* 12 (1981): 89–114; Brian Harding, "Epistemology and Eudaimonism in Augustine's *Contra Academicos*," *Augustinian Studies* 37/2 (2006): 247–274. For a "politicized" version of this general reading, see Augustine Curley, *Augustine's Critique of Skepticism* (New York: Studies in the Humanities Literature – Politics – Society, 1996).

[21] John O'Meara, "Neo-Platonism in the Conversion of Saint Augustine," *Dominican Studies* 3 (1950): 334–343; Ragnar Holte, *Béatitude et Sagesse*; Matthias Smalbrugge, "L'Argumentation Probabiliste d'Augustin," *Revue des Études Augustiniennes* 32 (1986): 41–55.

[22] Foley, "Cicero, Augustine, and the Philosophical Roots of the Cassiciacum Dialogues," *Revue des Études Augustiniennes* 45 (1999): 51–77. Similarly, John Mourant, "Augustine and the Academics" *Recherches Augustiniennes* 4 (1966): 86 claims that in *C. Acad.* Augustine sets out to refute the Academics because they provide an obstacle to *others'* belief, most importantly the work's dedicatee, Romanianus. See also John O'Meara, "Neo-Platonism in the conversion of Saint Augustine"; Ragnar Holte, *Béatitude et Sagesse*; Alven Michael Neiman, "The Argument of Augustine's *Contra Academicos*," *Modern Schoolman* 59 (1982): 255–279; Brian Harding, "Skepticism, Illumination and Christianity in Augustine's *Contra Academicos*," *Augustinian Studies* 34/2 (2003): 197–212.

obstacle to undertaking a course of liberal study;[23] Trelenberg, as an obstacle to laying the foundations of a demonstrative science;[24] Matthews, as an obstacle to further philosophical inquiry through a project of faith seeking understanding.[25] Yet all these scholars agree that Augustine saw skepticism as an obstacle, one which must be overcome before proceeding to non-skeptical projects. It is this last assumption that I call into question. To move beyond it, we must widen our focus from individual passages and get a handle on the text's broader dialectic.

An Alternative Reading: *C. Acad.* as a Study in Platonic Pedagogy

I suggest that the work's formal shift from debate to *oratio perpetua*[26] marks a shift in the type of argument at play.[27] *C. Acad.*'s longer first half presents what we might call a first-order debate in which Licentius and Alypius defend various Academic positions, while Trygetius and Augustine attack them. This process arrives at no definitive conclusion. With the move to *oratio perpetua*, Augustine steps out of the initial debates' dichotomies and reflects on what it was that allowed him and his companions to engage in debate in the first place. This second-order inquiry into inquiry, in turn, allows Augustine to draw various conclusions about the nature of human rationality.[28] Among these is the fact that rational thought

---

[23] Cary, "What Licentius learned"; Topping, "The Perils of Skepticism," 333.

[24] Jörg Trelenberg, *Augustins Schrift* De ordine (Tübingen: Mohr Siebeck, 2009).

[25] Gareth Matthews, *Thought's Ego in Augustine and Descartes* (Ithaca: Cornell University Press, 1992). See Ragnar Holte, *Béatitude et Sagesse*, for the statement of a similar position and review of this issue in earlier scholarship.

[26] Six of Augustine's seven complete dialogues end with a shift from debate to *oratio perpetua*. Alypius explicitly uses the rhetorical term at *C. Acad.* 3.14 as he asks Augustine to continue without him, and Augustine repeats it at 3.15 as he complies with Alypius' wish. The only other instance when the term is explicitly invoked is the very end of *De Mag.* where Adeodatus thanks his father for the speech he has just given (*De Mag.* 46). I take *C. Acad.*'s presentation to be programmatic: Augustine not only employs the formal feature that was to stay with him for the rest of his dialogues, he draws attention to the fact that he's doing so. The two works that lack this shift are *De Mus.*, which is the one surviving example of Augustine's disciplinary dialogues and *Sol.*, whose last book was never completed. See Chapters 4 and 5, respectively.

[27] Voss, *Der Dialog*, and Martin Claes, "Limitations to the *Exercitatio Mentis*: Changes in Rhetorical Style in Augustine's Dialogues," *Augustiniana* 57 (2007): 387–398 present the transition to *oratio perpetua* as marking a shift from reason to authority. Yet insofar as *C. Acad.*'s most powerful "rational" arguments are in its *oratio*, this shift can be symbolic at best.

[28] The terms "first-order" and "second-order" are my own. I invoke them to clarify what I take to be the all-important shift in Augustine's argument, as his text moves from inquiry into a given subject matter (first-order inquiry), to inquiry into the act of inquiry itself (second-order inquiry). Following recent conventions, we might think of the latter as "meta-inquiry." Augustine comes close to such a phrase at *De Ord.* 2.38, where he describes dialectic as the *disciplina disciplinarum*, which "teaches how to teach and how to learn, in which Reason shows herself, what she is, what she

presupposes norms, which are cognitive by the Academics' own standards, e.g. the disjunctive claim, "Zeno's definition is true or false."[29] With this, Augustine undermines the Academics' practice of arguing against the possibility of cognition. Nevertheless, he ends by suggesting a way forward that appears to him plausible (*probabile*) given this and other similar discoveries.[30] With this final suggestion, Augustine appropriates to his own ends the Academic practice of using plausibilities for philosophical inquiry. Academic practice thus serves a dual role in *C. Acad.*, as both the subject matter of the work's debates, and (in its somewhat altered form) as the methodology guiding Augustine to his final endorsement of a non-Academic way forward. This progression through (A) aporetic debate, (R) reflection on the act of debate and a final (P) plausible conclusion drives the dialectical drama of the work. Together, these three modes of argument advance a single approach to inquiry, which I will call ARP. To see how this is all meant to play out, we must take another look at how Augustine presents the Academics' project.

The work's two histories of the Academy invite readers to view the work's debates from two different perspectives. The "public history," discussed earlier, presents the development of the skeptical New Academy in a way that mirrors accounts given in Cicero's *Academica*.[31] In this first

---

wants, what she can do. She knows knowing." (*Haec docet docere, haec docet discere; in hac se ipsa ratio demonstrat, atque aperit quae sit, quid uelit, quid ualeat. Scit scire*). But I take dialectic to be merely one instance of second-order science: Dialectic is a formal discipline, with its own methods and concerns; the second-order inquiries of Augustine's *orationes perpetuae* follow different methods and pursue different ends. See Chapter 4 for discussion. We find a briefer, yet more fitting hint at *De quant. an.* 70, where Augustine shifts from debate into *oratio perpetua* and claims to be "untaught" (*indoctus*) when it comes to the matters at hand, which he nevertheless proceeds to discuss, as someone "certain in his own experience of what he is capable of" (*quid ipse ualeam, securus experior*). See Chapter 6.

[29] In what follows, I will use the phrase "cognitive norms" as shorthand for norms that may supply the content for cognitive impressions. The point of *C. Acad.* 3.21–29's list of such norms, I take it, is that they are employed by anyone engaged in rational thought and that by thinking about such norms, anyone may form a cognitive impression. See discussion in this chapter.

[30] Augustine first announces his intent to draw a *probabile* conclusion in *C. Acad.*'s second dedication to Romanianus, "And I will persuade you more easily of what I want, yet only to show it worthy of approval." (*tibi facile persuadebo quod uolo, probabiliter tamen*). *C. Acad.* 2.8. At *C. Acad.* 2.23 Augustine announces that the only difference between himself and the Academics is that "to them it seems worthy of approval that the truth cannot be found, but to me it seems worthy of approval that it can be." (*inter quos [Academicos] et me modo interim nihil distat, nisi quod illis probabile uisum est, non posse inueniri ueritatem; mihi autem inueniri posse probabile est*). Augustine declares his final victory at *C. Acad.* 3.30: "We are compelled to confess that it is much more worthy of approval that the Sage knows wisdom." (*cogimur confiteri multo esse probabilius, sapientem scire sapientiam*). Likewise, "now it is worthy of approval that the Sage knows something." (*iam probabile est nonnihil scire sapientem*). See also *C. Acad.* 2.29–30, 3.5 and 3.11–12.

[31] *Acad.* in fact gives several different accounts. For the historical accuracy of *C. Acad.* 2's public history and the question of what type of skepticism Augustine confronts in *C. Acad.*, see Eric

account, Augustine and Alypius set out how the Academics came to adopt their four characteristic practices. The founder of Stoicism, Zeno, begins this process – so the public history has it – by introducing his definition of the cognitive impression. The early Academics[32] had never considered the matter, but once it had been presented to them, they realized that cognition is in fact impossible and advocated withholding assent to all impressions. In response to the Stoics' inactivity argument, they then advocated the use of plausibilities for practical matters. In this way, the New Academy was born. Zeno's definition of the cognitive impression is at the heart of the matter, and given that the Academics accept it *in propria persona* and not merely as a dialectical move, it is thus a mitigated skepticism that they adopt.[33]

The secret history[34] revealed at *C. Acad.* 3.37–43 provides a very different perspective on these events.[35] Zeno appears in this account long before his Stoic days, as a student at the pre-skeptical, "early" Academy. Early Academic teaching, we are told, proceeded as a teacher constructed impasses out of his students' views as a means of concealing what he

Dubreucq, "Augustin et le scepticisme académicien," *Recherches de Science Religieuse* 86/3 (1998): 335–365; Charles Brittain, *Philo of Larissa: The Last of the Academic Skeptics* (Oxford: Oxford University Press, 2001): 242–246; Giovanni Catapano, "Quale scetticismo viene criticato de Agostino nel *Contra Academicos?*" *Quaestio* 6 (2006): 1–13. Such concerns are important for deciding whether or not *C. Acad.*'s refutation of Academic skepticism succeeds on the Academics' own terms. At present, my interest is not in this question but in how Augustine appropriates Academic arguments and practices, particularly as represented by Cicero's dialogues, for his own project. Unless otherwise noted, I use "Academics" to refer to Augustine's presentation rather than the historical figures.

[32] It will suit our purposes to look at three main stages of the Academy. The early Academy of Plato and his immediate successors subscribed to a positive body of doctrine, which we might think of as "Platonic." During the Hellenistic period, the skeptical New Academy argued against all claims to knowledge and advocated the withholding of assent. During the Imperial period, the "Platonist" revival of Plotinus *et al.* returned to the positive doctrines of Plato. The transitions between these stages of the Academy's life are what matters for *C. Acad.* Further subdivisions are set out at *C. Acad.* 2.15 & 3.39–41. For discussion of these somewhat convoluted stages of the historical Academy, see John Glucker, *Antiochus and the Late Academy*, (Göttingen: Vandenhoeck & Ruprecht, 1978).

[33] That is to say that they hold it to be true that cognition is impossible, as opposed to radical skeptics who adopt Zeno's criteria for merely dialectical purposes. See the Introduction in Charles Brittain, trans. *Cicero: On Academic Skepticism* (Indianapolis, IN: Hackett Publishing Company, Inc., 2006), viii–xlv.

[34] The term "secret history" is mine. Augustine introduces this account as what he believes rather than knows (*non quid sciam sed quid existimem*) at *C. Acad.* 3.37 and concludes at *C. Acad.* 3.43, "I have persuaded myself from time to time of this account of the Academics as plausible. (*Hoc mihi de Academicis interim probabiliter, ut potui, persuasi*). This is corroborated in the roughly contemporary *Ep.* 1.3, where Augustine refers to "what is at the end of *C. Acad.* 3 [as] perhaps more suspected than certain, yet nevertheless more useful than unbelievable" (*quod in extremo tertii libri suspiciosius fortasse quam certius, utilius tamen, ut arbitror, quam incredibilius*).

[35] The present chapter focuses on how Augustine uses these historical claims to frame his own project. Chapter 2 evaluates them as historical claims about Augustine's philosophical predecessors.

himself thought and of "un-teaching" (*dedocere*) whatever harmful opinions his students may have carried with them. All this is done to prepare students for the *mysteria* of Platonic doctrine. But for Zeno, the idea that all things are material proved too strong. He thus dropped out of the Academy and began his own Stoic school. When Zeno's materialist ideas started gaining favor among the masses, the then current head of the Academy, Arcesilaus, was moved to pity and took on these masses as his charge. Augustine explains:

> *Quam ob rem cum Zeno sua quadam de mundo et maxime de anima, propter quam uera philosophia uigilat, sententia delectaretur dicens eam esse mortalem nec quidquam esse praeter hunc sensibilem mundum nihilque in eo agi nisi corpore – nam et deum ipsum ignem putabat – prudentissime atque utilissime mihi uidetur Arcesilas, cum illud late serperet malum, occultasse penitus Academiae sententiam et quasi aurum inueniendum quandoque posteris obruisse. Quare cum in falsas opiniones ruere turba sit pronior et consuetudine corporum omnia esse corporea facillime sed noxie credatur, instituit uir acutissimus atque humanissimus dedocere potius quos patiebatur male doctos quam docere quos dociles non arbitrabatur. Inde illa omnia nata sunt quae nouae Academiae tribuuntur . . .*

> Therefore, since Zeno was seduced by a certain view of his own about the world and especially about the soul, about which true philosophy is ever vigilant, saying that the soul is mortal and that nothing exists beyond this sensible world and that nothing is accomplished in this world unless by a body – for he thought God himself to be fire – and since this evil spread far and wide, Arcesilaus seems to me most prudently and usefully to have hidden the Academy's view deeply and buried it as though gold to be found by posterity. Therefore, since the common mob is more prone to rush into false opinions and because of the familiarity of bodies believes more easily, but to their own detriment that all things are bodily, that most clear-sighted and humane man decided to un-teach those, whom he endured as being badly taught, rather than teach those whom he did not deem teachable. And from this was born all those things that are attributed to the New Academy. (*C. Acad.* 3.38.)

In this way, Arcesilaus brought early Academic practice onto the public stage, using Zeno's ideas to spin out impasses meant to un-teach materialism and to conceal his own (Platonic) ideas about intelligible reality.[36] The

---

[36] As with the Academics, I will limit my discussion of the Stoics and Platonists to the presentation of them by Augustine in *C. Acad.* There we find two basic philosophical orientations. Materialists, such as the Stoics or Manichees (as Augustine understands them) hold that everything that exists is material. Closely allied with this metaphysical position is a commitment to empiricism, i.e. the view that the bodily senses are the ultimate source of all thought. Intellectualists, such as the Platonists and catholic Christians (again, as Augustine understands them), hold that not everything that exists

results of this undertaking, to an external viewer, are the first three skeptical practices we have already seen: adopting Zeno's definition of the cognitive impression, arguing that cognition is impossible and arguing that assent is always irrational. Augustine proceeds to credit Arcesilaus' successor, Carneades, with instituting the use of *probabilia*, which he drew "from the very fonts of Plato" (*ab ipsis enim Platonis fontibus*).[37]

For the secret history, it is vital that in arguing against the possibility of cognition, Arcesilaus tacitly limits himself to impressions born of the bodily senses. He is well aware that the norms of everyday thought fulfill Zeno's requirements for cognition; he simply does not let on that he is aware of this. Yet there is a sense in which he hides his views in plain sight, for in the process of arguing that cognition is impossible, Arcesilaus uses cognitive norms of thought, whose origin he tacitly places in intelligible reality. The point is to show students that materialism cannot account for the kind of rational activity that human beings clearly engage in. By coming to realize their own rational capacities and the inability of Stoic theory to explain them, students are brought around to a perspective from which they can appreciate the explanatory power of Platonic intellectualism. Short of such preparation, they would be unable to recognize what it is that Platonic theory is meant to explain.

According to both histories, Zeno provides the impetus for the birth of the skeptical New Academy. On the first account, Stoic epistemology, in particular Zeno's definition of the cognitive impression is the crux of the issue, and by accepting it, the Academics came to exchange Platonic doctrine for a mitigated skepticism.[38] On the second account, the criteria set out in Zeno's definition pose no problem for Platonism, and it is Zeno's materialism that called for a change in early Academic practice.

---

is material: Things such as God and perhaps the rational soul, numbers, etc. exist but are not material; these immaterial realities exist in an "intelligible" world and serve as the ultimate object of at least some of our thoughts, i.e. the nonempirical ones. Augustine seems to assume a necessary correlation between empiricism and materialism, on the one hand, and intellectualism and the rejection of materialism on the other. From a historical perspective, such assumptions present a simplification of Stoicism and Platonism alike. That said, interpenetration of these issues remains controversial even today. For discussion, see Michael Frede, "The Stoic Notion of a *Lekton*" In *Language*, ed. Steven Everson (Cambridge: Cambridge University Press, 1994): 109–128; Gail Fine, "Knowledge and Belief in *Republic* 5–7." In *Plato* (Oxford: Oxford University Press, 2000): vol. 1, pp. 215–246.

[37] *C. Acad.* 3.40. The content of this doctrine contains a theory of two worlds: sensible and intelligible (*C. Acad.* 3.37). In Chapter 6, I discuss this theory, which Augustine uses to articulate a theory of graded virtues: civic, kathartic and contemplative.

[38] As Augustine concludes in his public history, "in this way the Academics appeared to take the impossibility of cognition from the Stoic Zeno's definition [of the cognitive impression]." (*Sed uerum non posse comprehendi ex illa Stoici Zenonis definitione arripuisse uidebantur*). *C. Acad.* 2.11.

This change was, however, superficial: None of Plato's doctrines was abandoned, and the early Academics were, for pedagogical reasons, already in the habit of concealing their own views and arguing for conclusions they did not themselves endorse. The only innovation of the New Academics, according to the secret history, is the public stage upon which such practices came to be carried out. At the end of the day, each historical account presents the New Academy as making exactly the same arguments; the difference comes down to the Academics' motivation for doing so.

The somewhat uninteresting orthodoxy of the public history has led scholars to pass it by as "merely didactic."[39] The secret history's unorthodox suggestion of crypto-Platonist Academic skeptics, while sometimes treated with antiquarian interest,[40] is often dismissed as simply bizarre.[41] Yet we should not let such appraisals blind us to the role these two histories serve within the text of *C. Acad.* itself, particularly given the contrast between the bland orthodoxy of the one and the bizarre unorthodoxy of the other. By articulating what that role is, we may begin to piece together the big project pursued in *C. Acad.* The first thing to note is that Augustine's two histories are not on par. The events set out in the public history may be integrated into the secret history's account, i.e. as the public perspective on Arcesilaus' crypto-Platonist exploits, but not *vice versa*. Furthermore, given that (according to the secret history) Arcesilaus took the public as his charge, these public and secret histories can be taken to describe the process of Platonist pedagogy from the perspective of the student and of the teacher, respectively. For the teacher, it is a process of concealing, un-teaching and eventually unveiling some treasured doctrine. For the student, it is a process of un-learning and self-discovery building to a final revelation. In practice, this plays out through a process of aporetic debate, reflection on the act of debating and the final revelation of a plausible conclusion, i.e. ARP. While a teacher such as Augustine has a synoptic view of this process from the start, his students will not fully understand what is happening until the end. This leads to various ironies: a student's attempt to refute his teacher actually plays into the teacher's plan; debates that fail to reach a conclusion nevertheless imply one through the act of debating; what really matters in a discussion of epistemology turns out to be one's metaphysics. I suggest that this is the broader context in

---

[39] Matthias Smalbrugge, "L'Argumentation Probabiliste."
[40] Carlos Levy, "Scepticisme et dogmatisme dans l'Académie: 'l'ésotérisme' d'Arcésilas." *Revue des Études Augustiniennes* 56 (1979): 335–348.
[41] John Rist, "Certainty, Belief and Understanding," 47, claims that this "historical curiosity" plays no role in *C. Acad.*'s treatment of skepticism.

which we should understand *C. Acad.*'s "refutation" of the Academics' skepticism.[42]

In what follows, I will argue that the various sections of *C. Acad.* add up to a study of this method. I begin with passages that model this method's three stages. I then turn to passages that articulate the theoretical underpinnings and implications of this method. By attributing two basic functions to this body of material – modelling and articulating – I present a coherent story for what has otherwise struck scholars as needless repetition. The payoff is a holistic reading of the text, which places concerns for refuting skepticism within a broader inquiry into the nature of philosophical inquiry.

Aporia: What Licentius Un-learned

Something resembling the public history's account of Academic skepticism is simply assumed at the start of *C. Acad.* 1, where Augustine's students Licentius and Trygetius argue respectively for and against the coherence of Arcesilaus' skeptical position. Their assumptions about the Academics' skepticism are corroborated at the start of *C. Acad.* 2 by the public history, which, in turn, prompts that book's debate over Carneades' use of plausibility. Augustine stresses that "*probabile*" and "*veri simile*" are merely alternative names for the same type of impression, and he argues that it is

---

[42] Looking at the work from the teacher's synoptic perspective, we can find new significance in the shift in speakers halfway through book 2's public history. In this passage, Augustine and Alypius respond to Licentius' request for information. At *C. Acad.* 2.10, Alypius asks Augustine to speak "in good faith" (*bona fide*), without lying or concealing anything. Augustine agrees and proceeds to spell out *what* the Academics argue but says nothing about *why* they do so. He ends by saying that he has spoken in good faith (*C. Acad.* 2.11) and invites Alypius to correct any errors or omissions (*C. Acad.* 2.12). Alypius complies by setting these arguments within the context of Stoic epistemology. Given that the public and secret histories agree on what the Academics argue but not on why, Augustine manages not to contradict himself or openly lie to his students, yet he has concealed things from them. This, however, is consistent with good faith. Augustine explains, "Good faith stems from the intention of the mind. For it ought to be clear that a confused person needs to be taught, and a deceitful person needs to be guarded against; of the two, the first needs a good teacher, the second a cautious student." (*Bona ergo fides est ex animi sententia. Homini enim homo falsus docendus, fallax cauendus debet uideri, quorum prius magistrum bonum, posterius discipulum cautum desiderat*). *C. Acad.* 2.12. Within the immediate context, this merely provides a way for Augustine to give Alypius the floor. Yet if we hold the public and secret histories up against each other, Augustine seems to be making a more substantial point: Good faith is a matter of one's intent and does not require full disclosure at all times. When it comes to confused individuals, such as Licentius and Trygetius who are still far from grasping the Academics' position as a whole, a "good teacher" is desirable. Augustine, following the lead of his crypto-Platonist Academics, understands that a good teacher will periodically conceal things from his students for pedagogical reasons. My thanks to Isabelle Bochet, "*Consentire sapientiae*: Going Beyond Skepticism in *C. Acad.*" (paper presented as part of the Townsend Lectures at Cornell University, Ithaca, New York, April 29, 2015) for drawing my attention to the significance of *bona fides* within the broader structure of the text.

impossible for Carneades to identify *veri similia* while lacking any acquaintance with *vera*.[43] By the end of the book, all agree that the Academics' use of plausibility is problematic, but it is not clear what a viable alternative would be. Toward the end of these debates, Augustine suggests that the absurd consequences of the Academics' arguments may be taken as evidence that the Academics did not actually subscribe to the views that they publicly endorsed.[44] Yet it is not until the secret history at the very end of *C. Acad.* 3 that Augustine reveals what the Academics' true commitments might have been.

The secret history invites Augustine's students (and readers) to reevaluate everything that came before from the standpoint of a Platonist teacher, to draw out the second-order consequences of *C. Acad.*'s first-order debates. The fact that *C. Acad.* 1 failed to reach any definitive conclusion, we now see, results from the empiricist assumptions that both Licentius and Trygetius employed in their debate.[45] Yet these young men unwittingly carried the solution with them all the while, insofar as both of them made use of cognitive norms to construct their arguments, however tainted by empiricism those arguments may have been. At *C. Acad.* 1.9

---

[43] Augustine sets out his argument at *C. Acad.* 2.16 by way of an analogy: "If someone claims your brother looks like his father yet is unacquainted with your father himself, won't such a person seem insane or simpleminded to you?" (*Si quisquam fratrem tuum uisum patris tui similem esse affirmet ipsumque tuum patrem non nouerit, nonne tibi insanus aut ineptus uidebitur?*) This thought experiment is elaborated at *C. Acad.* 2.19 and provides material for the rest of *C. Acad.* 2's debate.

[44] "For I don't think [the Academics] were men who didn't know how to impose names on things, but they seem to me to have chosen these terms for the purpose of hiding their own view from slower people and making it manifest to those who were more vigilant. And I will set out how and why this appears so to me, once I have first discussed those things men think were said by them as though they were adverse to human cognition ... For they seem to me to have been entirely serious and prudent men. But if there is anything which we will now be debating, it will be against those who believed that the Academics were adverse to the discovery of truth." (*non enim illos uiros eos fuisse arbitror, qui rebus nescirent nomina imponere, sed mihi haec uocabula uidentur elegisse et ad occultandam tardioribus et ad significandam uigilantioribus sententiam suam. Quod quare et quomodo mihi uideatur exponam, cum prius illa discussero, quae ab eis tanquam cognitionis humanae inimicis dicta homines putant... Nam illi mihi uidentur graues omnino ac prudentes uiri fuisse. Si quid est autem, quod nunc disputabimus, aduersus eos erit, qui Academicos inuentioni ueritatis aduersos fuisse crediderunt*). *C. Acad.* 2.24. This "prudence" of the Academics is invoked again at *C. Acad.* 3.36. Having reduced the Academics' use of *probabilia* to a laughable absurdity, Augustine asks somewhat rhetorically how the Academics themselves had not foreseen such results. He answers that they did, "most cleverly and prudently" (*Immo solertissime prudentissimeque uiderunt*). The secret history follows immediately as a kind of "error theory" explaining how these prudent Academics could come to endorse such ridiculous views in public. Within the secret history itself, Arcesilaus is said "most prudently" (*prudentissime*) to have hidden the views of the Academy. *C. Acad.* 3.38.

[45] With this, Augustine grants (the historical) Arcesilaus a circumscribed victory, insofar as he grants that his various skeptical arguments invoking dreams, madness and the like actually do undermine the possibility of empirically based cognition.

Licentius has made some progress in realizing this, as he declares, "I think that only God knows the Truth itself and perhaps the human soul once it has left behind this shadowy prison, which is the body." (*Veritatem autem illam solum Deum nosse arbitror aut forte hominis animam, cum hoc corpus, hoc est tenebrosum carcerem, dereliquerit*).[46] In this, Licentius has progressed from one Academic perspective, i.e. thinking that human beings cannot attain knowledge (or cognition), to thinking that they might be able to do so, provided that they use some nonbodily means.[47] This too Licentius presents as an Academic position. What he has not yet discovered is the Platonist perspective that human beings generally, and most importantly he himself, have access to intelligible reality *even while embodied*. From the perspective of *C. Acad.*'s crypto-Platonist curriculum, Licentius has cracked the Academics' skeptical facade, but he has not yet discovered what sits behind it.[48]

Reflection: Augustine's Discovery

In the *oratio perpetua* that ends the work, Augustine exploits the opportunity for self-reflection that Licentius and Trygetius let slip by. Imagining Arcesilaus to be present, he allows his companions to "listen in" as he attempts to trap the father of Academic skepticism in a series of dilemmas:

---

[46] *C. Acad.* 1.9.

[47] In having Licentius move between these positions, Augustine, as author, seems to be working through different Academic conceptions of the afterlife. Mutually contradicting accounts from Cicero's *Hort.* are preserved by Augustine himself. Frg. 97 (Müller), preserved at *De Trin.* 14.26, echoes the end of Plato's *Ap.* 40c4–41c7 in claiming that one may continue *inquiring* after the truth in the afterlife. By contrast, Frg. 50 (Müller), preserved at *De Trin.* 14.12, claims that like the gods we will be happy in having *attained* the truth (*cognitione naturae et scientia*). The fragmentary remains of the *Hort.* make it impossible to be certain whether Cicero ascribed either view to the Academic skeptics themselves. These fragments thus make poor evidence either for or against thinking that Licentius has departed from normal skeptical Academic theses. For a discussion of the place of these fragments in *De Trin.*, see Goulven Madec, "L'*Hortensius* de Cicéron dans les livres XIII–XIV de *De Trinitate*," *Revue des Études Augustiniennes* 15 (1969): 167–173.

[48] As a side note to the present chapter's constructive project: If we step back for a moment and set *C. Acad.* within the broader context of the dialogues, there is a sense in which Licentius and Trygetius both correctly define wisdom, albeit wisdom of different grades. As Augustine hints at in *C. Acad.* 3 (see the discussion of purification later in this chapter) and lays bare in *De quant. an.* (see Chapter 6), the virtues come in three grades: civic, kathartic and contemplative. One way of viewing *C. Acad.* 1's debate is that Trygetius has correctly defined contemplative virtue as having found truth, while Licentius has correctly defined kathartic wisdom as the diligent search for truth. While the two grades each have a certain integrity unto themselves, kathartic virtue aims beyond itself to contemplative virtue. Augustine, the author, plays with this asymmetry – reminiscent of Socrates' discussion of human and divine wisdom in Plato's *Ap.* – over the course of *C. Acad.* 1's debate.

Tamen quod Zeno definiuit, quantum stulti possumus, discutiamus. Id uisum ait posse comprehendi, quod sic appareret, ut falsum apparere non posset. Manifestum est nihil aliud in perceptionem uenire. Hoc et ego, inquit Arcesilas, uideo et hoc ipso doceo nihil percipi. Non enim tale aliquid inueniri potest. [A] Fortasse abs te atque ab aliis stultis; at a sapiente cur non potest? Quamquam et ipsi stulto nihil responderi posse arbitror, si tibi dicat, ut illo memorabili acumine tuo hanc ipsam Zenonis definitionem refellas et ostendas eam etiam falsam esse posse; quod si non potueris, hanc ipsam quam percipias habes, si autem refelleris, unde a percipiendo impediaris non habes. Ego eam refelli posse non uideo et omnino uerissimam iudico. Itaque cum eam scio, quamuis sim stultus, nonnihil scio. [B] Sed fac illam cedere uersutiae tuae. Vtar complexione securissima. Aut enim uera est aut falsa. Si uera, bene teneo; si falsa, potest aliquid percipi, etiamsi habeat communia signa cum falso. Vnde, inquit, potest? Verissime igitur Zeno definiuit nec ei quisquis uel in hoc consensit, errauit. An paruae laudis et sinceritatis definitionem putabimus, quae contra eos, qui erant aduersum perceptionem multa dicturi, cum designaret quale esset quod percipi posset, se ipsam talem esse monstrauit? Ita comprehensibilibus rebus et definitio est et exemplum. [C] Vtrum, ait, etiam ipsa uera sit nescio; sed quia est probabilis, ideo eam sequens ostendo nihil esse tale, quale illa expressit posse comprehendi. Ostendis fortasse praeter ipsam et uides, ut arbitror, quid sequatur. Quodsi etiam eius incerti sumus, nec ita nos deserit scientia. Scimus enim aut ueram esse aut falsam; non igitur nihil scimus. [D] Quamquam numquam efficiet, ut ingratus sim, prorsus ego illam definitionem uerissimam iudico. Aut enim possunt percipi et falsa, quod uehementius Academici timent et re uera absurdum est, aut nec ea possunt, quae sunt falsis simillima; unde illa definitio uera est. Sed iam caetera uideamus.

But let us discuss Zeno's definition, insofar as we fools are able. For Zeno said that the impression that can be grasped appears in a way that a false impression cannot appear. For it is clear that nothing else can enter into cognition. "I see things this way too," says Arcesilaus, "and it is through this definition that I teach that nothing is grasped. For nothing of such a sort can be found." [A] Perhaps by you and other fools, but why is the Sage not able to do so? Yet I judge that you would be unable to respond to even the fool himself, if he should tell you to use that famous shrewdness of yours to refute Zeno's definition and show that even it can be false; but if you are not able to do this, then you have this definition itself as something you may grasp, yet if you do refute it, you no longer have it as a means of impeding cognition. I don't see how it can be refuted, and I judge it to be most true. And thus when I know it, though I am a fool, I know something. [B] But let this definition give way to your cunning. I will use a most secure dilemma. Zeno's definition is either true or false. If it is true, I win; if it is false, an impression can be grasped even if it has signs in common with a false impression. "But how's that possible?" he exclaimed. Therefore, Zeno defined it most truly, and no one who agreed with him in this regard erred.

Or will we consider this definition to be of little worth or merit, which in opposition to those who had many things to say against cognition, in the process of describing what kind of thing can be an object of cognition, showed itself to be just such a thing? Thus it is both a definition and an example of cognitive impressions. [C] "Whether or not the definition is true," says Arcesilaus, "I don't know. But because it is worthy of approval, by following it I show that there is nothing of the sort which the definition said can be grasped." Perhaps you show that there is nothing beyond the definition that can be an object of cognition, and I imagine you see what follows from that. But even if we are uncertain of the definition, knowledge does not abandon us. For we know that Zeno's definition is true or false, and thus we know something. [D] Yet it won't come about that I am ungrateful, and thus I judge this definition to be most true. For either false impressions can be grasped – which eventuality the Academics fear terribly and is in fact absurd – or not even those impressions which are most similar to false ones can be; therefore, the definition is true. But let us now look into other matters. (*C. Acad.* 3.21)

This passage presents not one but three different dilemmas, which I have labeled (A), (B) and (D). Blake Dutton differentiates between them and attempts to present each as a sound argument. In the end, he concludes that Augustine merely came close.[49] Nevertheless, by presenting these dilemmas, however flawed they may be, Augustine engages Arcesilaus in rational debate. And having done so, Augustine may point out, as he does at (C), that in the process of arguing that cognition is impossible, Arcesilaus agrees to the disjunctive claim, "Zeno's definition is true or false." Whichever disjunct ends up being the case, the larger disjunction is always true and therefore certain by Arcesilaus' own standards. With this, at long last, Augustine presents a viable counterexample to the skeptical argument that cognition is impossible.

Augustine declares this discovery sufficient to undermine Arcesilaus' arguments against the possibility of cognition.[50] Yet there is nothing special about this particular disjunction, and Augustine proceeds to list other instances of cognitive norms that would be employed by anyone inquiring into any of the three branches of philosophy: physics,[51] ethics[52] and logic.[53] The cumulative point is that cognition, far from being impossible to attain, is ubiquitous, inasmuch as cognitive norms are presupposed by most if not all acts of rational inquiry. This is the truth

---

[49] Dutton, "Augustine, Academic Skepticism, and Zeno's Definition." For a similar appraisal see Kirwan, "Against the Skeptics." See also Charles Brittain, *Philo*, 165–166, who takes the purpose of this passage to demonstrate that Zeno's definition is a possible object of cognition.

[50] *C. Acad.* 3.21.   [51] *C. Acad.* 3.23–6.   [52] *C. Acad.* 3.27–8.   [53] *C. Acad.* 3.29.

that Arcesilaus, as a Platonist teacher, hid in plain sight as he made use of cognitive norms to argue that cognition is impossible. It is by catching the self-contradiction implicit in this that the student advances in Arcesilaus' Platonist curriculum.

According to the secret history, it was Zeno's materialism that Arcesilaus set out to un-teach. At this point, we can piece together the basic shape of Arcesilaus' strategy. He begins by adopting Zeno's certainty criterion: For any impression that represents a state of affairs, if it is possible for another impression to have the same content but be brought about by a different state of affairs, then the initial impression cannot be grasped. From this, Arcesilaus argues that for any empirical impression, another impression could have been brought about by a state other than the one it represents, e.g. even if I actually am in Athens, and it appears to me that I am in Athens, it is still *possible* that I am dreaming and actually in Citium. By Zeno's standards, this is enough to render my true impression incognitive. Such is the case for any empirical impression. Yet through reflection on the act of inquiry, Arcesilaus' student may come to realize that various norms are presupposed by rational thought and that these are cognitive by Zeno's own standards.[54] Since no empirical impression is cognitive, it follows that such impressions must have a nonempirical source, and thus *contra Zenonem*, it follows that there must be some nonempirical source of cognition.

Even scholars who will accept the cognitive status of Augustine's counterexamples are still quick to point out the trivial nature of truths such as "if there are four elements, then there are not five elements," "3 x 3 = 9" and "this appears white to me," all of which fall far short of the wisdom

---

[54] It is not completely clear how common such impressions are meant to be. Augustine's argument focuses on Zeno's third criterion, the certainty requirement: Impressions of necessary truths cannot be brought about by states of affairs other than the ones they represent, for the simple reason that there are no states of affairs in which necessary truths do not obtain. That said, it seems quite possible that an impression representing such a necessary truth, could be formed *not* through intellectual perception of that truth itself, but simply by one person's listening to another talking about such matters. In this case, the impression formed meets Zeno's first and third criteria, but fails to meet the second. In terms of the Platonist argument that *C. Acad.* attributes to Arcesilaus, this would mean that day-to-day use of rational norms does not necessarily assume impressions that are already cognitive. Still, the use of such norms would provide an occasion for individuals to reflect on their own rational activities and thus exercise their intellectual capacities by forming new impressions through direct perception of the intellectual realities from which these norms derive. If this is right, then by undertaking the reflections on rational activity advocated within the Cassiciacum dialogues, an individual can improve his epistemic state not only by discerning which impressions to assent to, but by acquiring new and improved impressions, which are cognitive and derived from the intelligible world itself. This would put Augustine in line with a strategy advanced by Plotinus (see Chapter 2 for discussion), though the question of how human beings typically acquire the norms of thought is not broached in *C. Acad.*

whose attainment is *C. Acad.*'s ultimate concern.[55] Such criticisms miss the place these cognitive impressions occupy within *C. Acad.*'s broader constructive argument. What is at stake here is not the Sage's wisdom but basic prerequisites of human rationality.[56] Augustine's cognitive impressions are not meant to constitute the wisdom attained at the end of philosophical inquiry, or even the first principles from which such wisdom may be derived. They are the prerequisite tools of reasoning that make philosophical inquiry possible. This is the sense in which these impressions "pertain to" the three divisions of philosophy.[57]

[55] While Augustine claims that all such impressions are certain, he does not address the further question of why this is so. Disjunctions, mathematical truths and other logical necessities are all always true. In the case of impressions such as "I exist" and "I live," the state of affairs described by the impression is a necessary condition of the impression's being formed. The certainty of first-person statements of subjective states, e.g. I have the impression of a table, relies on substantive psychological views about the mind's transparency to itself, which Augustine does not discuss in *C. Acad.* For critique of this last category, see Christopher Kirwan, "Against the Skeptics"; Therese Fuhrer, "Skeptizismus und Subjektivität"; Gareth Matthews, *Thought's Ego* and *Augustine*, 15–22.

[56] The Stoics distinguished between individual cognitive impressions and knowledge, which is a holistic state composed of several cognitive impressions: see Cicero, *Acad.* 1.41–2. Augustine rejects this distinction at *Sol.* 1.19: "**Reason:** Therefore, if you have any learning about these things, you do not hesitate to call it "knowledge," do you? **Augustine:** I wouldn't hesitate, if the Stoics would allow it, for they attribute knowledge to no one but the Sage. However I don't deny that I grasp those things, and the Stoics grant this even to the state of folly; but I'm not afraid of these Stoics in the slightest. Without getting into such distinctions, I hold the things you asked about by means of knowledge. Go ahead, then, so that I can see what point you're getting at in asking these things." (*R. Ergo istarum rerum disciplinam, si qua tibi est, non dubitas uocare scientiam? A. Non, si Stoici sinant, qui scientiam tribuunt nulli, nisi sapienti. Perceptionem sane istorum me habere non nego, quam etiam stultitiae concedunt: sed nec istos quidquam pertimesco. Prorsus haec quae interrogasti scientia teneo: perge modo; uideam quorsum ista quaeris*). I take this to be a point about terminology, viz. Augustine is saying that he is not going to reserve "*scientia*" to refer only to a holistic state, but will use it to refer to any instance of cognition. Regardless of his use of technical language, Augustine retains the substantive distinction between a fool (*stultus*) who grasps various things and a sage (*sapiens*) who grasps wisdom. By conflating these two substantive categories, various scholars infer that *C. Acad.*'s list of cognitive impressions is meant to show that wisdom is possible, *insofar as these cognitive impressions constitute wisdom*. Such a conflation seems to underlie the "moral readings" of Harding *et al.*, according to whom the present argument does not work, as well as the estimation of John O'Meara, *Against the Academics* (Westminster: Ancient Christian Writers 12, 1950), that *C. Acad.*'s argumentation is confused and thus in need of Christ to show us the Truth.

[57] Augustine addresses this claim at *C. Acad.* 3.23 to the (quite dead) Academic skeptic, Carneades who, "say[s] that nothing can be grasped in philosophy." (*Nihil ais in philosophia posse percipi*). This position had already been set out in the public history at *C. Acad.* 2.11: "For the Academics thought that knowledge could not come to a human being, at least when it comes to knowledge of things pertaining to philosophy, for Carneades said that he didn't care about other things." (*Nam et Academicis placuit nec homini scientiam posse contingere earum duntaxat rerum, quae ad philosophiam pertinent*). I invoke the larger dialectical movement at work in *C. Acad.* and argue that the things pertaining to philosophy, which Augustine presents as certain, are merely those impressions that one uses to carry out philosophical inquiries. This is most obvious for what I am calling "norms of thought." Yet first-person statements also have their role in ethical and psychological inquiries, e.g. *C. Acad.* 3.1–4 where Augustine and Alypius debate whether we want life for the sake of wisdom or

In historical terms, Augustine's antiempiricist argument engages Hellenistic thinking about the common concepts. Within Stoic theory, human beings, simply by being placed in the world, naturally develop a set of cognitive impressions, which make rational thought possible. These impressions, known as the common concepts, are what separate human beings from brute animals.[58] When Augustine invokes Arcesilaus' critique of empiricism, the real issue is not whether *any* impression is cognitive – for all the fuss, no one is seriously worried about the oar that looks bent in water – rather, by using Arcesilaus' arguments to cast doubt on empirical impressions as a whole, Augustine casts doubt on the Stoics' empirical origin for the common concepts. By the Stoics' own standards, such doubt is sufficient to render incognitive the basis of human rationality itself.[59] This much is enough to arrive at skepticism, as the public history's Arcesilaus has done. Yet Augustine goes further, and, by suggesting a nonempirical source for the common concepts, he offers a Platonist resolution to a Hellenistic debate. We find a similar strategy in Plotinus. *Enneades* 5.3.1–5 and 5.5.1–2 invoke a certainty requirement for knowledge and proceed to argue that no representational thought, empirical thought included, can ever be certain. From this Plotinus concludes that knowledge, if there is any, must be nonrepresentational. This, in turn, sets the stage for his intellectualist account of knowledge. While Plotinus does not state his premises' provenance, his certainty requirement bears the stamp of the Stoic/Academic debate.[60] Augustine employs a similar strategy but makes the original context explicit. To this he adds rumors of an esoteric Platonist tradition and spins out an elaborate secret history of

wisdom for the sake of living. Later on, the trio of first-person cognitive impressions, "I exist," "I am alive" and "I think" provide the principle from which the grand speculations of *De lib. arbit.* depart. See Chapter 7.

[58] While the mechanism through which humans acquire these concepts may be innate, according to the Stoics, actual concepts such as "the good" and the principle of bivalence are arrived at through empirical means. See Dirk Obbink, "'What All Men Believe Must Be True': Common Conceptions and *Consensio Omnium*." In *Oxford Studies in Ancient Philosophy* 10 (1992) 193–231; Charles Brittain, "Common Sense: Concepts, Definitions and Meaning in and out of the Stoa." In *Language and Learning*, ed. Dorothea Frede & Brad Inwood (Cambridge: Cambridge University Press, 2005): 165–209.

[59] We find such an argument at Cicero, *Acad.* 2.26.

[60] Dominic O'Meara, "Scepticism and Ineffability in Plotinus," *Phronesis* 45/3 (2000): 241–242 points out the similarity of Plotinus' argument to one found at *C. Acad.* 3.22–6. On my reading, it is a version of Plotinus' argument that drives the work's dialectic at the most basic level. For discussion of this argument in Plotinus, see also Eyjólfur Kjalar Emilsson, "Cognition and Its Object." In *The Cambridge Companion to Plotinus*, ed. Lloyd Gerson (Cambridge: Cambridge University Press, 1996): 217–249 and R. T. Wallis, "Skepticism and Neoplatonism," *Aufstieg und Niedergang der Römischen Welt* 36/2 (1987): 911–954.

crypto-Platonist Academic skeptics. What is an isolated argument in Plotinus provides a possible model from which Augustine developed a method to structure each of his eight dialogues.[61]

A Plausible Conclusion: Platonic Intellectualism

What has Augustine accomplished with all this un-learning and self-reflection? In failing to reach a definitive conclusion, the debate of book 1 illustrated that certainty cannot be attained through the bodily senses. Granted, neither Licentius or Trygetius may have thought of himself as a staunch empiricist, so part of the progress came as Licentius began to articulate his everyday assumptions and then to take critical distance from them. Meanwhile, by reflecting on the act of debate, Augustine was able in book 3 to show that we all carry certainties around with us already, viz. the norms of rational thought. Together, these two discoveries suggest that the way forward sits neither with the Academics' skepticism nor the Stoics' empiricism, but with the intellectualist theory of the Platonists. In order for Augustine to show the certain truth of Platonism, he would have to establish that the views of these three schools *exhaust* all possible explanations for human access to the common concepts. This would bring *C. Acad.*'s overarching argument in line with a strategy developed in Hellenistic debates over the human final end.[62] At the end of the secret history, Augustine claims that in his day, the Stoics have died out, the Platonists and Peripatetics agree with one another, and people become Cynics simply for the "freedom and license" (*libertas atque licentia*) it affords.[63] Yet in this Augustine does not even pretend to have exhausted all possible positions. He has merely taken stock of the options available to him and chosen the one that best explains what went before, insofar as Platonic intellectualism sidesteps the empiricist assumptions that led to *aporia* in book 1 and provides a theoretical context for the self-reflective discoveries of book 3. This is all Augustine claims. His big conclusion, that wisdom can be found with the Platonists, is presented not as something he holds as certain, but

---

[61] See Chapter 2 for further discussion of Augustine's debt to Plotinus and the earlier Platonic tradition.

[62] This argument strategy exists in a Stoic form, which involves arguing that there are only nine conceivable highest ends and that eight of them fail to hold up to scrutiny, leaving the Stoic view of the end to be the only viable one. The Academics make use of the same general strategy, although they argue that the Stoics' end does not hold up either. See Keimpe Algra, "Chrysippus, Carneades, Cicero: The Ethical *Divisiones* in Cicero's *Lucullus*." In *Assent and Argument*, ed. Brad Inwood & Jaap Mansfeld (Leiden: Brill, 1997): 107–139.

[63] *C. Acad.* 2.42.

merely something that, *contra Academicos*, strikes Augustine as plausible.[64] Some scholars have seen Augustine as unduly modest or otherwise disingenuous in the way he sets out this conclusion.[65] I take Augustine's claims at face value, for the simple reason that the arguments he deploys in *C. Acad.* support conclusions at the level of assurance that he explicitly claims for them. By admitting this, we can start to see how Augustine's argument against the Academics' use of plausibility contributes to *C. Acad.*'s constructive project.

Book 2's debate revolves around evaluating a simple argument: If, as Cicero testified, a *veri simile* impression is simply a *probabile* impression under a different description,[66] then an Academic skeptic such as Carneades, insofar as he refuses to assent to any impression as *verum*, is not in a position to approve of any other impression as *veri simile*, for the simple reason that he has no basis to identify such an impression. Scholars take

---

[64] It has become generally recognized that Descartes relies on Augustine for his response to skepticism, and the standard reading of *C. Acad.* as simply a refutation of skepticism likely rests on the assumption that Augustine and Descartes are engaged in essentially the same project. Both begin by setting a certainty requirement as a means of clearing the slate, which they then start filling in again with certainties arrived at through self-reflection. Yet Descartes explicitly cuts himself off from the school philosophies presented by his particular historical circumstances, seeking an intellectual vacuum in which to construct a demonstrative science upon the basis of self-evident first principles. When Augustine moves from skeptical doubt to self-reflective certainty, it is as a means of choosing between the competing authorities that are available to him within his own particular time and place, and he proceeds to advocate assenting to authoritative doctrines whose truth is still uncertain. From a Cartesian perspective, Augustine retreats to dogmatism before reaching the finish line. Yet Descartes himself runs into serious problems when he attempts to move from self-evident foundations, through demonstrative deductions, to substantive conclusions about the world beyond his own mind. From an Augustinian perspective, Descartes extends a methodology beyond its breaking point and introduces a form of faith under the guise of science. For a review of the "Cartesian Circle," see Lex Newman, "Descartes' Epistemology," in *Stanford Encyclopedia of Philosophy*, last modified 2014. http://plato.stanford.edu/. For discussion of Descartes' debt to Augustine, see Gareth Matthews, *Thought's Ego*, and Stephen Menn, *Descartes and Augustine* (Cambridge: Cambridge University Press, 1998).

[65] Emmanuel Bermon, "'*Contra Academicos vel De Academicis*' (*Retract.* I, 1): saint Augustin et les *Academica* de Cicéron." *Revue des Etudes Anciennes* 111/1 (2009): 75–93, for instance, claims that Augustine does not merely hold it to be true that wisdom can be found, but that he himself has actually found it, though he veils his conclusions in terms of *stultitia* so that his students will not be overcome by his authority as a teacher. See Michael Foley, "Cicero and Augustine," for a similar view.

[66] *C. Acad.* 2.26 preserves Cicero's *Acad.* frg. 19 (Müller): "All things, the Academic said, which I thought should be called worthy of approval or truthlike, appear to me to be such. And if you want to call them by another name, I won't offer any resistance. For it is enough for me that you have accepted well what I'm saying, i.e. the things onto which I impose these names. For the wise man ought to be not a coiner of terms but an investigator of things." (*Talia*, inquit Academicus, *mihi uidentur omnia, quae probabilia uel ueri similia putaui nominanda; quae tu si alio nomine uis uocare, nihil repugno. Satis enim mihi est, te iam bene accepisse quid dicam, id est quibus rebus haec nomina imponam. Non enim uocabulorum opificem, sed rerum inquisitorem decet esse sapientem*).

this to be one of *C. Acad.*'s refutations of Academic skepticism, although not all are equally convinced of its success.[67] Rather than weigh in on the success of Augustine's argument, I call into question the more basic assumption that its purpose (or at least its sole purpose) is to refute Academic skepticism. All the argument attempts to show is that one Academic practice of refusing to assent to any impression as true is incompatible with another Academic practice of using plausible impressions for practical matters. It does not follow that a non-Academic cannot use plausible impressions. And we find Augustine doing just this at the end of *C. Acad.*, after he has assented to the truth of various cognitive impressions.

There is little doubt that Augustine endorses Platonism and catholic Christianity in the end.[68] The question is how he gets there *in this text*, what the implications of this process are, and what purpose is served by such a process in the first place. I've argued that Augustine follows the Academics in using plausible impressions in conditions of uncertainty. While this uncertainty is global for the Academics, Augustine argues that one can use plausible impressions only when one is certain of some things even if uncertain of others. In this case, the self-reflective truth that each of us carries around cognitive norms of thought, coupled with the impossibility of the bodily senses to produce anything cognitive, provides a footing for declaring Plato's intellectualism truthlike, insofar as it provides the best explanation of this truth, given the competing theories currently available.

Having set out what the overarching argument of *C. Acad.* is, we may now turn our attention to its implications for the broader projects at play in the work. With this, we can set aside worries about refuting the skeptics and turn to a different constellation of questions about psychology, education and the intersection of philosophy and religion.

The Psychological Underpinnings of Augustine's Method

Academic ideas about the *probabile* are rooted in Stoic psychology, in particular the Stoics' theory of perception. Three basic components of this theory are relevant for piecing together Augustine's project in *C. Acad.* First, for normal human adults, all perception involves propositional content: Vision is not the passive messenger of shapes and colors, but a

---

[67] For discussion, see Cristopher Kirwan, "Against the Skeptics," and Therese Fuhrer, "Das Kriterium der Wahrheit."

[68] The clearest statement of this comes at *C. Acad.* 3.43. See discussion later in this chapter.

function of the rational soul, which actively interprets shapes and colors as an integral part of the perceptual act itself, forming an impression with propositional content, which may be true or false, and judging it plausible or not. The second thing to note is that perception occurs through a series of stages. The impression's formation and the judgment of its plausibility are more-or-less autonomous processes. It is only once this has occurred that we are presented with a choice: We may assent to this impression as true and thus integrate it into our body of assents,[69] or we may withhold our assent. The third thing to note is that it is our body of prior assents that guides our initial formation of new impressions. It is the common concepts that make this possible: As the foundations of human rationality, they provide the basic categories through which human perception is structured. Yet it is not merely the common concepts but the individual's whole body of prior assents that conditions how he perceives the world. In an ideal situation, these additional assents are limited to impressions that are cognitive and include the set of impressions that constitute wisdom. In actual human civilization, an individual will likely assent to all manner of false and incognitive impressions. This leads him to perceive incorrectly, seeing pleasure as good (rather than indifferent), pain as bad, etc.[70]

Given this basic setup, it is impossible for me to change how my *current* impressions are formed: My prior assents dictate how this first stage will be carried out, and the only choice I have is to assent or not. Yet through assenting and refusing to assent to certain impressions, I can change my overall body of assents and thus change how my mind will form *subsequent* impressions. With this we have the psychological underpinnings of Augustine's method. Aporetic debates help us identify and articulate problematic impressions, born of everyday experience, and give us good reason to withhold or, more precisely, withdraw our assent to them. Reflection on our rational activities supplies us with new impressions and gives us reason to assent to them. By altering our body of assents in this way, we change the way we form initial impressions, by changing what our mind stamps as plausible or not. This, in turn, puts us in a state to think more fruitfully about the grand accounts that close each work. This, I argue, is the basic purpose of an Augustinian dialogue, as viewed from a psychological perspective.[71]

---

[69] By "assents," I mean the body of impressions that we take to be true. This may include impressions that are true or false, certain or uncertain, cognitive or incognitive.

[70] See Seneca, *Epistulae* 90 for one Stoic account of the fall from the Golden Age.

[71] Cf. Heath, *Unity in Greek Poetics*, 21–27 discusses the psychological dimension of Plato's dialogues, which, he argues, are unified around attempts to help individual students make progress in philosophical understanding and the attaining of virtue.

This process does not get us all the way to understanding or, in
C. Acad.'s terms, to cognition of Augustine's final accounts. Yet it does
get us closer. From a purely practical perspective, the person who perceives
Augustine's intellectualist accounts as plausible is more likely to carry on
inquiries through which he might eventually grasp them. From an epistemic perspective, this process makes our current beliefs compatible with
these intellectualist accounts. Truths such as "even non-Sages (*stulti*) grasp
norms of rational thought" hardly demonstrate the certain truth of a
truthlike conclusion such as, "the Sage grasps wisdom." Yet the discovery
of the non-Sage's cognition provides some reason, other things being
equal, for rejecting the skeptical idea that the Sage's wisdom consists not
in cognition but in the perfect searching for the Truth. As Augustine puts
it, the only thing holding him back from assenting to the possibility of
grasping wisdom was the Academics' arguments against the possibility of
cognition.[72] With these arguments overturned, he is justified in finding it
plausible that the Sage grasps wisdom, while he is further justified, given
C. Acad. 1's failed attempt to secure cognition on empiricist grounds, in
finding plausible the Platonists' account of why this may be so.

Philosophy as Purification[73]

In his secret history of the Academy, Augustine tells us that:

> *Haec et alia huius modi mihi uidentur inter successores eius [Platonis], quan-*
> *tum poterant, esse seruata et pro mysteriis custodita. Non enim aut facile ista*
> *percipiuntur nisi ab eis, qui se ab omnibus uitiis mundantes in aliam quam-*
> *dam plus quam humanam consuetudinem uindicarint, aut non grauiter*
> *peccat, quisquis ea sciens quoslibet homines docere uoluerit.*

> Among Plato's successors, [Plato's theory of intelligible reality] and other
> such matters appear to have been preserved and guarded as mysteries so far
> as they could. For these things are not easily grasped, except by those who

---

[72] At *C. Acad.* 3.30 he claims, "But there is nothing further that I desire, if it is now worthy of approval
that the wise person knows something. For the only reason it seemed truthlike that he ought to hold
back assent is that it was truthlike that nothing could be grasped. But with this removed (for the
wise person grasps wisdom, as is now conceded) no reason now remains why the wise person would
not assent certainly to wisdom itself." (*Quid autem amplius desiderem, nihil habeo, si iam probabile
est nonnihil scire sapientem. Non enim alia causa ueri simile uidebatur eum assensionem sustinere
debere, nisi quia erat ueri simile nihil posse comprehendi. Quo sublato – percipit enim sapiens uel ipsam,
ut iam conceditur, sapientiam – nulla iam causa remanebit, cur non assentiatur sapiens uel ipsi
sapientiae*).
[73] See Chapter 6, which sets the present discussion within the broader context of the grades of virtue:
civic, kathartic (i.e. purifying) and contemplative.

by purifying themselves from all vices assume a certain habit that is more than human, and a person who knows these things sins gravely when he wants to teach them to just anybody. (*C. Acad.* 3.38)

Philosophical purification is needed before one can approach such teachings, and Augustine presents the Platonist curriculum not as a body of principles to learn but as a process of reorienting the student.[74] In theory, this process is adapted to the particular needs of each individual student. In practice, various materialistic views of the world are what most students must be "un-taught." The spread of Stoicism is partly to blame for the ubiquity of materialist notions, yet Zeno's materialist ideas gained popularity because "the familiarity with bodies" (*consuetudo corporum*) made the masses prone to assent to such false opinions in the first place.[75] This "familiarity" may refer simply to things that we are "used to," our "associations." It may also refer to a love affair or sexual relations. These two meanings – analogous to the two senses of "intercourse" in English – are brought together in *C. Acad.*'s two dedications, which lay out *C. Acad.*'s basic strategy *in nuce*.

Augustine dedicates the work to his benefactor and fellow North African, Romanianus.[76] While still a Manichee, Augustine had led Romanianus to join the sect, which, in *C. Acad.*, he refers to simply as "that superstition" (*illa superstitio*).[77] Now that Augustine has abandoned the

---

[74] Cf. Plato, *R.* 518c, where Socrates transitions from the Sun, Line and Cave analogies to the Guardians' 50-year curriculum via the claim that education is not a matter of pouring knowledge into the soul but of turning it from darkness toward truth. Catapano uses *C. Acad.*1's various discussions to piece together a conception of philosophy of conversion and purification. Giovanni Catapano, "In philosophiae gremium confugere: Augustine's View of Philosophy in the First Book of his *Contra Academicos*," *Dionysius* 18 (2000): 45–68. Paul R. Kolbet, *Augustine and the Cure of Souls* (Notre Dame, 2010) helpfully situates Augustine within classical notions of philosophy as therapy for the soul. For the presence of protreptic themes within *C. Acad.*, see Valentin, "Protreptique," and Sophie Van der Meeren, "La sagesse 'droit chemin de la vie': une métaphore du *Contra Academicos* relue à la lumière du protreptique philosophique," *Revue des Études Augustiniennes* 53 (2007): 81–111. Generic classification of the protreptic genre is notoriously difficult; see Mark D. Jordan, "Ancient Philosophical Protreptic and the Problem of Persuasive Genres," *Rhetorica* 4/4 (1986): 309–333; Slings, Simon R. "Protreptic in Ancient Theories of Philosophical Literature." In *Greek Literary Theory after Aristotle*, ed. Jelle Abbenes, Simon Slings, Ineke Sluiter & Dirk Schenkeveld (Amsterdam: VU University Press, 1995): 173–192. While the description of *C. Acad.*'s overall structure has much in common with the protreptic genre, my goal is to understand how *C. Acad.* works. I argue that *De beata v.*, *De ord.* and all of Augustine's later dialogues work in roughly the same way. Whether or not that places all of Augustine's dialogues within the protreptic sub-genre is beyond my current concerns.

[75] *C. Acad.* 3.38.

[76] *C. Acad.* 1.1–4, 2.1–9. For discussion on the literary and philosophical sources of these two dedications, see Karin Schlapbach, "Ciceronisches und Neoplatonisches in den Proömien von Augustin, *Contra Academicos* 1 und 2." In *Zur Rezeption der hellenistischen Philosophie in der Spätantike*, ed. T. Fuhrer & M. Ehler (Stuttgart: Franz Steiner, 1999): 139–151.

[77] *C. Acad.* 1.3.

Manichees, he is eager to get Romanianus to follow his lead once again. *C. Acad.* functions as a palinode of sorts, distancing Augustine from his still recent Manichee past. Augustine begins his case by listing various material pleasures and honors, which he claims make men miserable.[78] He proceeds to suggest that philosophy may free one from such things, by teaching that nothing should be worshiped that can be perceived by the bodily senses.[79] If we take this opening suggestion with the secret history's closing discussion of the *consuetudo corporum*, we find Augustine identifying a moral failure (valuing material goods) as the cause of an intellectual failure (thinking that only material things exist).[80] Augustine takes stock of Romanianus' moral progress in this regard, and he uses the same account of the moral/intellectual dangers of materialism to frame his own recent choices: In committing himself to Platonist philosophy and the catholic faith, Augustine left behind both Manicheism and a career in rhetoric, the "windy profession" (*uentosa professio*) that praises material goods.[81]

The work's second dedication spells out the implications of the intellectual failure of materialism. Augustine explains to his former patron:

> *Sed quia siue uitae huius multis uariisque iactationibus, Romaniane, ut in eodem te probas, siue ingeniorum quodam stupore uel socordia uel tarditate torpentium siue desperatione inueniendi – quia non quam facile oculis ista lux, tam facile mentibus sapientiae sidus oboritur – siue etiam, qui error omnino populorum est, falsa opinione inuentae a se ueritatis nec diligenter homines quaerunt, si qui quaerunt, et a quaerendi uoluntate auertuntur, euenit, ut scientia raro paucisque proueniat, eoque fit, ut Academicorum arma, quando cum eis ad manus uenitur, nec mediocribus uiris sed acutis et bene eruditis inuicta et quasi uulcania uideantur.*

> But since, because of either [i] the many varied tribulations of this life, Romanianus, as you judge in your own life, or [ii] a certain mental stupor, laziness, or slowness of sluggish [minds], or [iii] despair of finding truth (for the star of wisdom does not rise before minds with the same ease as this [visible] light rises before our eyes) or [iv] the false opinion that one has already found the truth, which is the mistake of all peoples, people do not inquire after the truth diligently, if they inquire at all, and they are turned away from wanting to inquire, it happens that knowledge seldom comes to

---

[78] *C. Acad.* 1.2.

[79] *docet nihil omnino colendum esse totumque contemni oportere, quicquid mortalibus oculis cernitur, quicquid ullus sensus attingit.* (*C. Acad.* 1.3).

[80] This failure is "intellectual" both in the broad sense of "thinking false things" and in the narrower sense of "thinking the wrong things about intelligible reality," although if we accept Platonism, the two failings coincide.

[81] *C. Acad.* 1.3.

human beings and then only to the few. And for this reason, the Academics' weapons, when it comes to hand-to-hand combat with them, not only with middling men but with clear-sighted and well educated opponents, seem to be invincible and fashioned by Vulcan, as it were. (*C. Acad.* 2.1)

The first two of these obstacles – business and laziness – are fairly mundane. The second two provide a more philosophical dilemma: Since intelligible light is harder to see than physical light – particularly given the *consuetudo corporum* – many people, (iii), grow weary of searching for the truth and eventually despair of ever finding it (*desperare inueniendi*). Alternatively, (iv), the same familiarity with bodies may lead people to suppose falsely that they have already found the truth and thus stop looking for it. This last obstacle Augustine identifies as *superstitio* a few pages later.[82] Materialism as an intellectual failure thus derails the search for truth either through superstition or through despair. Having analyzed this set of problems, Augustine could proceed by treating the symptoms, and it is normally assumed that the goal of *C. Acad.* is to undermine despair by attacking Academic skepticism from every angle imaginable, leaving *superstitio* to be addressed through a similar barrage of anti-Manichee arguments in Augustine's later work, *De uera religione*. Yet *C. Acad.* addresses the cause of these problems as well. I would argue that the attack on materialism is *C. Acad.*'s more basic project. Through it, Augustine sets out to reorient those like Romanianus who perceive the world as just so much matter and to help them recognize their own connection to intelligible reality.

Faith and Philosophy

C. Acad.'s second dedication ends as Augustine advises Romanianus not to judge himself to know anything, unless he is as certain of it as he is that 1+2+3+4=10, and at the same time not to despair of ever grasping the truth in philosophy but rather to trust Him who said, "seek and ye shall find."[83] These seemingly contradictory instructions bring faith and philosophy into some sort of relation. We learn more at the end of the *oratio perpetua*, where Augustine claims to be led on by "the dual weight of authority and

---

[82] *C. Acad.* 2.8.

[83] *cauete, ne quid uos nosse arbitremini, nisi quod ita didiceritis saltem, ut nostis unum duo tria quatuor simul collecta in summam fieri decem. Sed item cauete, ne uos in philosophia ueritatem aut non cognituros aut nullo modo ita posse cognosci arbitremini. Nam mihi credite, uel potius illi credite, qui ait* quaerite et inuenietis [Matthew 7:7], *nec cognitionem desperandam esse et manifestiorem futuram, quam sunt illi numeri.* (*C. Acad.* 2.9).

reason" (*gemino pondere... auctoritatis atque rationis*), which he associates
with Christ and the Platonists, respectively.[84] Taking these two passages
together, we might be tempted to find a one-to-one relation between their
dichotomies: The reason of the Platonists counters superstition by teaching us not to count anything uncertain as known, while the authority of
Christ keeps us from falling into despair by giving us something to believe
in. Yet *C. Acad.* explicitly speaks of the weight of Platonist authority and
ends as Augustine claims to trust (*confido*) that it is with the Platonists that
understanding is to be found. These passages suggest that faith in authority
plays a part in the Platonists' method as well.[85] While this small portion of
text has been pored over within developmentalist debate,[86] its more basic
role within *C. Acad.* is to show that faith and philosophy work in harmony,
provided one subscribes to the correct version of each. We find an example
of this in the work's second discussion of the plausible, which Augustine
uses to construct an argument for the rationality of faith.

Augustine presents a thought experiment midway through his *oratio*.[87]
Two travelers ask for directions: The first rashly "assents" to one set of
directions but quickly reaches his destination; the second "approves" of a
different set of directions and gets thoroughly lost. Augustine concludes
that if the first one erred, then both of them did,[88] and he proceeds to spell

---

[84] "But no one doubts that we are impelled to learn by the dual weight of authority and reason.
Therefore I have resolved not to depart from the authority of Christ in any matter, for I do not find
a stronger one. But since I am moved in such a way that I impatiently desire to grasp what is true
not only by believing it but also by understanding, that which must be followed by the most subtle
reasoning, I trust will be found among the Platonists and that it will not disagree with our
Scriptures, rites and doctrines." (*Nulli autem dubium est gemino pondere nos impelli ad discendum
auctoritatis atque rationis. Mihi ergo certum est nusquam prorsus a Christi auctoritate discedere; non
enim reperio ualentiorem. Quod autem subtilissima ratione persequendum est – ita enim iam sum
affectus, ut quid sit uerum non credendo solum sed etiam intelligendo apprehendere impatienter
desiderem – apud Platonicos me interim, quod sacris nostris non repugnet, reperturum esse confido*).
C. Acad. 3.43.
[85] The relation between faith and reason in Augustine is complex, and a full treatment would require
looking to texts spread across the course of his entire career. For wide-ranging discussions, see
Frederick Van Fleteren, "Authority and Reason, Faith and Understanding in the Thought of St.
Augustine," *Augustinian Studies* 4 (1973): 33–71; Norman Kretzmann, "Faith Seeks,
Understanding Finds: Augustine's Charter for Christian Philosophy." In *Christian Philosophy*, ed.
Thomas Flint (Notre Dame: University of Notre Dame Press 1990): 1–36; John Rist, "Faith and
Reason." At present, I will look to this issue only insofar as it bears on the overall structure of the
Cassiciacum dialogues and plays a role within the method Augustine articulates in them. While the
dialogues make passing reference to faith as an alternative to the way of reason (*C. Acad.* 2.42 and
De ord. 2.27), I will focus on faith insofar as it is a part of philosophical inquiry of the sort Augustine
pursues in these works.
[86] See Introduction.   [87] *C. Acad.* 3.34–36.
[88] "It easier [to think] that both travelers err, than that that one [who approves but gets lost] does not."
(*facilius ambo errant, quam iste non errat*). *C. Acad.* 3.34.

out parallel examples of approval and assent in legal settings. Some scholars take this to be *C. Acad.*'s definitive refutation of skepticism.[89] We should, however, note that it comes after Augustine's long list of cognitive impressions that demonstrates that cognition is possible. Given that the Academics' argument against assent rested on their prior argument against the possibility of cognition, there is no need for another refutation of the Academics' use of *probabilia*. Defenders of the "moral reading" have argued that it is this later discussion of *probabilia* rather than the earlier "epistemological" discussion of cognition that constitutes *C. Acad.*'s real refutation.[90] Others have seen this later passage as simply an attempt at kicking the skeptics when they're down.[91] I suggest that Augustine sets his sights higher than either of these goals.

This thought experiment allows Augustine to augment the Stoic/Academic definition of error as assent to an incognitive impression. On the basis of this definition, the first traveler (who assented and arrived at his destination) errs, while the second (who approved and got lost) does not. This absurd consequence allows Augustine to argue that the Stoic/Academic definition is too narrow, insofar as it omits instances in which one fails to follow a true impression.[92] Given this expanded definition of error, both travelers err. This rather bleak outcome advances Augustine's constructive project, insofar as it allows him to introduce considerations beyond the avoidance of error (in its new expanded sense), at least when matters of action are concerned. In the case of the two travelers, the relevant consideration is whether one arrives at his destination or not: The first traveler commits an epistemic error, yet arrives at his destination; the second avoids this epistemic error but commits what we might call a "practical error" in getting thoroughly lost. It is, of course, best to avoid

---

[89] Brian Harding, "Epistemology and Eudaimonism"; John Heil, "Augustine's Attack on Skepticism"; David Mosher, "The Argument of St. Augustine's *Contra Academicos*."

[90] Harding, Heil and Mosher defend this line in opposition to what Harding has dubbed the "received reading." They find the main thrust of the work to be "moral" and cite the legal formulations of Augustine's thought experiment as the crux of the whole work's argument. Given the connection of wisdom and happiness in ancient eudaimonism, this opposition of epistemology and morality supposes a false dichotomy, as Sophie Van der Meeren, "La sagesse," has helpfully pointed out. What's more, the morality discussed by these scholars has more to do with civic behavior than with happiness/flourishing (*beata uita*) and thus falls far short of articulating the ultimate goal of Augustine's philosophical undertaking. See also Curley, *Augustine's Critique of Skepticism*, 81, for the claim that the *apraxia* argument is "political" rather than "philosophical."

[91] Christopher Kirwan, "Against the Skeptics."

[92] "For I think that not only he who follows a false path errs, but also he who fails to follow a true path." (*Non solum enim eum puto errare, qui falsam uiam sequitur, sed etiam eum, qui ueram non sequitur*). *C. Acad.* 3.34. "Following" is another term for approval. This choice of terms highlights the practical nature of the current argument.

both sorts of error, but in situations when this is impossible, Augustine argues that an individual is in some sense justified in committing an epistemic error (which the Stoics and Academics avoid at all costs), when by doing so he may escape a practical error.[93] Within *C. Acad.*, the further consideration relevant to action is whether one eventually attains wisdom or not. The person who reaches this goal escapes error by all definitions, and Augustine concludes that one is justified in erring (through assenting to the incognitive), when this may lead one out of error altogether. With this, Augustine shows that the Academics' strategy of limiting themselves to approval is both insufficient for avoiding error, since one must approve of the *right* impressions, and basically useless for identifying what those impressions are, given that we are starting out in a state other than wisdom. Augustine concludes that we are practically justified in accepting, even assenting to, positions about which we lack certainty (i.e. catholic Christianity and Platonic intellectualism) when doing so will bring us to certainty in the end. This is not a blind faith, however, as Augustine goes beyond standard Academic practice to develop a method of aporetic debate and reflection on our own rational activity to guide us in coming to see some positions as more plausible than others.[94]

Conclusion

At this point, I hope to have put *C. Acad.*'s refutation of skepticism into perspective. Scholars have been right to find antiskeptical arguments scattered throughout the work and to judge some of them more successful than others. But by setting these arguments within a broader pedagogical project, we shift the emphasis from whether these arguments succeed to why they succeed. This allows us to recognize that the nonempirical nature of book 3's norms of thought is just as important as their certainty; that book 2's argument against people who use plausible/truthlike impressions

---

[93] In the courtroom examples which follow, the practical error to be avoided is "sinning" (*peccare*). Proponents of the "moral" reading of *C. Acad.* have, in my view, been swept away by the rhetoric of the passage and as a result, seen the ethical implications of *C. Acad.* in too narrow (i.e. modern) terms of correct action, rather than the more robust (ancient) conception of happiness/human flourishing.

[94] Pascal offers a modern parallel to Augustine's broad strategy: given widespread uncertainty when it comes to matters of wisdom and God, it is rational for us, *ceteris paribus*, to make wagers and take ideas on faith when doing so may eventually lead us out of uncertainty. We find similar arguments in Augustine's later work, *De util. cred.* 25. See Isabelle Bochet, "Justifying Belief: The Use of Skeptical Arguments in the *De utilitate credendi*," (paper presented as part of the Townsend Lectures at Cornell University, Ithaca, New York, May 1, 2015).

while refusing to assent to any truth does not stop people who assent to some truths from doing so. Perhaps most importantly, we find that book 1's inconclusive debate advances the work's overall project in two central ways. Insofar as Licentius and Trygetius fail to reach a conclusion, they call attention to the shortcomings of empiricism. Yet insofar as they succeed at having a debate, they model rational activity that presupposes norms of thought that can be grasped as certain. All of this proceeds according to Augustine's master plan.

By taking on the terms of the Stoic/Academic debate, *C. Acad.* treats certainty as a kind of "holy grail," the ultimate object of all philosophical striving. In doing this, the text might seem to suggest that certainty is vital to Augustine's own epistemology as well. According to the secret history, though, the early Academics looked on the Stoic demand for certainty and were not terribly impressed. Certainty played no part in early Academic epistemology, and Arcesilaus adopted it only as a dialectical means of confronting the Stoics' materialism, which he saw as much more problematic. Likewise, the ultimate concern of *C. Acad.* is not certainty or even epistemology in general. Like Arcesilaus, Augustine uses these matters as fodder for a course of Platonic pedagogy whose goals are not apparent until the end.

C. Acad.'s most basic project goal, I suggest, is to model the search for wisdom and articulate a method for undertaking this search. At *C. Acad.* 3.43, Augustine announces that at age 33, he has not yet found wisdom, though he has devoted himself to the search and is spurred on "by the dual weight of authority and reason" (*gemino pondere ... auctoritatis atque rationis*). This passage situates *C. Acad.* within the two schemes that bind the Cassiciacum dialogues into a set, as it picks out one of the classical virtues, wisdom, and one of the terms from Wisdom 11:20's triad: measure, number, weight. Augustine combines these to underscore that wisdom is pursued through authority and reason working in tandem. This particular pairing will stay with Augustine throughout his career.[95] What *C. Acad.* has to tell us is that reason allows us to justify faith in authority, to choose which authority to believe and to approach that authority with a healthy skepticism. Beyond all the details of the Stoic/Academic debate, Licentius models the last of these beautifully. While he treats Augustine with all respect due a teacher, he looks for every means possible to defeat his teacher's position. As a Platonic teacher, this is exactly what Augustine hopes his students will do. Small wonder, then, that he is more pleased

---

[95] See Chapter 7 for *De lib. arbit.*'s discussion of "faith seeking understanding."

with Licentius for opposing him than he is with Trygetius, who seems to be his ally.

Of the four classical virtues, wisdom provides a suitable starting point for Augustine's new philosophical undertaking, inasmuch as *C. Acad.*'s exploration of this virtue confronts basic questions about the nature of philosophy. It also yields a method, ARP, which Augustine will use and develop throughout the rest of the Cassiciacum works and his dialogue corpus as a whole. Chapters 3–7 will substantiate this claim as I present a fresh reading of these works and their characteristic approach to philosophy as the pursuit of virtue. I argue that a process of ARP, in some form or another, is the key to understanding how each of these dialogues functions as a single, unified whole. Before we turn to this, though, Chapter 2 explores what it means for Augustine to claim a Platonic pedigree for his method.

From Plato to Augustine

Chapter 1 explored the implications of *C. Acad.*'s "secret history" of the Academy for understanding Augustine's own project. I argued that this passage is key to understanding the basic philosophical method employed in *C. Acad.* and Augustine's dialogue corpus generally. In this, I take *C. Acad.* to be a programmatic work, in which Augustine displays his chosen method for writing dialogues and claims a Platonic pedigree for it. Up to this point, I have set aside questions about the historical accuracy of the secret history's claims and focused on how Augustine's use of this history helps us understand Augustine's own project. Doing so let us see that the whole of *C. Acad.*, at the most basic level, proceeds through a distinctive combination of (A) aporetic debate and (R) reflection on rational activity leading to (P) a plausible conclusion. In Chapters 3–7, I will argue that this basic method, ARP, provides the structuring principle for all eight of Augustine's dialogues. By broadening our focus for a moment, we find that this basic method at the heart of Augustine's dialogues is plausibly at play in central portions of Plato's corpus as well. *Men.*'s paradox of inquiry, reflection on a geometry lesson and theory of recollection provide a particularly clear instance of an ARP-style argument. In this respect, Augustine has written dialogues that are more authentically "Platonic" in their methodological and rhetorical orientation than either the dialogues of Cicero or the treatises of Plotinus. This is surprising, given that Cicero and Plotinus read Plato's works directly, while, according to our current best scholarship, Augustine did not.[1] This realization need not alter how we read Augustine's dialogues. But it does have implications for how we think about his place within the history of ancient philosophy and the dialogue genre. The present chapter seeks to understand Augustine as part of the "Academic" tradition – which for him includes Socrates, Plato, Cicero

[1] Pierre Courcelle, *Les lettres grecques en Occident, de Macrobe à Cassiodore* (Paris: Bibliothèque des Écoles françaises et de Rome, 1943).

and Plotinus – and to suggest how he could use intermediary sources –
Cicero and Plotinus – to work back to their common origin.[2]

From the standpoint of method, there are two basic strands running
through the works of Plato and the subsequent tradition. The elenctic
method proceeds by refining concepts and unearthing contradictions
before descending into perplexity (*aporia*). Consistency is its main criterion
and "un-learning" is its goal. It is the characteristic mode of inquiry found
in what are usually thought of as Plato's "early" or "Socratic" works.[3] The
hypothetical method, by contrast, proceeds by refining questions and
entertaining provisional answers. Its criteria are varied but include reflection on rational activity. Its ultimate goal is holistic knowledge, but it is
willing to deal with provisional answers in the meanwhile. It is the
characteristic mode of Plato's "middle" works.[4] These two methods are
brought together in Plato's *Men.*, which opens via elenchus and ends via
the method of hypothesis.[5] They are separated again by Cicero, who
presents Academic skepticism as a formalized version of Socratic elenchus,
and Plotinus, whose dialectical approach presents a distillation of Plato's
hypothetical method.

My suggestion, in its broadest terms, is that Augustine put these two
strands back together creating something substantially akin to *Men.* in its
philosophical method. This tidy picture is complicated, first, insofar as the
split is not as clean as I have stated it here (Cicero's skeptical method, for
instance, embraces provisional answers in a way characteristic of the
hypothetical rather than the elenctic approach); and, second, insofar as
Augustine approaches these matters through what is effectively a conspir-
acy theory. While all he needs to say is that Plotinus' methodology can be

---

[2] In this, I simply accept Courcelle's conclusions. The similarities I point out here could also be used
to argue that Augustine had read more Plato than Courcelle admits. Such an outcome would be
compatible with the argument of this chapter.

[3] Richard Kraut, "Introduction to the Study of Plato." In *Cambridge Companion to Plato* (Cambridge:
Cambridge University Press, 1992), 1–50 lists the early dialogues as *Ap., Charmides, Crito,
Euthyphro, Grg., Hippias Minor, Ion, Laches, Protagoras, Euthydemus, Hippias Major, Lysis,
Menexenus* and *R.* 1.

[4] Kraut, "Introduction" gives *Men., Cratylus, Phd., Smp., R.* 2–10, *Phdr., Parmenides* and *Theaetetus* as
the middle dialogues. I will not be discussing Plato's "late" dialogues –*Ti., Critias, Sophist, Statesman,
Philebus* and *Laws* – which, in general terms, critique the theory of forms put forth in the middle
works. On one standard view, these three groupings – early, middle and late – trace the development of
Plato's thought over time. While this developmental scheme is not universally accepted, for our
purposes what matters is not the order that Plato wrote in but merely the fact that different works
employ different methods. I will thus use "early" and "middle" as shorthand for works that employ the
elenctic or hypothetical method, respectively, without committing to any particular chronology.

[5] For this reason *Men.* is commonly thought of as a transitional work straddling Plato's early and
middle periods.

combined with Cicero's, what he does say is that Cicero and Plotinus were in fact engaged in the same basic project and employed the same methodology. If, however, we grant that this is simply Augustine's way of using his predecessors' work to think with, we may discuss how the methods of Cicero and Plotinus can be brought together; we need not worry about whether either author intended us to do so. This should suffice for our own project of understanding Augustine's relation to his philosophical models, so as to suggest how he was able to capture *Men.* so successfully.[6]

In what follows, I begin by setting out these two strands – elenchus and hypothesis – within Plato himself. I draw on Gregory Vlastos for discussion of the elenchus and Hugh Benson for discussion of the hypothetical method. *Men.* provides my model for how the two methods may be combined in a single project. Turning to the later tradition, I address how it is possible for Cicero to be both an Academic skeptic and a Platonist, and I suggest that by reading Cicero's Academic skeptical dialogues in light of a Platonic passage in *Tusc.* 1, Augustine could have put together his Platonic method, ARP. I corroborate this reading by examining passages of Plotinus that might have suggested such an approach to Cicero in the first place. I end by spelling out the rhetorical implications of this methodological history, offering a new explanation grounded in this methodological survey of the Academy for Augustine's habit of ending dialogues via *oratio perpetua*.

Socratic Elenchus

Concerns for method are, for the most part, merely implicit in Plato's early dialogues. Nevertheless, a common method, which scholars have come to call the *elenchus* (from the Greek for "cross-examination"), can be teased out by analyzing the shape of each work's overarching argument. The works typically open as Socrates encounters someone who claims some

---

[6] Likewise for Plato himself: My goal is not to uncover what Plato intended for his various works, but how Augustine was able to approximate *Men.* on one particular reading of that work. The closest scholars come to evaluating Augustine's Platonic pedigree is to ask what Augustine's sources for this historical narrative might be: Pierre Hadot, "Le *Contra Academicos* de saint Augustin et l'histoire de l'Académie," *École Pratique des Hautes Études, section 5: Sciences religieuses* 77 (1969): 291–295; Carlos Levy, "Scepticisme et dogmatisme dans l'Académie: 'l'ésotérisme' d'Arcésilas," *Revue des Études Augustiniennes* 56 (1979): 335–348; Therese Fuhrer, *Contra Academicos*, 403–405; Charles Brittain, *Philo*, 242–246. In a slightly different vein, Emmanuel Bermon, "saint Augustin et les *Academica* de Cicéron," and Charles Brittain, "Augustine as a Reader of Cicero." In *Tolle Lege: Essays on Augustine and Medieval Philosophy* (Milwaukee: Marquette University Press, 2011), 81–114, address the question of whether Augustine himself believed the secret history.

kind of moral knowledge. Socrates asks this person to define a term or defend a thesis. His interlocutor makes a series of valiant attempts; Socrates shoots them all down. Their discussion finally collapses into *aporia*, and Socrates' interlocutor responds by either seeking guidance or storming off. In pointing out the problems with others' ideas, though, Socrates does not invoke any expert knowledge. He merely pits his interlocutor's beliefs against themselves. The best this can hope to accomplish is to test whether Socrates' interlocutor is consistent in his beliefs. Yet Socrates seems to go beyond this and uses some of his interlocutor's beliefs to declare some of the interlocutor's other beliefs *false*. Vlastos has dubbed this "the problem of the elenchus."[7] He gives the following formal analysis of a standard elenchus:[8]

(1)   The interlocutor states a thesis, say *p*, which Socrates considers false and targets for refutation.

(2)   Socrates secures further agreement to further premises, say *q* and *r* (each of which may stand for a conjunct of propositions). The agreement is *ad hoc*. Socrates argues from *q* and *r*, but not to them.

(3)   Socrates then argues, and the interlocutor agrees, that *q* and *r* entail *not-p*.

(4)   Thereupon Socrates claims that *not-p* has been proven true, *p* false.

The problem, as Vlastos points out, is that *q* and *r* are "logically unsecured within the argument."[9] Because of this, the furthest this argument may viably proceed is (3). In his early work, perhaps out of a principle of charity, Vlastos claimed that this was all Socrates was attempting to do. Over time, though, Vlastos came to see that this is not supported by the dialogues themselves, and he admitted that Socrates does in fact, albeit without warrant, proceed all the way to (4).[10] What should we make of dialogues that use flawed arguments only to arrive at perplexity?

Some scholars hold that exposing ignorance and confusion, i.e. proceeding to (3), is itself a philosophically valuable accomplishment. Benson, for instance, argues that the goal of the early dialogues is not to determine the truth but to test the individual's overall state of beliefs.[11] Tarrant claims that the dialogues are primarily testing people rather than trying to

[7] Gregory Vlastos, "The Socratic Elenchus." In *Plato*, vol. 1, ed. Gail Fine (Oxford: Oxford University Press, 1999), 36–63.

[8] Vlastos, "Elenchus," 46.   [9] Vlastos, "Elenchus," 47.   [10] Vlastos, "Elenchus," 51.

[11] Hugh Benson, *Socratic Wisdom: The Model of Knowledge in Plato's Early Dialogues* (Oxford, 2000).

establish beliefs.[12] Matthews goes so far as to analyze twelve different types and uses of perplexity in Plato and Aristotle.[13] And we should not forget that Socrates presents himself as the wisest human being insofar as he does not take himself to know things that he does not know.[14]

Other scholars hold that Socrates was aiming higher and meant to get all the way to knowledge, i.e. to proceed all the way to (4), by use of the elenchus. This is problematic, however, if the best the elenchus can show is consistency, and consistency is insufficient to secure knowledge. Vlastos responds by carving out a category of "elenctic knowledge," i.e. knowledge that is consistent enough to withstand elenctic scrutiny, which he posited was the goal of the elenchus.[15] This deflationary reading, however, sits ill with a number of other things Socrates says about knowledge, and Vlastos himself admits that elenctic knowledge would still be second-best to "certain knowledge."[16] In sum, it is unclear what Socrates (or Plato writing through him) hoped to accomplish via the elenchus, though there is good reason to worry that the elenchus might not be up to the task.

Plato's Method of Hypothesis

Plato makes these methodological concerns explicit in *Men.*, where he formulates a version of Vlastos' problem of the elenchus and responds to it. The first third of the dialogue follows the familiar form of an elenchus,[17] as Socrates engages Meno in a discussion of whether virtue can be taught. They both end up in *aporia*.[18] Yet rather than run off to another engagement, Meno fights back, pointing out that their effort is doomed to failure. The resulting "paradox of inquiry" can be put as follows:[19]

---

[12] Harold Tarrant, "Socratic Method and Socratic Truth." In *A Companion to Socrates*, ed. Sara Ahbel-Rappe and Rachana Kamtekar (Oxford: Oxford University Press, 2006), 254–272.

[13] Gareth Matthews, *Socratic Perplexity and the Nature of Philosophy* (Oxford: Oxford University Press, 1999).

[14] Plato, *Ap.* 23a–b.

[15] Gregory Vlastos, "Socrates' Disavowal of Knowledge." In *Plato*, vol. 2, ed. Gail Fine (Oxford: Oxford University Press, 1999), 64–92.

[16] Vlastos, "Socrates' Disavowal," 79. For a critique of Vlastos' attempt to find Plato consistently distinguishing between these two forms of knowledge, see Matthews, "Shared Perplexity: The Self-Stinging Stingray." In *Socratic Perplexity*, 43–52.

[17] Plato, *Men.* 70–80.   [18] Plato, *Men.* 79c.

[19] Plato, *Men.* 80d–e. More precisely, Meno poses one problem, Socrates restates it, and it is not entirely clear which version they then responded to. The literature on these few lines is immense. For a critical overview, see Dominic Scott, *Plato's Meno* (Cambridge: Cambridge University Press, 2006). I have presented a combined version, inserting Meno's version as the sub-dilemma (a)/(b) within Socrates' larger dilemma.

(1)   For any object of inquiry, X, person P either knows X or does not
      know X.
(2)   If P knows X, then P cannot inquire into X because P already
      knows X.
(3)   If P does not know X, then P cannot inquire into X because either
      (a)   P will not be able to start inquiring after X, or
      (b)   P will not be able to identify X if P happens across X.
(4)   Thus P cannot inquire into X.

The crux of the puzzle is that to engage in inquiry, one must have enough to
go on yet still have somewhere to go.[20] Insofar as X covers *any* object of
inquiry, this paradox offers a thoroughly damning critique of Socratic
method. (3b), in particular, captures Vlastos' worry about elenchus: Even if
Meno had stumbled across the truth at some point in his initial discussion
with Socrates, he lacks a secure basis to distinguish it from false beliefs that
may contradict it. Meno articulates this worry and sets it within a broader
puzzle about inquiry. Within *Men.*, this methodological interlude marks the
transition between an initial elenctic inquiry and a second inquiry employing
the method of hypothesis. It is for this reason that scholars take *Men.* to be a
transitional work between Plato's early and middle periods. What concerns us
for the moment, though, is how the interlude's discussion of method relates to
the work's second attempt at inquiry, and what this tells us about the relation
of Socratic elenchus to Plato's new method of hypothesis.

Benson offers a formal analysis of Plato's hypothetical method. Limiting
himself to explicit discussions of the method in *Men.* and *Phd.*, which he
fills out by analyzing instances of the method at work in *Men.*, *Phd.* and
Republic, Benson offers the following scheme:[21]

---

[20] Standard scholarly resolutions revolve around further specifying "know." If we take "know" to mean
"partly know," then (2) is false, since a person with partial knowledge can seek to attain fuller
knowledge through inquiry. (2) is only a problem if we take "know" to mean "fully know." But on
this reading, (3) is false since a person who does not *fully* know X may still know *something* about X,
and this may be sufficient for both starting an inquiry, (a), and for bringing it to a successful
conclusion, (b). Alternatively, we could step back and ask what "knowledge" consists in. Later in the
work, 98b, Socrates suggests that knowledge is true belief that has been tied down with "an account
of the reason why" (*aitias logismos*). If we take "know" in the paradox to refer to such a lofty
epistemic state, then we could claim again that (3) is false: a person may have true beliefs about a
subject without being able to give an account of why these beliefs are true. These true beliefs may,
again *contra* (3), provide a basis for starting, (a), and successfully completing, (b), an inquiry. From
another angle, we could take "know" to mean "latently knows," which renders (2) false; or as
"occurrently knows," which renders (3) false. For critical review of these various moves, see Gail
Fine, "Inquiry in the Meno." In *Plato on Knowledge and Forms* (Oxford: Oxford University Press,
2003), 200–226.

[21] Benson, *Clitophon's Challenge*, 244.

[T]he method consists of two stages when seeking to answer some question (Q1), a proof stage that in turn consists in two procedures:

[Pa]   Identify a second question (Q2) from whose most compelling answer (the hypothesis (H1)) the answer (A1) to the original question (Q1) can be obtained.

[Pb]   Show how A1 is obtained from H1; sometimes this will be immediate and trivial, sometimes not;

and a confirmation stage, which also consists of two procedures:

[Ca]   Test the things that start out from (*hormēthenta*) H1 for agreement or disagreement with each other.

[Cb]   Identify a second reduced question (Q3) from whose most compelling answer (the higher hypothesis (H2)) H1/A2 can be obtained, and continue this process until one reaches something adequate (*hikanon*).

This scheme is an idealized version of a method scattered across Plato's middle works. By Benson's own admission, (Pb) is sometimes passed over, leaving the reader to make connections.[22] Plato is likewise somewhat vague about what, (Ca), testing the *hormēthenta* (i.e. the consequences) of one's hypotheses actually amounts to. In different contexts he treats this as a means of looking for consistency within the hypothesis itself, within one's set of beliefs, or with everyday experience of the world.[23] (Pa) and (Cb) often proceed in tandem, amounting to the basic instruction to keep moving to higher questions until one arrives at something adequate. While the elenchus sometimes moves deeper/higher and sometimes merely moves sideways, the hypothetical method actively pursues the former. The notion of "adequate" in (Cb) is a bit vague, perhaps meaning no more than what will strike Socrates' interlocutors as sufficient for their purposes at the moment. Ideally, though, one will eventually make it back to an unhypothetical first starting point (*archē*), such as the form of the Good in *R.*[24] Given the emphasis on wide-ranging explanation, this *archē* confers a form of holistic knowledge.[25] According to Benson, though, one may correctly engage in this process without attaining this final goal, provided the inquirer recognizes that his highest hypothesis (Hn) is in fact a hypothesis,

[22] Benson, *Clitophon's Challenge*, 204–207.   [23] Benson, *Clitophon's Challenge*, 135–139.
[24] Benson, *Clitophon's Challenge*, 149.
[25] Cf. Gail Fine, "Knowledge and Belief in Plato's *Republic* 5–7." In *Plato*, vol. 1, 215–246, who argues that the form of the Good in *Rep.* may be seen as a predecessor to coherence theory in current epistemology.

i.e. a provisional response, awaiting confirmation and/or a *logos* based on an unhypothetical *archē*.[26]

In order to bring Benson's scheme more closely in line with our discussion of Augustine, let us simplify it to the following four stages:

Stage 1   Ascend through higher/more basic hypotheses.
Stage 2   State hypotheses as provisional.
Stage 3   Test the consequences of one's hypotheses for consistency.
Stage 4   Attain holistic knowledge.

In rough terms, Augustine's aporetic debates accomplish the same end as Stage 1; his reflection on rational activity provides a particular means of accomplishing Stage 3's testing; and his plausible conclusions reflect Stage 2's willingness to deal in provisional answers. While Augustine does not claim to arrive at knowledge in the dialogues, there is good reason to think that it is the holistic knowledge of Stage 4 that he is ultimately after.[27] And while the order of these stages is somewhat different in Plato and August-ine, I take this to be a rhetorical rather than a philosophical difference.[28]

Benson presents *Men.*'s second inquiry into virtue as an instance of this scheme:[29]

Stage 1   (Q1) Is virtue teachable? → If virtue is knowledge, then it is
                  teachable.
           (Q2) Is virtue knowledge? → If something is good, then it is
                  knowledge.
           (Q3) Is virtue good?
Stage 2   (A3) Virtue is good.
           (A2) Virtue is knowledge.
Stage 3   But there are no teachers of virtue.

The overall framework is taken from geometry. It is not a demonstrative proof, but a method for trying out candidate proofs. Hence the provisional nature of the undertaking. Within *Men.* the search goes off track in the confirmation stage. In the process of testing the hypothesis that virtue is

---

[26] While *R.* gestures at such a starting point, Socrates is clear that actually getting to it would require a "longer road" than the one he is now leading his companions down (*R.* 435c-d and 504b ff.). For discussion, see Mitchell Miller, "Beginning the 'Longer Way'." In *Cambridge Companion to Plato's Republic*, ed. G. R. F. Ferrari (Cambridge: Cambridge University Press, 2007), 310–344. *Smp.*, likewise, describes a ladder of loves reaching to the vision of Beauty itself, although Plato does not imply that this vision is somehow reached by merely reading *Smp.* itself.
[27] This is clearest in *De ordine*. See Chapter 4.   [28] See discussion at the end of this chapter.
[29] Benson, *Clitophon's Challenge*, 174. I have adjusted Benson's presentation to make it fit my simplified scheme.

knowledge, Socrates points out that it should follow from this that there are actually teachers of virtue, although the weight of empirical evidence seems to say otherwise. The consequences of the hypothesis (A2) are thus not in agreement with experience. While this particular line of argument fails to reach the holistic knowledge of Stage 4, this should not detract from our seeing the method at work. This particular example also highlights the fact that Plato does not explain how one identifies higher questions to ask. While the step from (Q1)'s conception of virtue as teachable to (Q2)'s conception of virtue as knowledge is obvious enough, the step from here to all goods being knowledge seems bizarre. Given that progress in this method largely depends on the ability to find the right questions, some guidance on how to go about this would be helpful.[30] I suggest that this underdeveloped aspect of Plato's method will be addressed by Cicero and Plotinus' practice of reflecting on rational activity.

Taken as a whole, *Men.* shows that elenchus and hypothesis may be joined within a single project. In this case, the opening elenchus clears the ground and convinces Meno of the need for further work, while the closing inquiry via the hypothetical method advances this project, albeit without reaching a final conclusion. As we turn to later authors who pulled elenchus and hypothesis apart, we should hold *Men.*'s moment of reconciliation in mind, as it suggests to us the possibilities for situating these two approaches to inquiry within a single project. By keeping our eyes open for what work an argument can accomplish, rather than what its author meant for it to accomplish, we may view the Academic tradition through the lens of Augustine's secret history.

Cicero: Skeptic or Platonist?

The straightest path connecting Augustine to Plato looks to Cicero's Academic skeptical dialogues for a formalized version of Socratic elenchus and to Plotinian dialectic as a distilled version of Plato's hypothetical method. Augustine's secret history complicates this tidy picture: By claiming that the Academic skeptics were really Platonists in disguise, Augustine suggests that Cicero was a Platonist rather than a skeptic, or, better, both a Platonist *and* a skeptic. While the latter view may seem contradictory, it is in one sense quite in line with Cicero's own commitments. To see how, we must first clarify what exactly is entailed by the Academic skepticism Cicero advocates.

---

[30] See Benson, *Clitophon's Challenge*, 124–126.

Sextus Empiricus, writing nearly two centuries after Cicero, divided philosophers into three groups: dogmatists, who think they have discovered the truth; Academics, who assert that the truth cannot be grasped; and skeptics, who are still investigating.[31] While the Academics' arguments against the possibility of cognition might give the sense that they take knowledge to be impossible, Sextus – who represented the rival, Pyrrhonean, skeptical school – was likely too quick to judge the Academics here.[32] The historical Academics present themselves as inquirers after the truth, i.e. "skeptics" in Sextus' sense, who are happy to critique the views of others as a means of searching for the answers to central philosophical questions. This basic orientation gives Cicero's *De natura deorum, De finibus* and *De divinatione* their basic shape. Each presents paired speeches arguing for and then against particular schools' views on a given subject. Each work ends as characters decide which of the views under discussion strikes them as most plausible (*probabile/veri simile*) given the considerations just laid on the table via debate. Take *N.D.* for instance: In book 1, the character Velleius presents a speech in support of Epicurean theology and Cotta presents an Academic refutation of it; Balbus speaks in favor of Stoic theology in book 2, which Cotta proceeds to refute in book 3. The work ends as Cicero reports, "Cotta's argument [against Balbus] seemed to Velleius to be more truthful, but in my eyes, Balbus' case seemed to come more closely to a semblance of the truth."[33] Having just heard a refutation of Stoicism presented by a fellow member of his Academic school, Cicero ends by siding with the Stoics. This apparent contradiction can be resolved by recognizing that Academic skepticism, as presented in the structure of Cicero's dialogues, is not a commitment to a body of first-order claims about the world but to a second-order attitude about what it means to hold a commitment in the first place. A Stoic and an Academic may thus subscribe to the same views about the gods or whatever else. The difference is that the Stoic holds his views to be the truth, while the Academic holds them to be truth-like or plausible, given current considerations.[34]

[31] Sextus, *Outlines of Pyrrhonism* 1.1–4.
[32] The most direct evidence is perhaps *N.D.* 1.12 in whose dedication Cicero states, "We Academics are not the type of philosophers who think that nothing is true."
[33] Cicero, *N.D.* 3.95.
[34] For discussion of Cicero's Academic skeptical approach to writing dialogues, see Malcolm Schofield, "Ciceronian Dialogue." In *The End of Dialogue in Antiquity*, ed. Simon Goldhill (Oxford: Oxford University Press, 2008), 64–84 and J. G. F. Powell, *Cicero the Philosopher* (Oxford: Oxford University Press, 1995).

Cicero presents his skeptical approach as a formalized version of the Socratic elenchus.[35] His paired speeches use the Roman law court as a model for an approach to challenging and defending hypotheses[36] or, to be more exact, to defending and *then* challenging. His Stoic and Epicurean characters are aware of the main counter-arguments to their positions and often respond to these challenges before their Academic interlocutors have had a chance to voice them. One gets the sense of a well-worn dispute, with the major moves worked out ahead of time. Cicero's works spend little time identifying higher/deeper questions, for the simple reason that they are already concerned with basic questions.[37] In this respect, they have little in common with Plato's hypothetical method. It is likewise unclear that they are aimed at the holistic knowledge that is the hypothetical method's ultimate goal. What Cicero does capture, though, is the hypothetical method's embrace of provisionality and its commitment to testing the consistency of hypotheses, which are typically supplied by other schools' views. In this sense, the overarching structure of Cicero's Academic skeptical dialogues combines elements of Plato's elenctic and hypothetical methods. Nevertheless, it omits key elements of the hypothetical method that are present in Augustine.

Cicero's *Tusc.* provides the missing piece of the puzzle.[38] Book 1 addresses the fear of death. The student figure, identified only as A. (which might mean *auditor, adulescens* or even *Atticus*), thinks that death is evil and to be feared. The teacher figure, M. (presumably *magister* or *Marcus*, i.e. Cicero), follows Socrates in Plato's *Ap.* by arguing that the soul either keeps on living after death[39] or is destroyed[40] and that neither of these eventualities is evil or to be feared.[41] In the work's dedication, M. presents himself as following Socratic method:

---

[35] See discussion of *Tusc.* 1.8 in this chapter.
[36] The views tested were typically Epicurean, Stoic or Antiochian. While these schools tended not to view their own views as hypotheses, the Academics treated them that way. In this, they carried on in a Socratic spirit.
[37] Thanks go to Charles Brittain, who in commenting on a draft of this chapter helped me view the already-played-out quality of Cicero's debates as a strength rather than a weakness.
[38] Thanks also go to Peter Osorio for help in reconstructing the argument of *Tusc.* 1 (personal communication, August 12–17, 2017).
[39] Cicero, *Tusc.* 1.17–78.   [40] Cicero, *Tusc.* 1.78–112.
[41] The argument is spread across the entire book, though a clear statement of its strategy is set out by A. at 1.26.

fiebat autem ita ut, cum is qui audire uellet dixisset, quid sibi uideretur, tum ego contra dicerem. haec est enim, ut scis, uetus et Socratica ratio contra alterius opinionem disserendi. nam ita facillime, quid ueri simillimum esset, inueniri posse Socrates arbitrabatur.

But it worked out that, when the person who wanted to hear [me speak][42] had said what seemed to him to be the case, I would then speak against him. For this, as you [Brutus] know is the old Socratic method of arguing against the opinion of another. For Socrates thought that what was most truth-like could thus be most easily discovered. (Cicero, *Tusc. Disp.* 1.8)

All of which he claims is an undertaking in "following plausible ideas" (*probabilia conjectura sequens*).[43] So far, so good, but this is still merely a Socratic method applied to Platonic ideas, not an application of Plato's hypothetical method. The key comes at *Tusc.* 1.50–78. Here, while pursuing the possibility that the soul survives death, M. shifts from an extended doxographical survey of cultural and philosophical views on death[44] to arguing for a Platonic position in a Platonic way.

The Platonic idea M. is after is the soul's immortality. His opponents are materialist philosophers for whom, according to M., "there is no reason for the immortality of the soul to seem incredible except that they are incapable of understanding and grasping in thought what sort of thing a soul lacking body would be" (*qualis sit animus uacans corpore*).[45] M.'s strategy for dealing with this shortcoming is to reflect on the activities of the soul and turn the tables on his opponents, arguing their conception of soul *while in a body* is insufficient to explain the activities that souls clearly carries out.[46] These activities include self-motion,[47] memory,[48] discovery[49] and withdrawing from the body.[50] In this, Cicero presents himself as a reader of Plato, as the four activities of soul correspond to central arguments from four of Plato's middle dialogues, each of which Cicero names. The argument from self-motion is drawn explicitly from *Phdr.* 245c–3. The basic idea is that the soul is aware of itself setting itself in motion, and whatever sets itself in motion never ceases to move; thus, the soul is immortal. This argument is, at best, underdetermined. The growth of trees or vines is, after all, a form of motion; likewise, for animals' pursuits and flights. At *Tusc.* 1.56, M. further specifies the activities of soul by focusing on the divine in human souls (*in animis hominum diuina*). It is at this point that

---

[42] Cf. Cicero, *De Finibus* 2.2.   [43] Cicero, *Tusc.* 1.17.   [44] Cicero, *Tusc.* 1.17–49.
[45] Cicero, *Tusc.* 1.50.
[46] Cicero, *Tusc.* 1.51–52. Charles Brittain, "Self-knowledge in Cicero and Augustine (*De Trinitate*, X, 5,7–10, 16)," *Medioevo* 37 (2012): 107–136, provides a helpful analysis of this stretch of text and argues that it provides the model for an argument Augustine presents for the soul's immateriality in his later treatise *De Trinitate* (10.7–16).
[47] Cicero, *Tusc.* 1.53–55.   [48] Cicero, *Tusc.* 1.57–61.   [49] Cicero, *Tusc.* 1.62–70.
[50] Cicero, *Tusc.* 1.70–76.

parallels to Plato's hypothetical method and Augustine's ARP become clearest. The argument from memory draws explicitly on *Men.*'s geometry lesson, pointing out that the mind's limitless capacity for memory cannot be explained in material terms (more on this later in this section). The argument from discovery likens Archimedes' creation of an orrery to the Demiurge's creation of the wandering stars at *Timaeus* 47.[51] At this point, the argument switches slightly. Invoking an argument from design, in which we infer the existence of a Creator that we cannot observe from a creation that we can observe, M. argues that it is just as valid to infer the existence of a soul that we cannot observe from its works – i.e. being active, being wise, discovery, memory (*uigere, sapere, inuenire, meminisse*) – which we can. The passage ends by invoking Socrates "on his final day of life," i.e. *Phd.* The activity in this case is withdrawing from the body, which M. spells out morally (not being too attached to material goods), epistemically (thinking without making use of bodily senses) and metaphysically (soul and body being pulled apart in death). Since the soul fares better the more it withdraws itself from the body morally and epistemically, M. argues, it makes sense to think of the soul and body as metaphysically distinct as well.

Tusc. 1.50–78 is in one sense an exercise in doxography. Yet it goes beyond merely writing up Plato's opinions and presents a characteristically Platonic approach to argument as well. If all we had to go on was this passage, we would think that Plato is centrally concerned with working out what we can learn by reflecting on our own rational activity. As far as soundbite summaries go, I could think of worse ways of summing Plato up. What's more, these dialogues – *Phdr., Men., Ti., Phaedo* – are among those that make the greatest use of the hypothetical method. If we add to this the elements of Socratic elenchus already embodied by Cicero's Academic skeptical approach, we start rounding out a more complete picture of a Platonic methodology within the works of Cicero.[52] The passage as a whole approaches the question of the soul's immortality by taking a step back and arguing for its divinity instead. In this, we see M. identifying deeper/higher questions, through the conditional, "if the soul is divine then the soul is immortal." The hypothesis on the table, then, is "yes, the soul is divine."[53] Given the overall Academic skeptical

---

[51] While English speakers tend to distinguish between "discovery" (i.e. of something already present) and "invention" (i.e. of something new), Latin tends to run the two together in the single term *inventio*, which M. uses here. Archimedes "*inuentio*" of the orrery nicely straddles the divide.

[52] Again, my point is not that Cicero intended his works to be read in this way, but rather that they can be thus read without putting too much strain on the arguments he presents.

[53] There is an assumption at play here, made explicit at *Tusc.* 1.51, that divine things are best, or perhaps only, understood as existing apart from a body. A fuller reconstruction of M.'s argument

stance and the role of this argument as simply one arm of a larger disjunctive argument, the divinity hypothesis is clearly being treated as provisional. While materialist philosophers have challenged this hypothesis, M.'s Plato defends it in three different works by reflecting on our own rational activity and arguing that the materialists' challenge simply does not hold up.[54] In this, M.'s Plato defends a hypothesis by showing that its consequences agree with facts about human rationality that are accessible to us through reflection on our own rational activity.

Benson notes that Plato is somewhat vague on how one should go about testing whether the consequences of a hypothesis agree. If we are to take *Tusc.* 1's presentation of Plato as a guide, the process is centrally concerned with reflection on rational activity. Put into my simplified version of Benson's scheme, the argument of *Tusc.* 1.50–81 runs . . .

Stage 1 (Q1) Is the soul immortal? → If the soul is divine then the soul is immortal.
(Q2) Is the soul divine?
Stage 2 (A2) The soul is divine.
Stage 3 The consequences of (A2) agree. This is demonstrated via reflection on. . .
(a) memory (*Men.*)
(b) discovery/thought (*Ti.*)
(c) withdrawing from the body (*Phd.*)
(A1) The soul is immortal.

Has this process proceeded to a sufficiently unhypothetical starting point? M.'s claim that it is "more difficult to think of" the soul performing these functions with a body (or perhaps with the kind of body that his particular materialist interlocutors imagine) than without one hardly rings of first principles. This is, therefore, still a provisional approach proceeding via plausibilities in "the old Socratic method." Put into *C. Acad.*'s terms, *Tusc.* 1.50–81 presents an application of Augustine's "Platonic" method, ARP:

may thus add another level of hypothesis. Matters are complicated somewhat given that "in a body" may mean either "in a human body" or "in anything material whatsoever," both of which feature at various points in the course of M.'s argument. Yet these complications merely add steps to an argument by hypothesis, they do not undermine the fact that M. is presenting an argument by hypothesis. Given that our focus is on method, rather than the details of doctrinal content, I thus leave readers with a streamlined version of this argument.
54 We might retroactively include *Phdr.*'s arugment from self-motion as well, by spelling out the particular kinds of motion in terms of the three arguments to follow. Whether or not we do so makes no difference to the purposes of this chapter. I thus give the more conservative reading here.

(A) An opening doxography[55] presents a bewildering assortment of views on soul and death.

(R) Reflection on rational activity provides a foothold amidst this controversy: the soul is capable of. . .

    (a) memory (*Men.*)

    (b) discovery/thought (*Ti.*)

    (c) withdrawing from the body (*Phd.*).

(P) Plato's account of the soul's divinity and immortality is deemed the most plausible response.

While Socrates only explicitly announces that the last third of *Men.* will proceed via hypothesis, Cicero's inclusion of that work's geometry lesson here suggests a way we might see the hypothetical method at play in *Men.*'s middle section on method as well.[56]

At this point it might be objected that I am making too much out of suggestions in *Tusc.* 1 that could be, but in no way need to be, pieced together into something resembling Plato's method of hypothesis. Even if we grant that Cicero's Academic skeptical approach, as Augustine understands it, is a second-order, methodological commitment that is compatible with adopting various first-order doctrinal commitments from the skeptics' rivals, why should Augustine find so much significance in a discussion of Plato that is expressed in one half of one arm of a disjunctive argument, itself taking up merely one of five books making up a single dialogue of Cicero? What of the Stoicism endorsed as most plausible at the end of *N.D.* or *Hortensius*' injunction to seek wisdom without committing oneself to any particular school?[57] An initial response is that *Tusc.* 1.50–81 is ultimately more about second-order method than first-order theory. Just as Plato's hypothetical method subsumes Socratic elenchus within itself, Cicero's skeptical dialogues may be read as part of a larger nonskeptical project.[58] Still, we might worry that I have merely shown that Augustine

---

[55] Cicero, *Tusc.* 1.17–49.

[56] According to this reading, *Men.*'s paradox of inquiry provides an initial *aporia*, the geometry lesson provides an object for Socrates' reflection on rational activity and the theory of recollection is presented as a plausible answer to both. This passage is not explicitly referred to as an application of the hypothetical method, perhaps because Plato uses it to introduce the hypothetical method itself. In any case, it is not considered by Benson, who limits his study to passages where the hypothetical method is explicitly invoked. For an extended "Augustinian" reading of *Men.*'s middle section, see my "Platonic Pedagogy in Augustine's Dialogues," *Ancient Philosophy* 34 (2014): 151–168.

[57] While *Hort.* is no longer extant, Augustine himself preserves this fragment at *Conf.* 3.7–8.

[58] This would be most closely in line with Unitarian readings of Plato, which see Plato himself putting Socratic works such as *Euthyphro* to hypothetical purposes that he simply does not make explicit in the text.

could have read Cicero in this way, though I have yet to give any
compelling reason for why he would have done so. For this, let us turn
to Plotinus, whose presentation of Platonic method fills out and corrobor-
ates the picture that I have presented thus far.

Plotinus' Self-Reflective Turn

The two ascents to a vision of God at *Conf.* 7.16–23 and 9.23–28 are
among Augustine's most memorable pieces of writing. They are also
heavily indebted to Plotinus' treatise "On Beauty" (*Enn.* 1.6). Both works
take the same basic trajectory: The failure to explain physical beauty in its
own terms moves the individual back upon his own mind and its ability to
judge whether something is beautiful or not; yet it soon becomes clear that
this act of judgment itself requires some standard of judgment, which is
not contingent on the individual's mind. *Conf.*'s ascents thus move from
the external objects judged, to the judging mind, to the mind's standards
of judgment, or, more pithily: outward, inward, upward.[59] While these
passages from *Conf.* are among Augustine's most famous, we find the same
basic trajectory in *De Mag.*'s argument for the Inner Teacher, *De lib. arbit.*
2's argument for God's existence, *C. Acad.*'s argument for Platonic intellectualism and *De Mus.* 6's argument for the mind's relation to intelligible
number. In short, "outward, inward, upward" is the basic shape of an
Augustinian dialogue. What matters for present purposes is that this
upward trajectory, which Augustine adopts from Plotinus, is itself a
distillation of Plato's hypothetical method.[60] What's more, it is a distillation that is centrally concerned with reflecting on rational activity. In this
regard, I suggest, Plotinus provides a means of corroborating our Platonic
reading of Cicero's Academic skeptical dialogue and a plausible explanation for why Augustine might have ventured such a reading in the
first place.

Scattered throughout *Enn.* are appeals for the reader to reflect on his
own rational activity. Plotinus remarks on this technique at *Enn.* 5.3.6.
Having completed a discussion of Intellect's self-knowledge, he asks, "has
then our argument demonstrated (*ho logos edeixen*) something of a kind

---

[59] See also Frederick Van Fleteren, "The Cassiciacum Dialogues and Augustine's Ascents at Milan,"
Mediaevalia 4 (1978): 59–82.
[60] In the present chapter, I focus on Augustine's methodological debt to his predecessors. In
Chapter 4's consideration of *De Mus.*, I return to the theoretical underpinnings of this method
and the role of beauty in rousing the soul to ascend.

which has the power to inspire confidence (*energeian pistikēn exein*)?" to
which he replies:

> No, it has necessity (*anagkē*) not persuasive force (*peithō*); for necessity is in
> Intellect but persuasive force in the soul. It does seem that we seek to persuade
> ourselves rather than to behold truth by pure Intellect. For while we were
> above in the nature of the Intellect, we were satisfied and [really] thought and
> saw, gathering all things into one . . . But since we have come to be here below
> again and in soul, we seek for some kind of persuasion (*peithō tina*), as if we
> wanted to contemplate the archetype in the image. (Plotinus, *Enn.* 5.3.6)[61]

Having made the general point about "contemplating the archetype in the
image," Plotinus proceeds to spell out how the main theme of the treatise
might be better understood if the soul were to attend to its own intellectual
nature and "then transpose the image to the true Intellect." While the
passage is cast in rather metaphysical terms, the basic idea is that demonstrative proofs from first principles are going to be of little use to those who
are accustomed to thinking in everyday terms (i.e. those operating at the
level of soul). Nevertheless, everyday thought is infused with intellectual
thinking; by noticing this, even the most mundane-minded person can
find a toehold to begin the ascent to higher modes of thought.

Plotinus ends the section, *Enn.* 5.3.9, by spelling out this process of
ascent. Ideally, one would strip from his self-conception everything born of
bodily life, as a way of exposing pure intellectual thought. If that should
prove too difficult, though, one should think about his "soul insofar as it
forms opinions" (*psychēn doxastikēn*) and think about what is entailed by
that. And if this should still prove too much, then one should start with
sense-perception (*aisthesin*) or even the generative soul (*psychēn gennōsan*)[62]
and work from there. This attempt to meet readers "where they are"
provides a breath of fresh air in discussions that can sometimes seem
oppressively abstract.[63] Still, we might worry that Plotinus' strategy for
speaking in everyday terms is itself theory-laden: The assumption that the
generative soul is in some ultimate sense intellectual is itself controversial.
Sara Rappe articulates this worry: "A supposedly unmediated and hence,
unbiased appeal to consciousness becomes a method of securing credibility
for what are obviously entrenched dogmas within the Platonic school.

---

[61] Translations of Plotinus from A.H. Armstrong, *Plotinus: Enneads* (Cambridge, MA: Harvard
University Press, 1988).
[62] I.e. the part of soul responsible for the life-functions of the body.
[63] See Chapter 4 of this book and my "Augustine and the Liberal Arts," *Arts and Humanities in Higher
Education* 21/1 (2012): 105–113 for discussion of a similar series of next best approaches presented
at *De ord.* 2.47.

Why bother to employ such a circuitous method?"[64] I suggest that Plotinus' self-reflective "thought experiments," as Rappe calls them, are a step in Plotinus' version of Plato's hypothetical method. The hypotheses under examination are elements of Plotinus' metaphysics (e.g. the hierarchy of Soul, Intellect, One). The fact that Plotinus prescribes such exercises to people who have not yet come to grasp intellectual first principles shows that these hypotheses are being treated as provisional. The purpose of his thought experiments is to judge the consequences of these hypotheses. The ultimate goal of all this is to attain holistic knowledge.[65] To substantiate this suggestion, let us turn to a treatise from the *Enn.* that was known to Augustine.

Plotinus' treatise "On Beauty" (*Enn.* 1.6) presents a distilled version of Diotema's "mysteries of love," from Plato's *Smp.* 203B–212C. The treatise's first half, *Enn.* 1.6.1–3, begins with beautiful bodies and ascends to soul. The second half, *Enn.* 1.6.5–9, begins with beautiful souls and ascends to the Intellect and the One. I suggest that each ascent presents an application of Plato's method of hypothesis or, to put it in my terms, a complete round of ARP. It will be sufficient for our purposes to walk through only the first of these. The work's first chapter addresses the question of what makes bodies beautiful. Plotinus suggests the common response, "good proportion" (*summetria*), but proceeds to point out that even if symmetry explains the beauty of wholes, it fails to explain the beauty of their parts or of noncomposite things such as light or lumps of gold, which people often find very beautiful. What's more, it is unclear how symmetry would apply to the beauty of virtue or knowledge. Having drawn out these *aporiai*, chapter 2 shifts our perspective: Rather than looking to the physical object to explain beauty, Plotinus calls attention to the soul, which judges bodies to be beautiful. He suggests that soul is akin to form (*eidos*) and when the soul recognizes the work of its kindred form in a body, it is excited by this and therefore finds that body beautiful. While form may sometimes manifest itself as symmetry, it need not always do so, and, even when it does, symmetry is just the effect of a more basic cause, viz. the structuring power of form on those bodies. None of this follows deductively from what came before. It is a hypothesis, introduced

[64] Sara Rappe, "Self-Knowledge and Subjectivity in the *Enneads*." In *Cambridge Companion to Plotinus*, ed. Lloyd Gerson, (Cambridge: Cambridge University Press, 1996), 250–274, 265.
[65] My reading is broadly in line with Rappe, "Self-knowledge," 265, who concludes that the ultimate goal of these self-reflective turns is not persuasion but participation, as "[t]he success of the thought experiment means for Plotinus a validation of the contemplative journey." On this reading, self-reflection is a spiritual exercise in the sense that it helps make the soul "fit" for intellectual thought, while also testing the soul's progress.

by "We say at least" (*phamen dê*), which Plotinus makes plausible by reflecting on an instance of rational activity in Chapter 3:

> How does the architect declare the house outside [himself] beautiful by fitting it to the form of house within him? The reason is that the house outside, apart from the stones, is the inner form divided by the external mass of matter, without parts but appearing in many forms. When sense-perception, then, sees the form in bodies binding and mastering the nature opposed to it, which is shapeless, and shape riding gloriously upon other shapes, it gathers into one that which appears dispersed and brings it back and takes it in, now without parts, to the soul's interior and presents it to that which is within as something in tune with it and fitting it and dear to it. (Plotinus, *Enn.* 1.6.3)[66]

While this hardly settles the matter once and for all, it does put 1.2.1's theory of form in a rather favorable light. Put another way, this reflection on the rational activity of an architect does not prove Plotinus' theory of form. Rather, it shows that the consequences of this theory harmonize with everyday experience. What's more, the theory's application may be extended: "just as when a good man sees a trace of virtue in the young, which is in tune with his own inner truth, the sight delights him."[67] While symmetry cannot explain all instances of physical beauty, Plotinus' account of form captures all of these and relevant cases of nonphysical beauty as well. It is the stronger hypothesis.

As with Plato, we find in Plotinus a shift in the question being addressed. Yet, as in Cicero, the particular shift happens via reflection on the rational activity of a human agent. Such reflection is central in the move to higher/more basic questions as well as the subsequent testing of those hypotheses' consequences. While the overall shape of Plato's hypothetical method is clear enough in both cases, the execution of this method in *Enn.* 1.6, as in *Tusc.* 1, shows a preference for the tighter approach in which reflection on rational activities provides the lynchpin for the process as a whole.

In broad terms, our survey of methodological developments has been a story of two strands – elenchus and hypothesis – coming together in *Men.*, separating in Cicero and Plotinus and coming back together in Augustine. The main challenge has been to provide a viable account of how Augustine could have recombined these two strands – which were presented to him as distinct approaches of two different authors – and successfully reconstructed a Platonic model that he himself had likely never encountered. In response, I have attempted to present elements of Cicero's and Plotinus' thought in ways that show their compatibility. At this point, we can put all these pieces

---

[66] Armstrong, translator.   [67] Plotinus, *Enn.* 1.6.3.

together. First of all, the elenchus may be employed as an initial stage within the hypothetical method. In *Men.* it shows the need for further argument; in *Tusc.* 1 it shows the shortcomings of materialist accounts of soul; in *Enn.* 1.6 it shows that we cannot explain the beauty of bodies merely in terms of beautiful bodies. In each case, a bit of Socratic perplexity provides the entry point for further inquiry by hypothesis. Cicero's formalized version of this Socratic approach, however, dealt in explicitly plausible, provisional answers. It is not too much of a stretch to think that someone introduced to philosophy through Cicero, as Augustine was, could develop a feel for this provisional approach. Plotinus' general commitment to Platonism might suggest Platonic doctrines are to him foregone conclusions rather than provisional hypotheses, yet the way he presents these doctrines in works such as *Enn.* 1.6 shows a method that is fundamentally in line with the method of hypothesis. Here we find a second point of contact between Cicero and Plotinus, as both can be read as engaging in the provisionality of Plato's hypothetical method. The final connection comes in the two authors' chosen means for testing hypotheses. While the arguments *pro et contra* of Cicero's Academic skeptical approach suggest a no-holds-barred approach to deciding between rival positions, *Tusc.* 1 presents a different approach, in which reflection on rational activity becomes the main criterion. What's more, Cicero presents this as an explicitly Platonic approach. It is a small step from here to recognizing the similarity between *Tusc.* 1's reflections on rational activity and those of *Enn.* 1.6. With these connections drawn, the rest falls into place. What emerges is an approach to philosophical inquiry that combines rigorous scrutiny, self-reflection and a willingness to trade in provisional answers. In short, it gives you Augustine's ARP.

At this point I hope to have shown that Augustine could have combined Cicero and Plotinus to produce something approximating Plato's *Men.* Even so, this alone does not explain why he undertook to do so by suggesting that Cicero and the Academic skeptics in general were actually Platonists in disguise. Several centuries separate Augustine and the last of the Academic skeptics. Allegiance to this group, or even its ideas, was not a live option in 386CE in the same way that allegiance to Manichaeism or Platonism was. The common assumption that in the late fourth-century a powerful skeptic lurked around every corner likely rests on modern readers taking the rhetoric of Augustine's *Conf.* too seriously.[68] Cicero was,

---

[68] Topping agrees that Augustine ultimately did not take skepticism to be so grave a threat, but treated it as something "in the air," for which he cites *Ep.* 1.2 as evidence. Ryan Topping, "The Perils of Skepticism."

however, the father of Latin philosophy and Augustine's main philosophical source. It might simply be that Augustine, the historical individual, was taken with Platonism and wanted to get the archetypal Roman philosopher on his side.[69] In the final analysis, we can only speculate about the actual motivations of historical figures. Yet we can think usefully about how they present their ideas. If we take *C. Acad.* as our guide, then Augustine has latched onto the fact that Platonists such as Plotinus provide a framework that fully embraces Academic practices while at the same time surpassing them. The Stoics can't pull this off. Neither can the Epicureans or any other school Cicero presents. In the final analysis, I take Augustine's theory of crypto-Platonist Academic skeptics to amount to this: Cicero's works can be fruitfully put to Platonist ends; let's read them that way and see where it takes us.

The Dialogue Genre: From Plato to Augustine

At this point, I have set out an account of the two strands of method at play in *Men.* and argued that Augustine could have pieced them together from the works of Cicero and Plotinus. The picture that has emerged is of a four-stage process that ascends through higher/more basic questions, presents a provisional hypothesis in response, tests what follows from that hypothesis through reflecting on rational activity and ultimately ends by attaining holistic knowledge. The first three stages are embodied in Augustine's own method, ARP, albeit in a different order. To put it in other terms, Augustine's sources consistently present Platonic method as a process of A-P-R: Why does Augustine change this to A-R-P? From a philosophical perspective I can't see how this change would make much difference. From a rhetorical perspective, however, it makes for very different structures. APR sets out problems, floats a solution and then defends it. ARP sets out problems, appears to change the topic by reflecting on rational activity and finally, when everyone is thoroughly confused, reveals some as-of-yet unconsidered theory that makes everything else make sense. Why would Augustine make this change, and what does it have to do with his dialogues' characteristic switch from debate to *oratio perpetua*? In addressing these rhetorical questions, I suggest we start from the experience of someone reading these authors' works for the first time.

Cicero was attempting to make philosophy palatable for the Roman elite. These were people who divided their time between leisure (*otium*) at their suburban villas and the business (*negotium*) of running a Republic,

---

[69] See *C. Acad.* 1.8 for Cicero's importance to Latin philosophy.

which for the most part involved giving speeches before courts and assemblies at Rome. His dialogues' villa settings and casts of notable statesmen would have been instantly familiar to his target readership. More importantly, his speeches *pro et contra* resonate with the Republican ethos of stating opposing views and then letting free citizens make up their own minds. Cicero's plausible conclusions are a masterstroke, in that they embrace this ethos and set it within an Academic skeptical framework. The overall experience is of critical detachment: Everyone knows the rules, and there are no real surprises as each character states his case. Along the way, the Stoics may say outrageous things, and many of the Academics' attacks are quite funny, but these are merely part of the game, the sort of thing one would expect from Cicero. While I might be overstating the case some-what, Cicero's works sit toward what we might call the forensic end of the rhetorical spectrum.

If Cicero plays the lawyer, Plotinus plays the mystagogue. The whole point of the hypothetical method, as applied in "On Beauty," is to disrupt familiar ways of doing things. With each step up to a higher/more basic question, we are called on to think about the familiar world in new ways. Philosophy becomes a type of mystery religion as assumptions are stripped away, and we come to realize the inner depths of what we ourselves bring to everyday experience.[70] While Cicero presents debates that are already cast in terms of basic questions, Plotinus' treatises do substantial philo-sophical work by identifying what these basic questions are. As with Plato, the reader never quite knows what will happen next. In somewhat more modern terms, Plotinus' *Enn.* sit somewhere between "mystical" poetry and a "mystery" novel, as everyday puzzles and intuitions become clues in the search for some higher/more basic understanding of reality.

When it comes to shaping readers' experience, Augustine draws elem-ents from both Cicero and Plotinus but gives them his own twist. The villa setting and plausible conclusions are the clearest Ciceronian nod.[71] But Cicero's cast of statesmen is replaced by a couple of teenagers and August-ine's mother.[72] The villa setting itself is then dispensed with after the Cassiciacum works. Like Plotinus, Augustine plays the mystagogue,

---

[70] Chapter 6 places this approach to philosophy within the broader context of Plotinus' grades of virtue: civic, kathartic and contemplative.

[71] See Dennis E. Trout, "Augustine at Cassiciacum: *Otium honestum* and the Social Dimensions of Conversion," *Vigiliae Christianae* 42/2 (1988): 132–146 and R. J. Halliburton, "The Inclination to Retirement – the Retreat of Cassiciacum and the 'Monastery' of Tagaste," *Studia Patristica* 5 (1962): 329–340.

[72] See Conybeare, *Irrational Augustine, passim.*

drawing out the spectacular in the ordinary and leading his companions to think about things in new ways. If anything, he makes more of the language of mysteries and purification than Plotinus himself does. I suggest that this may explain Augustine's choice to move his plausible conclusions to the end. In one respect, this move allows him to follow the overall shape of Cicero's skeptical dialogues,[73] which end with individuals making up their own minds. Yet, whereas Cicero's characters often end by finding different views plausible, by the end of one of Augustine's dialogues, it is obvious to everyone what the "right" answer is. The difference sits in how the two authors arrive at their plausible conclusions. Cicero presents entrenched arguments *pro et contra*; Augustine treats his conclusions as the hypotheses of a Platonic inquiry, which he supports via self-reflection before he even announces what his hypotheses are. Augustine's *aporiai* and self-reflection constitute *explananda* that he piles up so high that by the time he announces his secret conclusion, it is the only plausible explanation within the intellectual horizons of the work's characters. Rhetorically, Cicero is writing philosophical court cases; Augustine is writing philosophical whodunits.[74]

Within Augustine's own context, the choice to alter Plato's hypothetical method by moving the hypothesis to the end may also reflect the fact that in actual mystery cults, the central revelation came at the end, not the middle. Like fraternity inductions today, ancient mystery religion was likely quite disorienting: The Eleusinian mysteries, for instance, involved processions of boxes with hidden contents, bathing in the ocean with piglets, crossdressers yelling obscenities, blindfolds, crowded rooms and spectacular light shows. Yet, somehow, all of this came together in the end.[75] While Christianity, even in the early centuries, was more upfront with new members about what they were getting into, it still reserved certain secrets for the properly initiated. For Augustine, writing in the months between his conversion to catholic Christianity and his baptism by Ambrose, concerns for mystery cult and purification were likely equal parts lived experience and literary trope. In his dialogues, he plays these ideas for all they are worth.

---

[73] As opposed to the Platonist middle portion of *Tusc.* 1.

[74] After working on *C. Acad.* for several years, I had the opportunity to teach it in an undergraduate seminar on skepticism. I was pleased to find that the mystery-novel aspect came across for my students, some of whom knowingly read beyond one day's assignment, because they couldn't wait to find out how it would end.

[75] For discussion of the Rites at Eleusis, see Helene Foley, *The Homeric Hymn to Demeter* (Princeton: Princeton University Press, 1994), esp. 65–75.

As a final question, what can our discussion of philosophical method tell us about Augustine's habit of ending his dialogues via *oratio perpetua*?[76] In rough terms, these *orationes* function as Plotinian treatises stitched onto Ciceronian debates.[77] Just as *Men.* joins an opening elenchus and a final inquiry by hypothesis, a Ciceronian skeptical dialogue may serve as the first stage of a Plotinian ascent. Yet, in Augustine, the two halves become intimately joined. The initial debate is not set aside as the *oratio* proceeds to reflect on some unrelated action of human rationality; rather, the initial debate itself provides the object of the *oratio*'s reflections.[78] And while elenctic inquiries sometimes move upward through higher questions and sometimes sideways through simply different ones, Augustine favors the former approach, giving even the elenctic portions of his work something of a hypothetical flavor. While the realism of Augustine's debates has led some scholars to see them as real conversations rather than literary productions, by setting Augustine's works within their broader philosophical contexts we see that each work's debate sets the stage for its concluding *oratio* by moving through ever more basic questions, by identifying problems with everyday assumptions and by providing an instance of rational activity to serve as the object of subsequent reflection.[79]

---

[76] See Chapter 1 for review of the scholarship on this question.

[77] *Tusc.* 1, with its opening dedication (1.1-8), brief yet aporetic debate (1.9-19) and long *oratio* (1.18-119), presents at least a formal parallel to the Cassiciacum dialogues. What's more, unlike many of Cicero's other works, the debate's subject is more than mere banter. That said, the function of these sections, particularly the *oratio*, is sufficiently different than what we find in Augustine, that I do not find this parallel to be terribly telling.

[78] As we saw in the previous chapter, in attempting to prove knowledge impossible, the Academic skeptic uses norms of thought that can be known, while Augustine's reflection on this fact provides the stepping off point for his conclusion that it is plausible that knowledge can be known.

[79] In advancing this suggestion, I have limited myself to ideas we know to have been within Augustine's intellectual horizons. Still, the similarity between Augustine's closing *orationes* and the myths that Plato uses to close dialogues such *Gorgias, Phdr.* and *R.* deserves at least passing attention. In general terms, the speeches in which Plato presents these myths are basically expository. The closest parallel to Plato's concluding myths comes in Augustine's final plausible accounts, each of which provides an explanatory framework for everything that came before. The *oratio* that concludes *De an. quant. an.* is entirely taken up with presenting such an account, in this case a scheme of graded virtues. See Chapter 6. In each of Augustine's other finished dialogues, however, the final plausible account is merely the final stage of a larger *oratio* that sets the stage for it through the process of reflection we've discussed. What's more, on one reading at least, Plato's concluding myths do not so much complete the discussions that lead up to them as provide an alternative yet compatible way of approaching the same questions. See Gábor Betegh, "Tale, Theology and Teleology in *Phaedo.*" In *Plato's Myths*, ed. Catalin Partenie (Cambridge: Cambridge University Press, 2009), 77–100. Augustine's plausible accounts, by contrast, are much more closely integrated with everything that went before and constitute the final step in the overarching argument of each work. If the existence of Plato's concluding myths was known to Augustine and provided him an impetus to end his own dialogues with *orationes*, then it appears not to have provided much more than this. It strikes me as more plausible that Augustine's *orationes* spring from a creative combination of the rhetorical strategies of Cicero and Plotinus.

At the end of the day, Augustine's dialogues are aimed at "the cure of souls."[80] As Plotinus' treatises show, such a project can take a variety of literary forms. Still, the dialogue provides one of the most direct – dare we say "natural" – ways of tracking an individual's progress in coming to think about things differently. The debate over the historicity of the Cassiciacum dialogues reached a stalemate with O'Meara arguing that they are literary presentations of real conversations and Madec arguing that the individuals at Cassiciacum based their actual conversations on Cicero's literary model. Whether art imitates life or life art, the fact of the Cassiciacum community and Augustine's literary presentation of what went on there show a concern for engaging individuals where they are and helping them work toward something better. While we can only speculate as to what actually went on at Cassiciacum, it is tempting to imagine that Augustine's interactions with his friends, family and students helped him practice and refine the type of Platonic method that he presents via *C. Acad.*'s secret history of the Academy.

---

[80] Paul Kolbet, *Augustine and the Cure of Souls*, explores Augustine's explicit reflections on this idea, beginning with the early dialogues.

CHAPTER 3

The Measure of Happiness
De beata vita

De beata v. presents a three-day feast in honor of Augustine's birthday. The setting is the philosophical community that Augustine gathered around himself at a villa in Cassiciacum outside Milan. Nearly the entire group is there: Augustine's teenage students, Licentius and Trygetius, familiar from *C. Acad.* are present, Augustine's mother Monica, brother Navigius, son Adeodatus, who was around 14 at the time, and two cousins, Lastidianus and Rusticanus, who seem to be mostly along for the ride. Playing host, Augustine serves a feast "not only for our bodies but for our souls,"[1] by leading the assembled company through a philosophical discussion while they eat. Happiness is their theme, and Augustine leads the discussion mostly by asking questions. His companions express a wide array of positions, most of them obviously true. If anything, the lack of controversy seems to reduce their discussion to polite conversation, in which characters express views already held by all. If we are to take *De beata v.* to be a serious philosophical dialogue, one in which actual philosophical work is accomplished, we must uncover the dialectical texture underlying all this agreement. Only then can we determine what the point of the undertaking might be and evaluate the success of their effort.

The task of finding a single project running through *De beata v.* is further complicated, as characters flip back and forth between philosophical and theological perspectives, and it is far from clear how the different ways of looking at things are meant to fit together. Augustine's mother, Monica, is given pride of place as a kind of Christian oracle, who expounds great philosophical truths despite her lack of education.[2] While Augustine, as author, honors his mother in this presentation, what she has to say ultimately lines up with both the everyday intuitions of her dinner companions and the philosophical doctrines of centuries past. Monica's oracular utterances notwithstanding, the group's conversation proceeds to

---

[1] *De beata v.* 9.　　[2] For an extended discussion, see Conybeare, *Irrational Augustine.*

82

reproduce major moves of Hellenistic moral thought, with characters even engaging in a recognizably Stoic approach to syllogistic argument.[3] This neat setup gives the impression of philosophy in the Euclidean mode, as proofs are derived from self-evident principles. In the end, though, the conversation fails to accomplish its main task of articulating the necessary conditions for human happiness. At that point, Augustine takes over and presents an uninterrupted speech (*oratio perpetua*) arguing that relating one's mind to Christianity's Holy Trinity in the right way is both necessary and sufficient for human happiness.[4] This jarring transition from philosophical to theological terms carries with it a subtler slide from merely necessary conditions for happiness to necessary and sufficient ones. In effect, the work begins by asking one central question but ends by answering a different one. The resulting mismatch seems to undermine *De beata v.*'s argument at the most basic level.

Scholars have avoided these issues by simply not looking for a single argument stretching across *De beata v.* as a whole. A formal division between conversation and *oratio* separates the group's philosophical discussion from Augustine's theological speculations, and individual scholars have, with remarkable regularity, treated one part or the other but not both. What's more, the presence of Stoic material in the work's conversation, but not its *oratio*, strengthens the impression of a hard divide between the work's "philosophical" and "theological/dogmatic" halves.[5] Yet *De beata v.*,

---

[3] For discussion, see Sabine Harwardt, "Die Glücksfrage der Stoa in Augustins *De beata vita*: Übernahme und Anwendung stoischer Argumentationsmuster." In *Zur Rezeption der hellenistischen Philosophie in der Spätantike*, ed. Theresa Fuhrer & Michael Ehler (Stuttgart: Franz Steiner, 1999): 153–171, James Wetzel, *Augustine and the Limits of Virtue* (Cambridge: Cambridge University Press, 1992): 55–61 and Paul Van Geest, "Stoic against His Will? Augustine on the Good Life in *De Beata Vita* and the *Praeceptum*," *Augustiniana* 54 (2004): 533–550.

[4] Scholars interested in the development of Augustine's understanding of the Holy Trinity take this work as an initial benchmark. See Jacques Verhees, "Augustins Trinitätsverständnis in den Schriften aus Cassiciacum," *Recherches Augustiniennes* 10 (1975): 45–75, and Lewis Ayres, "'Giving Wings to Nicaea': Reconceiving Augustine's Earliest Trinitarian Theology," *Augustinian Studies* 38/1 (2007): 21–40.

[5] Harwardt, "Glücksfrage," focuses on the work's debates but ignores the end of the work entirely. Wetzel, *Limits of Virtue*, presents a helpful analysis of the debate's "Stoic tactics" but treats the closing discussion of the Trinity as something of a footnote. F. Asiedu, "The Wise Man and the Limits of Virtue in *De beata vita*: Stoic Self-Sufficiency or Augustinian Irony?" *Augustiniana* 49 (1999): 215–234, attempts to defend the role of the Trinity in *De beata v.* against Wetzel's reading but in the process misconstrues *De beata v.*'s debate. By contrast, Verhees, "Augustins Trinitätsverständnis," and Ayres, "Giving Wings to Nicaea," ignore the work's debates entirely, looking exclusively to the Trinitarian material of the *oratio perpetua*. Michael Foley, "Cicero and Augustine," likewise jumps to the end for the "*terra firma*" of divine revelation. Marrou, *Augustin et la fin de la culture*, 308–315, refuses even to acknowledge the presence of a concluding *oratio perpetua* in *De beata v.* On his reading of the Cassiciacum works, closing *orationes* provide Augustine a venue for offering his own positive contribution to the problem under discussion, while the works' initial

considered as a whole, clearly brings philosophy and theology into some relationship. I propose to take the work's apparent incoherence not as a problem to be avoided but as a challenge to find a model that will accommodate all of the text.

In what follows, I will argue that *De beata v.* follows the "Platonic" method set out in *C. Acad.*, which I have dubbed ARP.[6] In the case of *De beata v.*, the opening "first-order" inquiry into happiness and the self-reflective, "second-order" inquiry into inquiry provide a set of first- and second-order *explananda* for which Augustine's closing account of the Trinity provides an explanation. If Augustine fails to prove this final account on the basis of what went before, I suggest it is because he is not trying to do so. While *De beata v.* lacks the technical, Academic-skeptical terms employed in *C. Acad.*, I argue that parallels between the two works' overarching arguments and rhetorical structures invite us to see *De beata v.*'s conclusion as what *C. Acad.* would deem plausible (*probabile*). In this, we do not find a demonstrative argument that didn't go quite right, but rather a concerted effort to change how individuals perceive themselves and their place in the world. The point is to get them asking the questions for which Christian doctrine provides answers and to help them grasp the concepts in which these answers are expressed. I end by drawing out the implications of my reading and situating *De beata v.* within existing debates about ethical theory. I suggest that the work presents a compatibilist account about reason and religion, one which integrates what some have seen as "masculine" reason and "feminine" emotion, while also bridging the gap between active and contemplative conceptions of happiness through a scheme of graded virtues.

Christian Inspiration and Hellenistic Epistemology

Conversation begins as Augustine asks his companions whether they want to be happy. They respond with one voice that they do. Monica, however, is quick to add that this is not enough and that to be happy, one must

---

debates serve as dialectical exercises of some sort. Marrou apparently finds no positive contribution anywhere in *De beata v.* and declares the whole of it captious and full of dialectical jousting.

[6] This three-stage method proceeds as (A) aporetic/inconclusive debate highlights the shortcomings of characters' current beliefs, (R) reflection on the act of debating allows characters to learn about themselves as rational agents, and (P) a "plausible" account is revealed at the end, i.e. one that explains what went before yet is not proven true in the process. See Chapter 1 for my defense of this reading.

want good things and not bad things.[7] Augustine, as author, uses this opening scene to set out the two necessary conditions for happiness presented in Cicero's *Hort.* Meanwhile, Augustine, as a character within the work, is quick to point out that his mother, without any philosophical training, has taken the very "citadel of philosophy" (*arx philosophiae*). Various scholars have seen Monica acting as some kind of Christian oracle who can channel deep philosophical truths through inspiration alone.[8] Augustine describes her this way in the text,[9] yet we must note from the outset that her first and most important pronouncement is not some *magnum mysterium*; it is a truism that would be readily accepted by any rational human being on a moment's thought.[10] Aquinas' later distinction between natural and supernatural sources of first principles is not at play here.[11] The present task is, rather, to find an account of human psychology that may explain how Monica is able to be inspired in such a way. In Hellenistic terms, *De beata v.* begins by invoking two common concepts, i.e. impressions shared by all rational human beings that make rational thought possible.[12] One of these is put forth by Monica in her oracular mode. But contrary to scholarly trends, we should not assume that Hellenistic epistemology and Christian inspiration must be mutually exclusive. In the end, Augustine's account of the Trinity will find a place

---

[7] *De beata v.* 10.

[8] See McWilliam, "Cassiciacum Autobiography"; Jean Doignon, "'Vie heureuse' et perfection: Variantes philosophiques dans l'unisson d'Augustin et de Monique à la fin de *De beata vita*," *Revue des Études Augustiniennes* 41 (1995): 309–314; Larissa Seelbach, "'Wie sollte ich selbst da nicht mit Freuden Dein Schüler werden wollen?' – Augustin über Monnicas Weg zu Gott," *Augustiniana* 55 (2005): 297–319; Conybeare, *Irrational Augustine.*

[9] Upon reciting Cicero's words from the *Hort.*, "Monica so cried out in response to these words, that we completely forgot her sex and believed that some great man was sitting with us; I, however, understood, as much as I was able, from what and how great a font these things flowed." (*In quibus uerbis illa sic exclamabat, ut obliti penitus sexus eius magnum aliquem uirum considere nobiscum crederemus me interim, quantum poteram, intelligente, ex quo illa et quam diuino fonte manarent*). *De beata v.* 10.

[10] Or at least that is how it is presented. There is a substantive question as to whether the good things in question are good by some objective standard or good for the individual who wants them. The latter seems a less controversial condition for happiness, although it leaves open the question of wanting bad things. Debaters address this worry with their discussion of Sergius Orata (*De beata v.* 26–28). In the end, they claim that those who want bad things are miserable whether or not they get them.

[11] See Harding, "Skepticism, Illumination and Christianity," for an attempt to read Augustine's early thought in such a light. Such categories go hand in hand with Euclidean models and Aristotle's approach to demonstrative sciences. While Aquinas accomplished remarkable things by imposing such frameworks on Augustine's thought, Augustine himself is proceeding within a framework that is more indebted to Platonist and skeptical modes of thought. See Chapter 2 for discussion of his intellectual horizons.

[12] See Chapter 1 for discussion.

for both, as it offers at once a Christian explanation of our access to the common concepts and a naturalistic account of Monica's divine inspiration.[13]

The Fruits of Reflection: First- and Second-Order Truths

The conversation proceeds as the group attempts to identify what one must do to meet these two conditions for happiness, viz. having what one wants and having good things. Three main suggestions are entertained: having secure things, having wisdom and having God. The exact relationship between these suggestions is somewhat murky. None of these suggestions is ever rejected as false, although each progressive step seems to offer a more basic explanation than the last. If this stretch of text strikes us as somewhat stilted, it is because the group is still working through the common concepts. This part of the debate moves forward as debaters attempt to piece together a coherent account from ideas already agreed to by everyone involved.

However this conversation may strike us, we should note that Augustine's companions find it riveting. Licentius is flabbergasted when an argument challenges a belief they already held,[14] Monica is "dumbstruck for a bit" (*diu stupida*) when Augustine uses an idea from Adeodatus to spin out a puzzle,[15] and there is a good deal of crying out and even some impromptu hymn-singing when puzzles are resolved by invoking views the group already held.[16] At first glance, it may seem that Augustine, as

---

[13] In *C. Acad.*, Augustine drew attention to the Academics' use of the common concepts as norms of rational thought. This allowed him both to undermine the skeptical thesis that cognition is impossible and to secure a jumping off point for his final plausible account, which posits some kind of human access to an intelligible world. See Chapter 1. *De beata v.* continues this project, as its debates provide a wider array of common concepts, while this work's closing account provides a fuller picture of human psychology and its connection to the intelligible world.

[14] At *De beata v.* 15 Licentius contradicts himself in attempting to escape an anti-skeptical argument: "'Well then,' Licentius said laughing irritably, 'the person who does not have what he wants is happy.' But when I ordered that this be written, he shouted out, 'I didn't say that.' Likewise, when I nodded that it should be written, he said 'I did say it.'" (*Prorsus beatus est, inquit, qui quod uult non habet, quasi stomachanter arridens. Quod cum iuberem ut scriberetur: Non dixi, inquit exclamans. Quod item cum annuerem scribi: Dixi, inquit*).

[15] *De beata v.* 19.

[16] When Augustine presents an anti-skeptical argument as the first day's dessert, "At this, they all cried out at once, snatching the whole 'dish.' But Licentius more attentively and more cautiously feared giving his assent, and said, 'I snatched up this dessert with you, since indeed I cried out being moved by this conclusion.'" (*Hic repente illi quasi totum rapientes exclamauerunt. Sed Licentius attentius et cautius aduertens timuit adsensionem atque subiecit: Rapui quidem uobiscum, si quidem exclamaui illa conclusione commotus*). *De beata v.* 14. At *De beata v.* 27 Monica explains that Sergius Orata was miserable because he lacked wisdom, and "All cried out in wonder then, and I myself was

author, is merely attempting to liven up an otherwise dull line of argument, adding narrative details that help keep the reader's attention but do not substantively alter that line of argument. If we look more closely, however, we find that debaters' affective experiences of debate steer the course of the debate itself and do so at a fundamental level. In the end, these experiences help debaters realize their own desire for truth as a basic motivating force in their lives. This self-reflective discovery will provide a second-order *explanandum*, which will, in turn, be addressed by Augustine's concluding Trinitarian account, as he credits the Holy Spirit with the "admonition" (*admonitio*) which leads all human beings to the Truth (i.e. Christ).[17]

During the work's debate, the desire for truth is strong enough to influence debaters, even before they have articulated the fact that they feel such a desire. This is clearest in their discussion of Sergius Orata.[18] While investigating the first requirement for happiness – having what one wants – Augustine asks whether every unhappy person (*miser*) lacks (*eget*) something. He invokes the famously wealthy Orata as a thought experiment,[19] stipulating that the man had every desire satisfied, not by wisely reining in his desires but through simple good fortune. Licentius suggests that Orata was unhappy insofar as he feared losing his possessions. Augustine points out that it is lack, not fear, that is under question. Licentius is stumped, and Monica again steals the day by claiming the fact that Orata feared losing goods subject to fortune shows that he "lacks wisdom" (*eget sapientia*). The assembled company are delighted with this response. We should note, however, that this solution would not be readily accepted by absolutely anyone on a moment's thought: Orata himself would hardly admit to being miserable, were it pointed out that he lacked wisdom, which he never

---

more than a little joyful and delighted because it was by her that this most powerful thing, which I had intended to bring forth at the end as a great thing from the books of the philosophers, had been spoken; I therefore said, 'Do you see that many and varied doctrines are one thing, a soul most intent on God is another? For where do these things at which we wonder proceed from if not from there?' At this Licentius, delighted, cried out saying, 'Certainly nothing more true, nothing more divine could be said!'" (*Vbi cum omnes mirando exclamassent me ipso etiam non mediocriter alacri atque laeto, quod ab ea potissimum dictum esset, quod pro magno de philosophorum libris atque ultimum proferre paraueram: Videtisne, inquam, aliud esse multas variasque doctrinas, aliud animum adtentissimum in deum? nam unde ista, quae miramur, nisi inde procedunt? – Hic Licentius laetus exclamans: Prorsus, inquit, nihil verius, nihil diuinius dici potuit*). When Augustine reveals his account of the Trinity at the very end, Monica responds by blurting out a line of Ambrose (*De beata v.* 35), and the whole company is left "rejoicing and praising God" (*gaudentibus et laudantibus Deum*). *De beata v.* 36. See also *De beata v.* 10.

[17] *De beata v.* 34–35.   [18] *De beata v.* 26–28.

[19] See Jean Doignon, "Développements stoïcisants d'Augustin autour de l'*exemplum*' cicéronien d'Orata," *Signum Pietatis* 60 (1989): 53–61.

wanted in the first place. What Augustine's companions have felt, and Orata has missed, is their own desire for the truth,[20] a desire that has been stirred up through rational inquiry.[21] Even before they articulate this desire, they feel its pull during their debate and refuse to entertain "ignorance is bliss" as a serious position.

At this point, we have seen two fundamentally different ways in which *De beata v.*'s debaters have established truths. First of all, they use their direct access to common concepts, such as the initial requirements for happiness, viz. having what one wants and wanting good things. Such ideas would be readily agreed to by any rational adult on a moment's thought (even if that thought is sometimes sparked by a divinely inspired utterance). Yet this debate has also established, or at least begun to establish, another type of second-order truth about human psychology, a type of truth discovered through reflection on the act of inquiry itself: In this case, the fact that these debaters desire the truth. The relation between these two types of truths becomes interesting at the point when the work's debate begins to break down.

Aporia: Augustine's Puzzle about Seeking God

The debate's main line of inquiry stemmed from an attempt to show what scenario would satisfy the initial two requirements for happiness. The discussion moved in short order from having secure things to having wisdom to having God. This leads naturally to the question of what "having God" actually means. It is at this point that troubles arise. Various accounts are suggested,[22] although Adeodatus wins out with "the person who attends to God and holds himself to Him alone" (*qui Deum adtendit*

---

[20] Augustine eventually uses Scripture to justify this slide from Orata's not wanting *wisdom* to Orata's not realizing his own desire for the *truth*: both are ultimately a desire for God the Son. See next section.

[21] The desire for truth is presumably not created by means of inquiry. Debaters' immediate response to Augustine's opening question, "do you all want to be happy," for instance, shows that a desire was already present. It is rather that the process of inquiry makes the desire salient, more acute. This is what I mean by "stirred up." While the amount of crying this entails within the dialogue may strike modern readers as somewhat contrived, I take such displays of emotion to function merely as a means of showing the inner states of Augustine's companions. For a different discussion of crying in these works, see Conybeare, *Irrational Augustine*, chapter 3, and Curley, *Augustine's Critique of Skepticism*, who takes a Straussian approach, reading this crying as code for some hidden meaning.

[22] "The person who lives well; the person who does what God wants; the person who does not have an impure spirit." (*qui bene uitit... qui facit quae Deus uult... qui spiritum inmundum non habet*). *De beata v.* 12.

et ad ipsum solum se tenet).[23] But this raises a further puzzle, since the person who seeks God (*quaerit Deum*) fulfills the description of someone who attends to God (*attendit Deum*) in all relevant respects; yet insofar as this person seeks God, he clearly does not yet have God (*habet Deum*).[24] Such a person thus both does and does not have God. The problem is made even more acute, insofar as all involved have already accepted an argument, presented as the first day's "dessert," in which Augustine uses the same strategy to argue that the Academic skeptics cannot be happy in seeking the truth without finding it.[25]

The group attempts to resolve this puzzle by drawing more distinctions, yet in the end they fail to produce a satisfying resolution. It is this stretch of text in which *De beata v.*'s use of Stoic syllogistic is the clearest.[26] Here, as in the rest of the work, syllogistic logic is used to articulate and elaborate puzzles, yet in so doing, debaters never actually solve anything. At best their syllogisms move the problem back a step. This process eventually comes to an end, as debate collapses into *aporia*, and Augustine is left to proceed through *oratio perpetua*.

It was the process of working through first-order truths that led Augustine's companions into this *aporia*; it is the second-order reflection on this process as an instance of rational activity that will let Augustine lead them out again. As we saw, the Orata episode suggests two different relations to truth; Augustine looks to these to solve the puzzle of having God. On the one hand, those of us who are not wise still grasp some truths, e.g. the common concepts; yet it does not follow from this that we grasp the whole of truth, i.e. wisdom. Augustine suggests that it is our cognition of part of

---

[23] *De beata v.* 18. This is offered as an elaboration of what it means "not to have an impure spirit." For the discussion leading to this final formulation see *De beata v.* 12, 17–18.

[24] *De beata v.* 19.

[25] *De beata v.* 13–16. The analogy between these two arguments is made explicit at *De beata v.* 20: "'I would like to agree,' Navigius said, 'but I especially fear that you will conclude that the Academic, who still seeks, will be happy, the Academic who in terribly vulgar, yet still quite fitting Latin, as it seems to me, was dubbed in yesterday's conversation "an epileptic."'" (*Vellem, inquit Nauigius, consentire, sed illum uereor, qui adhuc quaerit, praesertim ne concludas beatum esse Academicum, qui hesterno sermone uulgari quidem et male Latino, sed aptissime sane, ut mihi uidetur, uerbo caducarius nominatus est*). The skeptical thesis attacked in this "dessert" is explicitly the one defended by Licentius in *C. Acad.* 1. This passage thus features prominently in attempts to establish the order of the Cassiciacum dialogues, although there is some dispute about how to take Licentius' response in it. I take Licentius' estimation at *De beata v.* 15 of Augustine's argument as "so trifling an allurement for boys" (*tam paruae puerorum inlecebrae*) to be a verbal echo of *C. Acad.* 2.28, where Alypius scolded Licentius for "having been moved by either juvenile or puerile fickleness" (*utrum iuuenali an puerili leuitate commotus*). This cross-reference undermines scholarly attempts to insert *De beata v.* between books 1 and 2 of *C. Acad.* and calls into question the whole project of rearranging the dialogues' individual books. See my "Order of Augustine's Cassiciacum Dialogues."

[26] For analysis, see Sabine Harwardt, "Argumentationsmuster."

truth that gives rise to our desire for the whole of truth. By applying various bits of Scripture, Augustine identifies wisdom and truth with the Son of God,[27] and he suggests that the happy person "has God" insofar as he grasps the whole of truth. Yet an individual may also "have God" by grasping part of truth and by this be moved/admonished to grasp the whole of truth. Augustine identifies this affective admonition as the work of the Holy Spirit.[28] A single person may thus simultaneously both have and not have God, albeit in these two different ways.[29] Augustine's identification of Christ with wisdom and the Holy Spirit with the admonition to truth thus provides a resolution to *De beata v.*'s puzzle about having God. Yet even if we grant these identifications and see how they resolve the puzzle, this hardly *proves* the truth of Augustine's Trinitarian account. To see what kind of justification, if any, Augustine gives for his conclusion, we must step back and look at the progression of *De beata v.* as a whole.

A Plausible Conclusion: Happiness and the Trinity

Augustine's final account of the Trinity's role in human happiness turns on ideas of measure (*modus*).[30] According to this account, God the Son, who is Wisdom, acts as "the measure of the soul" (*modus animi*); "having wisdom" and "having God" thus come out as the same, since the human

---

[27] "But what should we say wisdom is except the 'wisdom of God'? But we accept on the authority of divine Scripture that the Son of God is none other than the Wisdom of God [1 Corinthians 1:24], and the Son of God is himself certainly God ... But what do you think wisdom is but truth? For this has also been said, 'I am the Truth' [John 16:6]." (*Quae est autem dicenda sapientia nisi quae dei sapientia est? Accepimus autem etiam auctoritate diuina dei filium nihil esse aliud quam dei sapientiam et est dei filius profecto deus ... Sed quid putatis esse sapientiam nisi ueritatem? Etiam hoc enim dictum est:* ego sum ueritas). *De beata v.* 34.

[28] Jean Doignon, "La praxis de l'*admonitio* dans les Dialogues de Cassiciacum de saint Augustin," *Vetera Christianorum* 23 (1986): 21–37, traces the development of the *admonitio* as a rhetorical device and thus situates *De beata v.* against a backdrop of rhetorical tradition.

[29] Augustine's claim is not that cognition of part of truth is accomplished through the Holy Spirit. On *De beata v.*'s closing account, any and all truth is from the Son; it is, rather, the affective *admonitio* that results from this partial cognition that Augustine associates with the Holy Spirit. See next section. We find here an echo of *C. Acad.* 1's rival definitions of wisdom: searching for truth and having truth. See Chapter 1 for discussion and Chapter 6 for the broader context of Plotinus' grades of virtue. Set in Plotinian terms, the person who has God in the sense of seeing God attains kathartic wisdom; the person who has God in the sense of having the whole of truth, attains contemplative wisdom.

[30] See Augustine's *oratio perpetua* generally (*De beata v.* 30–35), which anchors this notion of measure in Latin vocabulary of fullness (*plenitudo, frugalitas*) and deficiency (*nequitia, egestas*). Particular attention is paid to Cicero and Terence at *De beata v.* 31–32. These notions are used to work out Augustine's account of the Trinity at *De beata v.* 34–35.

mind that conforms fully to this intelligible paradigm is perfectly structured by it and in this perfection finds happiness. Those minds that conform less than perfectly are nevertheless still subject to wisdom's structuring power, which is apparent in our use of the common concepts and in the Holy Spirit's *admonitio ad ueritatem*. The *modus animi* itself, finally, is grounded in "the highest measure" (*summus modus*), the measure without measure, God the Father, to whom God the Son perfectly conforms. As Augustine puts it:

> *Illa est igitur plena satietas animorum, hoc est beata uita, pie perfecteque cognoscere,* [i] *a quo inducaris in ueritatem,* [ii] *qua ueritate perfruaris,* [iii] *per quid conectaris summo modo. Quae tria unum deum intellegentibus unamque substantiam exclusis uanitatibus uariae superstitionis ostendunt.*

This full satiety of souls, i.e. human happiness, is thus to grasp piously and perfectly [i] by what you are led into Truth, [ii] what Truth you enjoy and [iii] through what you are connected to the highest measure. And these three reveal one God and one substance to intellectual people when the shadows of multiform superstition have been pushed away. (*De beata v.* 35)

While this is perhaps somewhat obscure, the point here is to see that the mind's relation to each person of the Trinity is bound up in its relation to Truth, i.e. the Son. Thus, (i) we are led to the Son by the Holy Spirit's admonition, (ii) the Son himself, as Wisdom=Truth, acts as *modus animi* to which the mind conforms, while (iii) the Son acts as our connection to the Father.[31]

The debate in *De beata v.* produces a series of *explananda*, to which Augustine's concluding account of the Trinity responds. At the start of the debate, it was decided that the two necessary conditions for happiness – having

---

[31] This reading solves an interpretive dilemma set out by Verhees, "Augustins Trinitätsverständnis": either the Persons of the Trinity are meant to answer each of these indirect questions, in which case, we find (i) the Father by whom one is called into the truth, (ii) the Son who is the truth one enjoys and (iii) the Holy Spirit through whom one is bound to the highest measure; or, alternatively, the *formulas* within these questions refer to the divine Persons, in which case, (i) the Holy Spirit/ admonition is this "leading" into Truth, (ii) the Son is (again) the Truth that one enjoys, while (iii) the Father is the highest measure to which one is bound. Verhees does not prefer one alternative over the other. My reading splits the difference, finding the Holy Spirit and Son in the answer to the first two questions and the Father in the formula of the last. Ayres, "Giving Wings to Nicaea," argues that the Trinitarianism expressed here and in the other Cassiciacum works is not "economic," i.e. Augustine is not concerned with the Trinity only insofar as it relates to human beings to bring about their salvation. I am only interested in sorting out Augustine's Trinitarian speculations insofar as doing so allows us to see how they function within this text. With that said, the project Augustine undertakes in *De beata v.* and the methodology he uses to pursue it strike me as necessitating an economic treatment of the Trinity. Augustine approaches the Trinity through reflection on the suppositions of his own rational activities, and this allows him to put forth a plausible account of the Trinity insofar as it relates to human moral psychology.

what one wants and wanting good things – would be fulfilled by one who has secure things, wisdom and/or God. In Augustine's closing account, the Father's status as *modus sine modo* grounds the eternal security of the Son as humanity's highest good. By identifying the Son with Wisdom and both of these with the *modus animi*, Augustine spells out "having wisdom" in terms of structuring one's mind according to a rational paradigm or measure. And by distinguishing between cognition of part of Wisdom=Truth=Christ, by which the mind is moved to seek cognition of the whole of Truth, and full cognition, which suffices for happiness, Augustine resolves the puzzle of how the person who seeks God both has God (i.e. the Holy Spirit) and does not have God (i.e. the Son).

This account also responds to the debate's second-order *explananda*. Augustine describes the Holy Spirit as an admonition flowing from the very font of truth and this truth as a ray (*iubar*) flowing from the secret sun, to which belongs (*huius*) every truth we speak.

> *Admonitio autem quaedam, quae nobiscum agit, ut deum recordemur, ut eum quaeramus, ut eum pulso omni fastidio sitiamus, de ipso ad nos fonte ueritatis emanat. Hoc interioribus luminibus nostris iubar sol ille secretus infundit. Huius est uerum omne, quod loquimur, etiam quando adhuc uel minus sanis uel repente apertis oculis audacter conuerti et totum intueri trepidamus, nihil-que aliud etiam hoc apparet esse quam deum nulla degeneratione impediente perfectum. Nam ibi totum atque omne perfectum est simulque est omnipoten-tissimus deus.*

> Yet a certain admonition, which endeavors to persuade us to recall God, to seek him, to thirst for him with every aversion driven away; this admonition flows to us from the very font of Truth. That secret sun pours this ray into our inner eyes. To this [sun] belongs every truth we speak, and even now when with eyes that are still less healthy or suddenly opened, we hesitate to be boldly turned to it and to look upon it whole, and this appears to be nothing else than God, perfect with no loss standing in the way. For there all is whole and perfect and at the same time the most powerful God. (*De beata v.* 35)

While Augustine joined ranks with the Stoics in accepting the existence of the common concepts, he parts ways with them in offering a nonempiricist account of how human beings have access to these foundations of ration-ality. It is not through sense perception, but by the Truth shining in our inner eyes (*interioribus luminibus*) that any human being comes to know truths such as "we all want to be happy." With this, everyday human psychology and Monica's moments of divine inspiration are brought under a single account. Many details are lacking from this account, e.g. what conditions must be met to bring about such "illumination" within an individual's mind, or how normal illumination differs from its inspired counterpart, if at all. Whether Augustine, the historical figure, had thoughts on such details in 386 or not, they do not find their way into this text.[32] The project of *De beata v.* is to draw connections not divisions, as it gives an account of human moral psychology at its most fundamental level. In describing the basic setup of the human mind – any human mind – Augustine argues that the mind's relation to God the Son is what ultimately makes human beings capable of acquiring any truth and that this presence of the divine in everyday human moral psychology is what explains why anyone is moved to seek the truth in the first place.

These are big claims. The argument of *De beata v.*, taken as a whole, is hardly going to win any converts to Nicene Christianity. In fact, non-Christian philosophers of many different allegiances would find aspects of Augustine's account at best unsupported and at worst sheer claptrap. While Augustine's companions seem content with how his account meets the challenges he set for it, Augustine at no point attempts to show that it is the only way one may resolve *De beata v.*'s puzzles or explain its *explananda*. What's more, initial debates proceeded from necessary conditions for happiness, while Augustine presents his final account as fulfilling conditions that are both necessary and sufficient. The overarching argument of *De beata v.* leaves us with three interpretive choices: We may follow the scholarly majority in simply not looking for an overarching argument; we may declare *De beata v.* to be a failure when it comes to providing such an argument; or we may look for a model of argument that fits what we find in this text.

I suggest that the philosophical method advanced in *C. Acad.*, i.e. ARP, provides a framework for making sense of the project advanced in *De beata v.* We find the same rhetorical structure, as an initial puzzle gives rise to aporetic debates followed by a passage of *oratio perpetua*. In Chapters 1 and 2, I argued that Augustine tailored the dialogue form to suit his own "Platonic" method, which moves through aporetic debate, to reflection on the act of debating and a final plausible conclusion. We have already seen the aporetic quality of *De beata v.*'s debate and the reflection on the act of inquiry that emerged over the course of the work's second half. While Augustine does not

---

[32] Such attempts to distinguish general and special grace play a role in debates over the status of Augustine's conversion. See Introduction for discussion. The present account of inner illumination is further elaborated in the concluding *oratio* to Augustine's *De Mag.* of 389CE, though I take that too to be offered as a merely plausible explanation of the various puzzles and self-reflective discoveries raised by that work's debate.

explicitly employ the technical Academic terminology in presenting his concluding account of the Trinity, we find a similar jump from self-reflective discoveries to a conclusion that does not follow in any strict sense, but could be described as "plausible" (*probabile*) insofar as it provides a theoretical context for such discoveries.[33] Given the lack of explicit Academic terms, I ask that my reading be judged by how well it succeeds, where others have failed, to make sense of *De beata v.* To this end, we must get a better sense of what it means for ideas to be "plausible" and how one goes about making them so.

Platonic Pedagogy in *De beata vita*

Augustine's account of the Trinity employs modes of thought that are far removed from everyday life. Augustine's companions, none of whom has much formal training in philosophy, must therefore engage in some conceptual work. In *C. Acad.*'s terms, they must be "purified" before they are ready to think about this account in any kind of intelligent way. In *C. Acad.* such purification was carried out by means of a course of un-learning and self-reflective discovery, through which students reject certain modes of thought and adopt others. All of this is meant to change how they perceive the world.

In the present chapter, we have traced *De beata v.*'s various self-reflective discoveries, yet it is still not completely clear what, if anything, has been "un-learned." By approaching *De beata v.* with such questions in mind, we may pick out a pedagogical project running beneath the surface of the work's inquiry into happiness. At the heart of the matter is Augustine's concept of measure, which is at once central to his discussion of the Trinity and the sort of thing to strike the uninitiated as so much metaphysical nonsense. The problem in *De beata v.*, as in *C. Acad.*, is that everyday life conditions us to empirical modes of thought that are antithetical to Augustine's intellectualist approach to philosophy.[34] Such modes of

---

[33] *C. Acad.* is the first work of the Cassiciacum set, and I take it to be programmatic in ways that the other works are not. That said, explicitly probabilistic language does show up at *Sol.* 1.15 and *De Mus.* 6.15. At *Retract.* 1.5.3 & 1.11.4, meanwhile, Augustine comments that ideas in *De imm. an.* were "*temere dictum*," which is in the same conceptual ballpark. For discussion, see "plausible conclusions" in the index.

[34] *C. Acad.* 3.38 credits the "familiarity of bodies" (*consuetudo corporum*) with the spread of the Stoic materialism. At *De beata v.* 36, Augustine claims that his account of the Trinity will be clear to intellectual people who have pushed back the shadows of superstition, cf. the dedication to *C. Acad.* 2, where superstition is identified with the Manichees' materialistic ideas.

thought must be un-learned if one is to think fruitfully about intellectualist doctrines such as Augustine's account of the Trinity.

The specific thing that must be un-learned in *De beata v.*, I suggest, is what "having" means. We have seen already how debaters entertained the prospect of having different *objects* – secure things, wisdom and God – as they attempted to find scenarios that would fulfill the initial requirements for happiness. What's less obvious is that, thanks to Augustine's prompt-ings, debaters have also (most likely unwittingly) entertained different notions of what it means for the *subject* to have something. This shift in what "having" consists in explains the debate's otherwise needless repeti-tion. On the first day,[35] debaters tacitly drew their notion of having from everyday experience. This notion focuses on the object possessed and treats secure things, wisdom and God as possessions on par with any other. On the second day,[36] Augustine forces this assumption to the surface by interpreting Adeodatus' account in bluntly "objective" ways. In this, Augustine advances the overall line of inquiry by running Adeodatus' suggestions into the ground. On the third day,[37] debaters return to the beginning and revisit having secure things and wisdom, yet this time their discussion begins from an analysis of the possessing subject's mind, as they describe the mind that has secure things as one that uses wisdom to rein in desires that cannot be fulfilled. In this, debaters begin to think about "having wisdom" in a new way. It is Augustine, however, who brings this project to its fruition, as he uses his *oratio perpetua*[38] to suggest that the mind that has wisdom is a mind that is "perfected," neither running into excesses of gluttony or falling into miserly deficiency. This is accomplished by the mind's conforming perfectly to its appropriate measure, which Augustine eventually identifies with Christ. Having wisdom and having God, at least God the Son, thus come out to the same. This model of the mind's conforming to its appropriate measure, which it may do either perfectly or imperfectly, in turn, provides Augustine the framework for explaining how a mind that is still imperfect may have God the Holy Spirit and be moved to make progress in coming to have God the Son.

In its broadest moves, *De beata v.* presents the gradual dawning of a new way of looking at things, as Augustine gradually leads his companions to frame questions of moral psychology in terms of measure and structure. In a sense, the answer has been on the table since the beginning, as the first day's seemingly irrelevant banter about Trygetius' eating habits[39]

---

[35] *De beata v.* 10–13.   [36] *De beata v.* 17–22.   [37] *De beata v.* 23–29.
[38] *De beata v.* 30–36.   [39] *De beata v.* 7–9.

introduced issues of measure and conformity, which at that point were applied to the body rather than the mind. Augustine's companions fail to make the requisite connections at the time, and their debate breaks down before such models may be successfully applied to questions of having wisdom and having God. Be that as it may, their debate (seemingly irrelevant banter included) has prepared them to hear what Augustine has to say. By leading them through a series of incomplete answers, unsolved puzzles, elation and distress, Augustine undertakes a process of rewriting his companions' assents,[40] thus changing how they perceive the world. Granted, this particular group of people may have been predisposed to accept an account of the Trinity's role in happiness. Yet by un-learning mundane notions about having and reflecting on the act of inquiry, they are made ready to see the explanatory power of a particular account of the Trinity, which would otherwise have struck them as so much pious gobbledygook.

Taking Stock: *De beata vita* and Ethical Theory

Using *C. Acad.*'s Platonic method, ARP, as a framework, I have presented a holistic reading of *De beata v.* This has helped us move beyond the impression of mere table talk to appreciate the scope of the work's project. We can get a better sense of this scope by tracing the work's trajectory along three basic axes: reason vs. religion, reason vs. emotion, and civic vs. contemplative virtue. Doing so will help us see the work's contribution to broader discussions of ethical theory.

It is hardly groundbreaking for someone situated against the background of Classical moral philosophy to claim that happiness amounts to having wisdom and living a life with (or akin to) the gods. This was readily agreed to by Stoics, Peripatetics, Platonists and even Epicureans in their own way.[41] Yet it is perhaps significant that *De beata v.*'s initial formulation of these ideas was reduced to absurdity through a recognizably Stoic approach to syllogistic argument. In *C. Acad.*, Augustine reimagined the history of Hellenistic philosophy, forcing Stoics to accept skeptical conclusions and skeptics to accept a form of Platonism that, in turn, harmonizes with catholic Christianity. All roads lead to Rome, as it were. By reading *De beata v.*'s debate in light of *C. Acad.*'s interschool machinations, we

---

[40] Augustine's appropriation of this Stoic technical terminology is set out explicitly in *C. Acad.* The basic idea is that one's set of assents (i.e. whatever one takes to be true) affects how one perceives the world, in particular what impressions or ideas strike one as plausible (*probabile*). See Chapter 1.

[41] See Holte, *Béatitude et Sagesse*, for Augustine's relation to classical discussion of the human final end.

may see Augustine suggesting that Stoic or even Hellenistic philosophy in general is implicitly self-defeating in a way that may prepare one for the Christian faith. The Stoics put forth the right conditions for happiness, yet they fail to realize that these conditions cannot be met within the confines of the materialist metaphysics and psychology that they also hold. In *De beata v.* Augustine uses the Stoics' own syllogistic manner of argument to bring this shortcoming to light. But he does this in a way that looks for continuity: Even the Stoics have been the recipients of God the Son's gift, which they recognize as the common concepts that make rationality possible. They simply don't understand where this gift comes from. In our terms, Augustine presents a compatibilist position regarding reason and religion.[42]

De beata v. takes a similarly integrative approach when it comes to reason and emotions. Kant cast a long shadow when he separated the two, basing ethics entirely on reason and making emotion irrelevant or even an obstacle to morally worthy action.[43] This distinction is often discussed today in terms of "masculine" reason and "feminine" emotions, such as care.[44] These perspectives have made their way into scholarly work on Augustine himself. Catherine Conybeare sees little value in the rational arguments presented in *De beata v.* and the other dialogues written at Cassiciacum, so she sets them aside to look for the works' irrational, "emotional logic" instead.[45] Brian Stock takes a more holistic approach, attempting to relate reason and emotion in the dialogues. He sees this to be a relationship of antagonism and suggests that emotions of petty rivalry that accompany dialogue between individuals are what prompt the shift to *oratio perpetua*, which may proceed rationally through "inner dialogue" free of the obstacle of emotion. So far as I can tell, none of these approaches fits *De beata v.* very well. While the work's conversation calls up emotional responses from the group, these emotions do not hinder the

---

[42] Aquinas will present a similar position centuries later, though his commitment to Aristotelian demonstrative science led him to frame the discussion in terms of arguments from first principles. Aquinas thus draws a sharp distinction between arguments based on reason and those based on revelation, even if he thinks they mostly come together in the end. Augustine does not concern himself with this Aristotelian framework. *De beata v.* relates reason and religion in the sense that Christianity provides a solution to questions that philosophers pose.

[43] For the interpretive dispute about the role of inclination (emotion) in Kant's moral theory, see Christine Korsgaard, "Introduction." In *Kant: Groundwork of the Metaphysics of Morals*, ed. Mary Gregor & Jens Timmermann (Cambridge: Cambridge University Press, 2012), ix–xxxvi.

[44] While this literature is vast, Carol Gilligan, *In a Different Voice: Psychological Theory and Women's Development* (Cambridge, MA: Harvard University Press, 1982) is perhaps still the most influential work.

[45] Conybeare, *Irrational Augustine*.

progress of their rational undertaking. They advance it. If we read the work as moving through a course of ARP, then the emotional desire for truth, recognized through self-reflection, is what ultimately allows Augustine to move beyond the *aporia* that "rational," syllogistic approaches raised but could not solve. This is not to say that emotion has triumphed over reason, but rather that emotion has been integrated into a larger project that embraces more than one mode of argument.

Each dialogue of the Cassiciacum set explores one of the classical virtues – wisdom, moderation, justice, courage – with the first three building their discussion around a key term from Wisdom 11:20's phrase, "measure, number, weight." *De beata v.* contributes to this bigger project through its exploration of moderation and its final account of Christ as the "measure" of the soul. But what kind of moderation or, more generally, what kind of virtue are we talking about here? Aristotle presented the virtues as human excellences, ways of being good at being human, and happiness as a flourishing life of excellent activity. Yet he spelled out what this means in two fundamentally different ways. Through most of *Nicomachean Ethics*, Aristotle considers humans as rational, embodied beings, living in communities and driven by biological urges. Flourishing, for a human so conceived, is essentially a balancing act, as individuals use the golden mean to ensure that whatever they do, they do well. Yet in the work's last few pages,[46] Aristotle suggests that human flourishing is perhaps the best activity of the best part of a human being, i.e. intellect. Under this description, happiness ends up being a kind of philosophical contemplation that finds merely instrumental value in all other aspects of life. The relation between these two types of virtue, traditionally called "civic" and "contemplative," has been a matter of controversy throughout the Classical period and beyond. Plotinus approached the problem by setting out apparent contradictions within the works of Plato and resolved them by setting out a graded scheme of virtues: civic virtues permit excellence in everyday human life; kathartic (purifying) virtues prepare individuals for a life that is more than human; contemplative or "real" virtues permit the most excellent excellence in which we attain the happiness of the gods. According to the presentation in Plotinus' treatise, "On Virtues" (*Enn.* 1.2), the lower grades of the virtues are simply derivative versions of the higher ones, while anyone who attains a virtue at a higher grade will automatically have the lower grades as well.[47]

---

[46] Aristotle, EN 10.6–8.   [47] For fuller discussion, see Chapter 6.

I suggest that *De beata v.* employs Plotinus' strategy for using kathartic virtue to bridge the gap between its civic and contemplative counterparts. The discussion starts out in everyday, "civic" terms, conceiving of happiness as simply having good things; Augustine's *oratio*, by contrast, ends with a contemplative vision of the Trinity. The progression from the one extreme to the other – i.e. from good things, to secure things, to wisdom, to God – models a process of "kathartic" turning. Augustine's Trinitarian account then explains this movement in terms of the Holy Spirit's *admonitio*, and, in the process, provides a way of substantializing Plotinus' suggestion that lower virtues are derivative versions of higher ones. According to Augustine's theory, contemplative virtue is the soul's fully conforming itself to Truth=Wisdom=Christ as the *modus animi*. The soul's partially conforming to Wisdom, in turn, produces the admonition to seek Truth=Wisdom=Christ. This is the work of the Holy Spirit and an instance of kathartic virtue. Meanwhile, this partial grasp also provides a store of truths that will be useful for everyday living. Civic virtue thus ends up being a sort of afterthought at the lowest rung of the ladder. Given this setup, it becomes obvious why the higher virtues contain the lower ones. A person of kathartic virtue, one who excels at turning from lower things to higher things, will hardly get upset if she does not have the season's newest gadget; and a person of contemplative virtue, who is utterly fulfilled by the vision of absolute Truth, will hold to that truth, while the pursuit of property and satisfaction of everyday desires will seem insignificant in comparison to far greater goods.[48]

This process of shattering contemplative virtue into lower grades, in turn, provides a framework for explaining how Augustine's companions may move from one thing they already believe to other things they already believe yet still make progress. Their aporetic debate, (A), does not point out false belief – they were right to want secure things, wisdom and God – so much as a faulty conception of what their true beliefs entail. Reflection on that debate, (R), does not introduce their desire for Truth as something surprising so much as clarify its implications.[49] Augustine's plausible account, (P), presents a group of Christians with a Christian worldview, yet in a way that lets them see the whole to which a number of parts

---

[48] Augustine elaborates this basic idea in *De lib. arbit.* 1's account of temporal and eternal law. See Chapter 7.
[49] Cf. Therese Fuhrer, "Augustins Frühdialoge als Inszenierung der Einheit von religiöser Praxis und philosophischem Dialog." In *Metaphysik und Religion*, ed. Theo Kobusch & Michael Erler (Munich: K. G. Saur, 2002): 309–322, who suggests that the dialogues' debates begin from religious intuitions.

belong. Just as the lower virtues come about through the disintegration of the contemplative, the work's move back to the contemplative comes about through a process of reintegration. This is the feast for the soul that Augustine has prepared for his guests, and it is brought about through a course of ARP.

Be that as it may, one may still object that *De beata v.* lacks the explicitly Academic terms used to set forth ARP in *C. Acad.* Augustine, however, frequently keeps his cards close to his chest for pedagogical or rhetorical reasons.[50] It seems clear to me that the present dialogue's aporetic debate, (A), accomplishes conceptual work, that its self-reflection, (R), helps sharpen characters' self-knowledge and that its closing account of the Trinity is plausible, (P), in the sense that it explains what went before, in that it sidesteps problematic concepts that led to *aporia* and provides a theoretical context for the work's self-reflective discoveries. If we will grant all that, then why not go the rest of the way and take Augustine to present his closing account as plausible in the full sense of explanatory yet uncertain? Doing so would bring *C. Acad.* and *De beata v.* in line methodologically, making the basic thought that *De beata v.*'s debate and reflection provide *explananda*, criteria for happiness, which Augustine's account of the Trinity fits, but in a way that leaves the door open to other possibilities. While the guests at Augustine's birthday feast may be content enough to give the Christian Trinity the last word, I suspect that Augustine could have prepared an alternative Platonist version easily enough. Whatever these historical individuals might have thought, reading the work's overall argument as leading to a plausible conclusion allows for a more pluralistic approach to questions of virtue and the good life. In some situations, uncertainty is liberating. By taking such an approach, Christians can commit to a view such as Augustine's account of the Trinity, yet still admit that other schemes could also fit the bill, whether they be religious or secular in origin. Whether we accept the particulars of *De beata v.*'s argument, its approach to arguing provides a powerful model for engaging with ethical questions today, as it provides guidelines for those working within particular traditions to walk a middle way between the religious right and secular left, taking their own tradition seriously while admitting that others are worth taking seriously too.

---

[50] This is most obvious in *C. Acad.*, where Augustine tells his companions that he has a design for their conversation but refuses to tell them what it is until the very end. In Chapter 1, I present *C. Acad.* as a kind of philosophical mystery novel.

CHAPTER 4

God's Classroom
De ordine and *De Musica*

The narrative of *De ord.* opens with an elaborate scene.[1] In the hours before dawn, Licentius shoos a mouse away, thus showing himself to be awake. Augustine asks him about the odd alternating sound coming from a nearby ditch. Licentius explains that the cause is a cycle of falling leaves that cause water to back up and then wash them away.[2] Trygetius joins in as their little *schola* moves in short order to a discussion of causes in general. Thanks to a misheard comment, Licentius commits to the view that all things are held in God's providential order (*ordo*)[3] and proceeds to thank Providence for initiating their conversation about providence:

> *Hic ille lecto etiam exiliens prae laetitia: Quis neget, deus magne, inquit, te cuncta ordine administrare? Quam se omnia tenent! quam ratis successionibus in nodos suos urgentur! quanta et quam multa facta sunt, ut haec loqueremur! quanta fiunt ut te inueniamus! Vnde enim hoc ipsum nisi ex rerum ordine manat et ducitur, quod euigilauimus, quod illum sonum aduertisti, quod quaesisti tecum causam, quod tu causam tantillae rei non inuenisti? Sorex etiam prodit, ut ego uigilans prodar. Postremo tuus etiam ipse sermo te fortasse id non agente – non enim cuiquam in potestate est, quid ueniat in mentem –, sic nescio quo modo circumagitur, ut me ipse doceat, quid tibi debeam respondere.*

> Then Licentius, jumping for joy out of bed, said, "Who could deny, Great God, that you govern all things by order? How all things hold fast together! With what calculated steps are all things moved along to their appropriate points of convergence! How many and what great things have been done so

---

[1] *De ord.* 1.6–19.   [2] *De ord.* 1.7.

[3] I will use both "providence" and "order" to translate the single Latin term, *ordo*. The term has a wide range of meanings within Augustine, not all of them directly moral. For wide-ranging discussions of such concepts, see Josef Rief, *Der Ordobegriff des jungen Augustinus* (Paderborn, 1962); Anne-Isabelle Bouton-Touboulic, *L'ordre caché*. I will be concerned with *ordo*, only insofar is it figures within *De ord.*'s overall argument, viz. "the basic structure of the world by virtue of which the world is good for human beings." See also Anne-Isabelle Bouton-Touboulic, "Dire l'ordre caché: Les discours sur l'ordre chez saint Augustin," *Revue des Études Augustiniennes* 52 (2006): 143–166. Here she argues that in *De ord.*, Augustine borrows strategies from biblical exegesis to describe the *ordo rerum* by engaging in analogical, apophatic, metaphorical and mimetic discourses.

that we would say these things! What great things are being done so that we might find you! For from where but the order of things do these things flow, in fact are driven along, namely that we were awake, that you [Augustine] heard that sound, that you asked yourself about its cause, that you didn't find the cause of such a trifling thing? Indeed a field mouse has shown up so that I might be shown awake. Finally, your own expression, even when you were perhaps not the person in control of it, for what comes into each person's mind is not in his power, this expression was turned around in some way or other, so that it itself might teach me what I should say to you in response." (*De ord.* 1.14)

While slightly contrived, this scene shows that Licentius is taking Augustine's Platonic lessons to heart, as he is coming to embrace puzzles readily and to work through them via reflection on his own rational activity.[4] The rest of book 1 is taken up with seeming distractions involving Licentius' singing in the outhouse and a barnyard cockfight. The conversation eventually resumes at the start of book 2. Augustine's mother, Monica, and friend, Alypius, join in; the problem of evil is broached; Licentius' mind wanders off for a while; Augustine hints at three different models for thinking about providence; in the end, though, the task proves too much for his companions, who are left scratching their heads. At this point Augustine chides all involved for approaching such questions outside the proper "order of instruction" (*ordo docendi*)[5] and launches into an elaborate speech, laying out a course of liberal study that could prepare his companions for more fruitful inquiries into providence. Along the way, he presents the first extant statement of the medieval *trivium* and *quadrivium*. Having done so, however, he immediately concedes that those who lack time or resources may shorten the course of seven disciplines to one or two, or simply skip them entirely. Having established and then undermined this course of study, Augustine describes the soul's ascent to God and thus draws the work to a close.

While all of Augustine's dialogues from Cassiciacum contain elements of scene-setting and shifts in subject matter, *De ord.* seems simply to

---

[4] "[Licentius said,] 'but just now you gave me a great thing to wonder at.' 'What's that?' I asked. 'That you were wondering about those matters [i.e. the clogged ditch],' he said. 'But what is the source from which wonder, or whatever the mother of this vice is, normally arise,' I asked, 'if not some unaccustomed thing which is outside the manifest order of things?' He replied, 'I accept [that something comes to be] outside the *manifest* order of things; for it seems to me that nothing can come to be outside of order.'" (*sed modo plane dedisti mihi magnum mirari. – Quidnam hoc est? inquam. – Quod tu, inquit, ista miratus es. – Vnde enim solet, inquam, oboriri admiratio aut quae huius uitii mater est nisi res insolita praeter manifestum causarum ordinem? – Et ille: 'Praeter manifestum', inquit, accipio; nam praeter ordinem nihil mihi fieri uidetur*). De ord. 1.8.

[5] *De ord.* 2.24.

ramble. The frequent intrusions involving plumbing problems, wandering minds, mice, chickens and other earthy details seem to affirm the scholarly suspicion that the text records an actual conversation, one that has not gone very well. Meanwhile, the shift from a discussion of providence to an *oratio* on the liberal disciplines, leaves the impression of two different works loosely joined by the general theme of "order," applied in an *ad hoc* manner to providence and teaching. Some have seen this loose joining described by Augustine in his later *Retractationes*:

> *Per idem tempus inter illos qui* De Academicis *scripti sunt, duos etiam libros* De ordine *scripsi, in quibus magna quaestio uersatur, utrum omnia bona et mala diuinae providentiae ordo contineat. Sed cum rem uiderem ad intellegendum difficilem, satis aegre ad eorum perceptionem, cum quibus agebam, disputando posse perduci, de ordine studendi loqui malui, quo a corporalibus ad incorporalia potest profici.*

> At the same time as those books *De Academicis*[6] were written, I also wrote two books *De ordine*, in which is treated the big question of whether the order of divine providence contains all good and evil things. But since I saw that the matter was difficult to understand and sufficiently troublesome for those with whom I was dealing to grasp through discussion, I chose instead to speak about the order of study, through which one can advance from corporeal things to incorporeal things. (*Retract.* 1.3.1)

At best, this strikes me as underdetermined. If we look for *De ord.*'s unity in terms of its content, then we are left with "the order of divine providence" and the "order of teaching." But if that is all that binds the work, then Augustine might just as well have attached this closing *oratio* to *De lib. arbit.*, which also discusses the order of divine providence. What's more, this reading tells us nothing about why an ascent to incorporeal things is a fitting response to the first half of this particular text. Augustine is, after all, something of a Platonist, and the ascent from bodies to intelligibles turns up one way or another in nearly all his philosophical works.[7]

Since a focus on content fails to show any robust unity in *De ord.*, we might do better by reframing our discussion around the work's underlying project. Why is Augustine's recommendation to study the liberal disciplines a fitting response to the failure of this particular debate? How exactly is Augustine's course of study meant to help his companions advance from

---

[6] This is Augustine's alternative title for the work we tend to refer to as *Contra Academicos*. He gives both titles at *Retract.* 1.1.1. See Chapter 1 for discussion.

[7] See Chapter 2 for the Platonist background to this "upward trajectory" in Augustine's dialogues and *Conf.*

corporeals to incorporeals? What status does Augustine afford his closing account of Unity, given everything that went before? These questions, I argue, may be answered by reading *De ord.* as an application of the Platonic method Augustine set out in *C. Acad.*, i.e. ARP.[8] I suggest that the discussion of providence ends in *aporia* because Augustine's companions fail to recognize the special place that rational humans occupy in the world's providential structure. They are thus unable to explain how that structure is good for humans in particular.[9] In response, Augustine presents the liberal disciplines as formalized versions of the kinds of inquiry human beings engage in by virtue of their rationality. By engaging in such activity and then reflecting on the process, Augustine's companions could arrive at the self-knowledge they need for more fruitful discussions of providence. What they would find, according to Augustine's *oratio*, is that human rationality is unity-seeking and that the appearance of disunity in the world strikes us as puzzling, prompting us to find the deeper unity underlying the world's apparent disorder. This self-reflective discovery, in turn, helps make plausible Augustine's final account of Unity as the first cause of everything. According to this account, human beings have two-fold relationship to the first cause. Insofar as we are bodily, our parts are held together in unified wholes. In this we are no different than Augustine's chickens. Yet insofar as we are rational, we may grasp Unity intellectually, i.e. by working through puzzles and finding deeper unity. The end of this process is a vision of Unity itself that Augustine identifies with God. This vision, as *De beata v.* argued, is the truest happiness possible for a human being. *De ord.*'s response to the question of providence, at the most basic level, is that the world is good for humans insofar as the basic structures of God, world and human psychology provide ubiquitous opportunities for us to draw closer to true happiness.

My reading of *De ord.* rearranges elements of recent scholarly readings to form a new overall picture. While nearly all scholars agree that the work's debate ends in *aporia*, there is no consensus as to why. According to Foley, Trygetius articulates a Plotinian theodicy according to which local evils are swallowed up in the goodness of the whole that is the intelligible world, yet Trygetius fails to answer a further question on the origin of evil.[10] In this we

---

[8] This method moves through three stages: (A) aporetic debate, (R) reflection on the act of debating and a final (P) plausible conclusion. See Chapter 1.

[9] Or, to put it in the terms of Gareth Matthews, *Thought's Ego*, Augustine's companions approach providence as a third-person problem, when they need to be thinking about it from a first-person perspective. See also Naoki Kamimura, "Self-Knowledge and the Disciplines '*in uita*' in Augustine's *De ordine*," *Patristica*, Suppl. vol. 2 (2006): 76–96.

[10] Foley, "Cicero and Augustine," 71–75.

agree. According to Cary and Trelenberg, however, Trygetius and Augustine's other companions fail to articulate even this Plotinian idea.[11] On my
reading, it is not Plotinus' holistic, intelligible knowledge that Augustine's
companions fail to grasp, but the fact that everyday experience prompts
them, insofar as they are rational human beings, to search for such knowledge
in the first place. This slight difference in approach has major implications
when it comes to the purpose of Augustine's liberal curriculum. According to
Cary, Foley and Trelenberg, understanding *De ord.*'s final answer on evil
requires one to attain holistic, intelligible knowledge. All three see this
knowledge as the crowning achievement of Augustine's course of liberal
study, and none has anything to say about Augustine's admission that we
may skip some or all of the seven disciplines if need be.[12] On my reading,
what matters is not the content of this intelligible knowledge but the
realization that experience leads us to seek it. For this the liberal arts are
useful but ultimately unnecessary. As for the status of the work's conclusion,
Trelenberg is the only scholar to agree with me that Augustine treats it as
plausible, though we disagree as to what the exact content of that conclusion
is. Foley argues that Augustine rejects the use of "probability" entirely,[13] Cary
does not discuss the epistemic status of the work's conclusion, while some
older scholars deny that the work has a conclusion at all.[14] While My reading
comes closest to Trelenberg's, yet by approaching *De ord.* as an application of
ARP, I situate Trelenberg's reading within a broader project and provide an
explanation for the great deal of self-reflection present in the text.

   To defend my holistic reading of *De ord.*, I argue in what follows that
Augustine treats the liberal disciplines as useful but ultimately unnecessary
starting points for philosophical inquiry. From here I consider *De ord.* as
the conclusion to the three "scenic dialogues" from Cassiciacum.[15] Questions of pedagogy figure prominently, as Augustine explores the psychological and metaphysical underpinning of human rationality, and I explore
how the three works' opening dedications help set what follows within this
broader Cassiciacum project. This broader picture, in turn, helps us
understand Augustine's proposal to write dialogues on all seven liberal

---

[11] Cary, "What Licentius Learned," 148–156; Trelenberg, De Ordine, 391–396.
[12] Foley discusses Augustine's liberal curriculum only in passing, yet his suggestion that one may
   approach holistic knowledge of the world by seeking holistic knowledge of the text of *De ord.* at
   least suggests alternatives to that curriculum.
[13] Foley, "Augustine and Cicero," 65–64.   [14] See Trelenberg, De ordine, 392 for review.
[15] That is *C. Acad.*, *De beata v.* and *De ord.*, which are the only three of Augustine's eight dialogues to
   include a narrative setting. Bernd Reiner Voss, *Der Dialog*, 197, coins the term "*szenisch Dialog*" to
   mark the difference.

disciplines and why he stopped after *De Rhetorica* and *De Mus.* I will close by considering the latter, which is the only text to have survived.

Thinking about Providence: Licentius Defends his Position

In dedicating *De ord.* to his friend Zenobius,[16] Augustine likens the world's providential structure to a mosaic: those who complain of disorder are simply standing too close to see the big picture. The same could be said of *De ord.*'s debate,[17] which seems tortured and sprawling for someone working through it. Yet if we step back far enough, a broader picture emerges that, I will argue, is elegant and to the point. Let us therefore start with the big picture and then walk through enough detail to show how *De Ord.*'s debate contributes to the work as a whole.

The explicit goal of *De ord.*'s debate is to defend Licentius' position that all things are contained in order[18] against a series of challenges from Augustine, whom Licentius invites to test his position.[19] All but the very last of these challenges can be met by a relatively small conceptual arsenal. On the one hand is the recognition that one can conceive of "order" according to three basic models:

(1) The sum of a thing's parts
(2) The harmony of opposites
(3) The relation to intelligible number

These three models are mutually compatible. In fact, the last provides the grounds for the first two. On the other hand is the recognition that human beings may bear two distinct relations to the word's providential order: insofar as we are bodily beings, we are governed by order like any other bodily being; yet insofar as we are rational beings, we may also come to understand this order intellectually. Toward the end of the debate, Augustine juxtaposes these three models in a little *oratio*.[20] Humanity's twofold relation to order is not articulated until Augustine's final *oratio* at *De ord.* 2.31,[21] yet it is illustrated

---

[16] *De ord.* 1.2.   [17] *De ord.* 1.11–19 and 2.2–24.   [18] *De ord.* 1.8.   [19] *De ord.* 1.9.
[20] *De ord.* 2.12–17.
[21] This distinction is set forth as a distinction made by "most learned men" (*doctissimi uiri*) between "reason" (*ratio*), as the power of the mind by which things are divided and combined, "rational things" (*rationalia*), which use or can use reason, and "reasonable things" (*rationabilia*), which are made through the use of reason. While Augustine focuses on humans as rational, his mention of the World Soul at *De ord.* 2.30 suggests that humans, as bodily beings, could be the product of a rational albeit nonhuman artisan. In any event, it is clear enough that life in the world makes human beings subject to the structuring forces of rational agents, whether themselves, other people or mysterious forces such as the World Soul.

within the debate itself by Licentius, whose mind is "absent" from the discussion from *De ord.* 2.10 to 2.18, even though he is bodily present.

The debate makes progress as Licentius and Trygetius come to articulate Augustine's three models of order and humanity's two relations to them. They do so by working through a series of four basic questions:

Question	Discussed at...
(Q1) How are mice and leaves moved by order?	*De ord.* 1.11–14
(Q2) How is the order of goods and evils itself good?	*De ord.* 1.15–19
(Q3) What does it mean to be with God?	*De ord.* 2.2–21
(Q4) How could God be just before there was evil to punish?	*De ord.* 2.22–24

The first three questions prompt Licentius and Trygetius to employ each of Augustine's three models of order, in turn. Augustine starts the process by answering his own question, Q1, suggesting that mice and leaves follow an order insofar as they move human beings to philosophical reflection. Licentius enthusiastically accepts this response, yet he understands it in terms of efficient causation and proceeds to describe the world as merely a sum of its parts. This prompts Augustine to raise the normative concern of Q2. Licentius answers this by invoking a harmony of opposites: order is good insofar as God uses order to love good and hate evil. This prompts Augustine to ask what exactly is subject to God's governance, which quickly raises more basic questions about what it means to be "with God," i.e. Q3. While Augustine holds out a couple of possibilities, Licentius takes up the idea that being with God amounts to knowing God. This raises a series of three further questions, discussed in this section, each of which could be resolved by articulating human beings' twofold relation to order. Licentius and Trygetius answer each of them, although it is unclear how far they understand what they are saying. Augustine draws the debate to a close by returning to Licentius' response to Q2 and asks whether God was just before there was any evil to punish, Q4. At this point, Monica has joined the discussion and gives a promising response, although she lacks the conceptual resources to flesh it out. Q4 thus goes unanswered within *De ord.*'s debate and is returned to only briefly in the *oratio* that follows.

When it comes to Q1 to Q3, Augustine's final answer has been clear from the start: The world is good for humans insofar as experience of apparent disorder moves human beings to philosophical reflection through which they draw closer to God. The trouble is that Licentius and Trygetius fail to understand this answer the way Augustine intends. They need to engage in some conceptual work and self-reflection before they will be ready to see what Augustine is claiming. On the assumption that *De ord.* pursues *C. Acad.*'s Platonic method, ARP, then the goal of its debate should be to "un-teach" the young men's problematic perspectives and to model rational activity that may, in turn, serve as an object for self-reflective discovery, all of which will help them see Augustine's account as plausible. Having set out a big-picture view of this debate and its intended end, let us narrow our focus to see how each part advances this overarching project.

Q1 and Q2 are addressed in book 1. Throughout their discussion, Licentius and Trygetius fail to understand the special role assigned to human reason within Augustine's account. Thus when Licentius accepts that mice and leaves are held in order insofar as they sparked the group's discussion of order (Augustine's suggested answer to Q1), Licentius proceeds to spell out a causal nexus through which God providentially micromanages the world. Yet this treats mice and men as effectively on par, insofar as it assumes that they play the same kind of role within the world's providential nexus of causes.[22] If we flip ahead to Augustine's little *oratio* for a moment, we find Augustine differentiating between three different models of order. Licentius' current concept of order – which amounts to a kind of micromanaging, efficient causation – is summed up through the following examples:

> *Quid enim carnifice tetrius? quid illo animo truculentius atque dirius? At inter ipsas leges locum necessarium tenet et in bene moderatae ciuitatis ordinem inseritur estque suo animo nocens, ordine autem alieno poena nocentium. Quid sordidius, quid inanius, dedecoris et turpitudinis plenius meretricibus, lenonibus caeterisque hoc genus pestibus dici potest? Aufer meretrices de rebus humanis, turbaueris omnia libidinibus; constitue matronarum loco, labe ac dedecore dehonestaueris.*

> For what is more loathsome than an executioner? What more savage and awful than that soul? But he holds a necessary place within the laws themselves, and he is inserted into the order of a well moderated city. He is guilty in his own soul, yet through an external order he [becomes] a penalty for [other] guilty people. What can be said to be more sordid, more worthless, more full of shame and disgrace than prostitutes, pimps and other plagues of this sort? Remove prostitutes from human affairs and you will throw all things into confusion through lusts; place them in a position of lawful wives and you will be disgraced with taint of ill-repute. (*De ord.* 2.12)

---

[22] *De ord.* 1.14 quoted in the previous section.

On this model, Providence is the great orchestrator of events, leading bloodthirsty individuals into situations where they may punish the guilty, and leading leaves into ditches where they may spark conversation. Augustine does not say that this account is wrong. Yet, from the standpoint of his final position, it is superficial if not simply unnecessary. Given the nature of human psychology, there is no need for providence to clog that particular ditch or bring out that particular mouse. Simply place a human being in a world of apparent disorder and that human being will start asking questions.[23] Augustine, as author, drives this home with the series of events set between the debates of books 1 and 2: Licentius' turning from poetry to philosophy,[24] Licentius' singing in the outhouse,[25] and the group's stopping to watch a cock fight.[26] At first glance, these events seem to delay the group from resuming their discussion. Yet, from a self-reflective perspective, they actually advance it, insofar as they illustrate the fact that literally anything can prompt a human being to philosophical reflection. It is the nature of human rationality, not external circumstances, that accounts for this. Take the cockfight, for instance. The group begins by asking questions about the event itself, "Why do all cocks act this way? Why do they fight for dominance over the hens subject to them?" (*cur sic omnes, cur propter dominationem in subiectas sibi feminas*). Yet they quickly take a self-reflective turn:

> *cur deinde nos ipsa pugnae facies aliquantum et praeter altiorem istam considerationem duceret in uoluptatem spectaculi, quid in nobis esset quod, a sensibus remota multa quaereret, quid rursum, quod ipsorum sensuum inuitatione caperetur.*

> Furthermore, why did the very beauty of the fight draw us away somewhat from that higher study and to the pleasure of the spectacle? What is there in us that seeks many things removed from the senses? What is it that is captivated by the invitation of the senses themselves? (*De ord.* 1.26)

These are all the right questions to ask, and they were prompted by some chickens.

Q2 brings normative considerations into the mix, asking whether the order that embraces all things is itself good. Given that Licentius has just

---

[23] Christian Schäfer, "*Aqua haeret*. A view on Augustine's technique of biographical self-observation in *De Ordine*," *Index Augustiniana* 51 (2001): 65–75, reads *De ord.*'s clogged ditch as a Platonist metaphor for evil as a disturbance in "the perpetual outflow of reality." While this is perhaps a stretch, it is in keeping with my basic point. More to the point is Karin Schlapbach, "Divination, Wissen und Autorität in Augustins Cassiciacum-Dialogen," *Museum Helveticum* 62 (2005): 84–98.

[24] *De ord.* 1.20–21.   [25] *De ord.* 1.22–24.   [26] *De ord.* 1.25–26.

affirmed that God micromanages the world through a totalizing nexus of
efficient causes, it appears to follow that God brings about evils, as
Trygetius is quick to point out.²⁷ It is at this point that Licentius invokes
a harmony of opposites, claiming that it is according to order that God
loves good and hates evil.²⁸ This has the unwanted implication that evil
must exist if God is to be just, as Augustine eventually points out with Q4.
The more immediate concern, and the one that is more central to *De ord.*
as a whole, is that Licentius' answer fails to appreciate the distinctively
human good at the heart of providence. Licentius is thinking of God as a
kind of poet, who arranges events in clever, elegant ways. In his little
oratio, Augustine presents this harmony-of-opposites model thus:

> *Soloecismos et barbarismos quos uocant, poetae adamauerunt; quae schemata et
> metaplasmos mutatis appellare nominibus quam manifesta uitia fugere mal-
> uerunt. Detrahe tamen ista carminibus, suauissima condimenta desiderabimus.
> Congere multa in unum locum, totum acre putidum rancidum fastidibo . . .
> Mentientes conclusiones aut irrepentes paulatim uel minuendo uel addendo in
> assensionem falsitatis quis non metuat, quis non oderit? Saepe tamen in
> disputationibus certis et suis sedibus colocatae tantum ualent, ut nescio quomodo
> per eas dulcescat ipsa deceptio.*

> Poets are exceedingly fond of what they call solecisms and barbarisms. Yet
> they prefer to change their names and call them tropes and metaplasms
> rather than avoid such obvious flaws of language. But take these away from
> poems and we will long for these most delightful spices. Collect many of
> them into a single place, and I will feel nauseous about a whole that is
> pungent, stinking and rank . . . Who does not fear lying conclusions or
> those that creep little by little through subtraction or addition into assent to
> falsity? Who does not hate them? Yet in certain arguments, when set in
> their appropriate places, these often have such force, that somehow the
> deception accomplished through them becomes sweet. (*De ord.* 2.13)

This is the stuff of redemption stories and the triumph over adversity.²⁹
Yet what ultimately makes the world good for human beings is not that it
is a good story; it is that the world provides opportunities for individuals to
come to true happiness. The point of philosophical reflection, of seeking
unity behind disorder, is that the end of the process is coming to know
Unity itself, which Augustine identifies with God. As the group saw in

---

²⁷ *De ord.* 1.17.   ²⁸ *De ord.* 1.18.
²⁹ In contemporary terms, we might see the contrast between Augustine's first two models as the
difference between "balancing off" goods and evils and "defeating" them within greater wholes. See
Roderick Chisholm, "The Defeat of Good and Evil." In *The Problem of Evil,* ed. Marilyn McCord
Adams & Robert Merrihew Adams (Oxford, 1990): 53–68.

De beata v., this is true happiness for a human being.[30] The harmonious antitheses within creation might reflect this Unity, yet it is not the existence of these antitheses or the fact that we are governed by them, but the knowledge to which they may eventually lead us that grounds the goodness of providence for human beings. In treating the world as a "good read," Licentius has set the bar too low.

Book 2 brings questions of human rationality to the fore, thus moving beyond Licentius' response to Q1. What's more, by focusing on the wise person's knowledge, the group invokes a distinctively human good, thus moving beyond Licentius' response to Q2. The trouble now is to square all this lofty talk of intellectual reality with everyday human life. Augustine drives this home through a series of three further questions. Each of them can be resolved by realizing that human beings are able to relate to intelligible paradigms such as numbers in two fundamentally different ways, i.e. by being governed by them (*regi/gubarnari*) and by understanding them (*intellegere*). While humans and chickens are both composed of chemicals in certain ratios, humans can grasp these ratios intellectually. Chickens cannot. At *De ord.* 2.4, Augustine offers both relations – being ruled and understanding – as possible definitions for what it means to be "with God" (*cum Deo*). Licentius, however, latches onto the second at the exclusion of the first. The one-sidedness of his perspective, in turn, prompts Augustine to present a list of further questions:

Question	Discussed at...
(Q3a) Can things which are with God change?	*De ord.* 2.3–7
(Q3b) Does the wise person know folly?	*De ord.* 2.8–10
(Q3c) Does the fool act according to order?	*De ord.* 2.11

In response to Q3a, Licentius argues that only the wise person's knowledge and the objects of that knowledge are not subject to change; everything else about the wise person does change. Q3b asks whether this wise person's knowledge includes knowledge of folly (*stultitia*), which is the opposite of wisdom. After all, the wise person would need to know folly in order to avoid it[31] or to teach others how to escape it.[32] At this

---

[30] At *De ord.* 2.20, Licentius cites this previous discussion. I take this as an invitation to see ideas from *De beata v.* at play here.
[31] *De ord.* 2.8.   [32] *De ord.* 2.9.

point, Trygetius steps in, "since Licentius is completely absent,"[33] and points
out that the person who thinks he is seeing darkness is in fact simply failing to
see; likewise, the person who thinks he knows foolishness simply fails to
know. While this "privation account" solves one problem, it seems to leave
the fool outside God's order. Q3c articulates this worry. Trygetius can't think
of a good analogy (*similitudo*) for thinking about this but, nevertheless,
proceeds to explain that if one looks at the fool's life with a narrow mind
(*angusto animo*), it appears unordered, "but if raising the eyes of his mind and
broadening his gaze, he surveys all things at once, he will find nothing that is
not ordered, distinguished and situated in its proper places."[34] Augustine
is delighted by this response, though he is not convinced that Trygetius grasps
the implications of what he has said. It is at this point that Augustine launches
into his little *oratio* with its three models of order. The last of these captures
Licentius' and Trygetius' talk of the wise person's knowledge:

> *Iam in musica, in geometria, in astrorum motibus, in numerorum necessitatibus ordo ita dominatur, ut, si quis quasi eius fontem atque ipsum penetrale uidere desideret, aut in his inueniat aut per haec eo sine ullo errore ducatur. Talis enim eruditio, si quis ea moderate utatur – nam nihil ibi quam nimium formidandum est –, talem philosophiae militem nutrit uel etiam ducem, ut ad summum illum modum, ultra quod requirere aliquid nec possit nec debeat nec cupiat, qua uult, euolet atque perueniat multosque perducat, unde iam, dum ipsis humanis rebus teneatur, sic eas despiciat cunctaque discernat, ut nullo modo eum moueat, cur alius optet liberos habere nec habeat, alius uxoris nimia fecunditate torqueatur ...*

> Now in music, in geometry, in astronomy, in the relationships between
> numbers, order has such dominion that if anyone should want to see its
> 'font and inner sanctuary,' he would either find it in these or he would be
> led there through these without any error. Such education, if one uses it
> moderately (for nothing is to be more feared in these matters than excess),
> will nourish a soldier of philosophy, or even a general, of such a sort, that he
> will fly up to where he wants to be and arrive at that highest measure,
> beyond which he neither can, nor ought nor desires to ask for anything else;
> and he will lead many to that place from which even then, while held by
> human affairs, he will look down on and discern such matters so that it will
> in no way disturb him that one person wants to have children but has none,
> while another is tortured by his wife's excessive fecundity. (*De ord.* 2.134)

---

[33] *Licentio prorsus absente* (*De ord.* 2.10). The text is somewhat vague about what this means. Yet when
Augustine calls him back at 2.17, he describes him as "occupied with some care or other for so long"
(*tam diu nescio qua cura occupatus*) and "a stranger to this conversation" (*alienus ab hoc sermone*).
The implication is merely that his mind has wandered off.

[34] *Si autem mentis oculos erigens atque diffundens simul uniuersa conlustret nihil non ordinatum suisque
semper ueluti sedibus distinctum dispositumque reperiet.* (*De ord.* 2.11).

While Trygetius could not think of any analogy, Augustine's three models offer "innumerable similes" (*innumerabilia [similia]*).[35] The point is to recognize that the fool, even though he lacks knowledge of order, is still governed by it, as can be described by one or more of Augustine's three models. The fool is thus "with God" in one sense yet not "with God" in another. Nevertheless, the fact that the fool is governed by order gives him a starting point to escape his folly by coming to know the intelligible paradigms that ultimately structure that order. All he must do is accept the invitations to reflection that everyday experience confronts him with.

Now that Augustine has set out his three models of order, we might expect him to return to Trygetius to see whether the young man can put all these pieces together. Instead, he calls Licentius back to see how much he has managed to work out on his own. To this end, Augustine rephrases Q3a in explicitly bodily terms: How can the wise person's mind not change location when his body does?[36] Licentius, however, is still not thinking of human beings as relating to order in two different ways. He recognizes that he can't get out of this one, anticipates Augustine's next question, "Does God govern things that are not well governed?"[37] and admits that he can't answer this either. Since this is simply a variant of Q3c, which Trygetius has already answered, Augustine tells Licentius to read the transcript and moves on.

Recalling Licentius' position at the end of book 1, that it is according to order that God loves good and hates evil, Augustine poses the debate's final question, Q4: How could God's order be just before there was evil to hate? At this point, Monica has returned and answers, "Evil, which came to be, in no way came to be from God's providential order, but God's justice did not allow it to be unordered and has returned and compelled it into an order suitable to it." (*ipsum malum quod, natum est, nullo modo dei ordine natum est, sed illa iustitia id inordinatum esse non siuit et in sibi meritum ordinem redegit et compulit*).[38] For whatever it is worth, this is basically the position defended by Augustine in *De lib. arbit.*[39] Still, Monica has not

---

[35] *De ord.* 2.12. We find the same rhetorical move at *C. Acad.* 3.21, where, after a quite long discussion, Augustine finally presents a counterexample to the skeptical claim that knowledge is impossible, yet proceeds immediately to give numerous other examples. *De ord.*'s opening scene is likewise presented as a divinely inspired moment, as a mouse and ditch draw the group into philosophical reflection. Yet it is followed by three other scenarios that perform exactly the same function. By presenting something divine and then making it look commonplace, Augustine draws his companions into recognizing the divine behind the everyday.
[36] *De ord.* 2.18–21.   [37] *De ord.* 2.21   [38] *De Ord.* 2.23.   [39] See Chapter 7.

grasped that work's central distinction between natures, which are created by God, and states, which result from the choices of human free will. Without such conceptual tools, she cannot elaborate her idea. *De ord.*'s debate thus draws to a close with Augustine's companions scratching their heads.

What exactly has this debate accomplished? First of all, we should note that the debate is more concerned with understanding providence than with defending it against the problem of evil. The two tasks are, of course, intimately related. Modern preoccupations, however, often get the emphasis wrong, e.g. Russel's translation of *De ordine* as *Divine Providence and the Problem of Evil*. Augustine's more famous *De lib. arbit.* opens by asking "whether God is author of evil," effectively picking up at Q4. The overarching argument of *De ord.* addresses the more basic question of what makes the world good for humans in the first place. As for this central task, Licentius and Trygetius have enriched their conceptual vocabularies, moving from a relatively simplistic model of the world as a sum of parts to more sophisticated models involving antitheses and, ultimately, intelligible paradigms. Licentius has also gained facility at reflecting on his own actions, thanking Providence for prompting their discussion of providence. He has not, however, realized that reflecting on his own mental absence might provide the distinction he needs to meet Augustine's challenges. Meanwhile, neither young man has managed to put all these pieces together. Yet this is, in part, the point. Licentius begins ready to defend his position, come what may. By the end, he is pointing out the problems with his own views and even anticipating objections for which he has no response. By embracing perplexity in this way, Licentius gets a better sense of what is at stake in their discussion and is prepared to entertain Augustine's final *oratio* in a more sophisticated manner.

Thinking about Thinking:
Augustine's Reflections on Liberal Study

The main challenge for any holistic reading of *De ord.* is to explain how its two halves, debate and *oratio*, go together. The first thing to note is that Augustine's closing *oratio* is thorough. The whole thing is structured around an elaborate *diuisio*, as its main topic, "order," is divided and subdivided into progressively more detailed subjects. The basic structure is as follows:

Oratio Perpetua (2.24–52)
    Order... (2.25–52)
- of life (2.25)
- of instruction (2.26–51)
  - authority (2.27)
  - reason (2.30–51)
    - rational things (2.31)
    - reasonable things (2.32–51)
      - in character (see 2.25)
      - in liberal disciplines (2.35–51)
        - in speaking: grammar, dialectic, rhetoric (2.35–38)
        - in delighting: music, geometry, astronomy, arithmetic (2.39–51)
          - for the use of life (2.39–46)
          - for contemplation (2.47–52)

Questions of providence do not resurface until the final section on contemplation.[40] What is the point of all the detail leading up to this? The most obvious place to look for an answer is the point where the text transitions from debate to *oratio*. Immediately following Monica's inchoate response to Q4, Augustine, as narrator, responds:

> *Hic ego, cum omnes cernerem studiosissime ac pro suis quemque uiribus deum quaerere sed ipsum, de quo agebamus, ordinem non tenere, quo ad illius ineffabilis maiestatis intellegentiam peruenitur: Oro uos, inquam, si, ut uideo, multum diligitis ordinem, ne nos praeposteros et inordinatos esse patiamini. Quamquam enim occultissima ratio se demonstraturam polliceatur nihil praeter diuinum ordinem fieri, tamen si quempiam ludi magistrum audiremus conantem docere puerum syllabas, quem prius litteras nemo docuisset, non dico ridendum tamquam stultum, sed uinciendum tamquam furiosum putaremus non ob aliud, opinor, nisi quod docendi ordinem non teneret.*

When I saw that all were seeking God most eagerly and according to their abilities, but that they were not holding to that very order which we were discussing, through which one may arrive at understanding of His ineffable majesty, I said, "I beg you, if you have great love for order, which I see you do, do not get ahead of yourselves and out of order. For although the most hidden reason promises to demonstrate that nothing happens outside of divine order, nevertheless, if we were to hear that some teacher was attempting to teach syllables to a boy whom no one had taught letters,

---

[40] *De ord.* 2.47–52.

I don't say that he should be laughed at as a fool, but we would think he should be tied up as a madman, for no other reason, I think, than that he wasn't holding to the order of instruction." (*De ord.* 2.24)

This gives the impression that there is a right way to go about inquiries into providence. Since the bulk of Augustine's *oratio* is taken up with a presentation of the liberal disciplines, Cary takes Augustine's point to be that we must learn the content of the *trivium* (grammar, dialectic, rhetoric) and *quadrivium* (music, geometry, astronomy, arithmetic) in order to understand the providential structures of the world around us.[41] This fits well with Licentius' initial conception of providence as a totalizing nexus of efficient causes. To understand such structures, the liberal disciplines would be invaluable. This reading does not, however, fit well with the end of Augustine's *oratio*. Having just completed the first extant statement of the medieval curriculum, Augustine continues:

> *Et ne quisquam latissimum aliquid nos complexos esse arbitretur, hoc dico planius atque breuius, ad istarum rerum cognitionem neminem aspirare debere sine illa quasi duplici scientia bonae disputationis potentiaeque numerorum. Si quis etiam hoc plurimum putat, solos numeros optime nouerit aut solam dialecticam. Si et hoc infinitum est, tantum perfecte sciat, quid sit unum in numeris quantumque ualeat nondum in illa summa lege summoque ordine rerum omnium, sed in his quae quotidie passim sentimus atque agimus.*

> And so that no one thinks that we have embraced too wide a project, I say more plainly and briefly that no one ought to aspire to grasp these things [i.e. philosophical matters] without the 'double knowledge' of good disputation [i.e. dialectic] and the power of numbers [i.e. arithmetic]. And if anyone thinks that this is still too much, let him know as well as possible numbers alone or only dialectic. And if this too proves unending, at least let him know thoroughly what unity is and what it achieves, if not in that highest law and highest order of all things, then in the things we constantly perceive and do in everyday life. (*De ord.* 2.47)

Having begun with a full course of liberal study, Augustine whittles down the number of required disciplines from seven to two to one, and then suggests that we may skip the liberal arts entirely and attend to unity as we encounter it in everyday life. This is not a useful strategy for making sense of the world as a nexus of efficient causes. On my reading, Augustine has nothing to say against the attempt to understand the particulars of the world around us. Yet he treats such knowledge as unnecessary for getting at the heart of providence, which turns on our ability to know God intellectually. Put simply, what ultimately matters is not Augustine's first

[41] Cary, "What Licentius Learned."

model, which Licentius assumes at the beginning, or even the second, which Licentius embraces at the end of book 1, but the third, which provides the most basic explanation of the structures that make the world a good for human beings.

In many cases, these three models may come together as one moves through the liberal disciplines and on to self-knowledge. Take, for instance, inquiry into planetary motion. An inquirer might begin by looking into the efficient causes of the planets' motions (model one); this, in turn, can lead to the realization that these motions are ruled by certain forces that are balanced in harmonic ratios (model two); this realization, in turn, can prompt a consideration of these harmonies in their own right (model three). Yet, while ancient and modern astronomers may agree on these questions of pure math (model three), they will likely disagree on its application to particular cases (model two), and they will give completely different explanations for the efficient causes involved (model one). Be that as it may, all astronomers, whether ancient or modern, seek an account whose equations will balance out, as a way of finding the unity underlying experience. That is all that matters for purposes of *De ord.*'s main argument. Augustine continues his discussion of contemplation by setting out this self-reflective discovery:

> *Hunc igitur ordinem tenens anima iam philosophiae tradita primo seipsam inspicit, et . . . ita secum loquetur: ego quodam meo motu interiore et occulto ea, quae discenda sunt, possum discernere uel connectere et haec uis mea ratio uocatur. Quid autem discernendum est, nisi quod aut unum putatur et non est aut certe non tam unum est quam putatur? item cur quid connectendum est, nisi ut unum fiat, quantum potest? Ergo et in discernendo et in connectendo unum uolo et unum amo, sed cum discerno, purgatum, cum conecto, integrum uolo. In illa parte uitantur aliena, in hac propria copulantur, ut unum aliquid perfectum fiat. Lapis ut esset lapis, omnes eius partes omnisque natura in unum solidata est. Quid arbor? Nonne arbor non esset, si una non esset? Quid membra cuiuslibet animantis ac uiscera et quidquid est eorum, e quibus constat? Certe si unitatis patiantur diuortium, non erit animal. Amici quid aliud quam unum esse conantur? Et quanto magis unum, tanto magis amici sunt.*

Therefore, the soul holding to this order and now drawn to philosophy, first looks into itself and . . . speaks with itself as follows, "I, by a certain inner and hidden motion of mine, am able to distinguish and combine those things which are to be learned, and this power is called my reason." What, however, must be distinguished except what is either thought to be one but is not or at least is not as much one as it is thought to be? Likewise, why must anything be combined except so that it may become one as much as it can? Therefore both in distinguishing and combining, it is unity [*unum*] that I want; it is unity that I love. But when I distinguish, I want something purified; when I combine I want something whole. In the one case, foreign things are shunned; in the other, things that belong are bound together so that one complete thing comes to be. A stone, so that it might be a stone, has all its parts and its entire nature fastened into one. What about a tree? It won't be a tree, if it isn't one, will it? What about the limbs of some animal and the guts, and whatever it is that an animal consists in? Surely if these parts should suffer a separation from unity, there will no longer be an animal. What else are friends trying for than to be one? And the more they are one, the more they are friends. (*De ord.* 2.48)

Given the setup of the text, the most obvious object for the soul's current reflections is Augustine's account of Reason creating the liberal disciplines.[42] Yet what matters here is the rational activity involved, not the particular content of one discipline or another. Nor do the liberal disciplines have a monopoly on the search for unity. Augustine's *oratio* itself uses the dialectical technique of division to set everything in its place, creating a nicely ordered whole. From this perspective, the thoroughness of Augustine's *oratio* stems not from the necessity of each step of the curriculum it sets out, but from a desire to "let the seams show" and thus emphasize the search for unity that the *oratio* embodies as an artifact of reason.

In emphasizing the activity of study over the content of study, my reading makes sense of why Augustine picks out the particular disciplines of dialectic and arithmetic for those who are short on time. This is easier to see for dialectic, which Augustine presents as the "discipline of disciplines" (*disciplina disciplinarum*) or what we today might call a "meta-discipline." Within his account of the liberal discipline's genesis, Dialectic – momentarily personified – is born when Reason has finished constructing Grammar[43] and then stops to reflect on what she was doing.

> *Illa igitur ratio perfecta dispositaque grammatica admonita est quaerere atque attendere hanc ipsam uim, qua peperit artem: nam eam definiendo distribuendo colligendo non solum digesserat atque ordinauerat uerum ab omni etiam falsitatis irreptione defenderat. Quando ergo transiret ad alia fabricanda, nisi ipsa sua prius quasi quaedam machinamenta et instrumenta distingueret notaret digereret proderetque ipsam disciplinam disciplinarum, quam dialecticam uocant? Haec docet docere, haec docet discere; in hac se ipsa ratio demonstrat atque aperit quae sit, quid uelit, quid ualeat. Scit scire: sola scientes facere non solum uult sed etiam potest.*

Therefore, since Grammar had been completed and arranged, Reason was admonished to turn her attention and inquire into this power itself through which she gave birth to this art. For by defining, dividing and collecting, she had not only arranged Grammar and set it in order but also defended it from every attempt of falsity to creep in. How therefore could she pass on to

---

[42] *De ord.* 2.35–46.   [43] *De ord.* 2.35–37.

creating other things, before she had distinguished, noted and arranged her own tools and devices, so to speak, and produced that discipline of disciplines, which they call Dialectic? Dialectic teaches how to teach and how to learn. In her, Reason shows herself and makes clear what she is, what she wants, what she is capable of. Dialectic knows what knowing is; it alone not only wants to make people know but is also able. (*De ord.* 2.38)

Dialectic is inherently self-reflective and makes a fitting starting point for a project of thinking about thinking. Augustine presents arithmetic, the science of numbers, in a similarly self-reflective light.[44] For him, it is not a prerequisite to the other numerical disciplines. It is what one arrives at by reflecting on the activities that one uses while studying music, geometry and astronomy. In the end, though, neither dialectic nor arithmetic is necessary. The liberal disciplines are simply formalized versions of activities that flow naturally from human reason. By presenting these disciplines as expressions of human reason and employing dialectical tools to structure that presentation, Augustine models a process of reflecting on rational activity and invites his companions to consider their own discussion from a self-reflective perspective. By doing so, they would realize that the fact that mice move men to philosophical inquiry tells us more about men than mice, that human beings occupy a special place in the world's providential order and that the combination of world and human rationality provides a path for human beings to draw closer to God in a distinctively human way.[45]

The Providence of Thought: A Plausible Account of Unity

Augustine presents his discovery that human reason is unity-seeking as the result of self-reflection, available to any individual, regardless of background or education. If we grant him this conclusion, we may still wonder how it gets us to the work's final account of providence. So far we have been tracking Augustine's discussion of contemplation, which begins with the soul reflecting on its own activities.[46] This discussion proceeds as the soul turns to inquire into its own nature and its relation to reason[47] and

---

[44] *De ord.* 2.43.
[45] Additional evidence for my reading can be found at *De ord.* 2.30, where Augustine claims, "though people strive to act entirely rationally in matters that are prone to deceive, all but a very few are ignorant of what reason is and what kind of a thing it is." (*Itaque cum in rebus ipsis fallacibus ratione totum agere homines moliantur, quid sit ipsa ratio et qualis sit, nisi perpauci prorsus ignorant*). For present purposes it is the latter that is important. Likewise, at *De ord.* 2.45, Augustine points out that while native Italians harass him about his pronunciation of certain words, "they are rebuked [by him] about the nature of pronunciation itself." (*quod ad ipsum sonum attinet, reprehenduntur*).
[46] *De ord.* 2.47–49.   [47] *De ord.* 2.50.

then "ventures to see God."[48] To put this all together we must read a bit between the lines.

In coming to see God, the soul attains the "vision of Beauty, through imitation of which other things are beautiful and in comparison with which other things are foul" (*aspectum pulchritudinis, cuius imitatione pulchra, cuius conparatione foeda sunt cetera*).[49] In the preceding discussion of the liberal disciplines, Augustine drew a distinction between disciplines used for speech (grammar, dialectic, rhetoric) and those used for delight (music, geometry, astronomy, arithmetic). What was delightful about the latter was in each case a numeric ratio. In juxtaposing these discussions, Augustine suggests the following argument:[50]

(1)   A ratio exists when two numbers are held together in a unified relationship [analytic].
(2)   The more perfectly unified the ratios in a body are, the more beautiful we find that body [via self-reflection; e.g. on musical instruments more or less in tune].[51]
(3)   Thus, unity is the cause of the beauty in bodies and is more beautiful than they.

What reason does *De ord.* give us for accepting this argument? Sandpaper, after all, might be the cause of wood becoming smooth, but it does not follow from this that sandpaper is smoother than the wood it makes smooth. We might overcome this challenge by understanding "cause" in a formal rather than efficient sense. Yet what does any of this have to do with God?

In preceding chapters, I argued that the scenic dialogues from Cassiciacum – *C. Acad., De beata v., De ord.* – are each constructed around key terms from Wisdom 11:20's triad: measure, number, weight. *C. Acad.*'s overarching argument concludes that it is plausible (*probabile*) that wisdom can be found and the search is sped on by "the dual weight of reason and authority." *De beata v.* concluded that happiness is attained by conforming one's mind to Christ=Truth as the "measure of the soul." While *De beata v.* lacks *C. Acad.*'s technical terms for plausibility, both works present conclusions that are not demonstratively proven yet still richly explanatory

---

[48]   *De ord.* 2.51.   [49]   *De ord.* 2.51.
[50]   The general ascent from particular beauties to Beauty itself should be familiar from Plotinus, *Enn.* 1.6 "On Beauty," which is itself a reworking of Diotema's speech from Plato's *Smp.* See Chapter 2. Augustine presents an explicit version of this argument in his slightly later work, *De Mus.* 6.36. See discussion later in this chapter.
[51]   See *De ord.* 2.33–34.

of the aporetic debates and self-reflection that came before. I have thus argued for taking both works as pursuing a course of ARP. *De ord.*, I suggest, completes the triad with its account of Unity as first cause, "number" in the structuring of the world and the world's invitations to seek Unity as what grounds its goodness for human beings. We have traced the aporetic debates and self-reflective turns through which Augustine leads his companions to the final revelation of this account. Given the parallel argument structures of this dialogue and the other two, I suggest reading *De ord.*'s concluding account in the same light: not as a demonstrative argument that did not go quite right, but as a framework providing rich explanation for issues the dialogue as a whole has brought to our attention. The use of Wisdom 11:20 helps identify this Plotinian Unity/One with the God of Christian Scripture. Put another way, *De ord.*'s debates, narrative episodes and closing *oratio* prepare us to better understand what Scripture is saying when it claims that God is One. Yet it does so, not via direct scriptural exegesis, but through a process of reflecting on human psychology and raising questions about our everyday experience of the world.

Meanwhile, each of the Cassiciacum dialogues – *Sol.* Included – explores one of the classical virtues. *C. Acad.* is centrally concerned with wisdom and *De beata v.* with moderation. *De ord.* continues the project with its exploration of justice. This will be obvious enough to those who see *De ord.* as centrally concerned with the problem of evil and theodicy, which is quite literally a "defense of God's justice." Yet the problem of evil figured only in Q2, which was passed by rather quickly and Q4, which is sidestepped in this work. I suggest that *De ord.* aims at the more basic goal of understanding God's justice toward humanity by articulating what makes the world good for humans in the first place. That is not to say that responding to the problem of evil is unimportant. Yet "in the sight of such great Beauty," the problem of evil, which amounts to a set of worries about blame, punishment and retributive justice, seems trivial and even "foul in comparison." Among the goals of *De ord.* is to turn Licentius and Trygetius away from thinking about God as merely some great puppet master or judge meting out judgment and toward a vision of the Beauty behind the world.

The Cassiciacum Project

Questions of providence figure centrally in the dedication of all three of Augustine's scenic dialogues, yet providence does not become an explicit object of a main work's discussion until *De ord.* The dedications to

C. Acad. and *De beata v.* thus stand apart from the works they introduce, insofar as they seem to open with the wrong topic and weave in their works' central concerns only briefly. *De ord.*, by contrast, opens with providence and stays with providence. Yet, as we've seen, the account of providence it presents turns on the fact that everyday experience, particularly experience of disorder, may turn human beings to philosophical reflection. In this, Augustine presents philosophical inquiry as a process that comes naturally to human beings, flowing from their rational desire to find unity in the world. It follows from this that the main task for a teacher of philosophy is not to impart new knowledge but merely to remove obstacles to this natural process. From this perspective, it makes sense that *C. Acad.* should present its Platonic pedagogical method, ARP, as a form of "purification." Yet *De ord.* goes beyond *C. Acad.* by grounding this method in the basic structure of the world, by presenting that structure as a providential gift from God and by calling attention to the role of everyday experiences, particularly disconcerting ones, in calling individuals to philosophical reflection. This last idea is given a moral spin in the dialogues' dedications, which recount ways that seeming ill fortunes, such as the loss of material wealth and honors, are in fact good fortunes insofar as they can turn individuals to real goods. Augustine presents this as "return to oneself." The prime example of this in the dedications is Augustine himself, whose chest pains helped him leave his career in rhetoric and commit himself to philosophy. The scenic dialogues display the fruit of this new commitment. Concerns for pedagogy feature centrally, as the three works present Augustine removing obstacles and encouraging his companions as they turn to philosophy and return to themselves. The dialogues' opening dedications and *De ord.*'s closing *oratio* provide bookends for the set, insofar as the naturalness of philosophy, the obstacle of everyday goods, benefits of "ill fortune" and the return to the self sum up Augustine's big-picture vision for the community gathered at Cassiciacum.[52] This study seeks to present a holistic reading of these works. Let us turn now to their dedications, which I have so far mostly ignored, to show how each situates the text it introduces within the project advanced by the set as a whole.

---

[52] In speaking of this community, I am speaking merely of the dialogues' literary depiction of that community, not the actual group of people gathered at Cassiciacum. See Introduction for review of the scholarly debate over the dialogues' historical status.

Each of *C. Acad.*'s first two books opens with a dedication to August-ine's patron, Licentius' father, Romanianus. The first of these perfectly encapsulates the big-picture account of providence set out in *De ord.* but has little directly to do with *C. Acad.*'s discussion of wisdom. Augustine opens by claiming that in this life no one enters the "harbor of wisdom," where secure goods are to be found, unless he is blown there by a reversal of fortune of the sort people usually consider bad. Everything that happens is in keeping with the whole, as Philosophy promises to teach those who have been properly initiated. Augustine encourages Romanianus to respond to these invitations of seeming ill fortune and he prays that God will "restore you [Romanianus] to yourself."[53] This brief overview ties together *De ord.*'s providential call to philosophical reflection, *De beata v.*'s secure goods attained through wisdom and *C. Acad.*'s account of philoso-phy as a mystery religion designed to purify "initiates." Augustine con-tinues by cataloguing the material goods and honors that make the masses think Romanianus is happy, but in fact make him miserable. A recent reversal of fortune, however, offers a way to awaken Romanianus' divine spirit.[54] Augustine presents himself as an example of someone whom worldly goods tried to ensnare, while he was "daily singing their praises" as a rhetorician. Chest pains, however, compelled him to give up his "puffed-up profession," and he has now turned to philosophy. This philosophy, he continues, freed him from "that superstition" into which Augustine threw himself and Romanianus alike, for philosophy teaches that nothing accessible to the bodily senses should be worshipped; it promises to reveal the true and hidden God, and it even gives glimpses of him through the clouds.[55] Licentius shares this way of life with him, and Augustine presents the discussion that follows as a model for Romanianus to imitate.[56]

If we were to judge by this opening, the obstacle to be overcome in *C. Acad.* is not the Academic skeptics, who have yet to be even hinted at, but worldly success and the superstition that Augustine once shared with Romanianus. Elsewhere, Augustine identifies this superstition as Mani-chaeism, which he characterizes by its radical materialism.[57] In the over-arching argument of *C. Acad.*, as I read it, the Stoics' commitment to materialism is what caused the Academics to take their skeptical stance. This materialism presents a formalized version of the empiricist ways of thinking, born of everyday experience, that Licentius and Trygetius start

---

[53] *C. Acad.* 1.1.   [54] *C. Acad.* 1.1–3.   [55] *C. Acad.* 1.3.   [56] *C. Acad.* 1.4.
[57] See *De utilitate credendi* 2 and *Conf.* 4.1 & 6.12.

out with, and Augustine sets out to un-teach. The *oratio* that closes
C. Acad. 3 traces how the Stoics' metaphysical error (materialism) led to
an epistemological error (empiricism) and thus kept them from finding
wisdom. The dedication to *C. Acad.* 1 brings out the ethical aspect of this
problem, as Augustine likens his windy profession, which praises material
goods, to the superstition that worships a material God. On my reading,
C. Acad. presents a course of ARP designed to un-teach empiricist assumptions and draw attention to the knowledge presupposed by rational
thought. The point of all this is to purify Augustine's students for initiation into Platonic intellectualism.[58] The dedication to *C. Acad.* 1 sets
what I take to be the central project of *C. Acad.* within the broader context
of what I take to be the central project of *De ord.* If we are looking for
bookends for the scenic dialogues as a set, I don't know what more we
could ask for.

   C. Acad.'s second dedication opens by elaborating a list of four obstacles
encountered in the journey to the "harbor of philosophy,"[59] which
Augustine proceeds to apply to Romanianus' case. When it comes, first,
to the upheavals of everyday life, Romanianus' mind is "like a thunderbolt
wrapped up in clouds of domestic affairs,"[60] the implication being that a
thunderbolt can cut through a cloud if it really wants to. Moral and
intellectual shortcomings, second, should pose no issue for Romanianus,
who has demonstrated his virtue by supporting Augustine's studies for
years and encouraging him to found the philosophical community at
Cassiciacum.[61] Augustine holds himself up again as an example of someone who is returning to himself through philosophy. He is beginning to
find truth, he is confident that he will eventually arrive at "its higher
measure,"[62] and he is realizing that his boyhood religion, i.e. catholic
Christianity, is not as foolish as he had thought. This progress has come
as an encounter with "certain books," identified at *De beata v.* 4 as
Plotinus', which in an explosion akin to "exotic incense" (*bonas res arab-
icas*) made all worldly honors look petty by comparison.[63] Augustine
extends the comparison through an allegory of Philosophy's sister, Philocaly – literally "Love of Beauty" – who has been "dragged down from the

[58] See Karin Schlapbach, "Ciceronisches und Neoplatonisches in den Proömien von Augustin, *Contra Academicos* 1 und 2." In *Zur Rezeption der hellenistischen Philosophie in der Spätantike*, ed. Theresa Fuhrer & Michael Ehler (Stuttgart: Franz Steiner, 1999), 139–151 .
[59] *C. Acad.* 2.1.   [60] *C. Acad.* 2.2.   [61] *C. Acad.* 2.3–4.
[62] Cf. *De beata v.* 34's Trinitarian account of the Holy Spirit as the soul's admonition to truth, Christ=Truth as the measure of the soul and the Father as the highest measure.
[63] *C. Acad.* 2.5.

heights by the birdlime of lust" yet accounts for whatever is noble in nonphilosophical life. Even Romanianus' "adversary," if he were to recognize that Philocaly and Philosophy were born of the same father, Wisdom, would turn to the true Beauty of Wisdom.[64] While it is unclear who this adversary is,[65] Augustine here presents *De beata v.*'s move from everyday concepts of happiness to true happiness in conforming one's mind to God as the Measure of the soul, as well as *De ord.*'s move from everyday beauty to the greatest Beauty in the vision of God as Unity. All of which builds up to Augustine's basic message, "Let us return to ourselves!"[66]

The final two obstacles form a dilemma, as one may give up searching for truth either by despairing that it can be found or by thinking oneself already to have found it.[67] In Chapter 1, I argue that materialism is at the root of both problems. It was the Stoics' materialism that the Academics employed to argue against the possibility of knowledge, while it is the Manichee "superstition" that claims to have found the truth in a similarly materialistic account of God and the world. Augustine presents *C. Acad.* as a remedy to despair and promises another work, likely his *De vera religione* (390CE), to address the specifics of the Manichee superstition. He ends saying that he is busy "purifying himself of hollow and harmful opinions," and he offers Romanianus the seemingly contradictory advice not to count anything known unless he is as certain of it as that $1+2+3+4=10$, while at the same time trusting Him who said, "Seek and you shall find," i.e. Christ.[68] On the one hand, this advice encapsulates the work's Platonic method, whose demand for certainty clears away any empirical claims to knowledge while leaving intact various truths, such as $1+2+3+4=10$, whose certainty may be plausibly explained by the mechanisms of Platonic intellectualism. At the same time, it suggests that Christianity will stand up to this rigorous approach, while Manichaeism will not, thus hinting at *C. Acad.* 3.43's conclusion that wisdom can be found if we are sped on by the "dual weight of reason and authority" and its estimation that Platonism and Christianity are not opposed.

De beata v.'s dedication to Theodorus[69] develops *C. Acad.* 2.1's "harbor of philosophy" into an elaborate allegory. We find out that this harbor sits at the "hinterland of happiness" and no one gets there unless blown off the wrong course and onto the right one by the tempests of seemingly ill fortune.[70] For some this route is relatively direct; some get lost at sea for a

[64] *C. Acad.* 2.6–7. [65] Fuhrer 1997 *ad loc.* [66] *C. Acad.* 2.8. [67] *C. Acad.* 2.8.
[68] *C. Acad.* 2.9.
[69] For discussion of Theodorus see James O'Donnell, *Augustine* Confessions: *Volume 2: Commentary, Books 1–7* (Oxford: Oxford University Press, 1992) *ad* 7.9.13.
[70] *De beata v.* 1.

time; others fall somewhere in between.[71] Yet standing before the harbor is
the mountain of vainglory, from whose heights certain people delight to
look down on others. It is a quite attractive sight and sometimes lures away
people who have already made it into the harbor of philosophy.[72] Augustine, once more, provides himself as an example, recounting how reading
Cicero's *Hort.* at age 19 first got him "hot for philosophy" (*tanto amore
philosophiae succensus sum*) though he was led astray by a childish superstition and then held for a while by the Academics. Now, however, he has
found a Northstar in the sermons of Ambrose, who preaches an incorporeal God. The mountain of vainglory was also an issue for Augustine, who
could only renounce the charms of women and public honors after having
attained them. Reading Plotinus, though, and comparing his writings with
Christian teachings decided the matter, while an apparently inopportune
chest pain helped him complete his journey to the harbor.[73] Now that
Augustine has arrived at the port and gathered a group with him, i.e. the
Cassiciacum community, he is discovering that the harbor is itself large
enough to get lost in, so he asks for aid from Theodorus and dedicates to
him this discussion of happiness, which is, after all, a "gift of God."[74] He
ends by setting the scene, his birthday feast on the Ides of November.[75]

What are we to make of Augustine's image of the philosophical journey?
The first thing to note is that most of the journey is simply to get to
philosophy. Yet the harbor of philosophy is itself something to be trans-
versed en route to the hinterland of happiness. It is within this harbor that
Augustine situates himself and his companions. Each stage in this journey
to happiness ends up being a process of orientation, of finding the right
guides. Ambrose provides a "Northstar" with his Platonic/Christian ideas
of an incorporeal God. Meanwhile, by presenting three classes of sailors
who arrive at the port, Augustine suggests that there is more than one
viable route. Here he is speaking of the winds of fortune, but we could
easily extend this to *De ord.*'s discussion of the liberal arts, all or some of
which can be useful for returning individuals to themselves. In both texts,
I take Augustine to be expressing a sort of pluralism. Yet he makes it clear
that there are also many ways to go wrong. In the end, any and all viable
routes lead to a single end, the correct relationship to God, which the
Cassiciacum dialogues variously describe as Wisdom, Happiness and the
vision of Beauty. The talk of good fortune that appears bad, finally,
introduces an element of perspective. In this case, it is a narrative

[71] *De beata v.* 2.   [72] *De beata v.* 3.   [73] *De beata v.* 4.
[74] I.e. the literal meaning of "Theodorus." *De beata v.* 5.   [75] *De beata v.* 6.

perspective, as it is only after the storms of chest pains and reversals of fortune that a traveler realizes he started out on the wrong course.

De ord.'s dedication opens with a dilemma: Life's evils suggest either that God's providence does not extend to human affairs or else that these evils are committed according to God's will.[76] Or, more colorfully, how can a flea be so wonderfully constructed while human life is such a mess? Augustine's response is that anyone who sees this as an insuperable problem has become lost in life's details and needs to take a step back.[77] The problem is that such people lack self-knowledge. They must, therefore, take on a habit of withdrawing from the senses and returning to themselves. This, in turn, can be done by "burning away" everyday opinions in solitude or else "healing them through the liberal disciplines." (*Quod hi tantum adsequuntur, qui plagas quasdam opinionum, quas uitae quotidianae cursus infligit, aut solitudine inurunt, aut liberalibus medicant disciplinis*).[78] With this we find the *aporia* and self-reflection of *C. Acad.*'s ARP coupled with the liberal disciplines that *De ord.* presents as useful, albeit unnecessary, for such pursuits. The person who does this will come to understand that the beauty of the "uni-verse" (*uniuersitas*) derives from the 'Unity' (*unum*) after which it is named.[79] With this, Augustine introduces the remaining element of Wisdom 11:20's triad: number. He expresses hopes that Zenobius,[80] to whom the work is dedicated, will give himself to the order of learning laid out here,[81] quickly relates that chest pains have led him to take up philosophy at the villa of their mutual friend, Verecundus, and explains the use of a note-taker to record their conversations.[82]

What are we to make of these four dedications when it comes to presenting a holistic reading of Augustine's scenic dialogues from Cassiciacum? Along with the villa setting, these dedications are the dialogues' most self-consciously Ciceronian element. Like the dedications to Cicero's dialogues, they are mostly taken up with selling the reader on the fundamental value and nature of philosophy. Cicero, however, approached his dedications as more or less independent works sometimes quite literally pasted onto dialogues.[83] As a result, they often bear little direct relation to

---

[76] *De ord.* 1.1.

[77] *De ord.* 1.2. In this, he develops *De beata v.*'s narrative perspective through the visual metaphor of a mosaic.

[78] *De ord.* 1.3.   [79] *De ord.* 1.3.

[80] For the identity of Zenobius, see Trelenberg 2009, pp. 128–129.   [81] *De ord.* 1.4.

[82] *De ord.* 1.5.

[83] At *Epistulae ad Atticum* 16.6.4, Cicero recounts how he keeps a collection of prefaces and accidentally used one for two works. He thus requests that Atticus cut out the existing preface to

the discussions they introduce, which present interschool debates on various subjects. By contrast, Augustine's dialogues are themselves concerned with basic questions about the value and nature of philosophy. *De ord.*'s dedication poses basic questions about the goodness of the world and purpose of philosophical inquiry, its debate works through these questions and its closing *oratio* ultimately answers them. The relationship of the other dialogues' dedications to the works they introduce is not so one-to-one, because Augustine writes all four dedications in light of the whole set whose overarching project is not clear until the end of *De ord.*

De Musica and Augustine's Disciplinary Dialogues

I have presented a holistic reading of *De ord.* and the set of works to which it belongs. In doing so, I have argued that *De ord.*'s discussions of providence and the liberal arts are brought together in the more basic project of setting out a certain approach to philosophical pedagogy. When it comes to this more basic project, I have argued that the liberal disciplines are useful, insofar as they serve as formalized versions of processes of inquiry that comes naturally to human beings. The liberal arts are, however, ultimately not necessary, since the world itself serves as a God-given classroom. Moving forward, I suggest that this reading of *De ord.* can help explain what Augustine was hoping to accomplish when he set out the next year to write dialogues on the seven liberal disciplines, and why he abandoned the project after completing only two.

A standard scholarly narrative, as set by Peter Brown, takes Augustine's choice to abandon his works on the liberal disciplines as evidence of a profound intellectual crisis.[84] According to Brown, Augustine did not fully understand what he signed on for when he decided to be baptized, and it was only after becoming more familiar with the Bible that he realized the implications of Adam's fall and the futility of unaided human reason.[85] On my reading, Augustine's original impetus for writing on the disciplines was the opportunity for self-reflection they provided, not the detailed content of the particular disciplines used along the way. Once Augustine had written two such works, there was little to be gained *in terms of self-reflection* by

---

the copy of *De gloria* Cicero had sent and replace it with a new one he has composed to replace it. See Schofield, "Ciceronian Dialogue," 76ff for discussion.

[84] Brown, *Augustine* (first published in 1967). Markus presents this as a process of "disenchantment." For more recent versions of this developmentalist account, see BeDuhn, *Manichaean Dilemma* and Dobell, *Intellectual Conversion*.

[85] Brown, "The Lost Future," in *Augustine*, 139–150.

repeating the process another five times. In this respect, the project was doomed from the start, and there is no need to invoke a radical change of heart.[86] To judge between my perspective and Brown's, we should return to the texts themselves. Unfortunately, Augustine lost the original manuscript of *De Rhetorica*, and a text that is sometimes identified as his sketch for *De Dialectica* has little to recommend its authenticity.[87] *De Mus.*, however, survives and provides us a model for Augustine's proposed subgenre of "disciplinary dialogues."[88]

From a formal perspective, *De Mus.* is unique. It lacks the Cassiciacum works' characteristic dedication, but begins simply as the Teacher (*Magister*) asks his Student (*Discipulus*) a question.[89] In this, *De Mus.* is like Augustine's later dialogues: *De quant. an.*, *De Mag.* and *De lib. arbit.* Yet *De Mus.* is unlike any other complete dialogue of Augustine in that it lacks a concluding *oratio*.[90] Be that as it may, we do find a radical shift in subject matter, as a five-book inquiry into poetic meter gives way to book 6's inquiry into the psychological and metaphysical underpinnings that made the preceding inquiry into meter possible. Augustine presents book 6 as the point of the undertaking.[91] *De Mus.* is thus a self-reflective project of thinking about thinking. This much is fairly clear. What has not been acknowledged is that *De Mus.* 6 also contains language of plausibility at key points. I argue that this book employs a form of ARP as its basic philosophical method. While Augustine's other dialogues use a shift from

---

[86] At least as far as the disciplinary dialogues are concerned. There might be other reasons to argue for a change of heart. My current goal is not to defend any particular narrative of Augustine's development as an author, but to look critically at how the disciplinary dialogues have been used as evidences for such narratives.

[87] For discussion, see Belford Darrell Jackson, ed., *Augustine: De Dialectica* (Dordrecht: Synthese Historical Library, vol. 16, 1975). Regardless of this work's authenticity, we have *De Mus.* in its entirety. I will thus focus my attention here.

[88] See Vivian Law, "St. Augustine's '*De grammatica*': Lost or Found?" *Recherches Augustiniennes* 19 (1984): 155–183; William Jordan, "Augustine on Music." In *Grace, Politics and Desire: Essays on Augustine*, ed. Hugo Anthony Meynell (Calgary, University of Calgary Press, 1990): 123–135.

[89] Namely, "What foot is 'modus?'" (*Modus, qui pes est?*). *De Mus.* 1.1. *Sol.* is something of an anomaly in that it opens with a prayer to the Trinity. Yet, insofar as this functions as a dedication to God, it can be classed with the other Cassiciacum works.

[90] While *Sol.* also lacks an *oratio*, it is not complete. See Chapter 5 for my consideration of what this work's overarching argument would have been.

[91] See the Teacher's comments at *De Mus.* 6.1, as well as Augustine, *Ep.* 101, which recounts how Augustine sent a copy of book 6 alone to his friend Memorius. Marrou, *St. Augustin et la fin de la culture antique* (Bibl. des Ecoles d'Athènes et de Rome, cvix, 1939): 580–583 speculates that Augustine may have added *De Mus.* 6.1 to make the final book stand on its own. If this is so, then it reaffirms the idea of book 6 as special. It also supports the idea that the first-order disciplinary content, as presented in books 1–5, is useful, if ultimately unnecessary, for philosophical undertakings such as we find in book 6.

debate to *oratio* to mark a shift between the stages of ARP, *De Mus.*'s different tailoring of rhetorical structure to philosophical method can be accounted for by the demands of the "disciplinary dialogue," as set out in *De ord.*'s discussion of the liberal disciplines. While scholars typically take this portion of *De ord.* to announce Augustine's project of composing seven disciplinary dialogues,[92] it is not immediately clear what the nature of this project is. My reading takes a generally deflationary approach, as I argue that Augustine aims at plausibility rather than proof and treats the liberal disciplines as useful albeit unnecessary for someone setting out on philosophical inquiry. My hope is that this more provisional, more flexible Augustine will be all the more attractive for twenty-first-century readers.

Augustine follows *De ord.*'s discussion of the seven liberal disciplines with a series of abridgements, as we have seen. The passage concludes as follows:

> *Excipit enim hanc eruditionem iam ipsa philosophiae disciplina et in ea nihil plus inueniet, quam quid sit unum, sed longe altius longeque diuinius. Cuius duplex quaestio est: una de anima, altera de deo. Prima efficit, ut nosmet ipsos nouerimus, altera, ut originem nostram. Illa nobis dulcior, ista carior, illa nos dignos beata uita, beatos haec facit, prima est illa discentibus, ista iam doctis. Hic est ordo studiorum sapientiae, per quem fit quisque idoneus ad intellegendum ordinem rerum, id est ad dignoscendos duos mundos et ipsum parentem uniuersitatis, cuius nulla scientia est in anima nisi scire, quomodo eum nesciat.*

> For the discipline of philosophy itself now takes up this learning [i.e. from some combination of liberal disciplines or simply attending to unity in the world] and finds in it nothing more than what unity is, though in a far more divine way. For Philosophy pursues a twofold inquiry: one into the soul, the other into God. The first makes us know ourselves; the second makes us know our origin. The first is sweeter to us; the second is dearer. The first makes us worthy of happiness; the second makes us happy. The first is for those learning; the second is for the learned. This is the order of the studies of wisdom, through which each person becomes fit for understanding the order of the universe, i.e. for distinguishing between two worlds and the Father of the Universe, of whom the soul has no knowledge save knowing how [the soul] does not know Him. (*De ord.* 2.47)

For philosophical purposes, liberal study is useful insofar as it teaches us about expressions of unity in the world. This, in turn, provides the basis for the soul's inquiry into itself and its origin. In the end, though, this origin,

---

92 For a dispute about Augustine's possible sources see Ilsetraut Hadot, *Arts libéraux et philosophie dans la pensée antique* (Paris: Études Augustiniennes, 1948) and Danuta Schanzer, "Augustine's Disciplines: *Silent diutius Musae Varronis?* " In *Augustine and the Disciplines*, ed. Karla Pollmann & Mark Vessey, 71–112 (Oxford: Oxford University Press, 2005).

God, is in some sense beyond the soul's knowledge. I suggest that this script – inquiry into self, inquiry into cause, conclusion regarding a God who is not fully known – provides a template for cutting *De Mus.* 6 at its structural joints, dividing it into three and clarifying the centrality of ARP to the overarching project.

De Mus. 6 uses questions of number to frame its reflections on the activities involved in studying Music. The first third of the book – *De Mus.* 6.2–22 – looks into the numbers involved in sensing. The two characters begin by reflecting on the kinds of number involved in acts of speaking, hearing and taking delight in spoken sound. These are the basic activities that filled the preceding five books. The result is a list of five kinds of number: in the intent of the speaker, in the physical sound, in the sense of the hearer, in memory and in standards of judgment. Difficulties arise, however, when the two characters turn to ranking these kinds of number by merit.[93] On the one hand, numbers in physical sound seem to bring about the numbers in the sense of the hearer and thus should be ranked higher than they are in causal power. On the other hand, the idea that a body may have causal power over a soul runs counter to the basic intuitions of the Teacher and Student alike. The book's first main *aporia* thus takes the form of a simple question: How does hearing work if the body cannot act on the mind?[94] The teacher answers with what I take to be the book's central account of perception.[95] According to this, the soul works in the body, yet at times the body encounters resistance in the external world; in such cases, the soul must work harder and thus notices the difference. This is ultimately what perception is: the external world's resistance to the soul's activity in the body that the soul uses as a tool. There is much that could be said about this theory. What matters for our purposes is that the Teacher introduces it as something that "he thinks" (*sentio*)[96] and the result of "conjecture" (*coniectare*),[97] while the Student responds that his Teacher "seem[s] to be speaking plausibly" (*Probabiliter mihi dicere uideris*).[98] Using this plausible account of perception, they move past their *aporia* and complete their ranking, setting the numbers in physical sound below those in the sense of the hearer.[99]

---

[93] *De Mus.* 6.6–16.   [94] *De Mus.* 6.8.   [95] *De Mus.* 6.9–10.   [96] *De Mus.* 6.9.
[97] *De Mus.* 6.8.   [98] *De Mus.* 6.15.
[99] The resulting hierarchy ranks the five types of numbers thus: Judicial, i.e. the standards of what we find delightful; Advancing, i.e. from the intent of the speaker; Reacting, i.e. in the sense of the hearer; Memorial, i.e. in the memory of either the speaker or hearer; Sounding, i.e. in the physical sound (*De Mus.* 6.16). The remainder of the section argues that judicial numbers are immortal (*De Mus.* 6.17–22) and elaborates an account of memory's role in our use of such numbers in judging sounds (*De Mus.* 6.18–21).

If we take seriously the text's talk of plausibility, then we find all three aspects of ARP in the first third of *De Mus.* 6, albeit in a somewhat new order. In the Cassiciacum works, initial debates over wisdom, happiness and providence led to *aporia* and provided the instances of rational activity that Augustine subsequently reflected on to move past *aporia* to a plausible conclusion. By contrast, it is *De Mus.* 1–5's inquiry into poetic meter that provides an object for the Teacher's reflection, the fruit of which, when combined with an independent intuition that the body cannot act on the soul, generates the section's main *aporia*. The basic difference between *De Mus.* and the other dialogues is that discussions of wisdom, moderation and providence are already philosophical in their content. While *De Mus.* 1–5's discussion of meter employs processes worthy of philosophical reflection, the actual content of this debate – a rationalizing exposition of traditional poetic meter – is not philosophically significant. As *De ord.* puts it, all one needs take from a liberal discipline is that the world, in this case the world of spoken sound, is structured by number. The details are unimportant. Given this disconnect between the content of the initial debate and the Teacher's subsequent reflections on it, *De Mus.* lacks the tight structure of a Cassiciacum dialogue such as *C. Acad.* in which a discussion of wisdom ends in *aporia*, reflection on that discussion of wisdom provides a way past *aporia*, and all of this sets the stage for a plausible conclusion about wisdom. Instead, *De Mus.* comes closer to Plato's *Men.*, where a discussion of virtue is interrupted by a geometry lesson, which Socrates then reflects on to advance his discussion of virtue.[100] The end result is *aporia* that follows from reflection, rather than setting the stage for it, though the concluding plausible account responds to both in ways that are by now familiar.[101]

If, to borrow *De ord.*'s terms, the first third of *De Mus.* 6 presents the soul's inquiry into itself, then the next third – *De Mus.* 6.23–34 – presents the soul's inquiry into its origin or cause. The section opens as the Teacher asks whether there are any kinds of number above those involved in sensing. He reflects that it is one thing to be delighted by the senses, another to judge something by reason. In light of this he introduces a new class of judicial numbers and demotes the numbers involved in delight, which they had been calling judicial, to the status of "sensuous."[102] With this, questions about the nature of human reason are put squarely on the table. The Student, however, is

---

[100] See my "Platonic Pedagogy" for discussion of this contrast.
[101] To put it in terms from Chapters 1 and 2, if *C. Acad.* presents us with A-R-P and Plato's *Men.* presents us with A-P-R, then Augustine gives us R-A-P in this dialogue, *De Mus.*
[102] *De Mus.* 6.23–34.

skeptical of this new distinction and fears that when the soul judges and delights it does so by a single type of number that exists eternally above the human mind.[103] The task of this section, then, is to work out the soul's relationship to these numbers above it, i.e. the soul's cause. With this, we have a new *aporia*, which the Teacher addresses through concerted reflection on everything that went before. The passage starts, "Come now and consider the strength and power of reason, insofar as we are able from its activities" (*Age, nunc aspice in uim potentiamque rationis, quantum ex operibus eius aspicere possumus.*)[104] We could not ask for a clearer statement of reflection on rational activity. The Teacher proceeds to give a synopsis of books 1–5, which he presents as Reason's discovery of meter. Yet, he does not stop there:

> *Postremo attendit quid in his moderandis, operandis, sentiendis, retinendis ageret anima, cuius caput ipsa esset: hosque omnes animales numeros a corporalibus separauit: seque ipsam haec omnia neque animaduertere, neque distinguere, neque recte numerare sine quibusdam suis numeris potuisse cognouit, eosque caeteris inferioris ordinis iudiciaria quadam aestimatione praeposuit.*

> Lastly, Reason turned its attention to what the soul, of which it is the head, was doing in measuring, enacting, sensing and remembering these things. It separated all these spiritual numbers from bodily ones. It recognized that it itself could neither notice, distinguish nor rightly enumerate all these things unless by numbers of its own, and it set those numbers above others of an inferior order by means of a kind of judicial appraisal. (*De Mus.* 6.25)

This provides a nice synopsis of the activities involved in the first third of *De Mus.* 6. If we can characterize the shift from book 5 to book 6 as a move from thinking about meter to thinking about thinking about meter, then book 6's middle third presents a doubly self-reflective project of thinking about thinking about thinking about meter. In effect, the Student expresses confusion about what "judging numbers" entails, and the Teacher responds: It's what we were just doing! The point of all this is to clarify the soul's relationship to its cause, God. The section proceeds as the Teacher builds up to the following argument:[105]

(1)   What the soul loves about sensible beauty is equality.
(2)   If the soul loves equality, it must know equality.
(3)   The soul cannot know equality from bodies, since equality is eternal and bodies are changing.
(4)   Thus, the soul is given equality from God, who is eternal and unchanging.

---

[103] *De Mus.* 6.23.   [104] *De Mus.* 6.25.   [105] *De Mus.* 6.36.

I argued above that a version of this argument is what ties together the various pieces of *De ord.*'s final account. While *De Mus*. does not invoke any explicit language of plausibility at this point, we should note that it relies on the tacit premise, which the Teacher does nothing to secure, that bodies and God are the only possible sources for the soul's knowledge of equality. Augustine built an analogous argument in *C. Acad.* 3, where he invoked our knowledge of norms of thought, which could not be accounted for empirically, to conclude that we have access to intelligible sources of thought. That conclusion was explicitly presented as plausible. Given the work's closely analogous structures and the use of plausibilistic terminology earlier in the present book, I suggest taking this passage as also arguing for a plausible conclusion, that is to say a richly explanatory yet uncertain response to what came before. If this is right, then we have all three elements of ARP present in the work's second third as well, this time in something closer to the Cassiciacum form, inasmuch as the preceding discussion, *De Mus*. 6.2–22, both generates the *aporia* addressed here and models the rational activity that the Teacher reflects on to move past this *aporia*.

The book's final third – *De Mus*. 6.37–59 – draws on Christian ideas of the Fall and Salvation to work out the moral-psychological implications of the discussion up to this point. In this we do not find another round of ARP, so much as an elaboration of theological ideas within the framework established through the proceeding two rounds of ARP. This section moves through a series of three questions:

Question	Discussed at...
How does the soul fall into vice?	*De Mus*. 6.37–42
How is the soul saved from vice?	*De Mus*. 6.43–50.
What is the nature of the soul's final, saved state?	*De Mus*. 6.51–55.

Augustine ends the work – *De Mus*. 6.56–59 – with a brief account of God's creation of the world *ex nihilo*, which, in turn, provides the stage upon which this drama of the soul's fall and salvation plays out. The four main stages of this last section are intimately connected and Augustine begins the first of them by invoking the psychological account from *De Mus*. 6.9–10, which was already explicitly presented as plausible. I take this internal cross-reference to indicate that everything to follow is presented as plausible as well.

De Mus. 6's last third[106] is most easily grasped if we start with its concluding account of creation:

> *Nos tantum meminerimus, quod ad susceptam praesentem disputationem maxime pertinet, id agi per prouidentiam Dei, per quam cuncta creauit et regit, ut etiam peccatrix et aerumnosa anima numeris agatur, et numeros agat usque ad infimam carnis corruptionem: qui certe numeri minus minusque pulchri esse possunt, penitus uero carere pulchritudine non possunt. Deus autem summe bonus, et summe iustus, nulli inuidet pulchritudini, quae siue damnatione animae, siue regressione, siue permansione fabricatur. Numerus autem et ab uno incipit, et aequalitate ac similitudine pulcher est, et ordine copulatur. Quamobrem quisquis fatetur nullam esse naturam, quae non ut sit quidquid est, appetat unitatem, suique similis in quantum potest esse conetur, atque ordinem proprium uel locis uel temporibus, uel in corpore quodam libramento salutem suam teneat: debet fateri ab uno principio per aequalem illi ac similem speciem diuitiis bonitatis eius, qua inter se unum et de uno unum carissima, ut ita dicam, caritate iunguntur, omnia facta esse atque condita quaecumque sunt, in quantumcumque sunt.*

> But let us recall as much as pertains to the present discussion we have undertaken, namely that this [salvation and perfection of souls] is done through God's providence, through which He created and rules all things, so that even the sinful and wretched soul is ruled by numbers and bears them all the way to the deepest infirmity of the flesh. These numbers can be less and less beautiful, but they cannot lack beauty entirely. But God, most good and most just, envies no beauty whether it be created by the soul's damnation or return or abiding. What's more, number begins from one, it is beautiful through equality and similarity, and it is bound by order. Therefore, whoever confesses that every nature, so that it might be whatever it is, not only desires unity, but also tries to make itself similar to itself as much as it can and holds its own salvation to be a proper order of places, times or a body of a certain gravity – whoever confesses this ought to confess that all things, whatever they are and as much as they are, have been created and joined together from a single principle, through equality to it and a beauty similar to the riches of its goodness, through which all things are joined into one, both as a group and as from one, by a charity most dear, so to speak. (*De Mus.* 6.56)

Augustine proceeds to explain that it is through God's creation of the world from nothing that each and every thing received the stamp of number, which, in turn, provides the ultimate grounds for explaining how the lines of inquiry that make up *De Mus.* as a whole were possible in the first place.[107] This account of creation "ought to be confessed" by

---

[106] *De Mus.* 6.56–59.   [107] *De Mus.* 6.57–58.

anyone who realizes that individual things are unity-seeking (cf. Augustine's chickens from *De ord.* 2.48, which will no longer be chickens if they
lose the unity of their organs). As in *De ord.*, I take all of this to be a
plausible explanation that sidesteps the pitfalls of preceding *aporiai* and
provides a theoretical context for the work's self-reflective discoveries.
What matters for the last third of *De Mus.* 6 is the introduction of a
Pauline virtue, "charity/love" (*caritas*).[108]

Love provides the key for *De Mus.*'s final account of the soul's fall and
salvation. The previous section concluded that our desire for equality
means that we have received knowledge of equality from God himself.
The present section opens by asking how the soul could ever fall from this
contemplation of God.[109] The answer is pride,[110] which in this case
amounts to getting so caught up in applying numbers to bodily things
that we lose track of where we draw these numbers from. From here, the
Teacher asks how the soul might return to God and proceeds to explain
that Scriptures' command to "love God" means that we should refer all
actions back to God.[111] This involves a certain detachment from everyday
life, letting bodily pleasures pale in comparison to the delight we find in
God himself. This love of God will give us moderation by putting bodily
pleasures into perspective, courage by setting eternal joys over those death
can take away, and justice by rightly ordering our desires based on the
intrinsic goodness of things;[112] prudence, meanwhile, simply is this rightly
ordered state, in which the soul sets itself below eternal things and above
temporal ones.[113] In short, *caritas* is the root of all the classical virtues. The
last third of this section asks whether these virtues will be present in the
soul's perfected state.[114] In this the Teacher invokes a distinction between
"kathartic" virtues that purify us, making us perfect, and "contemplative"
virtues, which embody that perfection.[115] At first the Student cannot see
how these virtues would have any place in the vision of God. His Teacher,
however, brings him around to see that these same virtues have truer
forms: Prudence comes about as the soul looks upon God and forgets
about temporal vanities;[116] justice consists in holding to God's eternal law

---

[108] This is drawn from 1 Corinthians 13:13's triad "faith, hope, charity." I argue in Chapter 5 that the
whole triad provides a structuring principle for the overarching project of *Sol. + De imm. an.*
[109] *De Mus.* 6.37–42.   [110] *De Mus.* 6.39–40.   [111] *De Mus.* 6.43–50.   [112] *De Mus.* 6.50.
[113] *De Mus.* 6.37. This last point is greatly elaborated in *De lib. arbit.* The basic point is that God is
worth more than humans and humans are worth more than things. We should thus love God more
than humans and humans more than things. See Chapter 7.
[114] *De Mus.* 6.51–55.   [115] Augustine elaborates this distinction in *De quant. an.* See Chapter 6.
[116] *De Mus.* 6.52.

and not falling into sin; temperance consists in fixing one's love in God and living chastely away from all pollution;[117] courage flows from the eternal security of God.[118] In short, the love of God is the origin of the Classical virtues all the more clearly in their perfected forms. The love that flows from the one source of all things and binds all things into one thus provides the basis for the human soul's final happiness. In presenting all this, however, the Teacher is explicitly building on a plausible account of perception, and I suggest we take all of his closing account to be presented in the same light.

De Mus.'s account of *caritas* brings us as close as the dialogues get to Platonic ideas of *eros*. While my focus has been on how Augustine presents his theories, a brief word on these theories' content seems in order. On the surface, the pederastic culture of Plato's *Smp.* and *Phdr.* seems a far cry from Augustine's struggles with celibacy as he explores Christian asceticism. But we should not allow cultural difference to blind us from what's really going on here. While the love of beautiful bodies is the first rung on *Smp.*'s "ladder of love,"[119] it is merely a step along the way to love of character, knowledge and eventually Beauty itself. This ladder sums up *Smp.*'s broader discussion of what separates the good lover (*erastēs*) from the bad, all of which comes down to what the lover loves more: the body or the soul of his beloved (*erōmenos*).[120] Similar considerations are woven throughout *Phdr.* as Socrates engages Lysias, via a written speech in the possession of Phaedrus, on the difference between good and bad lovers. Here too, we find that the good lover is the one who nurtures his beloved's virtue as the two of them seek spiritual goods together. The process is not always placid. In *Phdr.*, Socrates described the *eros* that rouses the soul to recollect forms as a species of "madness" (*mania*).[121] At *Smp.* 215A–222C, a drunken Alcibiades "praises" Socrates by describing their courtship's bewildering combination of frustration and fascination. Plato's *Lysis* is a guide book in how to flirt with younger men at the gym, in which Socrates recommends confusing the object of one's affections through aporetic discussion. At the root of all of this are the insights, first, that moral education and intimate relationships go hand-in-hand, second, that both love and education are often confusing and, finally, that experiences of beauty – which are often tied up in experiences of love – somehow point

---

[117] *De Mus.* 6.53.   [118] *De Mus.* 6.54.   [119] Plato, *Smp.* 210a–211d.
[120] See especially the speech of Pausanias with its distinction between Heavenly and Common Aphrodite (*Smp.* 180c–185e).
[121] Plato, *Phdr.* 249D. Socrates goes on to describe the soul's growing wings as a painful process, not unlike teething, which involves throbbing and itching (Plato, *Phdr.* 251C).

beyond themselves to something higher. To my mind, this is simply ARP playing out within the context of ancient pederasty, as a particular form of erotic *aporia* and self-reflection on the experience of beauty point beyond themselves to experiences of Beauty that may be fleeting, provisional and, at least for the moment, best articulated in terms of the plausible.

In Augustine, this same basic approach is translated into the context of late fourth-century Christianity. The intimate teacher–student relationships of ancient pederasty are transplanted to communities organized around various ascetic ideals and even familial relationships, perhaps best exemplified in *De Mag.*, which presents a discussion between Augustine and his late son, Adeodatus.[122] While instances of *aporia* and self-reflection fill the dialogues, it is *De beata v.* that first brings in elements of desire, as thinking about the famously wealthy yet unphilosophical Sergius Orata helps the group realize its desire for truth, which Augustine's closing *oratio* identifies as the *admonitio ad ueritatem* of the Holy Spirit.[123] *De Mus.* uses experience of beauty or "delight" (*delectatio*) as an entry point to this constellation of ideas.[124] While *De Mus.* 1–5 may not pursue explicitly philosophical questions, i.e. it does not inquire directly into the soul or its cause, it sets the stage for them through a sustained exploration of sensory delight. In broad terms, the work's rational reconstruction of Latin poetic meters moves gradually from delight at the sound of metered poetry embedded in the work to a more intellectual delight, as the Student and Teacher articulate the numerical relationships underpinning these sounds. While not very explicit, by the end of five books of this, the text even invites a third, self-reflective form of delight at the fact that one is taking intellectual delight at understanding the numerical ratios underpinning these sounds. This comes to a head in the section's grand finale, which – if I'm reading it correctly – uses the Pythagorean Theorem to explain why dactylic hexameter is the most noble meter.[125] It is hard not to grin at the audacity of this undertaking and the fact that we readers, along with Augustine's characters, are entertaining such ideas in the first place. This passage naturally gives way to the explicit self-reflection of book 6, which eventually explains all such delight through the role of *caritas* as a

---

[122] For discussion of this relationship, see Erika Kidd, "Making Sense of Virgil in *De Magistro*," *Augustinian Studies* 46/2 (2015) 211–224.

[123] See Chapter 3.

[124] In this, Augustine expands on the suggestion underlying *De ord.* 2.39–51's proto-*quadrivium* of music, geometry, astronomy and arithmetic that it is number that delights us in experiences of sensory beauty.

[125] *De Mus.* 5.20–28.

fundamental principle of Creation. In this, we come full circle: Just as *Phdr.*'s opening sets a flirtatious, erotically charged stage for the subsequent discussion of *eros, De Mus.* 1–5 invites the reader into experiences of delight at various elements of Creation, both sensible and intellectual, thus setting the stage for a final account of the *caritas* at the heart of Augustine's experiments in new forms of Christian community.

Now that we have set out a reading of the project pursued in *De Mus.*, what are we to make of its lack of a concluding *oratio*? Up to this point, I have argued that the rhetorical structure of Augustine's other dialogues serves to mark a shift between stages of ARP. It might be objected that *De Mus.*'s different rhetorical structure implies that a different philosophical method is at play. Against this, I argue that Augustine's application of ARP to the liberal disciplines simply called for a different rhetorical strategy. The crux of the issue is that ARP is a philosophical method, while, to judge by *De Mus.*, a disciplinary dialogue does not become philosophical until its initial exposition of disciplinary content is over. At that point, the text turns to *De ord.* 2.47's "twofold inquiry" into the soul and its origin. In doing so, *De Mus.*'s teacher and student pursue two complete courses of ARP and complete the work by using their findings to construct a scriptural account of Creation, Fall and Salvation. The role of *caritas* in this scriptural conclusion, meanwhile, shows that like the Cassiciacum works, *De Mus.* is ultimately concerned with exploring a virtue, albeit a Christian rather than Classical one. While the transitions between stages of ARP are not marked by the other dialogues' shift into *oratio*, language of self-reflection and plausibility is invoked at key structural points within book 6's three main sections, giving a fairly clear nod to what Augustine, as author, is up to. Granted, the use of multiple rounds of ARP in a single work is a departure from what we have seen so far. Yet I argue in Chapter 5 that we find something similar in *Sol.* + *De. imm. an.* What's more, *De Mus.* 6 is an even clearer forerunner to *De lib. arbit.*, whose three books move, respectively, through two rounds of ARP and a plausible, scriptural account of the Fall.[126] All of this is simply to say that ARP is not a template to be slavishly followed, but a general way of approaching matters, which Augustine develops and adapts to structure each of his dialogues as different situations require.

---

[126] Each book of *De lib. arbit.* is rich with internal complexity. At root, however, book 1 represents the soul's reflection on itself, book 2 the soul's reflection on its source and book 3 an attempt to use these reflections to guide a plausible reading of Scripture. See Chapter 7.

At this point I hope to have shown how *De Mus.* pursues the project of liberal study set out in *De ord.* According to this, the liberal disciplines are useful but ultimately not necessary for philosophical inquiry. As should now be clear, one need not know about the technical details of pyrrhics, trochees and spondees to follow book 6's discussion; a general idea that rhythm is a matter of number and some experience of rhythmical speech will suffice. This somewhat weak connection of *De Mus.*'s final book to those that precede it, in turn, helps explain why Augustine abandoned the project. Books 1–5 are, from a philosophical perspective, somewhat problematic. While it is worthwhile to create experiences of delight for readers to then reflect upon, it is hard to imagine that the *self-reflective* conclusions of works on geometry, astronomy, grammar or rhetoric would be all that different than what we already find in *De Mus.* 6.[127] As Augustine has already put it in *De Ord.*: In all such sensory experiences, it is number that delights. Why bother repeating the process, having reached this realization once? Matters might be different for dialectic and arithmetic, which Augustine presents as inherently self-reflective disciplines, though the self-reflective ending of *De Mus.* (and presumably that of the now lost *De Rhet.*) gets to the same level of philosophical thought eventually. This thought, in turn, is further explored in Augustine's later nondisciplinary dialogues. To me, *pace* Brown, this does not indicate a change of heart so much as a refinement of strategy. Augustine's is a brilliantly self-reflective and speculative mind. His choice to set aside the disciplinary dialogues for those that open with philosophical questions may merely be a decision to cut to the chase. Whatever Augustine, the man, may have changed his mind about as time went on, his decision to abandon the disciplinary dialogues can be sufficiently explained in terms of the philosophical project he set out in *De ord.* at the start of his philosophical career.

---

[127] *De ord.* 2.43 presents arithmetic, the study of number, not as a prerequisite to music, geometry and astronomy but their culmination. The passage is quite short and leaves much unexplained. An entire work devoted to arithmetic would presumably have started with a discussion of the pure math, in this case probably a lot of fractions, which is meant to capture what we find beautiful in music, visible forms and visible motions. This, however, is purely speculative on my part.

CHAPTER 5

An Advanced Course
Soliloquia + De immortalitate animae

Sol. provides a behind-the-scenes view of Cassiciacum, as Augustine invites readers to listen in on his conversations with himself. As he puts it:

> *Voluenti mihi multa ac uaria mecum diu ac per multos dies sedulo quaerenti memetipsum ac bonum meum, quidue mali euitandum esset, ait mihi subito siue ego ipse siue alius quis extrinsecus, siue intrinsecus, nescio; nam hoc ipsum est quod magnopere scire molior...*

> While I was pondering many different things by myself for a long while and for many days diligently seeking myself, and what my good was, and what evil was to be avoided, suddenly I myself or someone else spoke to me, whether from outside or from within I do not know, for this is exactly what I am striving greatly to know. (*Sol.* 1.1)

The ensuing conversation between Augustine and "Reason" (*Ratio*) is a sufficiently innovative use of the dialogue genre that Augustine actually coins the term "soliloquy" (*soliloquium*) to describe it.[1] This "inner dialogue" set the groundwork for Boethius' *Consolatio Philosophiae*,[2] and the two works together provided a literary model for centuries to come.[3] *Sol.*'s discussion of death and the soul's immortality engages a tradition of consolation literature that began with Plato's *Phd.* and continued through book one of Cicero's *Tusc.*[4] Its musings on the nature of truth provide the

---

[1] During a methodological interlude at *Sol.* 2.14, Reason explains, "we have chosen conversations of this sort, which since we are talking with ourselves alone, I would like to be called and entitled *Soliloquies*. It is a new and perhaps harsh term, but suitable enough for indicating the matter." (*elegerimus huiusmodi sermocinationes; quae quoniam cum solis nobis loquimur, Soliloquia uocari et inscribi uolo, nouo quidem et fortasse duro nomine, sed ad rem demonstrandam satis idoneo*). Cf. Lewis and Short, *A Latin Dictionary, ad loc.*

[2] See Seth Leher, *Boethius and Dialogue: Literary Method in "The Consolation of Philosophy"* (Princeton: Princeton University Press, 1985), 90, 152 and 204.

[3] See Brian Stock, "The Genre of the Soliloquy." In *Augustine's Inner Dialogue* (Cambridge: Cambridge University Press, 2010), 63–76.

[4] While we cannot be certain how much Plato, if any, Augustine read directly, *Tusc.* 1 was surely among his intermediary sources. Augustine looks to its presentation of *Men.* and *Phd.* to guide *Sol.*'s

raw material for Anselm's *De veritate* and Medieval discussions of truth more generally,[5] while its autobiographical candor gives a foretaste of Augustine's own *Conf.*

Given the importance of *Sol.* in the grand history of philosophical literature, it is perhaps surprising that Augustine never finished writing it. He recounts in *Retract.*:

> *Inter haec scripsi etiam duo uolumina secundum studium meum et amorem ratione indagandae ueritatis de his rebus quas maxime scire cupiebam, me interrogans mihique respondens, tamquam duo essemus, ratio et ego, cum solus essem, unde hoc opus Soliloquia nominaui. Sed imperfectum remansit, ita tamen ut in primo libro quaereretur et utcumque appareret, qualis esse debeat qui uult percipere sapientiam, quae utique non sensu corporis sed mente percipitur, et quadam ratiocinatione in libri fine colligitur, ea quae uere sunt esse immortalia. In secundo autem de immortalitate animae diu res agitur et non peragitur.*

At the same time as these[6] I wrote two books in line with my zeal and love for tracking down by reason the truth about these matters which I most of all wanted to know; I asked the questions, and I responded as though I were two people – Reason and myself – although I was alone. Because of this, I called the work *Soliloquies*. But it has remained unfinished. Nevertheless, in book 1 the question is posed, and to some extent resolved, what kind of person one ought to be if he wants to grasp wisdom, which is grasped in no way by the bodily senses but rather by the mind. At the end of the book it is argued by a bit of reasoning that those things which truly exist are immortal. In book 2, however, the issue of the soul's immortality is discussed at length but not brought to completion. (*Retract.* 1.4.1)

> *Post libros Soliloquiorum iam de agro Mediolanum reuersus, scripsi librum De immortalitate animae, quod mihi quasi commonitorium esse uolueram propter Soliloquia terminanda, quae imperfecta remanserant. Sed nescio quomodo me inuito exiit in manus hominum, et inter mea opuscula nominatur. Qui primo ratiocinationum contortione atque breuitate sic obscurus est, ut fatiget cum legitur etiam intentionem meam, uixque intellegatur a me ipso.*

After writing my *Soliloquies* and returning to Milan from the countryside, I wrote one book, *On the Immortality of the Soul*, which I meant to be a kind of reminder to myself for bringing my *Solioquies*, which had remained unfinished, to completion. But somehow against my will it made its way

---

reflections on rational activity. See Chapter 2 for discussion of *Tusc.*'s role in shaping Augustine's view of Platonic practice.

[5] *Sol.* 2.29's presentation of the truth of a false statement, for instance, provides the basic kernel for Anselm's distinction between first and second rectitude.

[6] This refers either to the two books of *De ord.* or the whole of the scenic dialogues from Cassiciacum. Either way, this places the composition of *Sol.* in 386CE.

into people's hands and is counted among my works. Thanks to the brevity
and intertwining of its arguments it is so obscure that reading it taxes even
my concentration, and I myself can scarcely understand it. (*Retract.* 1.5.1)

In short, *Sol.* ends on a dialectical cliffhanger, and *De imm. an.* is so
obscure that even Augustine had trouble following it. The current chapter
is written for the intrepid reader, intent on reading the whole of *Sol.* + *De
imm. an.*[7] To this end, I present a reconstruction of the work's overarching
argument and the rhetorical structure of the never-written *Sol.* 3. On my
reading, this final book develops an account of the soul as a metaphysical
straddler: one foot in eternity, the other in time.[8] This account, in turn,
provides an explanatory framework for making sense of *Sol.* 2's main
argument, which on its own terms is likely to have struck Augustine's
contemporaries as questionable and modern audiences as bizarre. I suggest
that *De imm. an.* "completes" *Sol.* by doing conceptual work necessary to
clarify those aspects of *Sol.* 2's arguments that are likely to be
misunderstood.

Older scholarship on *Sol.* has focused on alternately identifying and
reconstructing the supposed Neoplatonist sources for book 2's argument.
Christian Tornau gives a useful critique of the often circular nature of such
undertakings.[9] More recent scholars have taken up the task of identifying
how *Sol.* and *De imm. an.* are meant to form a single work. My focus will
be on these more recent readings. At one extreme, Phillip Cary argues that
the central argument of *Sol.* 2 is "simply inept" and "doomed to failure"
insofar as Augustine had yet to grasp either Neoplatonism or Christian
doctrine sufficiently.[10] Giovanni Catapano takes a more moderate
approach, arguing that the first half of *De imm. an.* strengthens the
argument of *Sol.* 2, while the second half of *De imm. an.* makes it
superfluous.[11] Tornau himself presents the most positive reading, arguing
that *De imm. an.* succeeds in defending the argument of *Sol.* 2, provided
we grant Augustine some typically Platonist assumptions.

---

[7] The main task of this study is to read Augustine's dialogues as unified wholes. I will thus focus on
the composite work, which I will refer to as "*Sol.* + *De imm. an.*"

[8] For a fuller presentation of this view, see my "From Augustine to the Carolingian Renaissance." In
Cambridge Companion to Medieval Ethics, ed. Thomas Williams (Cambridge: Cambridge University
Press, forthcoming).

[9] Christian Tornau, "*Ratio in subiecto*? The Sources of Augustine's Proof for the Immortality of the Soul
in the *Soliloquia* and its defense in *De immortalitate animae*," *Phronesis* 62 (2017): 319–354.

[10] Phillip Cary, "An Abandoned Proof." In *Augustine's Invention of the Inner Self: The Legacy of a
Christian Platonist* (Oxford: Oxford University Press, 2000), 95–104.

[11] Giovanni Catapano, "Augustine's Treatise *De Immortalitate Animae* and the Proof of the Soul's
Immortality in *Soliloquia*," *Documenti e studi sulla tradizione filosofica medievale* 25 (2014): 67–84.

My reconstruction depends on treating *Sol.* + *De imm. an.* as part of the Cassiciacum set. In previous chapters, I argued that each of the earlier dialogues explores one of the classical virtues – wisdom, moderation, justice, courage – through a course of ARP[12] built around a Scriptural cue from Wisdom 11:20's 'number, measure, weight.' So far we have seen *C. Acad.*'s "dual weight of reason and authority" speed on the search for wisdom, *De beata v.* ground happiness and moderation in Christ the "measure of the soul," and *De ord.* invoke the numerical structure of the world to explain God's justice. By process of elimination, we should expect the central thread of *Sol.* + *De imm. an.* to be concerned with courage. This alone helps put the work's concern with the immortality of the soul into perspective. Meanwhile, 1 Corinthians 13:13's triad "faith, hope, love" figures prominently throughout *Sol.*,[13] in the place of Wisdom 11:20's "measure, number, weight," which has been used up. I suggest that this new scriptural triad, the so-called Christian or Pauline virtues, dictates the basic structure of *Sol.* + *De imm. an.* by providing the cue for what we might call three complete "rounds" of ARP. This represents a methodological development on the other Cassiciacum dialogues, each of which was structured around a single round, yet it finds parallels in the nearly contemporary *De Mus.* 6 and somewhat later *De lib. arbit.*[14] Within the Cassiciacum set, this methodological development reflects the fact that Augustine, who elsewhere plays the teacher, here presents himself as a student, albeit a more advanced student than those we have seen so far. By approaching *Sol.* + *De imm. an.* in this way, I hope to achieve a kind of reflexive equilibrium, using the earlier works as models for this last one while using this last one as partly defining the context for understanding what came before.[15]

---

[12] In Chapter 1, I argue that Augustine uses *C. Acad.* to set out a method according to which (A) aporetic debate and (R) reflection on the act of debating which lead to a (P) plausible conclusion. For the sake of convenience, I have dubbed this three-stage method ARP.

[13] Since Paul's term "*caritas*" has no verb form in Latin, Augustine uses "*amo*" when needed. While *amor* and *caritas* are sometimes contrasted, Augustine does not seem interested in doing so in *Sol.* For the sake of modern English idiom, which also lacks a verb for "charity," I will refer to "*caritas*" and forms of "*amor*" simply as "love." A similar problem exists for talking about faith in Latin, insofar as the noun form "*fides*" lacks a verb form while the verb form "*credere*" lacks a noun form. Since Augustine seems uninterested in contrasting these in *Sol.*, I will follow him in using "faith" and forms of "believe" interchangeably.

[14] See Chapters 4 and 7, respectively.

[15] Tornau, "*Ratio in subiecto*," attempts to make sense of *Sol.* + *De imm. an.* by setting it against debates among late antique Platonists and commentators on Aristotle. I, by contrast, approach the same work against the backdrop of Augustine's other dialogues from Cassiciacum. We have come to effectively the same conclusions working independently of one another.

Opening Prayer and Overview of the Work (*Sol.* 1.2–7)

Each of the scenic dialogues from Cassiciacum opens with a dedication to some important figure in Augustine's life. *Sol.* opens with a prayer to the Trinity. Whatever else Augustine hopes to accomplish with this prayer, it functions like the other dedications by situating the work within the body of thought presented by the dialogues as a set. *Sol.*, however, presents a more advanced perspective. The earlier dedications stress the beginning stages of inquiry, focusing on the opportunities for inquiry and challenges to it that the material world presents. *Sol.* takes a top-down approach, focusing on God as humanity's first cause and ultimate end. Nevertheless, these are merely two perspectives on the same body of thought. The prayer opens by invoking the Father as "God, creator of the Universe" (*Deus uniuersitatis conditor*),[16] a nod to *De ord.*'s closing account of Unity as first cause "from whom the Universe is named" (*uniuersitatis ... quae profecto ab uno cognominata est*).[17] *C. Acad.*'s two-worlds theory[18] is employed to invoke the Son as "intelligible light," "whose kingdom is the whole world which the bodily sense does not know" (*Deus intellegibilis lux ... Deus, cuius regnum est totus mundus, quem sensus ignorat*).[19] *De beata v.*'s Trinitarian account is used to invoke the Holy Spirit as "God through whom we are admonished to be watchful" (*Deus, a quo admonemur, ut uigilemus*),[20] and provides the basic outline that the prayer as a whole elaborates.

What we don't find in the earlier dialogues is *Sol.*'s central concern with the Pauline virtues. Augustine addresses the Son as "God, to whom faith arouses us, hope raises us, and love joins us" (*Deus, cui nos fides excitat, spes erigit, caritas iungit*).[21] He employs the same virtues in setting out his prayer's request:

> *Ad te mihi redeundum esse sentio; pateat mihi pulsanti ianua tua; quomodo ad te perueniatur, doce me. Nihil aliud habeo quam uoluntatem, nihil aliud scio nisi fluxa et caduca spernenda esse, certa et aeterna requirenda. Hoc facio, pater, quia hoc solum noui; sed unde ad te perueniatur, ignoro. Tu mihi suggere, tu ostende, tu uiaticum praebe. Si fide te inueniunt qui ad te refugiunt, fidem da, si uirtute, uirtutem, si scientia, scientiam. Auge in me fidem, auge spem, auge caritatem. O admiranda et singularis bonitas tua!*

---

[16] *Sol.* 1.2.   [17] *De ord.* 1.3.
[18] Namely, the theory that distinguishes between the sensible and intelligible worlds. This is sketched at *C. Acad.* 3.37; see Chapter 2 for discussion.
[19] *Sol.* 1.3.   [20] *Sol.* 1.3.   [21] *Sol.* 1.3.

> I sense that I should return to you: open when I knock at your doors; teach me how one arrives at you. I have nothing but my will. I know nothing save that changing, mortal things should be shunned and that secure, eternal things should be sought. I am doing this, Father, because I know only this, but how one arrives at you, I don't know. Advise me, show me, supply me for the journey. If by faith those who flee to you find you, then give me faith; if by virtue, give me virtue; if by knowledge, knowledge. Increase in me faith; increase in me hope; increase in me love. O how wonderful and unique is your goodness! (*Sol.* 1.5)

As in the scenic dialogues, the basic task here is to orient oneself, to find the proper guidance. Yet in *Sol.*, Augustine looks to faith, hope and love for this guidance. In *C. Acad.*, Augustine uses the language of the mystery cult to present philosophy as a form of purification. He invokes the same idea here to draw *Sol.*'s opening prayer to a close, "If I desire nothing other than you, then let me find you, Father, I pray. If, however, there is in me a desire for anything superfluous, then cleanse me and make me fit for seeing you." (*Si nihil aliud desidero quam te, inueniam te iam, quaeso, Pater. Si autem est in me superflui alicuius appetitio, tu ipse me munda, et fac idoneum ad uidendum te*).[22] At this point, Reason asks Augustine to summarize what he's asked for, and he responds, "I want to know God and the soul." (*Deum et animam scire cupio*).[23] This is a clear reference to *De ord.* 2.47, where Augustine defined philosophy as a "twofold inquiry into the soul and God" (*Cuius duplex quaestio est: una de anima, altera de Deo*).[24] The parallel between texts suggests that *Sol.* is treating philosophy and Christian virtues as somehow working in tandem. The question is: How? I argue that *Sol.* proceeds according to the philosophical method set out in *C. Acad.*, i.e. ARP, while using to the Christian virtues to structure its application. This results in three complete "rounds" of ARP, each one focused, in turn, on one of the Christian virtues with the overarching aim of purifying Augustine and bringing him courage in the face of death.

The fusion of Platonic method and Christian virtues dictates the structure of *Sol.* + *De imm. an.* at the most basic level. Round 1 looks to faith and extends across *Sol.* 1.7–15. Round 2 looks to love and occupies the rest of book one, i.e. *Sol.* 1.16–30. Both passages are concerned with testing Augustine's desire to know God and the soul, or, as *Retract.* 1.4.1 puts it, "what kind of person one ought to be if he wants to grasp wisdom." Round 3 looks to hope and extends across the rest of the work. As *Retract.* 1.4.1 puts it, "the issue of the soul's immortality is discussed at length" through the whole of *Sol.* 2, though this discussion is completed only in *De imm.*

---

[22] *Sol.* 1.6.   [23] *Sol.* 2.7.   [24] *De ord.* 2.47. See Chapter 4 for discussion.

an. On my reading, *De imm. an.* 1–9 continues the discussion by uncovering a basic conceptual problem in *Sol.* 2's main argument. This, in turn, sets the stage for *De imm. an.* 10–25, which presents a sequence of three basic questions, the first two of which are resolved through moments of self-reflection marked as the text invokes the person who "has reflected well on himself" (*se bene inspexit*). Here, I suggest, we find two "subrounds" of ARP, focused respectively on the soul and its cause, followed by the elaboration of a final plausible account. In this way, *De imm. an.* 10–25 follows the pattern set out in *De ord.* 2.47 and employed in *De Mus.* 6 and *De lib. arbit.* Let us now turn to Augustine's discussion with Reason, walking through each round in turn, and then step back to take stock.

Round 1: Faith (*Sol.* 1.7–15)

The whole work is summed up in the phrase, "I want to know God and the soul." To most of us, this would suggest two basic topics: God and the soul. But Augustine, ever the close reader, finds a further question in what "to know" might mean in this context. After all, Augustine doesn't know anything like God, and so he doesn't know what kind of knowledge of God will be enough. This leads to immediate *aporia*, and Round 1 proceeds with questions of "faith" and epistemology more broadly. With a nod to Plato's *Men.*, Reason leads Augustine through a quick geometry lesson on lines and spheres[25] and then reflects on the process:

> R. - At si aeque illud atque hoc nosti et tamen inter se, ut fateris, plurimum
> differunt, est ergo differentium rerum scientia indifferens?
> A. - Quis enim negauit?
> R. - Tu paulo ante. Nam cum te rogassem, quomodo uelis deum nosse, ut possis
> dicere: 'satis est', respondisti te ideo nequire hoc explicare, quia nihil haberes
> perceptum similiter atque deum cupis percipere; nihil enim te scire deo simile.

> **Reason:** But if you know both [the line and the sphere], and nevertheless they differ greatly from each other, as you admit, is there then a [sort of] knowledge of different things that does not differ?
> **Augustine:** Who would deny that?
> **Reason:** You did just a little while ago! For when I asked you how you wished to know God so that you could say, "This is enough," you responded that you couldn't explain this, since you hadn't grasped anything in the way you want to grasp God since you don't know anything like God. (*Sol.* 1.10)

---

[25] For *Men.*'s geometry lesson, see *Tusc. Disp.* 1.57–61.

The point of all this is to un-teach Augustine's assumption that different objects of knowledge require different types of knowing. This, in turn, sets the stage for Reason's account of intellectual vision: just as we see geometrical truths with the eyes of our mind, the same eyes may eventually come to "see" God, provided that we properly purify ourselves first. The passage elaborates the fusion of Platonic purification and the Pauline virtues:

> R. - *Promittit enim Ratio, quae tecum loquitur, ita se demonstraturam deum tuae menti, ut oculis sol demonstratur. Nam mentis quasi sui sunt oculi sensus animae; disciplinarum autem quaeque certissima talia sunt, qualia illa quae sole illustrantur, ut uideri possint, ueluti terra est atque terrena omnia. Deus autem est ipse qui illustrat. Ego autem Ratio ita sum in mentibus, ut in oculis est aspectus. Non enim hoc est habere oculos quod aspicere aut item hoc est aspicere quod uidere. Ergo animae tribus quibusdam rebus opus est: ut oculos habeat, quibus iam bene uti possit, ut aspiciat, ut uideat. Oculi sani mens est ab omni labe corporis pura, id est a cupiditatibus rerum mortalium iam remota atque purgata. Quod ei nihil aliud praestat quam fides primo. Quod enim adhuc ei demonstrari non potest uitiis inquinatae atque aegrotanti, quia uidere nequit nisi sana, si non credat aliter se non esse uisuram, non dat operam suae sanitati. Sed quid, si credat quidem ita se rem habere, ut dicitur, atque ita se, si uidere potuerit, esse uisuram, sanari se tamen posse desperet. Nonne se prorsus abicit atque contemnit nec praeceptis medici obtemperat?*
> A. - *Omnino ita est, praesertim quia ea praecepta necesse est ut morbus dura sentiat.*
> R. - *Ergo fidei spes adicienda est.*
> A. - *Ita credo.*
> R. - *Quid, si et credat ita se habere omnia, et se speret posse sanari, ipsam tamen quae promittitur lucem non amet, non desideret suisque tenebris, quae iam consuetudine iucundae sunt, se arbitretur debere interim esse contentam? Nonne medicum illum nihilominus respuit?*
> A. - *Prorsus ita est.*
> R. - *Ergo tertia caritas necessaria est.*
> A. - *Nihil omnino tam necessarium.*
> R. - *Sine tribus istis igitur anima nulla sanatur, ut possit deum suum uidere, id est intellegere.*

Reason: Reason, who is speaking with you, promises to display God to your mind just as the sun is displayed to your eyes. For the senses of the soul are, as it were, the eyes of the mind; the most certain matters of the disciplines [e.g. geometry] are like those things that are illuminated by the sun, so that they can be seen, for instance the earth and all earthly things. But it is God Himself who illuminates. I, Reason, however, am in minds in the way that sight is in the eyes. Now to have eyes is not the same as to look and to look at something is not the same as to see. Thus the soul needs three things: [i] that the soul has eyes which it can use well, [ii] that it looks and [iii] that it sees. Healthy eyes are a mind cleansed of every taint of the body, that is, already removed and purified from desires for mortal things.

And nothing but *faith* grants this in the first place. For this cannot be shown to a soul sick and polluted with vices, since only a healthy soul can see. Unless the soul *believes* that it will not see otherwise, it does not care for its health. But what if the mind believes things to be as I've said and that it will see if it is able, but it *despairs* [i.e. forsakes hope] of being able to be healthy? Won't it despise itself, give up and refuse to obey the doctor's orders?

Augustine: That's it exactly, particularly since the sickness must find these orders harsh.

Reason: So *hope* must be added to faith?

Augustine: I believe so.

Reason: What if the mind believes all this and hopes that it can be healed yet does not *love* that light which is promised, does not long for it and even judges that it should in the meanwhile be content with that darkness that has become pleasant through familiarity? Won't it no less reject its medicine?

Augustine: Certainly.

Reason: Thus *love* is a third necessity.

Augustine: Nothing else is so necessary.

Reason: Without these three, therefore, no soul is made healthy so that it may see, that is understand, its God. (*Sol.* 1.12)

Paul's idea, as Reason presents it, is that faith, hope and love are all necessary for bringing us to see God. Augustine replies that Reason's account of purification sounds "plausible" (*probabile*), but he "wouldn't dare to say he knows anything that Reason has said beyond the bit about the line and sphere" (*nam praeter illa duo de linea et pila nihil abs te dictum est, quod me scire audeam dicere*).[26] In this, we find a textual marker for a complete round of ARP in something less than a complete dialogue. In terms of virtues, we find no explicit mention of courage (*fortitudo*) anywhere in *Sol.* or *De imm. an.* Yet we do get talk of despair, and the fear of death comes up throughout the work. My suggestion is that all three Pauline virtues, or at the very least hope and love, play the role of courage in the system of virtues articulated in these works. With this, the stage is set for the next round.

Round 2: Love (*Sol.* 1.16–30)

Having set out a provisional, plausible account of what "to know" means in "I want to know God and the soul," Augustine moves on to "I want." In a

---

[26] *Sol.* 1.15.

passage reminiscent of *Conf.* 10, Augustine takes stock of his own progress in overcoming various kinds of temptation.[27] He is generally quite pleased with himself, yet in a moment of casuistry worthy of the best undergraduate mind, he presents the following dilemma. As Reason has explained, Augustine will see wisdom only if he first loves earthly things only for the sake of seeing wisdom, for instance if he comes to love money *only* insofar as it allows him to devote his time to philosophy. Yet it turns out that Augustine will be able to love earthly things in this way only if he first sees wisdom. He is stuck in a Catch-22, and it is clearly not his fault that he hasn't advanced further than he has.[28] Reason responds that Augustine's nighttime thoughts suggest he is not quite so over sex as he had claimed. Reason concludes that Augustine's current state is healthy only in comparison with a worse disease.[29] At this point Augustine starts to cry.[30] In terms of purification, Reason's tough-love approach has cut through Augustine's self-deception and helped him view his current state more objectively. Even so, the Catch-22 stands, and Augustine suggests that a "shortcut" (*compendium*) to wisdom could help him out of his rut, since a quick glimpse would help him love wisdom and put earthly things into perspective.[31] Reason complies and, in what has to be one of the few times in history that a syllogism has been tossed out like a piece of chocolate, quickly proves that only Truth is immortal, and only immortal things really exist.[32] This cheers Augustine up somewhat, and book 2 draws to a close. In terms of plausibility, Reason's proof seems to be accepted *as a proof.* As *Retract.* 1.4.1 puts it, "At the end of the book it is argued (*colligitur*) by a bit of reasoning that those things which truly exist are immortal." Yet what Augustine cares about in *Sol.* isn't whether Truth is immortal and really exists, it is whether Augustine himself is ever going to see this Truth. Still, the fact that Reason's little argument gave Augustine a partial glimpse of Truth encourages him in his search for the whole of Truth, strengthens his love for this Truth and makes his eventual attainment of this Truth seem a bit more plausible. But we're not there yet.[33]

Round 3: Hope (*Sol.* 2 and *De imm. an.*)

Round 3 takes hope head on with its discussion of the soul's state after death. Augustine begins by stating that he is certain that he now exists,

---

[27] *Sol.* 1.16–23.   [28] *Sol.* 1.24–26.   [29] *Sol.* 1.25.   [30] *Sol.* 1.26.   [31] *Sol.* 1.26.
[32] *Sol.* 1.28–29.
[33] We might compare *De beata v.*, where an individual's partial grasp of truth is connected to the Holy Spirit's admonition to seek the whole of Truth, i.e. Christ. See Chapter 3.

that he is now alive and that he knows various things, e.g. that he exists and is alive. What worries him is whether he will keep existing, living and knowing after death.[34] If he can show that he'll keep living, then it is obvious that he will keep existing; what really worries him is whether he will be able to have knowledge after death, in particular knowledge of God. With this, we have finally moved on to one of the objects of Augustine's desire "to know God and the soul." The rest of *Sol.* 2 is spent laying out pieces of an argument for the soul's immortality. Reason does not, however, make it clear what this argument is until the end of the book.[35] Let us start with this concluding argument as providing context for what leads up to it:

(1) If X is in a subject, Y, and X lasts forever, then Y lasts forever [*Sol.* 2.22–23]
(2) Every discipline is in the soul as a subject [*Sol.* 2.22]
(3) Thus, the soul lasts forever if the discipline lasts forever [from (1) & (2)]
(4) A discipline is Truth [*Sol.* 2.7–21, esp. 19–21]
(5) Truth lasts forever [*Sol.* 2.2]
(6) Thus, the soul lasts forever [from (3), (4) & (5)]
(7) The soul can never be said to be dead [*Sol.* 2.23]
(8) Thus, the soul is immortal [from (6) & (7)]

We might grant (1) as a straightforward metaphysical point. Reason presents (2) and (7) as more or less true by definition: A discipline (*disciplina*) is something to be learned (*disci*), and a soul that is dead is simply not a soul. The crux of the argument comes in (4) and (5). Augustine and Reason get to (4) through an inquiry into the nature of truth and falsity. They begin with sensible examples, suggesting that a true tree is one that appears to be what it is, while a false tree is one that appears to be something other than what it is, for instance, a wall. This leads to the problem that trees might not exist when no one is observing them. Augustine and Reason eventually set aside concerns for appearances and focus on the liberal disciplines (grammar, dialectic, geometry and so on),

---

[34] *Sol.* 2.1. This is the first instance of the so-called Augustinian "*cogito.*" Both Augustine and Descartes are interested in the fact that one cannot be wrong in thinking "I think" or "I exist." Yet Descartes uses these first-person truths as the basis for demonstrative arguments. Augustine uses them as the self-reflective start of an inquiry into one's own nature. The same triad – I exist, I live, I know – appears at *De lib. arbit.* 2.7, where it provides the stepping off point for an elaborate exploration of moral psychology. See Chapter 7 for discussion.

[35] *Sol.* 2.24.

which are true, in that they teach only truths and can be used to distinguish truth from falsity in their various domains of study. So it is in this sense that a discipline is Truth. And (5) is supported by the quick argument that even if the world ceased to exist, it would be true that the world had ceased to exist, therefore Truth lasts forever.

The problem with this argument is that it seems to rest on an equivocation. One way of untangling this is to say that (2), "every discipline is in the soul as a subject," and (5), "truth lasts forever," conflate the faculty of reason and the object of reason by way of (4), "a discipline is truth." On this reading, Augustine has merely bumbled. A somewhat more convoluted approach would start from the thought, "disciplines are truth in that they teach truths" and argue by analogy, "truth is the structure of the world in that it provides structure to the world and will outlast the world." The latter reading, while more complicated, brings out the more serious question of whether the processes involved in the liberal disciplines, by which we think about the world, are the same processes by which the world is itself structured or perhaps created. Put simply, the argument raises worries about scientific realism. On either reading, though, the central argument of *Sol.* 2 seems fundamentally flawed. On this point, Cary, Catapano and Tornau agree. We should note, however, that *Sol.* 2's discussion is incomplete.

De imm. an. 1–9 restates *Sol.* 2's main argument but this time stresses that a discipline can only exist in something alive (*in eo quod uiuit*). This moment of clarity, however, generates a further series of puzzles. The text proceeds[36] to give variations on *Sol.* 2's main argument, all of which involve *ratio* as a key feature. In the end, these arguments simply move the equivocation back a step, as *ratio* is treated variously as the "ratio" between bodily elements, the "ratio" between abstract numbers, the "discipline" of arithmetic, the abstract "structure" of logic and the human faculty of "reason." Given that *De imm. an.* is a sketch, it is not immediately obvious what a charitable reading of this passage would look like. Normally, we would try to present arguments as favorably as possible on their own terms; on the other hand, all the other dialogues from Cassiciacum have descended into confusion well before they were over. Given that *De imm. an.* 10 raises the question, "What is reason?" I suggest that the arguments of 1–9 are intentionally flawed and advance the work's overall

---

[36] Given that this is a sketch, there is no indication as to which character says what. While I have suspicions about this, for the time being I will simply endow the text with agency as though it were a character.

project by pinpointing what exactly Augustine needs to un-learn before he's ready for the work's final conclusion. This is the sense in which *De imm. an.* completes *Sol.* 2's discussion. If *Sol.* 3 was meant to end with an *oratio, De imm. an.* 10 would be a good place for it to start.

De imm. an. 10 distinguishes between three possible meanings of "*ratio*": the soul's capacity to see the truth, the soul's seeing the truth and the truth seen by the soul. This distinction, in turn, makes it possible for *De imm. an.* 11 to articulate the worry that has been riding under the surface since the end of *Sol.* 2, i.e. whether the truth, which we agree is eternal, is separable from the soul, which sees it. This question, in turn, initiates a string of three basic puzzles that structure the rest of the work. The first two of these turn on clearly marked moments of self-reflection. I take this to indicate two sub-rounds of ARP intended to clarify the soul's relationship to bodies and to intelligibles, respectively, thus setting the stage for a final account of soul as a metaphysical straddler with one foot planted firmly in either world.[37]

In suggesting that the soul and truth might be separable substances, *De imm. an.* 11–15 raises the possibility that the soul is immortal only when it has disciplinary Truth in it and that a soul that fell into total ignorance would become mortal. Having set out this *aporia*, the text continues, "whoever has reflected well on himself" (*qui se bene inspexit*) will realize that every soul is superior to every body.[38] In discussing other instances of ARP, I've argued that self-reflective discoveries are anchored on specific stretches of debate: *C. Acad.*'s insight, for instance, that we can be certain that rational thought uses certainties because we've just been arguing with a skeptic who has been using certainties to argue that certainty is impossible. In *De imm. an.* we don't have the normal banter to help see what portion of debate Augustine, or more likely Reason, has in mind. That said, the dialectic leading to the current *aporia* has displayed the soul's ability to do all sorts of things that bodies cannot do: It can hold past, present and future together through intentional action, it can apply eternal standards of reason to objects that exist in time, either creatively through

---

[37] I agree with Cary, "An Abandoned Proof," both that *De imm. an.* 1–8 presents variants of the same argument put forth in *Sol.* 2 and also that *De imm. an.* 10–11 brings problems with this line of argument to the surface. Yet Cary, who assumes that Augustine wrote as a way of figuring things out, concludes that it was at this point that Augustine (the author) realized that his project was doomed. I, by contrast, take the *aporia* presented in this passage to be simply one stage in a bigger project defined by ARP. It is perhaps telling that in declaring the work doomed to failure, Cary passes over the remaining two thirds of *De imm. an.* and their response to this initial *aporia*.

[38] *De imm. an.* 13.

art or critically through judgment and so on.[39] Whatever portion of text the speaker may have in mind, this moment of self-reflection provides a premise for a further argument:

(9)   Bodies must receive their form from something superior.
(10)   Every soul is superior to every body. [from self-reflection]
(11)   Thus, soul provides bodies with their form.
(12)   No body can be totally stripped of its form.
(13)   Thus, no soul can be destroyed.

There are a couple of issues here. If this argument proves anything, it proves the immortality of at least one soul, e.g. the World Soul that Plotinus held to imprint rational forms onto the natural material world. While that would be an interesting conclusion, we were trying to prove the immortality of Augustine's soul. Setting that aside, there's the deeper worry about combining (9) and (10) to get (11). For this to work as a proof, (10) would have to claim that soul is the only thing superior to body. Our moment of self-reflection hasn't given us anything like that. Still, if we step back and consider the options for things that are superior to bodies and which could be responsible for giving bodies their form, some kind of soul seems like a plausible candidate.[40]

In any event, it seems to be (9) that bothers Augustine, as *De imm. an.* 17 raises the worry that this form-giving thing we're calling "soul" is just a blending of the body's earth, air, fire and water. While today we might put this in terms of brain chemistry, this is a statement of the same general approach to material reductionism that is the default assumption for many today. In response, the text points out that the person who *se bene inspexit* realizes:

---

[39] This list at least partly aligns with Cicero's distillation of various Platonic dialogues in *Tusc.* 1. See Chapter 2.

[40] The possible existence of a World Soul is made explicit at *De imm. an.* 24 (discussed later in this chapter). It is unclear whether we should read this World Soul into the present argument. Tornau, "*Ratio in Subiecto*," 345–347, resists this move on the grounds that Augustine would engage in circular reasoning: basing the eternity of the World Soul on the world's sempiternity, which is itself secured through the eternity of the World Soul (personal communication, September 25, 2015). To avoid this problem, Tornau identifies God as the source of form invoked in the present argument and reconstructs the argument of *De imm. an.* 9–12 accordingly. On my reading, the present argument's contribution to the final account of *De imm. an.* 24 is not to prove, (13), that the soul cannot be destroyed, but merely to make plausible the idea, (11), that soul provides form to bodies. I have presented the argument in the somewhat more flawed, or at least underdetermined, form suggested by the text. Put another way, the present argument fails to prove the immortality of the soul, yet in the process it produces conceptual enrichment that ends up being useful for the work's final account.

(14)   The further one withdraws his thinking from the bodily senses, the better his understanding.

This moment of self-reflection might harken back to book 2, which went around in circles discussing false trees but finally made some progress when Augustine and Reason turned their attention to the liberal disciplines, which can deal with sensible things (like trees) but are not themselves sensible.[41] The second thing that self-reflection helps us realize is:

(15)   The objects of proper understanding are not themselves bodily and exist most fully (*maxime*) because they are always the same.

This could look back to a number of spots in the preceding debates; the geometry lesson from book 1 is an obvious place to start. Together, these two self-reflective insights display the soul's ability to contemplate intelligibles and thus show the soul to be linked to them "in some marvelous, incorporeal way" (*miro quodam . . . incorporali modo*).[42] This is meant to address the worry that the soul might merely be a blending of the bodies' four elements. As solutions go, it's a bit vague or, at the very least, provisional. Nevertheless, it serves to underscore some shortcomings of material reductionism and invites us to look for alternative explanations.

De imm. an. 18–25 takes up this invitation through a final *aporia*: If all we can say is that the soul is linked to intelligibles "somehow," and we've already stated that bodies cannot exist without some link to intelligible form, is it then possible that the soul's connection to truth could wane to the point that the soul became a body?[43] *De imm. an.* 24 responds by combining the two provisional conclusions leading up to this point into a final account in which each and every soul acts as an intermediary between eternal truth and changeable bodies:

> *Hoc autem ordine intellegitur a summa essentia speciem corpori per animam tribui, qua est, in quantumcumque est. Per animam ergo corpus subsistit et eo ipso est quo animatur, siue uniuersaliter, ut mundus, siue particulariter, ut unumquodque animal intra mundum.*

In accordance with this order we understand that form is imparted from the highest essence [i.e. God] through the soul to a body, through which the

---

[41]   *Tusc.* 1.70–76 presents "withdrawing from the body" as the activity reflected upon in Plato's *Phd.* See Chapter 2 for discussion.

[42]   *De imm. an.* 17.

[43]   While this is perhaps the strangest of the work's many strange ideas, it has precedence in Plato's discussion of ghosts at *Phd.* 80a–84c, with its famous line that pleasure and pain "nail the soul to the body."

body exists inasmuch as it exists. Body, therefore, has its subsistence through soul and exists thanks to that very thing in virtue of which it is ensouled, either in the universal way that the world is ensouled or in the particular way that each animal within the world is. (*De imm. an.* 24)

While *De imm. an.* 11–15 might have shown us something about the World Soul, *De imm. an.* 25 shows that it is in the nature of all souls, most importantly Augustine's soul, to be metaphysical straddlers between intelligible and material modes of existence.[44] In response to the text's last puzzle, souls might become *more* bodily (e.g. in the sense that they get preoccupied with temporal, bodily affairs) but the connection to intelligible truth is part of the soul's nature. The soul can thus never become a mere body.

So what can we say about how *De imm. an.* completes *Sol.* 2's discussion? At the end of *Sol.* 2, it seemed that Reason's argument rested on an equivocation, insofar as it treated "Truth" as both the structure of the world and the processes that living beings use to think about that structure. At the end of *De imm. an.*, we are presented with a substantive theory that provides a context for that equivocation: The reason there are rational structures in the world is that a living being put them there, whether the World Soul or some individual soul. Along the way, however, we have refined our concept of what a soul is. *Sol.* 2 treated a soul as something capable of learning a discipline. *De imm. an.* provides a more basic explanation for why that is: Souls are by nature connected to intelligible reality, and they by nature look to reflect this reality in the bodily world, either by imparting form (i.e. through human craft or the human-like craft of the World Soul) or by discovering form that was put there by some other soul.[45] In the end, the framework meant to clarify *Sol.* 2's argument does as much as the argument itself for showing why the soul is immortal. By coming to see the soul as a metaphysical straddler, we recognize that every soul has one foot planted in eternity. It is simply not in the nature of such a thing to die.[46]

---

[44] Tornau, "*Ratio in subiecto*" helpfully explains this account against the backdrop of Platonist models of causation and double causation.

[45] This hearkens back to Plotinus' theory in "On Beauty" that the soul is akin to form and delights when it encounters form in the world around it. See Chapter 2.

[46] My reconstruction of *De imm. an.*'s final position is basically in line with Tornau's, "*Ratio in subiecto.*" Cary, "An Abandoned Argument," 103, claims, "what Augustine obviously wants to do in his proof for the immortality of the soul is to show that the inherent imperishability of Truth 'rubs off' on the soul in which is it present." Yet Cary also claims that the main argument of *Sol.* 2 got the causal priority backward, making Truth rely on soul rather than the other way around. Whether or

Should we follow the model of the other Cassiciacum dialogues and take this conclusion to be offered as something plausible rather than proven? While there is no explicit language of plausibility in *De imm. an.*, its ending has the distinction of being the only passage referred to in *Retract.* as "rashly spoken" (*temere dictum*), and the portion of *De imm. an.* 24 quoted earlier is cited as the prime offender.[47] This bit of Stoic jargon suggests that we are in the general neighborhood of the plausible.[48] Beyond questions of textual cues, though, I have argued that the structure of *De imm. an.* follows the familiar jump from *aporia* and self-reflection to a final account that explains what came before, albeit in ways that fall short of proof. While such a conclusion may be merely provisional, it is enough to give Augustine good reason to think that the soul will keep on existing, living and knowing after death. This, in turn, gives him reason to hope that he will eventually come to see God with the eye of his mind. And it is this hope that was the point of Round 3 all along.

The Rhetorical Structure of "*Sol.* 3"

Sol. + *De imm. an.*'s multiple rounds of ARP represent a methodological development on Augustine's earlier dialogues. Each of these earlier works proceeded through a single round of ARP built around a term from Wisdom 11:20's triad: measure, number, weight. *Sol.* + *De imm. an.*, by contrast, pursues multiple rounds of ARP built around 1 Corinthians 13:13's triad: faith, hope, love. In this sense, *Sol.* + *De imm. an.* undertakes an amount of work comparable to the other three dialogues combined, albeit in a more distilled form. Its exploration of hope, meanwhile, with its two sub-rounds of ARP followed by the elaboration of a plausible account

---

not that is the case, the concluding account of *De imm. an.* 24, which Cary does not discuss, presents the picture Cary wants Augustine to present. Catapano, "*De Immortalitate Animae*," 82–84, claims that the first half of *De imm. an.* strengthens the argument of *Sol.* 2, while the second half of *De imm. an.* makes that argument superfluous. In this, Catapano points out what Cary has missed. Yet Catapano proceeds to argue that, if Augustine had finished *Sol.*, he would have needed to rewrite *Sol.* 2 to put them in line with the conclusions of this hypothetical "*Sol.* 3." My reading of the proposed *Sol.* 2–3 as application of ARP makes this unnecessary. Within such a structure, the argument of *Sol.* 2 advances the project by presenting problematic arguments that, in turn, call for the conceptual enrichment of *Sol.* 3.

[47] *Retract.* 1.5.3 & 1.11.4. While the second passage comes in a discussion of *De Mus.*, it refers to the passage from *De imm. an.* by name.

[48] Within Hellenistic debates, the Stoics defined rashness as assent to any impression that falls short of objective certainty. The Academics, who argued that we could never be certain of anything, responded that within the class of uncertain impressions, some are more "plausible" than others. "Rashness" and "plausibility" are thus both concerned with beliefs about which we are uncertain, even if the latter takes a more pessimistic view of the whole affair. See Chapter 1 for discussion.

finds a close parallel in *De Mus.* 6 and *De lib. arbit.* All three works, in turn, follow the form set out in *De ord.* 2.47's depiction of philosophy as a twofold inquiry into the soul and its cause. In this case, *De imm. an.* 11–15 inquires into the nature of the soul as something that gives form to bodies; *De imm. an.* 17 inquires into the soul's relationship to intelligible reality, which is the cause responsible for soul being a form-giving thing; *De imm. an.* 18–25 then puts these together and elaborates an account of soul as a metaphysical straddler.[49]

Given the overarching structure of this argument, what rhetorical form would *Sol.* 3 have taken if Augustine had ever finished writing it? I have argued that *De imm. an.* 1–9 contains a series of equivocal arguments about *ratio* that sets the stage for "a new beginning of sorts" at *De imm. an.* 10.[50] Given the bantering tone of *Sol.*, we might imagine Reason offering one "reasonable" sounding argument after another and Augustine becoming progressively confused to the point where one of them states the underlying issue of what "*ratio*" actually means. If the work were to end with an *oratio perpetua*, this would be a likely place for it to start. This would put *Sol.* in line with the other Cassiciacum dialogues as well as *De quant. an.* and *De Mag.* Alternatively, we might think that parallels to the structure of *De Mus.* 6's argument might suggest that *Sol.* 3 would also have lacked a final *oratio*. This strikes me as unlikely given that the lack of an *oratio* in *De Mus.* 6 stems from its peculiar status as a disciplinary dialogue and the lack of explicitly philosophical argument in books 1–5. If we might look ahead somewhat, *De lib. arbit.* 2 provides yet a third model. As I will argue in Chapter 7, this book also pursues rounds within rounds of ARP, yet it presents the three stages of its plausible conclusion via three little *orationes* divided by passages of dialogue. We might imagine a similar threefold division here, as Reason suggests the soul's relation to bodies, the soul's relation to intelligibles and the final, combined account

---

[49] In one respect, different scholarly reconstructions of *De imm. an.*'s argument are simply attempts to cut the text at its natural joints. While I find the same broad structure here as Catapano, "*De Immortalitate*," and Tornau, "*Ratio in subiecto*," each of us situates the main internal divisions at slightly different places. I come closest to Tornau, who sees the book building up to *De imm. an.* 24's final account. By contrast, the commentary of Gerard Watson, *Saint Augustine: Soliloquies and Immortality of the Soul* (Warminster: Aris & Phillips, 1986), 198–213, presents *De imm. an.* as little more than a list of objections and responses. It is, of course, perfectly possible for the book to build to a conclusion *through* a list of objections and responses (something akin to Chapter 2 of *Utilitarianism*, where Mill explains what Utilitarianism is by working through others' objections). My point is that *De imm. an.* is much more than a mere list.

[50] Augustine uses the term, *quasi aliud . . . exordium*, to introduce his *oratio perpetua* at *C. Acad.* 3.15.

of the soul as a metaphysical straddler.[51] Whichever model we prefer, in setting out the overarching structure of *De imm. an.*'s argument, I hope to have identified the structural considerations that Augustine, as author, would have taken into account in giving *De imm. an.* its final literary form as *Sol. 3.*[52]

---

[51] If my reconstruction of the *oratio perpetua* that would have occupied "*Sol. 3*" is at all convincing, then it provides a challenge to Stock's argument in *Augustine's Inner Dialogue* that the shift from debate to *oratio* represents a shift from "open dialogue" between individuals to "inner dialogue" with oneself. The point of this shift, according to Stock, is to step beyond the petty rivalries and emotions of open dialogue and engage in more serious inner dialogue as modelled by *Sol.* On my reading, emotion is a part of the philosophical undertaking not an obstruction to it (see Chapter 3), and Augustine's supposedly placid model of inner dialogue, *Sol.*, has just as much emotion as the other dialogues. What's more, Stock does not account for the fact that *Sol.* is incomplete and likely would have had its own closing *oratio*, as I've argued. While the shift into *oratio* might represent symbolicly what Stock wants it to, his reading of the role of emotion in the works, so far as I can tell, does not capture their fundamental dialectic.

[52] Given the weight of Augustine's seven other complete dialogues, the lack of any recognizably scriptural language at the end of *De imm. an.* is somewhat odd. The other Cassiciacum dialogues culminate in plausible accounts centered on Wisdom 11:20's measure, number, weight; *De Mag.*'s theory of the inner teacher combines Pauline language of the inner man with the Gospels' account of Christ as Truth; *De Mus.* culminates in an account of creation, fall and salvation, which turns on ideas of love/charity; *De lib. arbit.* 3 invokes piety to guide a protracted reading of Genesis. While *Sol.* opens with quite a lot of theological material, and an exploration of hope guides the basic structure of *Sol.* 2 + *De imm. an.*, its final account of soul as a metaphysical straddler has little about it that is recognizably Christian. While it might seem to inhabit the same general conceptual space as *De Mus.*'s discussion of creation, the rather central role it assigns to a World Soul is more in keeping with Plotinus than with Scripture. Perhaps this is an instance when Augustine's optimism about the compatibility of Christianity and Platonism stumbled as he sought a scriptural hook for his account of the World Soul. Tornau, "*Ratio in Subiecto*," 351, makes a similar suggestion. This is, however, mere speculation on both our parts. What matters for present purposes is how Augustine might have finished the work, not why he failed to do so.

CHAPTER 6

Philosophy and Kathartic Virtue
De quantitate animae

The central goal of this study is to find a holistic reading of Augustine's dialogues. To this end, I have focused on questions of method and, following Heath, have focused on projects rather than themes as what binds each individual work into a unified whole.[1] In the process, issues of virtue have risen to the surface. I have argued that the dialogues from Cassiciacum use scriptural cues to explore the classical virtues: wisdom, moderation, justice and courage. This fact has guided my reconstruction of the single project advanced by *Sol.* + *De imm. an.* At this point, though, we might ask what Augustine, as author, is hoping to accomplish with these dialogues as a set. We have often seen him, as a character within individual dialogues, dropping hints about his plans for whatever conversation he is in at the moment yet not laying those plans bare until the end. In Chapter 4, I took a synoptic view of the scenic dialogues' pedagogical vision for the Cassiciacum community, as expressed in their dedications and *De ord.*'s closing *oratio*, which act as "book ends" for that set. In the present chapter, I suggest that a slightly later dialogue, "On the Soul's Greatness" (*De quantitate animae*), written in 388CE, provides a useful starting point for taking a similarly synoptic view of the virtues within the Cassiciacum set. Here we find Augustine drawing into a single system the hints he has been dropping all along that he is exploring the Platonist idea that virtue comes in grades: civic, kathartic/purifying and contemplative. In what follows, I draw these passages together and present them in light of *De quant. an.* This result is a picture of philosophy as purification.

De quant. an. presents a conversation between Augustine and his friend Evodius. It is not continuous with the Cassiciacum works' narrative, yet its discussion of the soul's greatness will be in many respects familiar to

---

[1] See Introduction for discussion of Heath, *Unity in Greek Poetics*, and the methods guiding my reading.

readers of the earlier dialogues, and the heavily self-reflective discussion of geometry at *De quant. an.* 8–24 may give some sense of what Augustine's never written *De Geometria* would have been like.[2] What concerns us for the moment, though, is its concluding *oratio, De quant. an.* 70–81, which presents a sevenfold scheme of the soul's activity. In the act of presenting the first three steps (*gradus*), Augustine himself becomes a soul reflecting on itself and its actions of (1) animating a body, (2) bringing perception to a body and (3) engaging in rational activity. This rational activity is "distinctively human" (*homini proprius*)[3] and includes all the first-order arts from writing to housebuilding. Yet a soul can rise above these everyday activities by (4) purifying itself of bodily attachments. The intended end of this purification is a state of tranquility that the soul maintains by (5) keeping itself pure. This, however, is merely a prerequisite to (6) looking for God with the mind's eye and ultimately (7) seeing God with the mind's eye. This sevenfold scheme presents an elaboration of the idea Plotinus sets out in his treatise, "On Virtues" (*Enn.* 1.2), that the virtues come in grades: Civic virtues allow us to get along in the material world; kathartic virtues "purify" us for a better world; contemplative, or "true," virtues constitute the true happiness of that better world.[4] Having set out his sevenfold system, Augustine continues:

> *Nam cum sint ista per tam multas Ecclesiae scripturas dispersa, quamquam ea non incommode collegisse uideamur, plene tamen intellegi nequeunt; nisi quisque in illorum septem quarto gradu fortiter agens, pietatemque custodiens . . . inquirat omnia singillatim.*

> For since these things were scattered across many writings of the Church, although we seem to have collected them in a not unuseful way, they nevertheless cannot be fully understood unless, by working vigorously at the fourth of these seven levels and guarding piety, . . . one looks into them all one at a time. (*De quant. an.* 78)

Whether or not this is an accurate depiction of the Church at large, it provides a useful framework for connecting ideas scattered across Augustine's own writings. *De ord.* 2.47's presentation of philosophy as a "twofold inquiry into God and the soul" is captured in this scheme in stages 4 and 6, respectively. A disciplinary dialogue such as *De Mus.* thus begins at stage 3,

---

[2] See Chapter 4 for discussion of Augustine's disciplinary dialogues. Cary, "Explorations of Divine Reason." In *Augustine's Invention*, 77–94, esp. 89–94, explores this suggestion.
[3] *De quant. an.* 72.
[4] See also Porphyry, *Sententiae* 32 and commentary of Luc Brisson, *Porphyre: Sentences* (Paris: Librarie Philosophique J. Vrin, 2005), tome 2, pp. 628–642.

as the Teacher engages his Student's soul in the rational activity of
studying music; from here it progresses to stage 4, as the student is brought
to know himself as something greater than the bodies he studies and on to
stage 6 through which it strives for knowledge of God, which is the
ultimate point of all of this, i.e. stage 7.[5] While reason is involved as early
as stage 3, what characterizes stage 4 is the self-reflective nature of reason's
gaze. This movement is captured in ARP itself, as aporetic debate that uses
reason (stage 3) gives way to reflection on the act of debating (stage 4) and
the search for what explains all of this (stage 6). While the ultimate goal is
certain knowledge in the direct vision of God, Augustine is content to deal
with the higher levels of rational activity in provisional, plausible terms as a
way of advancing the search at stage 6.[6] Having clearly set out this scheme
of graded virtues, we can now recognize the hints of it scattered throughout the Cassiciacum dialogues and refine our understanding of the project
these works advance.

The culminating point of *C. Acad.* came as Augustine set out an account
of Plato's two-worlds theory as a plausible response to everything that
came before. The central passage runs thus:

> *Sat est enim ad id, quod uolo, Platonem sensisse duos esse mundos, unum*
> *intellegibilem, in quo ipsa ueritas habitaret, istum autem sensibilem, quem*
> *manifestum est nos uisu tactuque sentire, itaque illum uerum, hunc ueri*
> *similem et ad illius imaginem factum, et ideo de illo in ea quae se cognosceret*
> *anima uelut expoliri et quasi serenari ueritatem, de hoc autem in stultorum*
> *animis non scientiam sed opinionem posse generari; quidquid tamen ageretur in*
> *hoc mundo per eas uirtutes, quas ciuiles uocabat, aliarum uerarum uirtutum*
> *similes, quae nisi paucis sapientibus ignotae essent, non posse nisi ueri simile*
> *nominari.*

> It is sufficient for my aims to say that Plato believed there to be two worlds:
> the one is intelligible, in which Truth itself abides, but the other is sensible,
> which is clearly what we sense with sight and touch. Thus the one is true,

---

[5] It is not clear to me whether we can identify a discrete stage 5 in *De Mus.*, or any other work, which
is not somehow reducible to stage 4 or 6. It may be that the moments of prayer that otherwise seem
simply to interrupt the flow of an argument are meant to play this role. We find a similar ambiguity
among the Platonists themselves, as Porphyry interjects a stage of "having been purified" between
Plotinus' kathartic and contemplative virtues. See Charles Brittain, "Attention Deficit in Plotinus
and Augustine: Psychological Problems in Christian and Platonist Theories of the Grades of Virtue,"
Proceedings of the Boston Area Colloquium in Ancient Philosophy 28 (2003): 223–263.

[6] Augustine's sevenfold scheme gives an early indication of the medieval love for elaborate hierarchies
and calls to mind the various ascents of the soul set out in *Conf.* This particular hierarchy, however, is
quite securely grounded in what went before. See Chapter 2 for my argument that ARP represents a
version of Plato's method of hypothesis as found in *Men.*, *Phd.* and *R.*, albeit a version that bears the
stamp of Augustine's more immediate sources, Cicero and Plotinus.

the other truthlike and made in its image. And thus truth about the former is polished up and shines forth, as it were, in the soul that knows itself. About the latter world, however, there can come to be not knowledge but opinion in the souls of foolish people. Nevertheless, whatever is done in this world through those virtues which Plato called "civic" – which are like the other true virtues which are unknown save to a few wise people – this can only be called truthlike. (*C. Acad.* 3.37)

Within the context of *C. Acad.*, it is not entirely clear what we are to make of these claims, which connect Plato's two-worlds theory, the Academic skeptics' use of truthlike or plausible impressions and a distinction between civic and true virtues. Within the broader context of the Cassiciacum set and *De quant. an.*, however, they suggest that the grades of virtue play a role in the dialogues from the very beginning. What's more, *C. Acad.*'s presentation of philosophy as a mystery religion dedicated to purifying initiates, if set beside *De quant. an.* 78's insistence on attending to grade 4, suggests that for Augustine the virtues of a philosopher are kathartic virtues. If this seems somewhat deflationary, we should bear in mind that kathartic virtues are directed beyond themselves toward higher virtues. But that is simply to say that philosophy is the pursuit of wisdom, while the attainment of wisdom is the higher state toward which philosophy is directed. In Plotinus' terms, a philosopher's kathartic wisdom is directed toward the Sage's true wisdom. Confusion about this distinction is what fueled the debate of *C. Acad.* 1, where Licentius argued that one could be both happy and wise in the pursuit of truth, while Trygetius argued that happiness and wisdom are found only in attaining the truth. In retrospect, they were both right, albeit about different grades of wisdom. Questions of intellectual sources and school allegiances aside, the extent to which both Licentius and Trygetius present compelling cases testifies to the power of the grades of virtue as an explanatory scheme.[7]

De beata v. plays on a similar ambiguity between grades of virtue. *De beata v.* 19 presents the puzzle that the person who has God is the person who seeks God, yet the person who seeks God does not yet have God. Augustine resolves this puzzle in his final *oratio* by distinguishing between the person who grasps the whole of Truth, which Scripture identifies as Christ, and the person whose partial grasp of truth admonishes him to attain the whole of Truth, which admonition Augustine identifies

---

[7] *C. Acad.* 1.11, for instance, is one of the most moving passages in the dialogues, as Licentius describes the pleasure of the previous day's intellectual pursuits despite the fact that they arrived at no conclusion. For a particularly apt discussion, see Blake Dutton, "Happiness, Wisdom and the Insufficiency of Inquiry." In *Augustine and Academic Skepticism*, 49–74.

with the action of the Holy Spirit. According to this account, the Holy Spirit provides the psychological basis for kathartic virtue, while Christ provides the basis for true virtue. The particular virtue being considered is moderation, and the whole of the work presents a "gradual" progression from everyday civic conceptions of moderation as the virtue that makes desire-satisfaction possible, to a contemplative conception of conforming one's mind to Truth=Christ as the "measure of the soul." Just as *C. Acad.* claimed that civic virtues are drawn from true ones, the progression of *De beata v.* shows that desire-satisfaction, even in the civic sense, ultimately depends on the relation of one's mind to Truth=Christ and is thus a side effect or lower-grade version of "true" moderation.

De ord. takes up similar ambiguities from yet another angle. The work's debates are by and large generated by Licentius and Trygetius failing to recognize that human beings bear two relations to the providential structures of the world. Like everything else, we are ruled by these structures, yet as rational beings we are also able to understand them. This ambiguity comes to a head at *De ord.* 2.2–21 as the young men attempt to reconcile the wise person's intellectual knowledge, which does not change, with his interactions with the changeable world, first and foremost as a teacher. Justice is the virtue under consideration, and the work starts out by conceiving of human beings as ruled like everything else. This raises the question of whether God is just in meting out rewards and punishments for human behavior. Yet the debate progresses as Augustine's companions come to think of humans as intellectual beings capable of the higher virtues tied up in understanding God's providential structure directly. With this, civic conceptions of justice give way to true/contemplative ones. Kathartic justice makes its way into the picture, in turn, through the work's central answer to the question of providence, viz. that the world is good for human beings insofar as the apparent disorder of experience moves human beings to seek deeper unity and thus draw closer to Unity itself, which is God. This bears some resemblance to what we now think of as soul-making theodicies, i.e. the idea that God is justified in permitting suffering because some higher virtues, such as endurance and compassion, can only develop in the face of suffering.[8] Yet such virtues are best suited to life in an imperfect world. *De ord.*'s account of providence passes by concerns for civic virtue and focuses on how the kathartic virtues may

---

[8] For a classic statement, see John Hick, "Soul-Making and Suffering." In *The Problem of Evil*, ed. Marilyn McCord Adams & Robert Merrihew Adams, 168–188 (Oxford: Oxford University Press, 1990).

prepare us for a more perfect life. And within the Cassiciacum set, *De ord.* builds on *De beata v.* by spelling out how the Holy Spirit's admonition to Truth follows from the basic structures of God, mind and world.

Sol. + *De imm. an.* completes the set with the most protracted exercise in ambiguity of all four. As we've seen, *Sol.* 2's main argument turns on an equivocal use of "truth" as both the structure of the world and the processes humans use to think about that structure. *De imm. an.* 1–9 shifts the equivocation over to *ratio*, which is treated as both the truth and the mind's capacity to see the truth. All of this sets the stage for the work's final account of human souls as metaphysical straddlers, which both sums up the distinctions of the previous dialogues and clarifies the basic goal of human pursuits: Given that we are by nature connected to both eternity and time, we should strive to become better acquainted with what is above and put its mandates first. If we do this, everything else will fall into place.[9] This is captured early on in Reason's account of intellectual vision:

> Thus the soul needs three things: [i] that it has eyes which it can use well, [ii] that it looks and [iii] that it sees. Healthy eyes are a mind cleansed of every taint of the body, that is, already removed and purified from desires for mortal things. (*Sol.* 1.25)[10]

The main virtue under consideration here is courage, whose civic form is traditionally associated with military contexts. Aristotle defines courage as a twofold mean about fear and confidence, aimed at the fine.[11] The Greek *andreia* literally means "manliness" and in several contexts could just as well be translated as "valor." *Sol.* + *De imm. an.* presents a more advanced course of study than the scenic dialogues, and civic conceptions of courage do not feature in this work. Instead, we start with a peculiarly kathartic, philosophical conception of what courage is for. In this case, the fear in question is not that death will be the end of the life as we know it; it is that Augustine may never come to know the Truth that he is after. We find a similar worry in the Platonists that once we shut off everything born of the bodily sense, we might find that there is simply nothing left. Plotinus and Porphyry developed faith (*pistis*) in intellectual reality as a peculiarly Platonist virtue.[12] Augustine, however, looks explicitly to Paul for a fuller

---

[9] This basic thought is elaborated in *De lib. arbit.* 1's account of temporal and eternal law. See Chapter 7.
[10] See Chapter 5 for Latin text.   [11] Aristotle, EN 3.6–9.
[12] For discussion of parallels between Plotinus, Porphyry and Augustine on this topic, see Robert Dodaro, "Augustine on the Statesman and the Two Cities." In *A Companion to Augustine*, ed. Mark Vessey, 386–397 (Oxford: Blackwell Publishing, 2012), esp. 393–397.

arsenal of faith, hope and love to combat his fear that death may cut short his search for God. In sum, each of the Cassiciacum dialogues, at the most basic level, strives toward true virtue through a philosophical process that *De quant. an.* identifies with kathartic virtue and structures around a process of ARP.[13]

We might clarify Augustine's contribution to discussions of virtue theory by comparing the dialogues' pursuit of true virtue with what we find in Aristotle. Their approaches differ in two main regards. First, Aristotle presents virtue as the excellence of human nature, although he is notoriously vague about what aspect of human nature is relevant. The vast majority of *EN* operates under the assumption that virtue is an excellence of the whole human soul: nutritive, sensitive and rational. This leads to a conception of virtue – and thus of flourishing – which encompasses a wide range of embodied human life. Yet at EN 10.7–8, mere pages before the end of the work, Aristotle suggests that human virtue might be the excellence of the most excellent part of our nature, i.e. reason, and presents a view of flourishing as the life of contemplation. This is, of course, an early statement of the problem that the Platonists' grades of virtue are meant to resolve, and Augustine follows Plotinus by presenting civic virtue as simply a degraded form of the contemplative, while kathartic virtue bridges the gap.

Second, and more importantly, EN 2 argues that, when it comes to the embodied virtues of character, we become virtuous by performing virtuous deeds. This process of habituation begins in childhood and depends rather heavily on one's teachers having correct views about what is good for a human being, which, ideally, rest on their having correct views of what human nature is. Given his commitment to endoxic method, Aristotle assumes that most teachers' views will be correct enough, while the task of moral philosophy is to systemize and correct everyday views about human nature and human ends. EN 10.9 draws the work to a close as Aristotle argues that proper education requires proper laws about how to raise our young. This, in turn, sets the agenda for his *Politics*. For the individual

---

[13] The one issue Tornau, "*Ratio in Subiecto*," and I part ways on is the ultimate goal of *Sol.* + *De imm. an.* While Tornau, 336–338, recognizes the philosophical relevance of the work's roundabout approach to argument, he sees these exercises as basically spiritual exercises meant to prepare the work's junior partner, i.e. Augustine, for the work's main argument, which Tornau takes to be its proof of the soul's immortality. I take the work's inquiry into immortality to be merely an occasion for pursuing the greater goal of exploring and instilling a particular kind of courage. The distinction is a rather subtle one, although my reading has the advantage of explaining the otherwise odd fact, pointed out by Catapano, that *De imm. an.* defends the argument of *Sol.* 2 in a way that makes that argument superfluous.

who was improperly raised, Aristotle holds out little hope for a flourishing, virtuous adult life.

While Augustine recognizes the importance of habit,[14] he is more optimistic about the prospects for adults to change. It is here that the power of ARP becomes apparent. Aristotle assumes that we become X by practicing X; this one-to-one approach requires a teacher to push us in the right direction. *C. Acad.*'s crypto-Platonist teachers operate by pushing students in the wrong direction. The success of the method depends not on the teacher having the right view of human nature, but on the fact that the student is by nature human. Aporetic debates engage our rational faculties and prompt us to extricate ourselves from problematic assumptions. Reflection on those debates turns the student's rational faculties onto themselves so that reason may become known to itself through its activities. Plausible conclusions, meanwhile, provide a provisional framework while we work through a process of more aporetic scrutiny and more self-reflection. While familiarity with philosophical applications of the liberal arts might speed the process along, the liberal arts themselves are merely formalized versions of processes that flow from human nature. The dialogues thus present Monica, an uneducated woman, uttering the deep truths of learned men,[15] and the young Licentius as a model for his father to imitate, since "no age may complain that it is excluded from Philosophy's breasts." (*Philosophia ... a cuius uberibus se nulla aetas quereretur excludi*).[16] The dialogues themselves are centrally concerned with modelling this process and articulating the method through which it is carried out.[17] The teacher they present is not Aristotle's learned professor or seasoned coach but a Socratic stingray who embraces perplexity and presents himself as a student engaged in the search for a higher form of living.[18]

In the Cassiciacum dialogues, this search for true virtue is structured in the dialogues around cues taken from Scripture. This shows us something about what Augustine thought of Scripture in 386. Wisdom 11:20's "measure, number, weight" supplies the key images for the scenic dialogues,

---

[14] See, for instance, *De ord.* 2.25's discussion of the order of life. [15] *De beata v.* 10.

[16] *C. Acad.* 1.4. See Conclusion for discussion of the relevance of age to the process of philosophy.

[17] It is perhaps for this reason that studies that look to the dialogues for "Augustine's early view," rather than how he presents that view, have so thoroughly failed to appreciate the pedagogical value and sophistication of these works. See Introduction.

[18] Or as one of my students, Kolten Ellis, put it upon reading a draft of this chapter, "Augustine's idea is that the process of looking for answers makes us better people" (Rollins College Philosophy & Religion Club, September 23, 2015).

while 1 Corinthians 13:13's "faith, hope, love" structures the three rounds of ARP spread across *Sol.* + *De imm. an.* While the paucity of scriptural reference in these dialogues has led scholars like Alfaric to see them as more Platonist than Christian,[19] I would turn the tables. Just as *Conf.* devotes two whole books to exploring the first line of *Genesis*, the scenic dialogues, six books in total, present a protracted meditation on a single phrase from *Wisdom. Sol.* + *De imm. an.*, in turn, devotes three books to a single phrase from Paul. If anything, Augustine is paying less attention to Scripture as time goes on. But rather than trying to gauge how Christian Augustine was – particularly when that is understood in terms of how often he quotes Scripture – we would do better to ask what he is doing with that Christianity. At the most basic level, the Cassiciacum dialogues use Christian Scripture as a means of purification, a tool for helping us come to know the soul and God as we reorder our lives around what is truly human in us.

---

[19] See Introduction for review of this scholarly debate.

CHAPTER 7

Piety, Pride and the Problem of Evil
De libero arbitrio

De libero arbitrio is perhaps Augustine's most famous dialogue among philosophers, and rightly so. This work sets out the "Augustinian" solution to the problem of evil. Its proof for God's existence is a clear forerunner of Anselm's ontological argument. Its method of "faith seeking understanding," meanwhile, has been an inspiration to rationally minded Christians for centuries. The last of Augustine's seven dialogues, *De lib. arbit.* presents Augustine's attempt to lead his friend Evodius to an understanding of evil along the same path that Augustine himself travelled. Evodius was not part of the Cassiciacum community that made up the cast of *C. Acad.*, and in many ways, this last dialogue seems a far cry from the first. Here Augustine looks to Isaiah, not the Academy, for methodological guidance. The early works were infused with skeptical language and methods but short on Scripture. *De lib. arbit.* is thick with Scripture and seems opposed to skepticism at the deepest level. On any standard reading, book 2 does not argue that God "plausibly" exists. It sets out to prove that God in fact does exist. Book 3's turn to Genesis for an explanation of evil seems a far cry from the early dialogues' critical search for truth. In short, with *De lib. arbit.* Augustine appears to be engaged in a new project. As a result, even readers who are willing to accept my analysis of the earlier dialogues' methodology may be reluctant to see *De lib. arbit.* as cast in the same mold. The present chapter gives my response to this worry. In what follows I argue that the apparent differences between the first and the last of Augustine's dialogues are simply apparent and little more.

The first step in moving beneath surface appearances is to note that *De lib. arbit.* has also struck many scholars as a rather badly organized work. Readers commonly complain of the needless repetition between its first two books and of the descent from philosophical rigor to sermonizing in the third.[1] While its tone is more "churched" than what came before, I argue that the key to

---

[1] These supposed flaws are often attributed to the fact that Augustine wrote the three books over a number of years. Simon Harrison lays out these worries in "Dissecting *de libero arbitrio*." In

reading *De lib. arbit.* as a single, tightly unified whole is to see its method of faith seeking understanding as a development of the "Platonic" method set out in *C. Acad.* This three-stage method, which I have dubbed "ARP," uses aporetic debate to "un-teach" problematic assumptions, and reflection on the rational activity as a means of acquiring self-knowledge. Both, in turn, set the stage for a final plausible conclusion, which, in Academic-skeptical fashion, is presented as richly explanatory of what came before yet still lacking the certainty of proof.[2] In previous chapters, I argued that Augustine's earliest dialogues – *C. Acad., De beata v.* and *De ord.* – were each structured around a single round of ARP. *Sol.* + *De imm. an.* extended the method by building multiple rounds of ARP around the Pauline virtues: faith, hope, love. *De Mus.* 6, in turn, presents a threefold pattern – set out at *De. ord.* 2.47 – in which two complete rounds of ARP structure inquiries into the soul and its source, God, which together set the stage for a concluding elaboration of a closing scriptural account.

    De lib. arbit.'s three books present the pattern of *Sol.* + *De imm. an.* and *De Mus.* 6 writ large. Books 1 and 2 each move through a complete course of ARP, as they inquire into the soul and God, respectively. These discussions, in turn, serve to construct a framework that is used to guide book 3's reading of Genesis. Each of the work's three books is framed around a different formulation of the problem of evil (POE). POE 1 asks whether God is to be blamed for moral evil. Augustine responds in book 1 by setting out an account of human free will as the origin of sin and of human beings, not God, bringing suffering onto themselves by breaking the mandates of eternal law. POE 2 asks whether God was wrong to give humans the free will that made sin possible in the first place. Augustine responds in book two by elaborating an account of God as the source of all goods, arguing that free will is one of these goods and concluding that sin is simply the result of human beings turning their will toward lower goods, such as bodily pleasure, in a way that shuts them off to higher goods, such

---

Augustine's Way into the Will (Oxford: Oxford University Press, 2006), 17–27, and he responds to them in "The Integrity of *de libero arbitrio,*" *ibid.,* 28–62. My aim is not to challenge Harrison's reading, which I find quite insightful, but to supplement it by setting *De lib. arbit.* within the context of Augustine's dialogue corpus as a whole. The payoff is to see that features of the work noted by Harrison reflect larger patterns at play in the corpus. See also Scott MacDonald, "Augustine." In *A Companion to the Middle Ages,* ed. Jorge Gracia & Timothy Noone, 154–171 (Oxford: Blackwell Publishing Ltd, 2003), who sets *De lib. arbit.* within the context of Augustine's thought more broadly. While MacDonald focuses on theory over method, my focus will be on method over theory.
[2] See Chapter 1 for reconstruction of this method and Chapter 2 for consideration of its status as "Platonic."

as virtue. POE 3 asks what the cause of this perverse movement of will away from higher goods might be. Augustine responds in book 3 by looking to Genesis and tracing a historical account of sin all the way back to Adam's fall and Lucifer's pride. The three books thus advance a single plausible account of sin, which is presented in three stages: *De lib. arbit.* 1 focuses on the human soul, *De lib. arbit.* 2 focuses on God, and *De lib. arbit.* 3 sets them both within a broader scriptural narrative.

Just as each of the earlier dialogues is built around a certain virtue,[3] the three books of *De lib. arbit.* are ultimately built around an exploration of piety (*pietas*). For a Latin speaker, this refers to the correct attitude of gratitude toward a benefactor, whether human or divine. Within *De lib. arbit.*, Augustine defines it as an attitude of thankfulness for goods given, an effort to think of God in the highest terms possible and a willingness to take responsibility for one's own shortcomings. He presents it as the attitude one must have when looking to Scripture for answers to life's big questions, as he himself does in book 3. What's more, it is the attitude that the philosophical inquiries of books 1 and 2 encourage Evodius to take. Piety thus provides the central means for coming to the work's final answer to the problem of evil, while thinking about the problem of evil, in turn, provides an opportunity for instilling the virtue of piety. Pride is the answer Augustine finally gives to "whence evil?" The three books of *De lib. arbit.* thus pursue a tightly unified project, as they seek to instill the virtue that corrects the very vice they identify. What's more, they do so via a method that is continuous with that of Augustine's earliest dialogues.

By presenting a reading of *De lib. arbit.* as a unified whole and articulating its unnoticed contributions to virtue theory, I hope to update the use of the work in current discussions of POE. Put in what has become a standard form, this problem states that an omnipotent, omniscient, omnibenevolent (3-O) God is not compatible with the existence of evil in the world around us. Within debates over God's existence, the problem of evil provides powerful ammunition for the atheist camp. Theists, in turn, have looked to Augustine's "free will defense" as a way of placing the blame for evil squarely on human shoulders and thus rendering the existence of a 3-O God consistent with the existence of evil that he permits but does not cause. That said, the POE debate has taken many twists and turns over the centuries, and changing preoccupations have shaped how particular generations have approached Augustine's work. The second half

---

[3] Wisdom in *C. Acad.*; moderation in *De beata v.*; justice in *De ord.*; courage in *Sol.* + *De imm. an.*; love/charity in *De Mus.*; the grades of virtue in *De quant. an.* See Chapters 1, 3–5.

of the twentieth century presents a particularly pronounced example of this, with its strong focus on questions of logical consistency. At the start of the twenty-first century, however, the debate took a turn by introducing questions of explanatory power. As a result, the time is ripe for reevaluating *De lib. arbit.*'s discussion of evil. Its explanatory frameworks, exploration of piety and particular fusion of philosophy and Scripture have more to tell us than twentieth-century discussions of POE have recognized. Let us begin by reviewing this debate as a way of framing existing approaches to *De lib. arbit.* and the new approach I advocate here.

The POE Debate from Mackie to Adams

In an infamous 1955 article, "Evil and Omnipotence," John Mackie invoked the existence of evil in an attempt to prove that God does not exist and that belief in God is positively irrational.[4] Mackie threw down the gauntlet perhaps a bit too hard, and theists were quick to respond that the best he could show was the logical incompatibility of the claims (1) "God exists" and (2) "evil exists," *provided* that (3) there is no morally sufficient reason for God to permit evil.[5] From this point on, the "logical" debate over POE took up a search for possible morally sufficient reasons for God to permit evil. Given the focus on logical consistency, it made little difference where these reasons came from or whether any of them were God's actual reasons for permitting evil. This set the agenda for late-twentieth-century readings of *De lib. arbit.* Plantinga's 1974 *God, Evil and Freedom* pursues this project with analytic abandon.[6] In the end, his account of "transworld depravity" (the idea that any possible soul might be disposed to sin at least once) may suffice to satisfy the terms of the logical debate, yet it left some wondering whether we'd lost track of the point.

If demanding God's actual reason for permitting evil sets the bar too high, particularly within a debate over God's existence, individuals came to desire at least some evidence that the reasons being bandied back and forth

---

[4] John L. Mackie, "Evil and Omnipotence," *Mind* 64 (1955): 200–212. I refer the reader to the very useful volume ed. by Marilyn McCord Adams & Robert Adams, *The Problem of Evil* (Oxford: Oxford University Press, 1990), which collects Mackie's article (chapter 1) and other key texts from the twentieth-century debate. For an accessible but critical introduction to the problem, see Chad Meister, *Evil: A Guide to the Perplexed* (London: Continuum, 2012).

[5] Nelson Pike. "Hume on Evil," *The Philosophical Review* 72 (1963): 180–197. Chapter 2 in Adams & Adams.

[6] Alvin Plantinga. "God, Evil, and the Metaphysics of Freedom" from chapter 9 (pp. 164–193) of *The Nature of Necessity* (Oxford: Clarendon Press, 1974). Chapter 5 in Adams & Adams.

might be correct. With this, the "evidentiary" debate was born.[7] From one perspective, this was progress. Yet, in a sense, it was merely a return to Mackie's attempts at proof, albeit proof aimed at probability. Such an effort supposes that our current understanding of the world's deep structures is more or less correct. For those more pessimistic about the prospects for human knowledge, however, the evidentiary debate merely amounts to a more complicated return to the drawing board.

Marilyn Adams' 1999 book, *Horrendous Evils and the Goodness of God*, revives the terms of the logical debate, yet with the added demand for conceptually rich explanations of how God may defeat the world's worst evils by organically integrating them into individuals' lives.[8] With this, the generic 3-O God of what she calls "standard restricted theism" is set aside for the particularities of actual religious tradition. Adams presents herself as a skeptical realist about theological questions. She takes there to be a truth of the matter when it comes to God's morally sufficient reasons for permitting evil, but she distances herself from claims to know what those reasons are. Her demand for explanation and historically grounded detail goes beyond mere logical consistency. Yet explanation is not evidence, at least not in the terms set out by the evidentiary debate. Her middle-way approach resets the terms of the debate, asking whether actual religions' detailed accounts of God's interactions with humanity can plausibly *explain* why God would permit the evil we see in the world around us.

From an epistemological standpoint, the recent POE debate follows moves that come surprisingly close to the inter-school of the Hellenistic period. The Stoics advocated a way of life in which the wise person never did, said or thought anything in the absence of absolute certainty. The Academic skeptics attacked this ideal as unrealistic for human beings and developed a way of life that dealt instead in plausibilities (*probabilia*), which is to say ideas with explanatory power that are nevertheless uncertain. While the Academics never denied that the truth exists, they never affirmed it either.[9] Augustine owes much to the Academics. While he parts ways with them when he affirms the existence of truth and takes himself to

---

[7] See William Rowe, "The Problem of Evil and Some Varieties of Atheism," *American Philosophical Quarterly* 16 (1979): 335–341. Chapter 7 in Adams & Adams. See also Daniel Howard-Snyder, *The Evidential Argument from Evil* (Indianapolis: Indiana University Press, 1996) for a collection of articles on either side of the debate.

[8] Marilyn McCord Adams. *Horrendous Evils and the Goodness of God* (Ithaca: Cornell University Press, 1999). See part one "Deconstructing a Problem" for her critical review of the twentieth-century debate, pp. 5–55.

[9] *Pace* Sextus, PH 1.1–4. See Chapter 1 for discussion.

know some things for certain, he retains a skeptical worry about our ability to get the whole picture right. In this, he takes a skeptical realist position broadly akin to Adams'. Most importantly, his philosophical method seeks not certainty but explanation, or, as *De lib. arbit.* puts it, his is a project of "faith seeking understanding."[10]

We will never be able to read an ancient text in a way completely unbiased by our current perspectives, yet we are often presented with more than one current perspective to choose from. I suggest that approaching *De lib. arbit.* in the spirit of Adams will allow us to set individual arguments into their overarching context and show the epistemic status of their particular claims. This will help us deepen our understanding of what *De lib. arbit.*'s response to POE actually is. *De lib. arbit.*'s project of faith seeking understanding, meanwhile, provides a model not just for dealing with evil but for approaching a range of problems about which certainty still escapes us and for doing so from within a traditional perspective, be it religious or not.

Aporia, Reflection, Plausibility (ARP) and the Rule of Piety

While a concern for piety is at work from the start of *De lib. arbit.*, Augustine does not draw attention to it until the beginning of book 3, where the discussion between Augustine and Evodius gives way to the scriptural exegesis of Augustine's concluding *oratio.*[11] Let us begin at this turning point to lay out the goal of what came before. *De lib. arbit.* 3 opens with Evodius caught in a dilemma: He is committed to two claims, yet so far as he can tell, these claims contradict each other:[12]

(1) God foreknows everything that will be.
(2) We sin not by necessity but by the will.

"Necessity" is the ancient term for determinism. In our terms, Evodius is expressing a puzzle in logical determinism, i.e. that the present truth of

---

[10] Eleanore Stump, *Wandering in Darkness* (Oxford: Oxford University Press, 2010), presents the same general call for conceptual enrichments as Adams, in this case with a focus on narrative theory, which she anchors in recent developments in neuroscience. Her response to evil takes its inspiration from Aquinas, however, and thus provides a looser point of reference for what I take to be the skeptical tenor of Augustine's approach.

[11] That said, he does drop hints, invoking piety at *De lib. arbit.* 1.5, 1.14, 1.35 and 2.54. Without the perspective of the whole, however, it is nearly impossible to see what the significance of these hints is. To my knowledge, no scholar has yet connected the dots to articulate the centrality of piety to the work as a whole.

[12] *De lib. arbit.* 3.4.

God's foreknowledge determines our future choices and thus renders our will unfree. There are various ways of disarming such puzzles (first articulated by Aristotle at *De Interpretatione* 9). Augustine points out that Evodius' problem rests on a further assumption:[13]

(3) Everything God foreknows happens not by the will but by necessity.

Having articulated this assumption, Augustine proceeds to refute it, arguing first that it makes no difference that it is *God's* foreknowledge: otherwise, God's foreknowledge would take away God's own freedom, which is surely absurd.[14] Augustine's second, more substantive argument is that Evodius has things backward: Just as it is my willing X in the past that makes my current memory of my past will true, so it is my future will for Y that makes God's present foreknowledge of my future will true.[15] When it comes to either remembering or foreknowing a will, the will in question is the truthmaker, as we would say today. While foreknowledge inverts the typical temporal priority in which a truthmaker precedes knowledge in time, we should not slip into thinking that the causal priority, in which a truthmaker precedes knowledge in explanation, has also been inverted. I will refer to this as Augustine's first-order response to Evodius' puzzle about logical determinism.

While that may be interesting in its own right, what matters for the broader structure of *De lib. arbit.* is not Augustine's solution to this particular puzzle but his reflections on the attitudes with which different people approach this puzzle.[16] When faced with Evodius' initial dilemma, some people are quicker to excuse their sins than to confess them and simply reject (2). Such people embrace fatalism and use God's inerrant foreknowledge of their sins as an excuse not to strive for anything better. Other people try to escape this dilemma by rejecting (1) on the grounds that the world is ruled by "blind chance" rather than God's divine providence. This, however, is a problematic claim for a Christian to make. A subset of this group thus tries to "fix" the problem by concluding that God's providence is merely "weak, unjust or evil" (*uel infirmam uel iniustam uel malam*),[17] yet in doing so, they merely slip into deeper

---

[13] *De lib. arbit.* 3.6.   [14] *De lib. arbit.* 3.10.   [15] *De lib. arbit.* 3.10–11.
[16] *De lib. arbit.* 3.5.
[17] *De lib. arbit.* 3.5. For those of us used to thinking about logical determinism in exclusively descriptive terms, it makes little sense to claim that God's foreknowledge is "unjust or evil." The odd slip into normative language is likely due to the Latin term *prouidentia*, which means either "foresight" (descriptive) or "oversight" (normative). Augustine's discussion is quite condensed, and he seems uninterested in pulling these two meanings apart. While this is problematic for his first-order solution

confusion. Augustine's diagnosis is that all these groups inquire "in an impious way" (*non pie*).[18] The "rule of piety" (*regula pietatis*) requires us instead always (i) to think of God in the highest terms possible, (ii) to thank God for the goods He's given us, even if they are not the greatest goods, and (iii) to acknowledge our sins and look to God for healing.[19] When it comes to Evodius' worries about logical determinism, holding to the rule of piety will strengthen our belief in both (1) and (2) and encourage us to understand how we maintain both claims without contradiction, e.g. by articulating and then rejecting (3).

While Augustine uses logical determinism to introduce his rule of piety, he presents piety as the correct attitude for inquiry into a broad range of philosophical questions. Those who embrace it, "would be neither puffed up when discoveries have been made nor bothered when discoveries have not been made; in coming to know, they would become better prepared for seeing and in not knowing they would become more favorably disposed toward searching." (*ut neque inuentis rebus inflati neque non inuentis turbulenti et cognoscendo instructiores fierent ad uidendum et ad quaerendum ignorando mitiores*).[20] With progress comes an "inflated ego." By thinking of themselves as wise, some people shut themselves off from rigorous scrutiny and become complacent in their (other) unexamined beliefs. Yet rigorous scrutiny can leave others simply distraught. By realizing that they were mistaken in some of their beliefs, they conclude that they were mistaken in all of their beliefs and are left at a total loss about how to proceed. Those who would engage in serious philosophical inquiry must walk a fine line. As we saw with Evodius' puzzle of logical determinism, the rule of piety helps individuals find this middle way.

While the language is somewhat different, we find an analogous problem spelled out in Augustine's earliest dialogue, *C. Acad.* In the opening dedication to book 2, Augustine warns his patron, Romanianus, to beware of two ways that a philosophical inquiry may go off course:

to the puzzle, his second-order reflections, so far as I can tell, hold up to scrutiny when read either normatively or descriptively. For further discussion, see Christian Parma, Pronoia *und* Providentia: *Der Vorsehungsbegriff Plotins und Augustins* (Leiden: Brill, 1971).

[18] Peter King's 2000 Cambridge translation of *De lib. arbit.* renders this "not . . . in a religious way" and elsewhere renders "*pietas*" as "religiousness." In contemporary English, "pious" and "piety" call up various connotations that King is presumably looking to avoid. But given that piety is more recognizably a virtue than religiousness, I have chosen to risk using "piety." As Socrates showed us over and over again, it is one thing to understand the name of virtue, but it is another thing to understand its essence. Ideally, *De lib. arbit.* can challenge contemporary understandings of what piety actually is and help us see why it might be considered an attractive virtue for individuals who normally cringe at the connotations of the English term.

[19] *De lib. arbit.* 3.5.   [20] *De lib. arbit.* 3.5.

But since, because of either [i] the many varied tribulations of this life, Romanianus, as you judge in your own life, or [ii] a certain mental stupor, laziness, or slowness of sluggish [minds], or [iii] despair of finding truth (for the star of wisdom does not rise before minds with the same ease as this [visible] light rises before our eyes) or [iv] the false opinion that one has already found the truth, which is the mistake of all peoples, people do not inquire after the truth diligently, if they inquire at all, and they are turned away from wanting to inquire, it happens that knowledge seldom comes to human beings and then only to the few. (*C. Acad.* 2.1)[21]

After laying out mundane obstacles, [i] and [ii], August sets out a dilemma vaguely reminiscent of *Men.*'s paradox of inquiry, explaining that inquiry can go off track either [i] by despairing at finding the truth or [ii] by falsely thinking that one has already found the truth, a state Augustine identifies with "superstition" at *C. Acad.* 2.8. In Chapter 1, I argued that *C. Acad.*'s Platonic method, ARP, is developed to overcome just such a dilemma. Aporetic debate clears away superstition, reflection on the act of debating shows that human beings are not totally without resources, and Augustine's concluding *orationes* give plausible explanations for why that is so. While *De lib. arbit.*'s language of "piety" is more overtly religious, its strategy for carrying out a fruitful inquiry into the problem of evil is, at root, the same.

The philosophical fruits of *De lib. arbit.* 1 and 2 add up to an elaborate hierarchy of goods. Through a combination of critical scrutiny and self-reflection, Augustine and Evodius classify and rank various goods as small, intermediate and great (e.g. physical pleasure, free will and justice, respectively). These hierarchies, in turn, help un-teach Evodius' everyday assumptions, first, that the world's evil amounts to nothing more than physical suffering and, second, that the best possible world would be one made up of only the best possible goods. In the course of constructing these hierarchies, *De lib. arbit.* 1 analyzes sin in terms of human beings freely choosing lesser goods over greater ones, while *De lib. arbit.* 2 argues that God is the ultimate source of all goods – small, intermediate and great. The rule of piety, with which Augustine opens *De lib. arbit.* 3, is simply the appropriate response to the conclusions of *De lib. arbit.* 1 and 2: that God is that than which nothing is higher, that human goods – even the intermediary and lower ones – are from God and that I am to blame for my own sin.

---

[21] See Chapter 1 for Latin text and discussion.

In the final analysis, the rule of piety is a reality check. By invoking it, Augustine invites us to join in *De lib. arbit.* 3's exploration of Christian Scripture, as he elaborates an account of humanity's middling position in creation as the image of God, albeit a fallen image. By being honest about ourselves, both our capabilities and our shortcomings, we stand a chance of finding a solution to POE in the pages of Scripture. In the final analysis, however, this will not prove the truth of Scripture. The dialectical debates and self-reflection of books 1 and 2, rather, put us in the right mindset to see how a scriptural narrative of creation, fall and redemption can explain the state of moral psychology in which we now find ourselves. Similar to Augustine's other dialogues, *De lib. arbit.*'s shift from debate to *oratio* marks the start of a "plausible" conclusion, which, in Adams' terms, provides a possible morally sufficient reason for God's permitting evil, one that is richly explanatory and grounded in the details of a particular religious tradition.

With this overview in place, let us now turn to the details. For those familiar with *De lib. arbit.* already, my discussion may seem to focus on the transitions between arguments more than the arguments themselves. My goal is to set out a holistic reading of the work's single project, one situated in and informed by Augustine's whole corpus of dialogues. As usual, my reading will stand or fall by how well it can make sense of the present text.

POE 1: Is God to Blame for Moral Evil? (*De lib. arbit.* 1.1–4)

The work opens with the question, "Is God the author of evil?" (*utrum deus non sit auctor mali*).[22] In this sense, at least, *De lib. arbit.* gets straight to the point. Unlike Augustine's Cassiciacum dialogues of 386CE, *De lib. arbit.* lacks the Ciceronian dedication and the Platonic scene painting. In the absence of these, our attention is focused immediately on the dialectical drama. A quick exchange clarifies that Evodius is interested in "evil done," what today we call "moral evil" (sin, crime) as opposed to "natural evil" (earthquakes, disease). With this, we have the work's first formulation of the problem of evil (POE 1): Is God to blame for the moral evil committed in the world? Augustine promises to guide Evodius through this problem "by the same route [he] used to escape" (*eo tecum agam ordine quem secutus euasi*).[23]

---

[22] *De lib. arbit.* 1.1.   [23] *De lib. arbit.* 1.4.

Inordinate Desire and Eternal Law (*De lib. arbit.* 1.5–15)

The first step is to say what "doing evil" consists in.[24] Evodius, like most of us, believes that adultery, murder and sacrilege are bad, yet Augustine responds that it is only by asking "why?" that we can move beyond mere belief and come to understand the nature of evil. Evodius begins with the obvious, "they're illegal." Augustine chides him for relying on authority (which merely supports beliefs) and points out that that the law may be wrong.[25] Evodius tries again, suggesting that such acts violate the mandate, "do unto others," but Augustine points out that this would make adultery permissible, provided the adulterer doesn't mind loaning out his wife to other adulterers.[26] Evodius is at a loss for words. Augustine suggests that "inordinate desire" (*libido*) is what makes each of these deeds evil. While the sexual connotation of "lust" is relevant to the adultery case, Augustine and Evodius proceed to apply it to murder, sacrilege and other nonsexual evils too.[27] The common denominator, Augustine suggests, is that all these acts are concerned with things that can be taken from a person against his or her will.[28] This is a crucial detail, as it draws attention to the fact that any form of punishment that one human being (or institution) can inflict on another human being involves taking things from that person against his or her will. If an individual didn't love such things in the first place, he would not suffer – in a strong sense – when they were taken away. While the government may punish me by taking away my property, for instance, I will only suffer as a result if I am overly attached to or love material goods in the first place. Evildoers love exactly this sort of thing. They thus make themselves susceptible to suffering when they are punished for their crimes.

With this, Augustine has presented the first stage of his account of temporal and eternal law. According to this, it is a basic fact of moral psychology that all and only evildoers are susceptible to suffer punishment. Since this is true at all times and in all places, Augustine deems it a mandate of eternal law. Particular human governments make use of this fact, as they work out their various legal codes and match particular punishments to particular crimes. Since these modes of punishment vary from place to place and time to time, Augustine deems them a matter of temporal law, which draws its justice from eternal law.[29] In our terms, this

---

[24] *De lib. arbit.* 1.5.   [25] *De lib. arbit.* 1.6.   [26] *De lib. arbit.* 1.7.   [27] *De lib. arbit.* 1.8–9.
[28] *De lib. arbit.* 1.11.   [29] *De lib. arbit.* 1.15.

is a pluralist account.[30] Eternal law provides an absolutist framework, which is unchanging and universally applicable. It provides the basic foundation for Augustine's moral psychology. Yet Augustine also treats temporal laws as actual laws that individuals should follow. In this, he integrates a relativistic element that may differ across cultures and change over time.

The point of this discussion is to understand how God is not to be blamed for the existence of moral evil in the world. At this point, we've learned that inordinate desire is the cause of moral evil, and people who act on such desire make themselves vulnerable to suffering temporal punishment. Yet this merely moves the question back a step: It might be that God, as Creator, is ultimately responsible for individuals' inordinate desires. To guard against this possibility, Augustine must show that it is the individual human being, and no one else, who is responsible for his or her own desires. Augustine addresses this more refined POE 1 on two different fronts: The first looks at the human will in relation to the rest of the world;[31] the second focuses on the will itself.[32]

The Will Alone Enslaves Itself to Lust (*De lib. arbit.* 1.16–22)

Augustine's first line of defense is essentially to argue that nothing of lesser power than the human individual *could* force that individual into inordinate desire, while nothing equal to or greater than that individual in power (e.g. God) *would* do so. The individual is thus responsible for his own inordinate desire, or, more colorfully, "enslaving himself to lust."[33] Augustine, as he often does, backs into this argument. He closed the previous discussion by summing up eternal law as "that by which it is just for all things to be most ordered" (*ea est, qua iustum est, ut omnia sint ordinatissima*).[34] He then proceeds to expand on the theme of order,[35] spelling out a ranked list of what has power over what. In doing so, he collects all the candidates for what may enslave the human mind to lust

---

[30] Susan Wolf, "Two Levels of Pluralism," *Ethics* 102/4 (1992): 785–798, offers a helpful discussion of pluralism as a middle way between absolutism and relativism.

[31] *De lib. arbit.* 1.16–22.   [32] *De lib. arbit.* 1.23–30.   [33] *De lib. arbit.* 1.21.

[34] *De lib. arbit.* 1.15.

[35] Following distinctions drawn by Heath, *Unity in Greek Poetics*, I'd point out that these two passages are connected both at the surface level of what the text is talking about (order) and in terms of what the text is doing (addressing POE 1). While the latter is what's really driving the discussion, the former is the immediately apparent connection. In more or less Socratic form, Augustine is encircling Evodius with one big argument, although it's not until the end that Evodius realizes this. All of this adds to the theater of the piece and is carefully calculated to build toward the book's climax. See Introduction for discussion of Heath.

into one neat "hierarchy of power" and then picks them off one group at a time.

The basic contours of this hierarchy are drawn from Augustine's favorite triad of self-reflective certainties: I exist, I live, I know (*sum, uiuo, noui*).[36] Among other things, these three certainties are impervious to skeptical attack: Anyone who can form the thought "I exist, I live, I know (e.g. that I exist and am alive)" satisfies even the Academics' requirements for certainty and has good reason for rejecting the global skepticism that they publicly preach.[37] Within *De lib. arbit.* 1, the first thing to note is that existing, living and knowing are nested activities: Everything that lives exists but not *vice versa*, while everything that knows lives (and thus also exists) but not *vice versa*. This defines a hierarchy of merely existent things (e.g. rocks), merely living things (plants and nonhuman animals) and rational beings (humans and God).[38] In a sense, existing, living and knowing are merely three modes of being, each fuller than the last. While this seems to be a merely descriptive classification, its normative implications sit just beneath the surface. In *De lib. arbit.* 2, Augustine will point out that no living thing would choose merely to exist and no rational being would choose merely to live. The fuller modes of being are in fact better modes of being. The second thing to note is that living things have power over merely existing things but not *vice versa*, and rational beings have power over both. If we grant that having power over a thing means, minimally, making it serve the purposes of one's will, then it is clear that merely existing things cannot have power over anything, except metaphorically. The more interesting relationship is between humans

---

[36] *De lib. arbit.* 1.16–17.

[37] Thanks to Descartes, whose "*cogito ergo sum*" owes much to Augustine, this line of antiskeptical argument is even more famous than Augustine set out in his work against the Academic skeptics. This is ironic, since Augustine isn't even trying to refute global skepticism in *De lib. arbit.* The similar set of certainties – I live, I remember, I will (*uiuo, memini, uolo*) – occurs at *De Trinitate* 10.14, 13.7 and 15.21. In two of these passages, Augustine explicitly names the Academic skeptics, but he doesn't seem particularly worried about refuting global skepticism there either. While we, with our Cartesian preoccupations, might find it massively exciting that we have access to certainties that can overturn global skepticism, the overall arguments of *C. Acad.*, *De lib. arbit.* and *De Trin.* suggest that Augustine himself is more interested in using the fact that we can grasp such certainties as an entry point for a discussion of human psychology. In *C. Acad.*, he uses our access to norms of rationality to argue that at least some of our thoughts plausibly originate from intellectual, i.e. nonempirical, faculties. See Chapter 1. In *De Trin.*, he uses these three self-reflective certainties as a step toward understanding the human mind as a trinity of memory, understanding and will, which in turn is merely a step toward trying to understand the Holy Trinity of Father, Son and Holy Spirit.

[38] At *De lib. arbit.* 1.16, Augustine defines knowledge as "holding by reason that which is grasped" (*ratione habere perceptum*). It is through this definition that he slides from talking of "knowing beings" to "rational beings."

and nonhuman animals. We might think that certain animals, lions for instance, are sufficiently well equipped with claws, strength and speed that they could in fact bend human beings to their will. Yet, as Augustine points out, human beings do overcome physically more powerful animals, as we see in the case of lion trainers.[39] It is our reason that allows us to do this, and a human being that allows himself to be controlled by a mere animal has willingly given up the control that is his by nature. The last thing to note is that while most of our discussion of this *scala naturae* has compared discrete beings, Augustine initiated the discussion by listing the *self*-reflective certainties: I exist, I live, I know. Just as there are rational animals (i.e. humans) and nonrational animals out in the world, there are rational and nonrational faculties within each of us. That's why I can be so sure that I live and I know. And just as humans should have power over animals, the reason within me should have power over my nonrational desires and faculties. Such a soul is "completely in order," wise and strong.

At this point, we can return to POE 1. We have already established that moral evil is the result of inordinate desire/lust. The question is whether an individual evildoer is responsible for enslaving himself to lust or not. Having laid out a hierarchy of power, we can say that nothing lower than a human has power over a human being. If we give in to a desire for gold, the gold is not doing anything. We are. Similarly, if we allow ourselves to be controlled by animals, this only takes place because we allowed it.[40] Within the class of rational human beings, Augustine argues that wisdom and power work in tandem. While someone who is not wise might wish to enslave a wise person to lust, he could not do so, for the wise person's mind is stronger than the vicious person's. Augustine is a bit vague on why this is so, but perhaps he has in mind something like bribery, which works only with people who value short-term physical benefit over long-term integrity of character. Such tactics simply won't work to sway the wise. A wise person, by contrast, could perhaps enslave a vicious person's mind to lust, e.g. by a bribe, but he would not do so, since a wise person would see that this is wrong.[41] God, finally, who is wiser and more powerful than any human being, is most capable of enslaving a mind to lust, but would least

---

[39] *De lib. arbit.* 1.16–19.
[40] My family dog, Isis, for instance, would jump up and down in excitement whenever it occurred to her that she would like a biscuit. Over time, she successfully trained my parents to comply by giving her one. Augustine's response that my parents *allowed* the dog to train them seems a useful analysis of the situation.
[41] Likewise, a wise person, even if able to enslave another wise person, would not do so.

of all do so. The only conclusion left to draw is that the individual human being enslaves himself to lust. He alone is responsible for any evil he commits and for opening himself up to suffering the punishments of temporal laws. So, while evil is both committed and suffered in our world, it is committed and suffered only by those individuals who have given themselves over to lust for things that can be lost against their will. It is their own fault not God's.

A Good Will Suffices for Happiness (*De lib. arbit.* 1.23–30)

While this is all terribly impressive, Evodius points out that this solution to POE 1 relies on the assumption that the individual human started out wise.[42] While he is willing to admit that the human race was created wise in Eden, he has trouble with the idea that each and every evildoer since then has started out wise and then willingly gave himself over to lust. Augustine responds by presenting his second main line of defense. He begins with a fourth self-reflective certainty: I will. Evodius isn't immediately sure that he has a will. Augustine responds that there's no point in Evodius asking questions if he does not will to know their answers. Evodius concedes the point.[43] Augustine proceeds to argue that external goods – riches, honors, bodily pleasures – are good only insofar as one wills to use them well. In a move foreshadowing Kant,[44] he concludes that a good will is itself more valuable than any of these things that can be lost against one's will. All that one must do to have a good will, by contrast, is to will it.[45] Doing so brings with it the classical virtues: prudence, since a good will shows what should be sought and what avoided; bravery, because a person with a good will is not pained by losing things that can be lost against his will; moderation, because he is not enslaved to inordinate desires; justice, because he is not tempted away from giving each his due.[46] Evodius easily accepts that a virtuous life such as this would be happy in the robust sense of the best life available to a human being.[47] Building on the previous discussion of temporal and eternal law, we see that a good will places temporal goods, which can be lost against one's will,

---

[42] *De lib. arbit.* 1.23–24.   [43] *De lib. arbit.* 1.25.
[44] See Kant, *Groundwork of the Metaphysics of Morals*, section 1 (4:393–4:396).
[45] *De lib. arbit.* 1.26.
[46] *De lib. arbit.* 1.27. At *De Mus.* 6.37, 43–50 Augustine makes the similar argument that love (*caritas*) leads to all the virtues. See Chapter 4.
[47] *De lib. arbit.* 1.28.

below eternal goods, which cannot. What could such an eternal good be? First and foremost is a good will itself, which requires nothing more than to will to have a good will. Whether we started out wise or not, this is within our power. Anyone who chooses otherwise is responsible for the misery that ensues. Meanwhile:

> A. *Ex quo conficitur ut, quisquis recte honesteque uult uiuere, si id se uelle prae fugacibus bonis uelit, adsequatur tantam rem tanta facilitate, ut nihil aliud ei quam ipsum uelle sit habere quod uoluit.*
> E. *Vere tibi dico, uix me contineo quin exclamem laetitia, repente mihi oborto tam magno et tam in facili constituto bono.*
> A. *Atqui hoc ipsum gaudium quod huius boni adeptione gignitur, cum tranquille et quiete atque constanter erigit animum, beata uita dicitur; nisi tu putas aliud esse beate uiuere quam ueris bonis certisque gaudere.*
> E. *Ita sentio.*

Augustine: From which it follows that anyone who wants to live rightly and honorably, if he wants himself to want this before fleeting goods, obtains so great a possession with such great ease, that for him to have what he wants is nothing other than to want what he wants.
Evodius: To tell you the truth, I can scarcely contain myself from shouting out for joy, since such a great good has suddenly appeared to me and been so easily established!
Augustine: But indeed, this very joy, which comes about through obtaining this good, when it tranquilly, peacefully and constantly arouses the soul is called the happy life; unless you think that to live happily is anything other than to rejoice in true and certain goods.
Evodius: That's just what I think. (*De lib. arbit.* 1.29)

At this point, the problem of evil has faded into the background, as Evodius is swept away with the idea that true happiness is so close at hand.

In terms of the book's overarching structure, the discussion of POE 1 has stirred up and articulated Evodius' desire for a certain kind of life. Meanwhile, this very desire/will is an integral part of the kind of life desired. In this way, reflection on the act of inquiry, its affective dimensions in particular, has advanced the inquiry.[48] While we have seen various moments of self-reflection in book 1 (I exist, I live, I know, I will), I take this final desire for happiness to provide the structural turning point in book 1's course of ARP. The discussion continues:

[48] We find a similar move in *De beata v.*, where a discussion of happiness as desire satisfaction stirs up a desire for truth, which is taken as grounds for ruling out the possibility that "ignorance is bliss." See Chapter 3.

A. *Recte. sed censesne quemquam hominum non omnibus modis uelle atque optare uitam beatam?*
E. *Quis dubitat omnem hominem uelle?*
A. *Cur igitur eam non adipiscuntur omnes? Dixeramus enim atque conuenerat inter nos uoluntate illam mereri homines, uoluntate etiam miseram, et sic mereri ut accipiant. Nunc uero existit nescio qua repugnantia, et nisi diligenter dispiciamus, perturbare nititur superiorem tam euigilatam firmamque rationem. Quomodo enim uoluntate quisque miseram uitam patitur, cum omnino nemo uelit misere uiuere?*

Augustine: Right. But do you think any human being does not in all ways want and choose the happy life?
Evodius: Who doubts that every human being wants this?
Augustine: Why then does everyone not arrive at it? For we said above, and it was agreed between us, that human beings earn happiness through the will, and they earn misery through the will, and thus they earn just as they get. But now there is some kind of contradiction, and unless we investigate diligently, it will endeavor to throw into confusion our earlier so carefully composed and steady reasoning. For how does anyone willingly suffer a miserable life when no one at all wants to live miserably? (*De lib. arbit.* 1.30)

The problem, Augustine proceeds to explain, is that a will can be "good" in two ways: willing to live happily and willing to live rightly. While everyone wills the former, many do not will the latter, which is in fact the more basic. He who successfully wills to live rightly does so, and happiness follows in its wake.

Rightly Ordered Loves (*De lib. arbit.* 1.31–35)

What does this will to live rightly actually amount to? Loving eternal goods before temporal ones. What are these eternal goods? A good place to start is the eternal law by which good people are rewarded with happiness, and evil people are rewarded with misery. Those who cannot embrace this basic setup of the world with joyous love are simply more enthralled with temporal goods than they would care to admit. Augustine proceeds to enumerate these temporal goods, which can be lost against one's will: bodily health, freedom, family, friends, one's country, honor, fame and property.[49] In the process he forces us to reevaluate our priorities, all as a means of moving us toward the proper attitude of piety.

At this point we may think that Augustine has simply set the bar too high. While many find the unbridled love of money distasteful, we tend to praise individuals who devote their lives to family, friends or country. Such desires

---

[49] *De lib. arbit.* 1.31.

hardly seem inordinate. The key, I suggest, sits in what Augustine means by
"love." He offers the thought experiment of a slave who kills his master to
escape torture (1.9–10). While there is nothing wrong with wanting to live
without being tortured, this desire becomes inordinate when it comes to
override more important aspects of one's life. Being tortured is bad. Being a
murderer is worse. The criterion for "more important" is the now familiar
question of whether a thing can be lost against one's will. Augustine draws
the Stoic conclusion that when one's desire and circumstances conflict, a
good person turns his desire away from what can be lost against his will, but
an evil person attempts to bend circumstances to meet his desire. While this
is hardly the mindset that brought institutional slavery to an end, it is decent
advice for getting through an individual life. "Loving" something in this
context means placing it before all other desires, structuring one's whole life
around it. While it is fine to desire the wellbeing of one's mother, for
instance, something has gone wrong when a person will do literally anything
for her, e.g. murder innocent people because she seems not to approve of
them. This is a perversion of a son's love for his mother, insofar as it puts
maintaining a mother's state of mind above every other end.[50]

So where do we stand relative to POE 1? *De lib. arbit.* opened with an
investigation of moral evil. By the end of book 1, the evils under consideration and their comparable goods have been relegated to the class of things
that can be lost against one's will. Health, freedom, family, friends, country
and even property, honor and fame are all in fact good, albeit secondary
goods, which are ill suited to serve as final ends around which to structure
one's life. Augustine concludes:

> *ille autem qui recte his utitur, ostendat quidem bona esse, sed non sibi – non enim*
> *eum bonum melioremue faciunt, sed ab eo potius fiunt–, et ideo non eis amore*
> *adglutinetur neque uelut membra sui animi faciat, quod fit amando, ne cum*
> *resecari coeperint, eum cruciatu ac tabe foedent, sed eis totus superferatur, et habere*
> *illa atque regere, cum opus est, paratus et amittere ac non habere paratior . . .*

> The one, however, who uses these rightly, shows that they are indeed goods
> but not *his* – for they do not make him good or better, but rather they come
> to be better through him. And thus he is not glued to them in love, nor do
> they become, as it were, limbs of his soul, which comes about through

---

[50] Modern audiences might think of Norman Bates from Alfred Hitchcock's film, *Psycho* (1960).
Augustine's slavery example is unfortunate, insofar as many today would think that escaping an
abusive master constitutes just cause for self-defense. If I am right in reading Augustine's account of
temporal and eternal law as a form of pluralism, he might respond that such killing in self-defense
would be justified in our time but not in his own.

loving, so that when they start to be cut loose, they do not befowl him with torment and infection, but he is borne totally above them and is prepared to hold and rule them, when there is need, and even more ready to send them away and not have them. (*De lib. arbit.* 1.33)

What can serve as a final end? That's still a bit vague, although we can be sure that it must be something that cannot be lost against one's will. Still, we've made progress in that we have refined the problem under consideration. The real problem with evil isn't that God permits good people to suffer robbery, torture or even murder. Truly good people do not "suffer" in these things at all. The real problem is that God allows inordinate desire to drive individuals to commit such crimes in the first place. Initial appearances to the contrary, evil doers are the real victims of the world's worst evil. Yet, as we've seen, such individuals are alone to blame for enslaving themselves to lust, which, Evodius concludes, they do "from the free choice of the will" (*ex libero uoluntatis arbitrio*).[51] At this point, Evodius is content to declare POE 1 solved. Yet this solution raises the obvious question: Is God to blame for giving us free will in the first place? With this, we arrive at POE 2, which is addressed in the work's next book.

Taking Stock of *De lib. arbit.* 1

Before turning to POE 2, let us step back and evaluate *De lib. arbit.*'s proposed solution to POE 1. Augustine began by articulating POE 1, "is God to blame for moral evil?"[52] and analyzed moral evil in terms of lust/inordinate desire, explaining how lust makes one susceptible to suffering temporal law's punishments.[53] From here he gave two arguments for why each evil human being is responsible for enslaving himself to lust.[54] Yet his second argument led to the conclusion that anyone who wills to be happy will be happy, which is clearly not the case.[55] Augustine responded to that puzzle with the plausible suggestion that we may achieve happiness by structuring our use of temporal goods, which can be lost against our will, around our love of eternal goods, which cannot be (1.30–35). With this account neatly laid out, it is obvious that human free will is to blame for the moral evil of the world. POE 1 solved.

Evodius finds this all quite appealing, yet Augustine's final account of rightly ordered loves hardly follows with deductive necessity from what went before. At best, he's shown that the love of eternal goods does not run

---

[51] *De lib arbit.* 1.35.   [52] *De lib. arbit.* 1.1–4.   [53] *De lib. arbit.* 1.5–15.
[54] *De lib. arbit.* 1.16–30.   [55] *De lib. arbit.* 1.30.

afoul of the problems that love of temporal goods does. Yet it may run afoul of other problems. A *Harry Potter* fan, for instance, may develop imaginary relationships with the faculty and students of Hogwarts, structuring his life around the demands of this imaginary world.[56] Such a commitment can only be taken away if the individual is willing to have it be. By *De lib. arbit.* 1's definitions, this would thus be an eternal good. Yet we would hardly say that such a fanatic is living the best life possible for a human being. At the very least, book 1's account of a suitable first good is underdetermined. While Augustine does not explicitly invoke the language of the Academic skeptics here, their concept of plausibility nicely sums up the book's final conclusion. This may strike some as a disappointment. To evaluate the success of *De lib. arbit.* 1 in its own terms, though, we must first articulate what the text is meant to accomplish.

Augustine presents *De lib. arbit.* 1 as an exercise in "faith seeking understanding."[57] The phrase comes from a mistranslated version of Isaiah 7:9, "Unless you believe, you will not understand."[58] While it is pointless to ask what Isaiah might have meant by this phrase – which he never actually said – Augustine treats faith seeking understanding as a process of setting beliefs within broader explanatory frameworks.[59] Evodius started out believing that theft, adultery and murder are instances of moral evil, that God is not responsible for such evils and perhaps even that human free will is the root of the problem. By the end of book 1, however, he has a much clearer understanding of how these ideas fit together. While he still might not be certain of the truth of this broader picture, he has come to see its explanatory power. To put it in *C. Acad.*'s terms, Evodius has "unlearned" mere faith (e.g. the idea that something is wrong because it is illegal) and opened himself up to Augustine's more richly, albeit uncertain, explanatory account of inordinate desire. As I have reconstructed book 1's argument, all of this has been accomplished through a course of ARP. The dialectical debate over the nature of evil helped refine POE 1 and show what is at stake. The process of inquiry, meanwhile, stirred up a desire in

---

[56] See the works of J. K. Rawlings. I thank Ronald Scott Novak, a student in my Evil seminar at Rollins College, for this particular example.

[57] *De lib. arbit.* 1.4.

[58] The Latin version available to Augustine at the time, which he cites at *De lib. arbit.* 1.4, is "*Nisi credideritis, non intellegetis.*" The Hebrew original says something closer to "Unless you believe, you will not stand firm," which is better captured by the Vulgate's translation, "*si non credideritis non permanebitis.*"

[59] For a more detailed analysis, see Norman Kretzmann, "Faith Seeks, Understanding Finds: Augustine's Charter for Christian Philosophy." In *Christian Philosophy*, ed. Thomas Flint, 1–36 (Notre Dame: University of Notre Dame Press, 1990).

Evodius for a higher kind of good. Reflection on this desire leads to an *aporia*, exposing the shortcomings of his thinking.[60] Augustine responds by suggesting a plausible account of using temporal goods for the sake of eternal loves. While this account is not demonstratively proven, it sidesteps initial, superficial assumptions that led Evodius into *aporia* and provides a theoretical framework for the book's self-reflective discoveries. As with any plausible solution, the progress made is still provisional. While book 1 has a degree of integrity unto itself, its final account solves one version of POE only to raise another. This progression from POE 1 to POE 2 constitutes the first of book 1's two main contributions to the project of *De lib. arbit.* as a whole.

The second contribution of *De lib. arbit.* 1 is to set the stage for Augustine's rule of piety. Anyone reading their discussion in the way I've suggested should feel Evodius' elation as he reflects on his desire for true happiness, share his disappointment as hope for this crashes into *aporia* and breathe a sigh of relief as Augustine explains where they went wrong. All of this is carefully orchestrated. Through such a process of perplexity and self-reflection we improve our understanding of ourselves as human and our place in the world. In so doing, we come to appreciate the goods we have been given and take responsibility for the evils we bring on ourselves. In short, we take on a more pious attitude and move forward in preparing ourselves for the scriptural explorations of *De lib. arbit.* 3.

POE 2: Was God Right to Give Free Will, through Which Moral Evil Is Possible? (*De lib. arbit.* 2.1–7)

De lib. arbit. 2 opens as Augustine and Evodius ask whether God was right to give us free will, through which moral evil is possible.[61] The obvious response is "yes," but that seems to conflict with the basic idea that God is just. Augustine proceeds to spell out this problem, which I've dubbed POE 2, in terms of three claims that generate the unwanted conclusion:

(1)   God exists.
(2)   All goods come from God.
(3)   Free will, which makes moral evil possible, is one of these goods.
(C)   Thus, God is responsible for moral evil.

Each of these claims is central to Christian belief. Evodius himself believes (1), (2) and (3), but wants to understand them in such a way that he can

---

[60] *De lib. arbit.* 1.30.   [61] *De lib. arbit.* 2.1.

see why God is not responsible for evil, which he also believes.[62] He would particularly like to know why God didn't give free will in such a way that it could only be used rightly, just as justice can only be used rightly.[63] In reply, Augustine leads Evodius through a long and intensely self-reflective discussion – *De lib. arbit.* 2.7–29 – and responds, in turn, to each of Evodius' problematic claims, which he rephrases at 2.7 as a series of questions:

Questions	Response at
(Q1) How is it clear that God exists?	*De lib. arbit.* 2.30–39
(Q2) Do all things, insofar as they are good, come from God?	*De lib. arbit.* 2.40–47
(Q3) Is free will to be counted among these goods?	*De lib. arbit.* 2.47–54

In this way, POE 2 provides the structure for the whole of book 2.

The middle chunk of this book – *De lib. arbit.* 2.7–39 – is normally taken to be Augustine's proof for the existence of God and the forerunner to both Anselm's so-called ontological argument[64] and the fourth of Aquinas' five ways.[65] That is fine, so far as it goes, yet I would point out that Augustine's version of this proof is imbedded in a larger structure that follows *C. Acad.*'s method, ARP. In this case, aporetic debate has been distilled into the opening passage,[66] in which POE 2 is spelled out as the three particular claims that are the root of the problem. While the book's proof proceeds through a series of arguments, the bulk of them ultimately just draws our attention to our own rational activity. Given the precedence of *C. Acad.* and the other dialogues, I hope that readers familiar with this passage will find it helpful to think of it as an epic course of self-reflection. Some readers, however, will be less willing to accept that book 2 is aimed at a merely plausible conclusion. After all, *De lib. arbit.* 2 offers a proof of God's existence, one which occupies an important place in the history of such proofs. This is one point at which *De lib. arbit.* seems simply to occupy a different thought world than *C. Acad.* To read *De lib. arbit.* 2 as some kind of provisional, skeptically inspired undertaking would be an affront to the grand traditions of rational theology.

I suggest that *De lib. arbit.* 2 offers two kinds of conclusion. Standard readings are right that Augustine takes himself to prove as certain that some highest being exists. Yet standard readings are wrong to stop there.

---

[62] *De lib. arbit.* 2.5.   [63] *De lib. arbit.* 2.4.   [64] Anselm, *Proslogion* 2–4.
[65] Aquinas, *Summa Theologiae* I.2.3.   [66] *De lib. arbit.* 2.1–7.

Having concluded that a highest being exists, Augustine proceeds to identify it with the God of Abraham as described by Scripture.[67] The jump from highest being to "God" relies on the authority of Scripture in ways that undermine Augustine's attempt to offer demonstrative proof. I suggest that Augustine is well aware of this, since the jump is clearly marked in the text: Augustine draws his first conclusion about a highest being through discussion with Evodius, yet he sets out his second conclusion about God via a short *oratio*. We find the same pattern repeated for his response to Q2 and Q3: Passages of dialogue treat God in the generic terms of restricted standard theism, while *orationes* invoke more nuanced accounts of the God of Scripture. In other words, the end of *De lib. arbit.* 2 alternates between the styles of Plantinga and of Adams. I suggest that these passages of dialogue with Evodius are meant to arrive at certainty, while the passages of *oratio* allow Augustine to go further, hinting at a broader explanatory framework that provides a context for these certainties without claiming to be certain of that context. In short, Augustine uses these *orationes* to present plausible conclusions. While this is somewhat more elaborate than what we've seen in the dialogues up to this point, it is a clear variation on the same literary form and philosophical method. Let us walk briefly through the stages of this argument and then step back to consider the advantages of recognizing the methodological continuities between *C. Acad.* and the middle book of *De lib. arbit.*

An Epic Course of Self-Reflection (*De lib. arbit.* 2.7–29)

The self-reflective middle of *De lib. arbit.* 2 supports Augustine's responses to all three of Evodius' questions. Yet he and Evodius approach this task with the first of them foremost in mind, viz. how is it clear that God exists?[68] In approaching this question, they offer a formal description of God as (a) higher than the highest element in human nature and (b) that than which nothing else is higher.[69] The task is to show that something exists that meets this description. Augustine suggests that if they find something higher than human nature, (a), then either this thing will meet condition (b) or something higher than it will meet (b) and thus (a) too by implication. Either way, something meets both conditions, and thus God

---

[67] In what follows, I will use "God" (with a capital G) as the proper name of Scripture's central figure, as opposed to a mere highest being or generic "god."

[68] At *De lib. arbit.* 2.47, Augustine comments that in answering Q1, they have answered Q2 and Q3 also.

[69] *De lib. arbit.* 2.14.

exists. The real task, then, is to find something that meets (a), and this will "suffice" to show that God exists.[70]

Their search moves through five broad stages. The first uses a protracted course of self-reflection to establish that reason is the highest element in human nature.[71] The second sets out secondary criteria for identifying something higher than human reason. Augustine argues that since an individual's reason (e.g. Evodius') is subject to change and is private to him, anything that is (c) eternal/unchanging and (d) common to all would be better than the best thing in that individual.[72] Augustine's full list of criteria for identifying God is thus:

(a)   Higher than the highest element in human nature
(b)   That than which nothing else is higher
(c)   Eternal/unchanging
(d)   Common

The third and fourth stages of Augustine's argument engage in further self-reflection to establish that number[73] and wisdom[74] meet Augustine's secondary criteria, (c) and (d), respectively. The fifth and final stage argues that number and wisdom are in fact the same thing, and cites Christian Scripture, which identifies both with God.[75] The first four of these stages, at least, amount to an extended course of self-reflection, which is meant to provide us with knowledge that is certain.

Stage one begins by once again invoking the self-reflective triad: I exist, I live, I know.[76] In book 1, Augustine used these three elements of human nature to rank human beings above nonrational animals and both above inanimate objects.[77] In book 2, he uses the same starting point to articulate and rank a human being's own perceptual and cognitive faculties.[78] Let's take a familiar example from seminar rooms: a cup of coffee. Each of my[79] five bodily senses takes this physical thing as its object, albeit each in its own way: I see the steam rising from its surface, feel its warmth in my hand, smell its savory aroma as it approaches my face, taste its full-bodied complexity and hear the dull clink as I set it back on the table. Yet there are many things that feel warm, e.g. a brick left in the sun, which I would not be tempted to drink from. As far as my sense of touch goes, however, warm is warm. There must therefore be some faculty of the mind, beyond the

---

[70] *De lib. arbit.* 2.14.   [71] *De lib. arbit.* 2.7–13.   [72] *De lib. arbit.* 2.14–19.
[73] *De lib. arbit.* 2.20–24.   [74] *De lib. arbit.* 2.25–29.   [75] *De lib. arbit.* 2.30–39.
[76] *De lib. arbit.* 2.7.   [77] *De lib. arbit.* 1.16–19.   [78] *De lib. arbit.* 2.8–10.
[79] Given the centrality of self-reflection to this line of thought, I will engage extensively in first-person writing, with the understanding that readers may form the same thoughts for themselves.

five senses, which coordinates the five senses. We might think that "reason" is the obvious candidate, yet Augustine points out that nonrational animals are just as capable of coordinating sense modalities. He thus posits an "inner sense" (*sensus interior*) as necessary for explaining both human and animal behavior. While this inner sense cannot be sensed by any of the five bodily senses, the inner sense can sense each of the bodily senses as well as their content.[80] Augustine invokes this asymmetry to show the superiority of the inner sense over the bodily senses. In a self-reflective twist, he then points out that in the course of their discussion, he and Evodius have been using reason to think about the inner sense, the bodily senses and their various objects. It thus follows that reason can take each of these as its object. Yet it is not possible for my inner sense, my bodily senses or my cup of coffee to take reason as its object. With this, Augustine spells out a new hierarchy of perception/cognition, beginning with physical objects and moving up through the bodily senses and inner sense to reason as the highest human faculty.[81]

Stage two takes up the search for something higher than human reason. Book 2's discussion up to this point has come to the same conclusion as book 1's. Both present reason as the pinnacle of human nature. Book 2 moved the discussion forward, though, by presenting human senses and reason as

---

[80] The fact that the inner sense coordinates the contents of the bodily senses makes it clear that the inner sense is aware of their content. That the inner sense is aware of the senses themselves becomes apparent when things go wrong. Imagine, for instance, that in the midst of a riveting discussion of evil, I absentmindedly reach for my coffee but miss. My inner sense realizes that I have failed to touch, and it will direct my gaze at the object so that I can make a second attempt. This time, sight and touch report successful content, and I proceed to sip my coffee. The inner sense is thus aware of the sense of touch itself, even when it fails to report anything.

[81] At the outset, I claimed that this whole passage is basically one protracted project in self-reflection. Yet in arguing for the existence of an inner sense from the fact that we cannot explain certain behaviors merely in terms of the bodily senses, Augustine may seem to be moving from *aporia* and self-reflection to a plausible explanation. We find an analogous move in *C. Acad.* 3, where the fact that we carry with us certain norms of thought that we could not acquire through the senses is used to set up a Platonic account of nonempirical intellectual faculties. I take this passage of *C. Acad.* 3 to be a paradigmatic case of the jump from *aporia* and self-reflection to a plausible conclusion. For the sake of consistency, it seems I should take *De lib. arbit.* 2's claims about the inner sense as merely plausible as well. The difference, I suggest, is in the degree of specification. If *C. Acad.* had stopped at "nonempirical," then Augustine would simply be stating the conclusion that necessarily followed from the foregoing combination of *aporia* and reflection. Yet *C. Acad.* keeps going by invoking details of Platonic intellectualism that are rendered merely plausible by what came before. Augustine's claims about the inner sense are not comparably loaded. When he invokes the inner sense, all he attributes to it are actions that cannot be explained by the bodily sense alone, yet cannot be attributed to reason either insofar as nonrational animals also perform them. "Inner sense" is thus a placeholder for whatever it is by which we carry out these actions. This passage, in the final analysis, amounts to a way to make us notice and think about our activities. I thus classify the whole passage as a protracted exercise in self-reflection.

faculties that take objects. Thus far, each object of reason discussed –
physical things, bodily senses, inner sense – has been lower than reason.
Insofar as we can think about thinking, it is also clear that reason can take an
object equal to itself, i.e. reason. The real question is whether reason can take
an object that is higher than itself. Augustine's strategy is to characterize
human reason in such a way that we can say what something better than it
would be like. The first thing to note is that human reason changes. Each of
us is born in a state little different from other animals, and our reason
develops over time. Augustine takes this to be a mark of imperfection and
suggests that something that is eternally complete and unchanging would be
better than changeable reason.[82] He also points out that human reason is
private in the sense that I have my own reason, which has been developed to
a certain degree, while you have your own reason, which has been developed
to a different degree. Reason's lower objects are likewise private: While you
and I both have sight and can see the same object, e.g. my coffee cup, we
cannot see exactly the same part of it, from the same angle, at the same time.
Likewise for the other senses:[83] in the case of sight, hearing and touch, one
perceiver simply gets in the other's way; in the case of taste and smell, both
of which Augustine understands to be kinds of nutrition, one act of
perception "uses up" the precise bit of the substance being perceived.[84]
Augustine presents this as a kind of limitation and suggests that something
common, which could be fully perceived by everyone simultaneously without being used up, would be superior to my private reason and its various
other objects. If we want to find something higher than the highest element
of human nature, i.e. something to meet criterion (b), we should thus look
for something that is eternally unchanging and common, i.e. something that
meets criteria (c) and (d).

Stage three begins as Evodius presents "number" as a candidate for
something eternal, common and thus higher than human reason.[85] This
seems obvious enough, given that the sum of seven and three has always
been, is now and ever shall be ten. What's more, my thinking about this in
no way precludes anyone else from thinking about this. Augustine, however, raises the worry that we come to know numbers through our bodily
senses, e.g. by counting apples in preschool. If this is right, then we derive
numbers from physical objects, which are changeable and private, and it
follows that numbers themselves must be changeable and private to some

---

[82] De lib. arbit. 2.14.   [83] De lib. arbit. 2.15–19.
[84] See De lib. arbit. 2.19 for an earthy discussion of nurses chewing food for infants.
[85] De lib. arbit. 2.20–24.

degree, too. Evodius is not impressed. Even if we get our knowledge of numbers through counting apples, he replies, it is by the "light of the mind," not images drawn from the senses, that we judge whether one's math is correct.[86] Augustine commends him for this but points out that he need not even admit that we learn numbers through the senses. He points out, first, that all numbers ultimately derive from "one." Turning the empiricist's worry against him, Augustine also points out that each and every physical object is composed of parts: Even atoms have a top, middle and bottom, each of which has a top, middle and bottom, and so on. When we look to physical things, we find plurality not unity. "For when I seek unity in a body, and I have no doubt that I do not find it, I do at any rate know what I am seeking there, what I am not finding there and that it cannot be found there or, better yet, is totally not there to start with." (*Cum enim quaero unum in corpore et me non inuenire non dubito, noui utique quid ibi quaeram et quid ibi non inueniam et non posse inueniri uel potius omnino ibi non esse*).[87] Empiricism cannot adequately explain our grasp of numbers, which Augustine concludes must be intellectual in origin.[88] The empiricist challenge is thus set aside, and the work's first candidate for something higher than the highest element of human nature has been established.

While stage three and stage four both proceed via rational inquiry and reflection, Augustine links the two of them by setting them within a broader scriptural context. As Ecclesiastes 7:26 points out, "My heart and I have gone around so that I might search out and think about and know wisdom and number." This passage serves two purposes within the immediate context. First, it presents something that Evodius already believes, or presumably would believe if pressed. The discussion up to this point has thus brought Evodius to understand why number is a fitting object of searching out, thinking about and knowing. Second, it links number with wisdom, which is Augustine's second candidate for something higher than human reason. While most of us are comfortable granting that there is just one right answer for any given problem in arithmetic, many would be less comfortable thinking about wisdom (*sapientia*) in such black-and-white terms. We might agree that wisdom

---

[86] Evodius has apparently read Augustine's *De Mag.* or is at least familiar with the Platonic tropes about the "light of truth," which he here applies to mathematics.

[87] *De lib. arbit.* 2.22.

[88] With this, Augustine gives a short version of *C. Acad.*'s central argument that we acquire the norms of rational thought through intellectual, not empirical, means. For present purposes, though, he does not stress the intelligible or causal status of numbers, but their commonality and eternity.

is the knowledge through which we attain happiness (*beata*), or, as Augustine puts it, "the truth in which the highest good is seen and grasped" (*ueritatem in qua cernitur et tenetur summum bonum*).[89] Yet different people find happiness in different things. Evodius lists military service, farming, money making and philosophy. Scripture notwithstanding, "wisdom" seems like a poor candidate for a single thing common to all rational minds.

Stage four responds to this worry by seeking to establish a single, common wisdom amid all this diversity of opinion.[90] The basic problem, as I reconstruct Augustine's argument, is that we normally conceptualize wisdom as a body of first-order normative knowledge: If engaged in phalanx warfare, circle around the enemy and come at them from behind; if vines are producing few grapes, prune them; buy cheap and sell dear. Since people disagree about which bits of first-order advice are relevant to happiness, we arrive at *aporia* about the unity of wisdom. Augustine moves beyond this *aporia* by inviting us to reflect on the second-order criteria by which we think about happiness and judge whether or not we have attained it.[91] While we might disagree about what happiness and wisdom consist in, we can be certain that we all have the desire to be happy and wise. What's more, we do not have to take a poll to be certain that everyone wants to be happy and wise.[92] This is a bold claim. Yet if we're honest with ourselves, we should admit that Augustine has a point. If a person claims that he doesn't want to be happy, we assume that he's either lying or has misunderstood what we mean by "happy." We thus press him until he admits what we already know he has to admit: that he in fact does want to be happy. Even before we're happy, Augustine explains, we have a basic grasp, a "notion" (*notio*) of happiness through which we recognize that we want to be happy.[93] What's more, we all have the same basic notion, which is why we won't accept disagreement on whether someone wants to be happy, even if we disagree about what happiness consists in. Likewise for wisdom. In drawing these conclusions, Augustine has not relied on any particular first-order account of happiness. In fact, he invokes Plato's Sun analogy to distinguish between the "objects" of first-order accounts of happiness and the single "light of wisdom" in which we view them.[94] As with number, we might seem to learn about other people's

---

[89] *De lib. arbit.* 2.26.   [90] *De lib. arbit.* 2.25–29.
[91] In contemporary terms, he avoids an impasse in normative theory by pushing the discussion into metaethics.
[92] *De lib. arbit.* 2.28.   [93] *De lib. arbit.* 2.26.   [94] *De lib. arbit.* 2.27.

desires for happiness through experience of particular cases, i.e. by talking with people. Augustine describes such "notions" as the "rules and certain beacons of virtues" (*regulas et quaedam lumina uirtutum*),[95] i.e. basic certainties shared by all rational beings, which serve as norms of rational thought. Yet these notions are not arrived at by inference from particular cases; they follow from the structure of rationality itself, as will be obvious to anyone who thinks about it long enough.[96] Augustine thus presents wisdom as a second candidate for something higher than the highest element of human nature. With this, *De lib. arbit.*'s self-reflective project is complete.

Q1: How Is It Clear That God Exists? (*De lib. arbit.* 2.30–39)

At this point, Augustine and Evodius have established that reason is the highest element of human nature, and they have identified both number and wisdom as, (a), higher than that. It is unclear whether these two higher realities amount to the same thing, whether one is higher than the other or whether some further reality is higher than both. None of this matters to the argument, though, since Evodius has already agreed that whatever the hierarchy stops at, we can call that God. By *De lib. arbit.* 2.30, Augustine thus has everything he needs to respond to Q1: How is it clear that God exists? We should note, however, that he does not conclude his line of

---

[95] *De lib. arbit.* 2.29.

[96] In claiming shared notions of happiness and wisdom, Augustine has invoked the Stoic doctrine of common concepts (Gr: *proleipseis, ennoiai*). As strict empiricists, the Stoics held that we acquired these norms through bodily experience, albeit with the aid of providence and certain innate dispositions. See Chapter 1. Through his characteristic combination of *aporia* and self-reflection, Augustine takes a Platonist route to the same conclusion. The fact that everyone wants to be happy is not the conclusion of philosophical inquiry, it is the presupposition, and we can be certain of its truth by simply thinking about the structure of our rational thought and desires, all of which presuppose this basic, structuring idea. Having discussed happiness and wisdom with some care, Augustine proceeds to list several other notions pertaining to ethical inquiry (*De lib arbit.* 2.28–29): (a) one should live justly; (b) lower things should be subordinate to better things; (c) equal things should be compared to equal things; (d) one's own things should be attributed to each; (e) the uncorrupted is better than the corrupted; (f) the eternal is better than the temporal; (g) the inviolable is better than the violable; (h) the mind should be turned from corruption toward uncorruption; (i) a life that is not turned away from a sure and honorable way of thinking is better than one that is easily shattered and overthrown by temporal misfortunes. We might find some of these dubious, yet Augustine claims that these notions are common to all rational beings. The majority of these notions have in fact been central in guiding *De lib. arbit.*'s inquiry up to this point. Augustine has spelled out several hierarchies over the course of *De lib. arbit.* 1 and 2: whether you agree with his rankings or not, you are invoking (b) and (c) in doing so. *De lib. arbit.* 1's discussion of temporal and eternal law presupposed the very basic (e), (g) and (i), while (f) and (h) are simply refinements of them. Having already used these notions, we should now be in a position to embrace the claim that these notions are presupposed by the act of ethical inquiry.

thought until 2.39. A passage of *oratio perpetua* (2.30–39) sits between the end of stage four and Augustine's final response to Q1. In the course of this speech, Augustine describes God as Trinity,[97] Incarnate Redeemer[98] and Object of delight.[99] While book 2's argument may prove the existence of a highest being, as presented by restricted generic theism, it at best shows the plausibility of Augustine's more richly detailed depiction of this highest being as presented by Scripture.[100] This ambiguity is reflected in the conclusion to the discussion of Q2:

> A. *Est enim deus, et uere summeque est. Quod iam non solum indubitatum, quantum arbitror, fide retinemus, sed etiam certa, quamuis adhuc tenuissima, forma cognitionis adtingimus. Quod quaestioni susceptae sufficit ut cetera quae ad rem pertinent, explicare possimus, nisi quid habes aduersus ista quae opponas.*
> E. *Ego uero incredibili omnino et quam tibi uerbis explicare non possum laetitia perfusus accipio ista, et clamo esse certissima.*

> **Augustine:** For God exists, truly and in the highest degree. This we now hold not only by faith as something undoubted, so far as I see it, but we even touch with a form of understanding[101] which is certain even if still very thin. This suffices for the inquiry we have set out on, as we can disentangle the other things that pertain to this matter, unless you have anything against these things, which you might want to oppose.
> **Evodius:** I am just so overwhelmed by a completely unbelievable joy which I cannot express to you in words! I accept the things you are saying and cry out that they are most certain. (*De lib. arbit.* 2.39)

What exactly is Augustine referring to as the object of his "very thin yet certain" understanding? And why does Evodius respond that he is "most certain"? If Augustine has the existence of Scripture's God in mind, then he has offered a quite bad proof and should not be claiming certainty.[102] If he has in mind some generic highest being, then the rich particulars of Augustine's *oratio* are an unnecessary and potentially misleading distraction.[103]

---

[97] *De lib. arbit.* 2.39.   [98] *De lib. arbit.* 2.37.   [99] *De lib. arbit.* 2.35.

[100] The idea that God is the object of delight is equally at home within Platonism, as Augustine makes clear by invoking a Platonic sun analogy at *De lib. arbit.* 2.36. The idea that we should take delight in God is thus not *exclusively* scriptural, yet I would not go so far as to call it part of restricted standard theism.

[101] While I have been translating "*cognitio*" as "grasp" in Stoic contexts, the contrast here with "*fide*" and the work's overall method of "faith seeking understanding" suggest "understanding" as the better translation.

[102] By Augustine's own standards at *C. Acad.* 2.1.9, this would amount to superstition. See Chapter 1.

[103] From the standpoint of the work's proof, they could just as well be removed or replaced by a description of the Manichees' Light God, Allah or even Zeus, under the right description.

The key, I suggest, sits in recognizing that Augustine takes both the particular and generic depictions of God to refer to one and the same God. "Highest being" is one quality of the God of Scripture. Augustine has succeeded in making Evodius certain that God, under the description "highest being," exists. Yet Scripture says quite a lot more about God too. Book 2's argument has not proven these further details, and their understanding is thus "slight." Nevertheless, the self-reflective project up to this point has brought Evodius to a new level of self-knowledge for which scriptural descriptions of God provide a richly explanatory context. In approaching "that which is higher than the highest thing in human nature" via number and wisdom, Augustine leads Evodius to poke his head into a higher world. What he finds are realities that are eternal and common to all rational beings. Augustine embraces the idea of commonality to present Christ as the Truth (*ueritas*), who "welcomes all her [*sic*] lovers who are in no way envious of each other" (*Omnes amatores suos nullo modo sibi inuidos recipit*).[104] That this Truth is one person of a Triune God responsible for creating the universe is, in *De lib. arbit.*'s terms, still a matter of faith. Yet, given what's led up to this point, it would certainly explain a lot. In *C. Acad.*'s terms, the *oratio* of *De lib. arbit.* 2.30–39 presents a plausible conclusion to the book's reflections. As for the broader project of *De lib. arbit.*, book 1 characterized eternal goods as those that cannot be lost against our will; at *De lib. arbit.* 2.37–38, Augustine explains why this is the case. His explanation operates on two fronts.

First, *De lib. arbit.* 2's reflections on number and wisdom bring lofty ideas of eternity down to earth. While we typically don't think about it, our everyday thought is suffused with eternal goods. Book 2's extended reflection on rational activity makes us take notice and sets the implications of this discovery within *De lib. arbit.* 1's discussion of happiness. Augustine explains:

> *Nemo autem securus est in iis bonis quae potest inuitus amittere. Veritatem autem atque sapientiam nemo amittit inuitus. Non enim locis separari ab ea quisquam potest, sed ea, quae dicitur a ueritate atque sapientia separatio, peruersa uoluntas est, qua inferiora diliguntur. Nemo autem uult aliquid nolens.*

> No one, however, is secure in those goods which he can lose against his will. No one, however, loses truth or wisdom against his will. For one cannot be spatially separated from them, but what is called separation from truth and wisdom is [in fact] a perverse will through which we love lower things. No one, however, wants something unwillingly. (*De lib. arbit.* 2.37)

---

[104] *De lib. arbit.* 2.37.

De lib. arbit. 1.30–35 claimed that we may attain happiness by properly submitting temporal goods to eternal goods. In presenting number and wisdom as eternal standards of judgment, *De lib. arbit.* 2 makes this account much more plausible. If I dent the rim of my salad bowl, the appropriate response is not to revise my concept of the circle, it is to fix the salad bowl. It is the nature of eternal goods to act as standards for temporal ones but not *vice versa*. When it comes to ethical matters, if the way I lead my life encourages me to revise my belief about the beacons of virtues, something has gone seriously wrong. Acts of self-indulgence (that "one more round") always involve some good, yet it is inevitably some lesser, short-term good that is chosen over some greater, long-term good (e.g. being sharp in the morning so that I can get lots of writing done). While we are perfectly capable of thinking along such lines, we cannot consistently do so while consciously endorsing the notion, "lesser things should be subordinate to better things."[105]

Second, *De lib. arbit.* 2 introduces the idea that eternal goods are common: The fact that one person possesses an eternal good does not stop someone else from doing so. This helps explain *De lib. arbit.* 1.25–29's conclusion that happiness is, in some sense, within the reach of every individual. It also provides a response to the worry, raised earlier, that someone might attain happiness by structuring his life around the demands of the imaginary world of Hogwarts. Book 1 characterized eternal goods merely as those that cannot be lost against one's will. This was problematic, insofar as it allowed personal fantasies to count as eternal good. Book 2's discussion of number and wisdom places objective parameters on what may pass as an eternal good. Christianity's God of Truth can plausibly meet these standards. One may need Scripture to see the connection between number, wisdom, truth and God, yet once this connection is suggested, any rational individual can, in principle, come to see the coherence and explanatory power of this account. In most instances, this will not be true of the Hogwarts fanatic. Still, we might imagine a case where a Hogwarts fanatic of a philosophical persuasion could structure his fantasies around notions of number, wisdom and truth that are shared by all people. One might even think that good fiction invites such thinking. In these cases, it is hard to see what's wrong with structuring one's life around Hogwarts, if doing so can in fact provide a framework for working out appropriate relations between temporal and eternal goods. Whatever Augustine, the man, would have thought of this, the argument that *De lib. arbit.* has presented up to this

---

[105] *De lib. arbit.* 2.29.

point leaves open the possibility of more than one way of living up to eternal standards. This is not to say that anything goes. My suspicion is that any two frameworks that converge around eternal goods of the sort *De lib. arbit.* has laid out, will be structurally similar in robust ways. In any event, at this point in the work, our understanding is slight, and the framework Augustine has constructed still lacks detail. This, however, is merely Augustine's response to the first of *De lib. arbit.* 2's three *aporiai*. Further parameters will be set and explanatory connections made as he and Evodius progress in their search for understanding.

Q2: Are All Things, Insofar As They Are Good, from God? (*De lib. arbit.* 2.40–46)

Augustine approaches Q2 by returning to the idea that each of us carries around notions of happiness and wisdom, which he here calls "glimmerings along our shadowy path" (*in hoc tenebroso itinere coruscantibus*).[106] Extending the journey metaphor, he cites Wisdom 6:17, "Wisdom shows herself favorably to them along the road, and in all providence does she meet with them."[107] Augustine explains, "For wherever you turn, Wisdom speaks to you by means of certain footprints which she has impressed upon her works." (*Quoquo enim te uerteris, uestigiis quibusdam quae operibus suis inpressit loquitur tibi*).[108] The immediate point is dynamic: every good thing in the world points in the right direction on our journey to Wisdom/Number/God.[109] Yet the bigger point is static: The fact that all goods point beyond themselves is the case because every created good is ultimately from God.

Augustine elaborates this point in terms of number, which he applies to the hierarchy of beings that he's been developing since book 1. Physical bodies, he explains, are shaped by number, as are the rhythmic, "measured" motions of animate bodies. A rational craftsman has number in mind, which he imposes on bodies through some kind of measured motion. Finally, there is the number that the craftsman looks to as a standard of judgment. This final number, as was suggested in *De lib. arbit.* 2.30–39's plausible account, either is God or is from God. The end result is an expanded hierarchy, where the familiar list of beings and their characteristic activities are associated with a particular type of number.

---

[106] *De lib. arbit.* 2.41. This "dark path" might be a reference to *C. Acad.* 1.9's "shadowy prison" (*tenebrosum carcerem*), i.e. the body.
[107] Cited at *De lib. arbit.* 2.41.   [108] *De lib. arbit.* 2.41.
[109] This sums up what I take to be *De ord.*'s ultimate account of providence. See Chapter 4.

Type of number	Characteristic activity	Type of being
Number/Form/Wisdom	Being a Standard of Judgement	God or from God
Numbers in Mind of Craftsman	Understanding	Humans
Numbers in Bodily Motion	Living	Animals and Plants
Numbers in Bodies	Existing	Physical Objects

This scheme is meant to embrace every possible good. Good things (apples, golden retrievers, human beings) fall into the rightmost column. Good properties (the taste of an apple, the speed of a retriever, the virtue of a human being) fall into the middle column, insofar as they are ways that things carry out their characteristic activities *well.*

The next step is to claim that the goodness of things and the goodness of properties ultimately both rely on number, i.e. that dependency runs right to left on our chart. Augustine argues:

> *Intuere caelum et terram et mare et quaecumque in eis uel desuper fulgent uel deorsum repunt uel uolant uel natant. Formas habent quia numeros habent; adime illis haec, nihil erunt. A quo ergo sunt nisi a quo numerus? quandoquidem in tantum illis est esse in quantum numerosa esse?*

> Look upon heaven, earth, sea and whatever in them either flashes down from above, crawls down below or flies or swims. They have forms because they have numbers. Take these numbers away from them, and they will be nothing. Therefore from what do they exist if not that from which number exists, since indeed being belongs to these things to the degree that they are endowed with number? (*De lib. arbit.* 2.42)

If talk of "degrees of being" strikes us as odd, we should keep in mind that this is a completely general argument. For any physical thing, up to and including human beings insofar as we have bodies, it will be more beautiful and better at being the kind of thing it is, which is to say it will exist more fully, to the extent that it embodies numerical proportionality. While "*forma*" in this context clearly bears the meaning "shape," it also carries the secondary sense of "beautiful form" or "shapeliness." There are clear Platonic and Pythagorean echoes in his talk of number and form, yet the basic thought is quite general. For anyone with more or less Classical sensibilities, physical beauty is a matter of proportionality. Living beings, whether plants, animals or humans, flourish to the extent that their bodily humors are balanced. Animals flourish insofar as their movements are suitably measured. Humans flourish in a particular way when their understanding conforms to eternal standards of number and wisdom. So if existing, living and understanding are all modes of being, then something has being to a greater or lesser degree to the extent that it carried out well its characteristic mode of being.

The final step is to argue that all these numbers depend on God, i.e. that dependency in the leftmost column runs from bottom to top. Human craftsmen provide a promising model, insofar as the act of building employs all four classes of number: Objective standards guide the craftsman's intention, which guides the movement of his body, which imposes number on physical objects. Yet it is not clear that every good quality or thing can be set within this scheme. As Augustine points out at *De ord.* 2.49, sparrows build circular nests and bees create hexagonal combs, yet neither uses anything resembling human understanding. Natural objects in general embody number, yet the fact that they are natural means that no builder, human or animal put that number there. Given what Augustine has said here, it seems possible that there are at least two orders of number in the world: one that runs through human craft and another that does not.[110]

Augustine elsewhere presents two strategies for dealing with this problem. The first is to turn from cases of building to cases of judgment: While no human or animal imposed the hexagonal structure on a beryl crystal, the fact that human beings can use number to judge such a crystal shows that the number in human understanding and the higher number that humans look to as a standard are superior to the number in the crystal. This is the strategy invoked in *De Mus.* 6. Yet since our current task is to show that all goods are from (i.e. created by) God, talk of judgment misses the point. The second strategy for connecting the number that either is God or is from God to the number in bodies is to posit an unseen World Soul. Augustine toys with this idea at *De ord.* 2.49 and at *De imm. an.* 14–15. This soul of the world acts as a humanlike agent, which is responsible for imposing number on crystals, moving the limbs of sparrows and bees to create their geometrical dwellings, and possibly also the actions of the human body that we think of as autonomous. While the World Soul is a Platonist idea, which Augustine does not specifically invoke in this passage, his talk of Wisdom, Providence and God as Creator comes quite close. For instance:

> *Vae qui derelinquunt te ducem et oberrant in uestigiis tuis, qui nutus tuos pro te amant et obliuiscuntur quid innuas, o suauissima lux purgatae mentis sapientia! non enim cessas innuere nobis quae et quanta sis, et nutus tui sunt omne creaturarum decus. Et artifex enim quodammodo innuit spectatori operis sui de*

---

[110] His most extended engagement with this problem comes in *De Mus.* 6, where characters differentiate between several different types of numbers. See Chapter 4.

ipsa operis pulchritudine, ne ibi totus haereat, sed speciem corporis fabricati sic
percurrat oculis, ut in eum qui fabricauerit recurrat affectu. Similes autem sunt,
qui ea quae facis pro te amant, hominibus, qui, cum audiunt aliquem
facundum sapientem, dum nimis suauitatem uocis eius et structuras syllabarum
apte locatarum auide audiunt, amittunt sententiarum principatum, cuius illa
uerba tamquam signa sonuerunt.

Woe to those who abandon you as their leader and wander about your footsteps, who love your intimations instead of you and forget what you intimate, Wisdom, thou sweetest light of a purified mind! For you do not stop intimating to us what and how great you are, and your intimations are every grace of created things. For a craftsman also in a certain way intimates to the viewer of his work about its very beauty so that he not linger there completely but run over the beauty of the crafted body with his eyes in such a way that he hastens back with affection to the one who crafted it. Those who love the things you make instead of you, however, are like people who, when they hear a wise person that speaks with fluency, while they listen too eagerly to the sweetness of his voice and the arrangements of his nicely spoken syllables, lose the principle of these sentences, of which his words sounded out as signs. (*De lib. arbit.* 2.43)

Human and divine creators are explicitly likened here. A Creator God who looks after sparrows would certainly fill the gap in Augustine's argument. Yet this fact alone hardly proves that such a Creator exists. Augustine is aware of this, as his worries about such problems in *De ord.* and *De Mus.* make clear. Rather than take Augustine to throw prior caution to the wind and knowingly present a bad argument for a Creator, it seems more charitable to conclude that he isn't arguing at all, at least not in the sense of offering proof. He is, rather, teasing out puzzles from *De lib. arbit.* 2.7–29's self-reflective hierarchies to motivate a particular account of Creation and to show its explanatory power for a wide range of phenomena. He is, once again, presenting a plausible conclusion.

Augustine ends by invoking more Scripture. So far he has presented a scheme in which a Creator God imposes number on Creation. While creatures (and their embodied numbers) come and go, God abideth ever. This is the point made in Psalm 101:27–28, "You shall change them, and they shall be changed; but you are the same and your years shall not fail," as well as Wisdom 7:27, which says of divine Number that "remaining in itself, it makes all things new."[111] We might find here an argument from contingency: If change is the taking on of new forms, and nothing can give form to itself, then it follows that there must be some unchanging form

---

[111] Both passages cited at *De lib. arbit.* 2.45.

that is prior to all changing forms (paraphrasing *De lib. arbit.* 2.45). As book 2's proof of God's existence, we can take Augustine's response to Q2 two ways. The portion of dialogue dealing with Q2 is quite short. Evodius responds to Augustine's second *oratio*:

> Satis mihi persuasum esse fateor, et quem ad modum manifestum fiat, quantum in hac uita atque inter tales quales nos sumus potest, deum esse, et ex deo esse omnia bona, quandoquidem omnia quae sunt, siue quae intellegunt et uiuunt et sunt sive quae tantum uiuunt et sunt siue quae tantum sunt, ex deo sunt.

> I confess that I have been persuaded, both [Q1] how it is clear that God exists – as much as it is possible in this life and among people such as us – and also [Q2] that all goods are from God: for indeed all things which are, whether those that understand and live and exist or those that only live and exist or those that only exist, are from God. (*De lib. arbit.* 2.47)

Evodius does not proceed, as he does elsewhere, to praise God as ultimate object of human happiness, as Providential Ruler of the world or even as the Creator of the world. All this is the stuff of plausibility. All he claims as clear (*manifestum*) is that all goods are from God insofar as all things are from God. While we could dress this "God" up in the rich descriptions of Scripture, all Evodius really needs to invoke here is a generic highest being upon which all lower beings are dependent. This, in turn, is all that Augustine can really claim to have proven certain given considerations up to this point. As with Q1, I thus conclude that Q2 also offers two kinds of conclusions: one generic and certain, the other richly descriptive and merely plausible.

Interlude: "Such Great Circles of Argument" (*De lib. arbit.* 2.47)

It is only at the end of book 2 that we wind our way back around to POE 2: Is God responsible for giving us free will, through which moral evil is possible? Augustine begins his discussion of Q3 – is free will a good from God? – by explaining this roundabout approach:

> Sed uidere debuisti etiam istam tertiam iam solutam. Propterea quippe tibi uideri dixeras dari non debuisse liberum uoluntatis arbitrium, quod eo quisque peccat. Cui sententiae tuae cum ego retulissem recte fieri non posse nisi eodem libero uoluntatis arbitrio, atque ad id potius hoc deum dedisse asseuerarem, respondisti liberam uoluntatem ita nobis dari debuisse ut iustitia data est, qua nemo uti nisi recte potest. Quae responsio tua in tantos circuitus disputationis nos ire compulit, quibus tibi probaremus et maiora et minora bona non esse nisi ex deo. Quod non tam dilucide ostendi posset, nisi prius aduersus opiniones impiae stultitiae qua dicit insipiens in corde suo: Non est deus,

206 Piety, Pride and the Problem of Evil

qualiscumque de re tanta pro modulo nostro inita ratio, eodem ipso deo in tam periculoso itinere nobis opitulante, in aliquid manifestum intenderetur.

But you ought to have seen that the third question [Q3] has now too been resolved. For you had said that it seemed to you that free choice of the will ought not to have been given because through it everyone sins [i.e. POE 2; *De lib. arbit.* 2.1]. And when I replied to this idea of yours that nothing can be done rightly unless by that same free choice of the will, and I showed that it was for this reason, rather, that God gave it [2.1–3], you responded that free will should have been given in the same way justice was, which no one can use unless rightly [2.4]. And this response compelled us to go in such great circles of argument, by which we proved to you that goods great and small do not exist unless from God [i.e. Q2; *De lib. arbit.* 2.40–46]. And this could not be shown very clearly unless first – against the opinions of impious folly by which the fool says in his heart, "There is no God," [i.e. Q1; *De lib. arbit.* 2.30–39; cf. Psalm 13:1 & 52:1] – whatever kind of reasoning about so great a matter had been undertaken in our meager way should be directed at something clear [i.e. the self-reflection of *De lib. arbit.* 2.7–30], while the very same God gives us aid on such a dangerous path. (*De lib. arbit.* 2.47)

In one sense, the answer has been on the table since the beginning. At the very start of book 2, Evodius grants that all goods are from God, that free will is a good and thus that it is justly given.[112] Yet he merely believes these things on authority. To bring him to understanding, "such great circles of argument" (*tantos circuitus disputationis*) were needed. The term might be a nod to Eccl. 7:26, cited at *De lib. arbit.* 2.24, "My heart and I have gone around [*circuiui*] so that I might search out and think about and know wisdom and number." I take "*circuitus disputationis*" to be as close as Augustine gets to a technical term for what I have dubbed a "round" of ARP. The term occurs at *Sol.* 2.25 in a similar sense. Here it seems to refer to the rounds of reflection and plausible conclusions, which he proceeds to name. This reading, however, must be qualified in two ways.

First, in analyzing particular passages as complete rounds of ARP, I am wary of attributing more precision to the text than it will support. By coining the term ARP, I have reified what is for Augustine a way of going about things. That said, there is a kind of completeness to be found in the process of moving through *aporia* and reflection to a plausible conclusion. Augustine seems to be referring to this completeness here, however inexactly. So, having "gone around" in "an indirect manner" (the two basic meanings of *circuitus*), we are back where we started. The point of all

---

[112] *De lib. arbit.* 2.1–4.

this was to arrive at understanding of the faith, which has been accomplished mostly by situating self-reflective discoveries within ever more sophisticated explanatory hierarchies. Augustine's main task in book 2's final exchange with Evodius is simply to connect the dots and show how all of this is relevant to the question at hand.

Second, in setting understanding as the goal of all these rounds of argument, we should not exclude certainty from Augustine's explanations. There is nothing wrong with us finding plausible those things about which we are certain. In fact, there would be something wrong with us if we did not! The point is that Augustine does not require certainty for something to be plausible. Conversely, he does not consider certainties to be merely plausible; this would be more skeptical than he is willing to be. In the course of dealing with Q1 and Q2, we found Augustine respecting these distinctions, as he offered two levels of response. In responding to each question, he provided a proof, aimed at certainty. These proofs dealt with God in generic terms and were presented via discussion with Evodius. Yet in each case, he set these explanations within broader frameworks, drawing details from Christian Scripture (and key Platonic texts) that were neither generic nor certain. These merely plausible explanations were presented via short passages of *oratio perpetua*. In what follows, I suggest that we find such a twofold response to Q3 too, as a passage of discussion attempts to draw certain conclusions[113] and a third short *oratio* sets these certainties within a broader, plausible framework.[114] In this case, though, it is not the description of God, but the detail with which we think about the will, that divides certain conclusions from plausible explanation. Having worked through this methodological interlude, let us begin with Augustine's certain conclusion before setting off into these deeper waters.

Q3: Is Free Will, Which Makes Moral Evil Possible, a Good from God? (*De lib. arbit.* 2.47–54)

Augustine proceeds by adding precision to the idea that goods come in degrees. He presents two criteria for ranking goods relative to each other. First, a good that can only be used rightly is better than one that can be used rightly or wrongly. Justice, for instance, can only be used rightly, and it is a greater good than feet, which can be used rightly or wrongly (presumably by bringing people somewhere they should or should not be). Yet it does not follow from this that feet are bad: They are merely

---

[113] *De lib. arbit.* 2.47–50.   [114] *De lib. arbit.* 2.51–54.

lesser goods.[115] Second, something without which we cannot live rightly is a greater good than something without which we can live rightly.[116] Again, we cannot live rightly without justice but we can live rightly without feet. Free will straddles the divide. Without it our choices would have no moral worth one way or the other. Like justice, free will is thus necessary for living rightly. Yet, like feet, free will can be used both rightly and wrongly. Putting this together, we get three grades of goodness:

Possible use	Type of thing	Grade of goodness
(1) Can be used only rightly	Justice	Great
(2) Can be used rightly or wrongly		
(a) Cannot live rightly without	Free will	Intermediate
(b) Can live rightly without	Feet	Small

While feet can be used wrongly and aren't even necessary for living rightly, no one would fault God for giving us feet. *A fortiori*, Evodius should not blame God for giving free will, which is a far greater good than feet, albeit not so great a good as justice.

At this point, Augustine has nudged Evodius from one basic intuition to another, both of which might ultimately be aesthetic in nature. Evodius started out assuming that the best possible world is one consisting of the best possible goods, and he concluded that a 3-O God should have made such a world. This was the thought underlying POE 2: Was God right to give free will, through which moral evil is possible? Through a roundabout course of argument, Augustine has now "un-taught" this idea and replaced it with an argument from plenitude, viz. that the best possible world is one consisting of as many kinds of goods as possible. On this second view:

> *Quare abundantia et magnitudo bonitatis dei non solum magna sed etiam media et minima bona esse praestitit. Magis laudanda est bonitas eius in magnis quam in mediis et magis in mediis quam in minimis bonis, sed magis in omnibus quam si non omnia tribuisset.*

> Therefore, the abundance and greatness of God's goodness is responsible for their being not only great goods but also intermediate and small ones. His goodness is more to be praised in great goods than in intermediate ones, and more in intermediate ones than in small ones, yet more in all goods than if he had not bestowed all goods. (*De lib. arbit.* 2.50)

---

[115] *De lib. arbit.* 2.50.   [116] *De lib. arbit.* 2.49.

To put it another way, Evodius started out by viewing the goodness of the world as the sum of the first-order goods in the world. Augustine augments this perspective by looking to the second-order good of the world's having a full range of goods. In any event, he has shown, to Evodius' satisfaction, that free will is a good, albeit an intermediary one, and that God was not wrong to give it even if it is not so great a good as justice. At this point, POE 2 has been resolved according to the terms set out, and Augustine's praise of God's abundant goodness seems a perfectly fitting place to draw book 2 to a close.

Augustine, however, keeps going. He proceeds via *oratio* to explain:

> *Voluntas ergo, quae medium bonum est, cum inheret incommutabili bono eique communi, non proprio, sicuti est illa de qua multum locuti sumus et nihil digne diximus ueritas, tenet homo beatam uitam; eaque ipsa uita beata, id est animi affectio inhaerentis incommutabili bono, proprium et primum est hominis bonum. In eo sunt etiam uirtutes omnes, quibus male uti nemo potest.*

> Therefore, when the will, which is an intermediate good, clings to the unchangeable common good, which is common not private, just as truth is, which we have spoken about quite a lot but not said anything worthy, a human being has the happy life. And this happy life, that is the favorable disposition of a rational soul clinging to the unchangeable good, is the first and distinctive human good. In it also are all the virtues which no one may use wrongly. (*De lib. arbit.* 2.52)

Here Augustine sets book 2's discussion of the common concepts within an ethical framework. Yet all that this earlier discussion showed was that conformity to these common standards is necessary for happiness. In his final *oratio* of book 2, Augustine suggests that holding to common standards, "such as truth," is sufficient for happiness as well. He proceeds to clarify: Just as each person's will is private to the individual, so is each individual's happiness and virtue. One person cannot be happy or virtuous through another's happiness or virtue:

> *sed coaptando animum illis incommutabilibus regulis luminibusque uirtutum quae incorruptibiliter uiuunt in ipsa ueritate sapientiaque communi, quibus et ille coaptauit et fixit animum quem istis uirtutibus praeditum sibi ad imitandum proposuit.*

> but by fitting the rational soul to those unchangeable rules and beacons of the virtues which live incorruptibly in the truth itself and in common wisdom, to which a person endowed with these virtues, whom one has set out to imitate, has also fitted and formed his soul. (*De lib. arbit.* 2.52)

Through the self-reflections leading to this point, we glimpsed pieces of wisdom that are necessary for happiness. Augustine now sets his sights on the whole of wisdom and suggests that grasping it will be sufficient for the happy life. We find an exactly analogous move in *De beata v.*, where Augustine gives good reason for thinking that conforming one's mind to eternal standards of measure is necessary for moderation and thus happiness, yet he concludes that fully conforming one's mind to eternal measure is also sufficient for happiness and then proceeds to identify this measure with the Persons of the Holy Trinity in various ways. That argument, like the current one, presents a pathetic attempt at proof. Yet, for reasons that should now be obvious, I do not take Augustine in either passage to be offering proof but, rather, presenting a preexisting account, which a course of *aporia* and reflection has prepared the reader to see as plausible.

Augustine spells out the implications of this richer account of the will.[117] All things created by God are good. When the mind holds to the eternal, it is rewarded with the highest good. When it turns from the eternal to the temporal, it finds yet more goods, albeit lesser ones, though it makes itself liable to suffering punishment when these goods are taken away.[118] God is gracious in giving all these goods, and since the will "voluntarily" turns from the greater to the lesser, God is also just in letting wills become subject to temporal punishment. What causes the will to make such an obviously bad choice? "If I were to respond to you, as you ask this, that I don't know, perhaps you would be somewhat sad, but nevertheless I would respond truly. For it is not possible to know what is nothing." (*Ita quaerenti tibi si respondeam nescire me, fortasse eris tristior, sed tamen uera responderim. Sciri enim non potest quod nihil est*).[119] Augustine clarifies that the will's movement from higher to lower goods is a "defective movement." Insofar as this is a movement, one toward some good, it is ordered and from God. Insofar as it is defective, it is from nothing, since "every defect is from nothing" (*omnis ... defectus ex nihilo est*).[120] In spelling this out, however, Augustine is not explaining anything; he is setting up a new puzzle, POE 3: What is the cause of the will's perverse movement away from higher things? Answering this will be the task of *De lib. arbit.* 3.

Taking Stock: ARP in *De lib. arbit.* 2

My goal in this chapter is to show that reading *De lib. arbit.* in terms of the Platonic method set out in *C. Acad.* allows us to make sense of the *De lib. arbit.* as a whole. I have suggested that book 3 presents a scriptural

[117] *De lib. arbit.* 2.53.   [118] Cf. *De lib. arbit.* 1's discussion of temporal and eternal law.
[119] *De lib. arbit.* 2.54.   [120] *De lib. arbit.* 2.54.

response to the problem of evil, which *De lib. arbit.* 1–2 prepares us to see as plausible through courses of aporetic debate and self-reflection. When it comes to the work's aporetic function, we have articulated three versions of POE and seen how each leads to the next. Books 1 and 2 are aporetic not in the sense that they provide no solutions, but in that each solves one problem only by raising another. The work thus proceeds by refining the problem and setting the stage for *De lib. arbit.* 3's eventual theodicy. At the same time, it works through a program of unlearning, as Evodius' initial conception of evil and happiness in terms of temporal goods is gradually replaced by a fuller conception of happiness and misery in terms of our relation to eternal goods. When it comes to self-reflection, I have offered an alternative perspective on *De lib. arbit.* 2's proof of God's existence. The self-reflective certainties of 2.7–29 set the stage not just for showing God's existence, i.e. Augustine's response to Q1, but for his response to Q2 and Q3 as well. I have argued that these responses operate on two distinct tracks. Through discussion with Evodius, Augustine proves that God is not to be faulted for giving us free will. This solution rests ultimately on self-reflective certainty and treats God and the will in quite generic terms. In the final analysis, this amounts to an argument from contingency and an argument from plenitude: All goods depend on some highest being, which has something to do with standards of judgment, for their being and their goodness; the world, meanwhile, is better for having a full range of goods rather than just great goods, so we have no grounds to complain that the intermediate good, free will, can be used badly. Yet this discussion is punctuated by three *orationes*, in which Augustine sets his solution within a richer explanatory framework. In this, he draws freely from Christian Scripture and Platonist doctrine to present a plausible account of a God of Truth who is the Maker and Ruler of Creation.

One or the other of Augustine's tracks will resonate more depending on readers' preoccupations. Scholars such as Plantinga have looked to the book's proofs for possible morally sufficient reasons for God's permitting evil. The generic terms in which these proofs are constructed were well suited for the twentieth-century discussion of standard restricted theism. Such readings would do well to pass over the work's *orationes*, which introduce complications that are unnecessary for considerations of standard restricted theism. Scholars such as Adams, by contrast, should be drawn to the *orationes* as well. Yet they should not look to these in isolation from the rest of the work. This would leave us with mere dogma, the "Augustinian" position of catechisms and patristic authority. It very much matters how we get to these conclusions, since it is through *aporia* and reflection that we come to see what Augustine's conclusions explain, and we are given good reason to find them plausible. This is, after all, a project of faith seeking understanding. For scholars who are sympathetic to Adams' skeptical realism, Augustine's roundabout courses of argument are worth taking seriously, both for what they help us understand about the problem of evil and for the model they provide us for working through other aspects of life in which certainty eludes us. At the end of the day, though, these *orationes* merely hint at a broader scriptural context. It is with book 3 that Augustine turns to Scripture in earnest and sets about elaborating a plausible scriptural response to the problem of evil.

POE 3: What Causes the Will's Perverse Movement away from Higher Things? (*De lib. arbit.* 3.1–5)

What philosophers sometimes refer to as "the problem of evil" is really a family of problems. *De lib. arbit.* 1 opened with Evodius wanting to know whether God is to be blamed for moral evil (POE 1). There Augustine argued that moral evil comes about because human beings use their free will to turn from eternal goods to temporal ones, thus enslaving themselves to lust. With this, POE 1 was answered yet in a way that raised POE 2: Is God to blame for giving us free will that makes moral evil possible? Book 2 proceeded to argue that free will is an intermediary good, God is to be praised for giving us a full range of goods, and sin is simply a perverse movement of the will from greater goods to lesser ones. This solution to POE 2 presents human beings as acting irrationally and contrary to their own best interest. I, for one, find this to be psychologically plausible. Nevertheless, this account raises the final question, POE 3: What is the cause of the will's perverse movement away from higher things? With this, the stage is set for book 3. If a college course in medieval philosophy is going to cut part of *De lib. arbit.*, book 3 is the favored choice. As Simon Harrison 2006, 28, puts it, this final book operates at a level of "transcendental" virtuosity. Less charitably, after the rigorous arguments of *De lib. arbit.* 1–2, book three may strike some as a sermon run amok. Unfortunately, stopping at book 3 leaves Augustine's response to POE woefully incomplete. My hope is that the following overview will be of use to philosophically oriented readers wishing to follow *De lib. arbit.*'s project through to the end.

The difficult thing about *De lib. arbit.* 3 is not that it lacks structure, but rather that it employs three different structuring principles that do not always line up neatly with each other. To make sense of this, I suggest we look at POE from a different angle for a moment, distinguishing between the "theoretical" POE as a problem discussed by philosophers of religion, and the "pastoral" POE as the wedge that can be driven between religious folks and their God by the experience of evil. The latter is much more personal, and in the midst of suffering, theoretical distinctions and carefully crafted arguments are often ineffectual, if not simply inappropriate. I suggest that *De lib. arbit.* 3 addresses both varieties of the problem and uses piety on both fronts. As we recall, the "rule of piety" requires us always (i) to think of God in the highest terms possible, (ii) to thank God for the goods He's given us, even if they are not the greatest goods, and (iii) to acknowledge our sins and look to God for healing.[121] This is the attitude that the philosophical frameworks constructed in books 1 and 2 are intended to cultivate. When it comes to offering a theoretical solution to POE 3, these frameworks guide Augustine's reading of Genesis as he pieces together and articulates a scriptural account of Creation and humanity's place within it. Central to this account, as we've started to see, is the capacity of the human free will to turn toward higher or lower goods. In the course of setting out this theoretical account, Augustine simultaneously addresses the pastoral problem through what I will call the work's "practical project" of raising Evodius' mind from lower things to higher things.[122] While the work's theoretical project is clear enough, Augustine opens book 3 on a practical tone:

> *Propterea quid opus est quaerere unde iste motus existat quo uoluntas auertitur ab incommutabili bono ad commutabile bonum, cum eum non nisi animi et uoluntarium et ob hoc culpabilem esse fateamur omnisque de hac re disciplina utilis ad id ualeat, ut eo motu improbato atque cohibito uoluntatem nostram ad fruendum sempiterno bono a lapsu temporalium convertamus?*

> Therefore, what need is there of seeking from where this motion emerges, by which the will is turned from unchangeable good to changeable good, when we confess that it belongs to nothing but the soul and is willed and is for this reason culpable, and every useful teaching about this matter results in this: By scorning and checking this motion, we turn our will from its fall into temporal goods and toward enjoying the everlasting good? (*De lib. arbit.* 3.2)

---

[121] *De lib. arbit.* 3.5 and 3.12.

[122] As with "piety," "pastoral" has connotations in English that are likely to be misleading here, as they sometimes involve compassion to the exclusion of rational thought. As with "piety," *De lib. arbit.* will hopefully challenge our ideas of what pastoral care might amount to. Yet given that the term "pastoral" does not figure in *De lib. arbit.* itself and "practical" more clearly sets *De lib. arbit.* against its classical background (cf. Aristotle, EN 2.2), I will speak in terms of Augustine's "practical project" in response to the "pastoral problem of evil."

In this we find a kind of spiritual exercise in which concerns for evil are eclipsed as one rises to higher goods. These two approaches to POE, theoretical and practical, provide the deep structure of book 3. At the same time, Augustine strings together individual sections of his presentation via surface-level transitions, some of which track the deep structure of the book and some of which don't. The result of laying these three structures – theoretical, practical, surface – on top of one another is a seeming mess.

What we really need for *De lib. arbit.* 3 is a synoptic view of what the book is trying to accomplish. If we step back, we realize that the book splits down the middle, presenting two long *orationes*, each introduced by a passage of discussion. The first of these introductory discussions[123] addresses a puzzle in logical determinism, as we discussed earlier; the second[124] takes up a puzzle in causal determinism. These two approaches – logical and causal – in turn set the stage for the *orationes* they introduce. The first *oratio*[125] approaches POE 3 from a logical or synchronic point of view, addressing the worry that the world's perfection requires human beings to sin. This amounts to a challenge and defense of the argument from plenitude set out at the end of book 2. As a response to POE 3 – what causes the will's perverse movement away from higher things? – this first *oratio* simply removes reasons for thinking that it is God. Yet this raises the further question: What, then, did cause this perverse movement of the will? The second *oratio*[126] approaches POE 3 in terms of efficient causation, tracing the preconditions of humanity's current sinful state back in time to Adam's Fall and Lucifer's before that. It is at this point that questions of narrative take center stage. Augustine's final answer to the theoretical POE is that Lucifer's pride is the causal beginning of all sin.[127] His answer to the practical problem, meanwhile, is to combat the effects of this pride by raising Evodius to a more pious mindset. Book 3 presents a huge amount of detailed content. In what follows, I will limit my discussion to showing how recognizing the role of piety will help us make sense of book 3 as a unified project and the natural culmination of books 1 and 2.

Logical Determinism and the Argument from Plenitude (*De lib. arbit.* 3.4–46)

Augustine introduces the rule of piety through second-order reflection on the different ways that people respond to logical determinism. As for his

[123] *De lib. arbit.* 3.4–11.   [124] *De lib. arbit.* 3.47–50.   [125] *De lib. arbit.* 3.12–46.
[126] *De lib. arbit.* 3.51–77.   [127] Ecclesiastes 10:15 cited and expanded upon at *De lib. arbit.* 3.76.

first-order response to the worry that God's foreknowledge is incompatible with humans' free choice to sin, Augustine explains that it makes no difference that God's foreknowledge is either God's[128] or knowledge.[129] Yet even if we accept these responses, discussed earlier, there is still the more basic worry that God is responsible for anything that necessarily takes place in His creation.[130] Augustine addresses this worry by spelling out a more elaborate version of the argument from plenitude set out at *De lib. arbit.* 2.50, this time drawing his catalogue of created beings from Scripture. His first *oratio* – *De lib. arbit.* 3.11–48 – is taken up with working through this argument and various objections to it.

The hierarchies that Augustine has been gradually articulating and elaborating since book 1 reach their culmination in the argument from plenitude at *De lib. arbit.* 3.13–17. Through a series of comparisons, e.g. a wandering horse is better than a stone that does not wander off,[131] Augustine spells out something like the following scheme:

General class	Subdivisions	Members
God	God	God
Free/rational beings ...	who can sin but don't	Angels & perfected humans
	who sometimes sin	Most humans now
	who always sin (now)	Devil and his minions
Brute animals	Brute animals	Horses, birds, etc.
Physical things	Light	Sun
		Moon
		Lamps
	Other than light	Fertile land
		Barren land
		A stone

This scheme provides the framework for a *reductio*: If we complain that the moon is not as great as the Sun, yet we acknowledge that a lamp is good, then we have contradicted ourselves and in the process broken the rule of piety. The solution: We should follow the rule of piety by thanking God for the Moon, whose goodness occupies a middle position between the good of the Sun and the good of a lamp. Likewise, we should not blame God for not making human beings to be like the Angels who cannot sin.

---

[128] *De lib. arbit.* 3.10.   [129] *De lib. arbit.* 3.10–11.
[130] *De lib. arbit.* 3.12. Evodius' initial worry seems to be that human beings all necessarily sin at some point (*De lib. arbit.* 3.9), although the text is somewhat vague on this point.
[131] *De lib. arbit.* 3.15.

We should, rather, thank God for making us better than the Devil and his minions, who are now perpetually locked into sin, as well as nonrational creatures, which are incapable of moral worth one way or the other. We should, in short, be thankful for God's goodness in creating such a full range of rational creatures and praise him for his justice in assigning each its lot: Good Angels are rewarded with unending blessedness; the Devil is punished with unending misery; and human beings are punished but given a chance to repent.[132] Augustine advanced this argument through various particular comparisons: Sun vs. Moon; horse vs. a stone. Still, the fact that these all fit into a single hierarchy suggests a single overarching argument: If we reject the rule of piety and complain that any part of creation wasn't created better than it is, then there will be no reason to stop until we get to that than which nothing is better, i.e. God. But this is simply to complain that God created anything. Since few of us would be willing to go that far, the rule of piety, which demands gratitude for our place in things, provides a more tenable alternative.

Having set out this argument, Augustine turns to two objections to it. The first, "I would rather not exist than be unhappy" (*non esse quam miserum me esse mallem*) seems to come out of nowhere. Augustine's initial reply, "you're lying!" (*mentiris*) may seem unhelpful, yet it does clarify what's at stake.[133] In presenting the argument from plenitude, Augustine is counting on his audience approaching the matter piously, as the arguments of *De lib. arbit.* 1–2 prepared them to do. Book 2 started from the self-reflective triad – I exist, I live, I know (*sum, uiuo, noui*) –[134] and proceeded to elaborate the hierarchy of goods at the heart of his argument from plenitude. The person who would rather not be than be unhappy denies the value of intermediary goods in this scheme. In response, Augustine introduces a fourth self-reflective certainty – I will (*uolo*) – and proceeds to argue that no one could will not to be.[135] What they actually want, according to Augustine, is peace (*quies*), which is not nonbeing but fullness of being. Still, the need to argue for the apparent is usually a sign that things have gone horribly wrong. Augustine thus proceeds to present an error theory, explaining how a process of habituation could leave people so confused that they come to misidentify their own desires.[136] Given the centrality of self-reflection to ARP generally, the

---

[132] *De lib. arbit.* 3.15.   [133] *De lib. arbit.* 3.18.   [134] *De lib. arbit.* 1.16–17.
[135] *De lib. arbit.* 3.19–22. This argument proceeds via a great number of fine distinctions. In his translation, Peter King has helpfully tracked the argument's different twists and turns.
[136] *De lib. arbit.* 3.23.

theoretical importance of this passage could not be greater.[137] As important as such theoretical issues are, what we're actually talking about here is
people who are suicidal, and Augustine's practical project starts taking over
midway through.[138] The end result is a prime example of the rambling,
sermonizing quality of book 3, which will strike us as lacking direction if
we do not recognize that the book pursues both a theoretical and a
practical project in tandem.

Having dealt with this first objection, Augustine reiterates that creation
is better for incorporating a full range of goods – great, intermediate and
small – than it would be if it contained only great ones.[139] This sets the
stage for Augustine's second objection: According to the argument from
plenitude, human sin seems necessary to complete the perfection of God's
creation, yet God, nevertheless, dishes out unhappiness as punishment for
that sin.[140] Augustine responds to this objection by arguing that the
perfection of creation does not, in fact, require human sin[141] and that
God should be praised whether humans sin or not.[142] This is the philosophical heart of Augustine's response to POE 3 construed as a problem in
logical, as opposed to causal, determinism. In constructing his response,
Augustine puts the theoretical frameworks of books 1 and 2 to the test.

The principle of plenitude is in some sense an aesthetic one, bound up
in classical ideas of unity in variety. Augustine's argument seems to place
aesthetic concerns above moral ones, justifying human sin and suffering
insofar as they are amusing or otherwise pleasing to God's aesthetic
sensibilities. Even if we grant that God's aesthetic sensibilities are correct,
this is a somewhat callous view of the Creator. Augustine's response is that
plenitude is a matter of natures not states: It is not a soul's state of sin that
adds to the whole, but the existence of souls whose nature allows them to
sin.[143] Within the class of created rational beings, one extreme is occupied
by good angels who are able always to avoid sin and are thus rewarded by
eternal happiness, while the Devil and his minions occupy the other
extreme, insofar as they are (now) unable to refrain from sin and thus
rewarded with eternal misery. Human beings occupy the middle rung,

---

[137] Those who simply deny Augustine's self-reflective starting points could bring his project to a dead
halt. We find a similar scenario at *De Trin.* There, Augustine claims that each of us knows himself,
yet this correct self-knowledge is obscured by additional false opinions. In this case, we fall into
error not through a lack of knowledge but through an excess of opinion. Augustine's solution there
is to use skeptical doubt to separate what we're certain of and what we're not certain of, as a way of
dividing our self-knowledge from mere opinions. See Charles Brittain, "Self Knowledge in Cicero
and Augustine (*De Trinitate*, X, 5, 7–10, 16)," *Medioevo* 37 (2012), 107–136.
[138] *De lib. arbit.* 3.20–21.   [139] *De lib. arbit.* 3.24–25.   [140] *De lib. arbit.* 3.25.
[141] *De lib. arbit.* 3.26–35.   [142] *De lib. arbit.* 3.36–46.   [143] *De lib. arbit.* 3.26.

insofar as we are able to sin or not sin, and we are duly rewarded with happiness or misery depending on our choice. With this basic point in place, Augustine proceeds to spell out a scriptural account of how the world's just and perfect order will be maintained, whether any creature, human or angelic, ever sins or not.[144] At bottom, this is a scriptural elaboration of book 1's account of eternal law, arguing that everything works out for the best. When someone is burnt alive, for instance: If the individual suffers this fate in pursuit of duty, then his death provides evidence of his courage and endurance; if the individual is a ruthless criminal, then we approve of his just punishment. Either way, the aesthetic and ethical order of the world is preserved. It is not, however, the physical act but the character of the individual that makes the difference.[145] Augustine proceeds to emphasize the aesthetic side of this account: When a slave is punished by being made to clean a sewer, a human being, who is a greater good, "adorns" (*ornat*) the sewer through his attentions, while the sewer, a lesser good, is employed in the just punishment for the slave's sin.[146] In this way, higher and lower goods are brought into a kind of unity and ordered beauty. Yet this does not make the slave's sin necessary, since there are other provisions in place for cleaning sewers. The same applies to angels, who are assigned various roles in creation as punishment or reward, even though God has other provisions in place and is perfectly capable of looking after creation on His own.[147] When it comes to human beings, "the wages of sin is death." Augustine proceeds to use Scripture to spell out book 1's account of the human will enslaving itself to lust: Properly ordered wills belong to God and are rewarded with eternal life; those who turn to lust belong to the Devil, who punishes them with death. While this is all completely just, God goes even further: Christ, who was sinless, allowed himself to be killed, thus voiding the contract with the Devil. By exploiting a loophole in his deal with the Devil,[148] Christ "ransoms us from death" in what theologians have come to call a ransom theory of the atonement. In terms of the worry we started out with, the perfection of Creation does not require that humans occupy a state of sin, merely that human nature be capable of sinning, and the justice of creation is maintained whatever its creatures end up doing.

Augustine concludes that God should be praised whether humans sin or not.[149] While the previous argument proceeded in a largely oratorical

---

[144] *De lib. arbit.* 3.27–35.   [145] *De lib. arbit.* 3.28.   [146] *De lib. arbit.* 3.27.
[147] *De lib. arbit.* 3.32–35.   [148] *De lib. arbit.* 3.29–35.   [149] *De lib. arbit.* 3.36–46.

manner, relying on parallelism and antithesis,[150] this one proceeds via the "briefest dilemma" (*breuissima complexione*).[151]

(1)   If we find fault with a thing, we praise its nature.
(2)   If we praise a thing, we praise its nature.
(3)   If we praise a creature's nature, we praise its Creator.
(C)   Thus, whether we praise or blame creatures, we praise their Creator.

The argument turns on (1), which assumes that we fault vice and that vice is simply the failure of a thing to live according to its nature. In effect, this argument gives us a philosophical distillation of the proceeding passage's more rhetorical presentation of God as the creator of natures not states. Augustine elaborates the point through scriptural terms of debt (*debitum*).[152] The passage turns on the fact that "*debeo*" may take either a direct object (e.g. *debeo drachmam/*"I owe a drachma") or an infinitive (e.g. *debeo ire/*"I ought to go"), while both may be joined with an ethical dative (e.g. *debeo tibi drachmam/*"I owe you a drachma"; *debeo tibi ire/*"I ought to go for your sake"). While English makes this seem rather complicated, the basic principle here is that when a benefactor gives a beneficiary some good, the beneficiary is indebted to that benefactor.[153] In this case, God gives human beings the ability to act rightly, i.e. through freely willing in a rightly ordered way; human beings thus owe it to God to act rightly. If we pay this debt then everyone is happy. If we don't pay this debt, then we've not held up our end of the bargain, and we are punished accordingly. Given that this particular benefactor freely gave all goods, God doesn't owe anyone anything.[154] With this, we have arrived at a pious perspective by another route: (a) acknowledging God as supreme, (b) thanking God for whatever goods He has given us, and (c) taking responsibility for our own shortcomings.[155] In terms of the work's broader project, this logic of debt presents a scripturally informed way of working out the details of the

---

[150] To take just one example, "the mortal flesh adorned the first man [Adam], so that the penalty would fit the sin. And it adorned our Lord, so that His mercy might free us from sin." *De lib arbit*. 3.28. While this makes an intuitive kind of sense, it will hardly satisfy most philosophers.

[151] *De lib. arbit.* 3.36–42.   [152] *De lib. arbit.* 3.42–46.

[153] Given the two basic meanings of *debeo*, "owe" and "ought," the passive participle form, *debitum*, is either "a thing owed," i.e. a "debt," or "a thing ought-ed," i.e. something that ought to be done. The substantive difference is slight: "ought" is for verbs, "owe" is for nouns. While English reserves separate words for each notion, Latin makes do with *debeo*.

[154] *De lib. arbit.* 3.45.

[155] Going into the details of this passage, which is quite convoluted, would go beyond the purposes of this chapter. That said, readers interested in evaluating Augustine's ransom theory and logic of debt will find it worth their while to compare *De lib. arbit.* 3.46 with chapter 8 of Anselm's *De libertate arbitrii*.

previous section's ransom theory, which is, in turn, a scriptural respelling of book 1's account of lust. Augustine's theoretical and practical projects come together in the end, as Augustine draws his conclusion that whatever happens in Creation, praise the Creator![156]

Causal Determinism and the Fall (*De lib. arbit.* 3.47–50)

Having listened to Augustine speak uninterrupted for roughly the length of book 1, Evodius finally speaks up. While he is now convinced that God is not to blame for causing us to sin, he still wants to know what the cause is, not just what it isn't. Augustine's *oratio* has only reinforced this desire, given that some angels sin, some don't, and individual human beings fall somewhere in between. What is the cause of one nature going one way and one going another? And Evodius doesn't want to hear "the will." At this point Augustine puts his foot down, accusing Evodius of wanting to go beyond the root of the matter:

> *Sed quae tandem esse poterit ante uoluntatem causa uoluntatis? Aut enim et ipsa uoluntas est et a radice ista uoluntatis non recedetur, aut non est uoluntas et peccatum nullum habet.*

> But what, tell me, will be able to be the cause of the will before the will? For either it is the will itself and it will not be separated from this root of the will, or it is not the will and it has no sin. (*De lib. arbit.* 3.49)

If all we readers are after is a possible morally sufficient reason for God permitting evil, we might as well stop reading here. Augustine, however, wants understanding, and while he refuses to admit a "cause" of sin beyond the will itself, he sympathizes with Evodius' more general demand for some kind of explanation, particularly given the difficulty each of us has avoiding sin and our generally poor track record as a species. While Augustine argued in his first *oratio* that God would be just, whatever happens in Creation, he argues in his second *oratio* that God has been just in Creation as it actually turned out, i.e. in the narrative presented in Scripture.

It is at this point that the book's three types of structure – theoretical, practical and surface – come together in a much tighter way. Augustine's second *oratio* proceeds through two main stages. *De lib. arbit.* 3.51–70 considers how it can be just that current human beings are afflicted with "ignorance and trouble" as punishment for our first ancestor's sin.

---

[156] *De lib. arbit.* 3.46.

In doing so, he considers four possible accounts of the soul's origin,[157] and responds to objections about the suffering of infants and animals.[158] *De lib. arbit.* 3.71–77, in turn, explains how Adam and Eve fell by giving in to temptation,[159] which was only possible because Lucifer had already fallen.[160] In terms of surface-level structure, the text moves backward in time, progressing steadily from one (efficient) cause to another. Lucifer's fall is the final puzzle. As the highest of all God's creatures, Lucifer enjoyed the most intimate relationship a creature could hope for with the highest good there is, and unlike human beings he was perfectly aware of this. Why would such an individual ever choose to turn from God to his own everlasting detriment? Augustine's answer to the theoretical POE is that pride made Lucifer turn from the highest good (God) to a lower good (Lucifer himself). Meanwhile, Augustine holds up the result of that pride as a practical, cautionary tale to encourage the piety he has been working to instill from the outset. With this the book's three structures – surface, theoretical and practical – align.

Augustine looks to Scripture for the idea that human beings are afflicted both by ignorance of the good and by trouble in holding to it, even when they know what the good is.[161] But we hardly need the Bible to tell us this. Through the debates and reflections of books 1 and 2, Evodius has come to understand complex hierarchies of goods and has started thinking of moral goodness in terms of the desires of the will rather than the laws of the state. While Evodius didn't begin this process totally ignorant of the good, he clearly had a lot to learn. And while he hasn't given in to criminal desires in the course of their conversation, he has been rather spotty in his desire for the highest good. This is one of the shortcomings that Augustine's practical project of instilling piety strives to correct. When Augustine suggests that we are afflicted by ignorance and trouble, this should not come as a new idea. Augustine's point, rather, is that Scripture puts its finger on a truth of human moral psychology, so we should listen to what else Scripture has to say about the matter. In short, the reflections and dialectical debates of books 1 and 2 have prepared us to realize the explanatory power, the plausibility, of book 3's scriptural account of original sin. To his credit, Augustine acknowledges the obvious objection to Scripture's account of inherited punishment:

[157] *De lib. arbit.* 3.56–66. [158] *De lib. arbit.* 3.67–70. [159] *De lib. arbit.* 3.71–74.
[160] *De lib. arbit.* 3.75–77. [161] *De lib. arbit.* 3.51–70.

Si Adam et Eua peccauerunt, quid nos miseri fecimus, ut cum ignorantiae caecitateet difficultatis cruciatibus nasceremur et primo erraremus nescientes quid nobis esset faciendum, deinde ubi nobis inciperent aperiri praecepta iustitiae, uellemus ea facere et retinente carnalis concupiscentiae nescio qua necessitate non ualeremus?

If Adam and Eve have sinned, what have we miserable people done to make it that we were born with the blindness of ignorance and the torments of trouble, and that we first went astray not knowing what we ought to do and then, when the precepts of justice started to be laid bare, we wanted to do those things but were unable thanks to some necessity of carnal longing holding us back? (*De lib. arbit.* 3.53)

Augustine presents this as a question "muttered" by people who are ready to lay blame on anything but themselves for sinning.[162] In this respect, I and likely most readers today have failed to live up to the rule of piety. But the point of this rule is not to beat us up for being unwilling to accept without question what appear to be morally repellent claims. The point is for us to question the faith and to try to understand how its moral shortcomings are merely apparent.

Our murmured complaint provides the prompt for the rest of the section.[163] Augustine begins by assuming that ignorance and trouble are "innate" (*natura*)[164] and then argues that such innate punishment is just, whichever of four possible accounts of the soul's origin is correct. The arguments he gives apply just as well if ignorance and trouble are acquired after birth, as Augustine mentions in passing.[165] The four accounts are as follows:

(1)   All souls are derived from a single original soul, i.e. Adam's.
(2)   Each soul is created individually at the same time as its body.
(3)   Souls preexist bodies, and individuals are sent into bodies as needed.
(4)   Souls preexist bodies, and individuals enter into bodies of their own accord.[166]

---

[162] *De lib. arbit.* 3.53.   [163] *De lib. arbit.* 3.56–66.

[164] As with "*debeo*," Latin's relatively limited vocabulary presents a complication here, as the single word "*natura*" in its ablative form can mean either "by nature" or "from birth." Augustine draws explicit attention to this, and clarifies that "strictly speaking" nature refers to humanity's created nature, i.e. before the fall. This is to be distinguished from "that nature in which we are born as mortal, ignorant and slave to flesh, due to the penalty from damnation" (*De lib. arbit.* 3.54). We might think of this as our fallen nature. Scripture uses "*natura*" in both senses, and Augustine follows suit. For the sake of simplicity, though, I will refer to the first as "natural" and the second as "innate."

[165] *De lib. arbit.* 3.70.

[166] Beyond the immediate concerns of *De lib. arbit.*, the origin of the soul is a problem for Augustine in that he is sympathetic to both Platonism, which in some versions affirms reincarnation, and Christianity, which does not. He addressed such a worry in *De Mag.*, where he presented an

The first and last options can be dealt with quickly. If each soul is derived from Adam's as though from a single "rootstock" (*propago*),[167] then there is a robust sense in which each of is Adam, and it is clear how we can be justly punished by God for a sin that we ourselves, in some sense, committed. So much for (1). Likewise, if each soul descends into a body of its own accord, (4), then we can hardly blame God for the ignorance and trouble that we brought on ourselves, not by sinning personally, but by choosing to enter bodies burdened with the penalty for Adam's sin. Augustine's response to (2) and (3) relies on the rule of piety's second injunction to thank God for even intermediate goods. In the case of (2), the fact that later souls were created at the low state to which the original humans descended highlights how far even the lowest rational creature surpasses the goodness of even the highest nonrational creature. Yet even in this fallen state, the soul has implanted in it "the natural judgment by which it puts wisdom ahead of error and peace ahead of trouble" "a natural judgement by which it prefers wisdom to error and peace to trouble" (*naturale iudicium quo sapientiam praeponat errori et quietem difficultati*),[168] i.e. the common concepts that featured centrally in book 2's reflections. Even if the soul is not guilty for being born into ignorance and trouble, God has provided ways for it to rise to a higher condition. Likewise for (3), God sends souls into the world as quasi-soldiers to "conquer the Devil" by struggling to bring creation back from the low state to which it has fallen. In either case, an individual soul is not born blameworthy but becomes blameworthy insofar as it fails to make use of this ability. This tough-love approach would make sense, provided that we were actually able to raise ourselves from our fallen state. Experience, however, suggests otherwise. Augustine's blanket response to all such worries is that Christ has overcome human sin for us.

> *Cum uero ubique sit praesens qui multis modis per creaturam sibi domino seruientem auersum uocet doceat credentem consoletur sperantem diligentem adhortetur conantem adiuuet exaudiat deprecantem, non tibi deputatur ad culpam quod inuitus ignoras, sed quod negligis quaerere quod ignores, neque illud quod uulnerata membra non colligis, sed quod uolentem sanare contemnis; ista tua propria peccata sunt.*

---

account of Christ as the Inner Teacher, who illuminates the mind as we come to learn new things. In doing so, Augustine removed the need for reincarnation that more literal versions of Platonic recollection present. Yet to remove the need for something is not to show that it does not exist. In the present scenario, theories (3) and (4) are at least compatible with reincarnation and have precedence in Plotinus' account of providence.

[167] *De lib. arbit.* 3.59.   [168] *De lib. arbit.* 3.56.

> But since there is present everywhere throughout a creation that is obedient
> to its Lord one who calls back the withdrawn, who instructs the faithful,
> who cheers the hopeful, who exhorts the diligent, who supports the one
> making an attempt and who hears the one praying, it is not counted as your
> fault that you are unwillingly ignorant but that you neglect to seek out what
> you do not know; nor is it counted as your fault that you do not bind up
> your wounded limbs but that you scorn the one who wants to heal you.
> These are your own sins. (*De lib. arbit.* 3.53)

In short, we go wrong insofar as we fail to heed piety's injunction, (3), to
accept our personal failings and to seek healing for our souls.

At this point, Augustine has argued that, however the details work out,
God is just in afflicting us with ignorance and trouble as punishment for
Adam's sin. The next step is to explain how Adam came to sin in the first
place. Augustine gets there, however, by answering a seemingly tangential
objection about infants who suffer and die before committing any sin.[169]
Ignorance and trouble may dispose these infants to sin, yet until they
actually do so, Augustine suggests that they can be counted neither good
nor bad, neither just nor sinful. While this neutral moral state is introduced
within a discussion of ignorance and trouble, it provides a key conceptual
enrichment that Augustine will exploit to approach the question of how the
first humans fell.[170] Given the preceding discussion of infants, the answer
should be obvious: Adam and Eve were originally created neither foolish nor
wise but occupied a middle state. That said, they were rational, which means
that they could freely accept a "precept" (*praeceptum*) of wisdom and thus
become wise or reject it and become fools.[171] Even in this neutral state, the
ability to become wise sets humans above nonrational creatures. Whichever
way humans choose, they do so with their own free will and are thus

---

[169] *De lib. arbit.* 3.66–70.
[170] *De lib. arbit.* 3.71–77. Augustine suggests that the death of children can serve other purposes, e.g.
punishing or correcting their parents. He suggests that God might even make it up to such
children in the afterlife, as he did for the Holy Innocents murdered by Herod (*De lib. arbit.* 3.68).
While this discussion of the afterlife represents an early version of a Limbo doctrine, what matters
for present purposes is the state of young children this side of the grave. Augustine completes the
passage by raising an objection about animal suffering (*De lib. arbit.* 3.69–70). Yet he brushes aside
the complaint, suggesting that those who raise it mistake the good of an animal, that by nature
must age and die, with the good of a star, that lasts forever. That said, there is a lesson to be learned
here: Those who pay attention "piously and diligently" (*pie et diligenter*) will see that pain is merely
the animal's way of avoiding division and thus seeking unity. Likewise, even inanimate things seek
unity through a kind of stability, while rational human beings seek unity of knowledge by avoiding
ambiguity. The work's practical project thus asserts itself here. And with a nod to *De ord.* 2.47,
Augustine suggests that creatures, each seeking unity in its own way, "suggest and declare the unity
of their Creator" (*unitatem insinuare atque praedicare creatoris*). *De lib. arbit.* 3.70.
[171] *De lib. arbit.* 3.72.

responsible for the consequences. Yet, like infants, the original humans were neither just nor sinful until they chose for themselves.[172] As it worked out, they chose to reject wisdom and thus brought ignorance, trouble and death unto themselves and their descendants.

The question at this point is why rejecting the precept of wisdom would have looked like an appealing option in the first place, even if it was not an overpowering one. To answer this, Augustine looks to Genesis' story of the apple for an allegorical depiction of humanity's first choice.[173] Invoking Stoic psychological theory, he suggests that any choice amounts to assenting or rejecting "some impression" (*aliquod uisum*).[174] God's precept of wisdom represents an impression from higher (i.e. eternal) things, while the serpent's suggestion represents an impression from lower (i.e. temporal) things. While Adam had no control over which impressions came into his mind, his will was free to choose between them. And by choosing lower things over higher ones, he made the wrong choice, as should be abundantly clear to those of us who have made our way through *De lib. arbit.* 1 and 2. Given that this is an allegorical interpretation, you might think that God and the serpent in this story merely represent humanity's rational and sensory faculties. Yet Augustine, never one to stop with just one level of interpretation, proceeds to ask why the serpent was going around giving such dangerous suggestions in the first place. With this we arrive at *De lib. arbit.*'s final puzzle.[175]

Scripture depicts Lucifer as the absolute pinnacle of God's creation. In terms of his nature, Lucifer was, is and ever will be a very great good.[176] What's more, his original state was of direct intimacy with the Trinity Himself, the highest happiness any creature could ever obtain. Unlike us, Lucifer was afflicted with neither ignorance nor trouble. And unlike the first humans, there was not some other serpent to whisper suggestions into his ear. What could possibly motivate a rational creature, enjoying the highest possible good and knowing full well that he's doing so, to throw it away for all eternity? What could have suggested "the plan that impiety should be pursued" (*appetendae impietatis consilum*)?[177] At this point, we must bring a bit more psychological detail onto the table. As we saw with Adam, impressions can come from below, through the bodily senses or from above

---

[172] *De lib. arbit.* 3.71–73.   [173] *De lib. arbit.* 3.74.   [174] *De lib. arbit.* 3.74.
[175] *De lib. arbit.* 3.75–77.
[176] This is a basic point of difference between Augustine's catholic explanation of evil and the Manichees' dualism which presents good and evil as two opposed substances.
[177] *De lib. arbit.* 3.75.

through reason. Yet, as we saw in *De lib. arbit.* 2.9, reason can also become aware of itself. With this framework in place, Augustine suggests:

> *Vt autem in contemplatione summae sapientiae – quae utique animus non est, nam incommutabilis est –, etiam se ipsum qui est commutabilis animus intueatur et sibi ipse quodammodo ueniat in mentem, non fit nisi differentia qua non est quod deus et tamen aliquid est quod possit placere post deum. Melior est autem cum obliuiscitur sui prae caritate incommutabilis dei uel se ipsum penitus in illius comparatione contemnit. Si autem tamquam obuius placet sibi ad peruerse imitandum deum ut potestate sua frui uelit, tanto fit minor quanto se cupit esse maiorem. Et hoc est,* Initium omnis peccati superbia *et* Initium superbiae hominis apostatare a deo.

> But although in the contemplation of that highest wisdom – which certainly is not the soul, for it is unchangeable – the soul which is changeable also sees itself and somehow comes into its own mind, this only happens through the difference by which the soul is not what God is, but nevertheless is something that can please next to God. Yet it is better, when the soul forgets itself in comparison to the love of the unchangeable God, or holds itself in complete contempt in comparison with Him. If, however, it resolves to imitate God perversely, getting in its own way, so to speak, so that it wants to enjoy its own power, the more it wants itself to be greater, then the lesser it becomes. And this is "pride, the beginning of all sin" [Sirach 10:15], and "Departing from God is the beginning of man's pride" [Sirach 10:14]. (*De lib. arbit.* 3.76)

In the end, it turns out that Lucifer was his own serpent, as a moment of self-reflection presented a lower good for him to will in place of the highest good. As the highest created good, Lucifer occupied the position of penultimate good next to God. If anyone was going to go astray by willing himself before God, Lucifer seems a plausible candidate.

When it comes to providing a theoretical answer to POE 3, there is nowhere further to go. God created Lucifer as a very great good, yet Lucifer freely chose himself over God and thus fell into sin. Pride (*superbia*) was the cause of this fall, and envy (*inuidia*) followed in its wake, moving Lucifer to tempt the first humans away from God, successfully it turns out, thus raining down ignorance, trouble and death upon their descendants. Given his fondness for delegating tasks, God struck a deal with Lucifer whereby all subsequent sinners – i.e. all human beings beyond a certain age – would pass into his dominion for punishment. Yet God eventually overturned this deal by submitting Himself to death, while being free of sin and thus ransoming us from death. Any sinful human thus has the option of siding with Christ and rising from death and sin to eternal life with God. Or, more psychologically, human beings can structure their lives around temporal goods or eternal ones; since most of us go about this the wrong way, placing temporal goods before eternal ones, the eternal God entered time, so that He might lead us from lesser goods to greater goods one step at a time.

When it comes to *De lib. arbit.*'s practical project, Lucifer provides an example for us to recoil from. In setting himself above God, Lucifer shatters the rule of piety: failing to think of God in the highest way possible, failing to thank God for the goods he has been given, and failing to acknowledge his own shortcomings, however minor they were at the start. In this sense, pride and piety sit at opposite ends of the continuum. Yet even here God preserved the perfection of the universe not only by allowing Lucifer to punish sinful humans, but also by letting Lucifer's own torments stand for all time as a warning against the pursuit of lower things.[178] By resorting to scriptural narrative in the end, Augustine is not merely trying to scare us into eating our vegetables. Having worked through *De lib. arbit.* 1–2's dialectical and self-reflective discussions, we are in a position to understand the moral psychology underlying Augustine's account of pride and the self-destructive irrationality of turning away from eternal goods, of preferring the Devil's torments to the happiness found in eternal goods:

> *Tanta est autem pulchritudo iustitiae, tanta iucunditas lucis aeternae, hoc est incommutabilis ueritatis atque sapientiae, ut, etiam si non liceret amplius in ea manere quam unius diei mora, propter hoc solum innumerabiles anni huius uitae pleni deliciis et circumfluentia temporalium bonorum recte meritoque contemnerentur. Non enim falso aut paruo affectu dictum est:* Quoniam melior est dies unus in atriis tuis super milia. *Quamquam et alio sensu possit intellegi ut milia dierum in temporis mutabilitate intellegantur, unius autem diei nomine incommutabilitas aeternitatis uocetur.*

> But so great is the beauty of justice, so great is the delight of eternal light, that is to say, of unchangeable truth and wisdom, that, even if it were not permitted to remain in it more than the span of a single day, on account of this alone innumerable years of this life filled with delights and abundance of temporal goods would rightly and deservedly be held in contempt. For neither falsely nor with little good will has it been said, "For one day in your courts is better than a thousand." Although this can also be understood in another sense, so that "a thousand days" are understood in the changeability of time, but the unchangeableness of eternity is called by the name, "one day." (*De lib. arbit.* 3.77)

With this image of eternal bliss, Augustine draws *De lib. arbit.* to a close.

---

[178] *De lib. arbit.* 3.76.

Taking Stock: Augustine's Dialogues from *C. Acad.* to *De lib. arbit.*

In this chapter I have responded to the impression that *De lib. arbit.* is engaged in a project that is fundamentally different from the Platonic method set out in *C. Acad.* and pursued in Augustine's earliest dialogues. Now that we have walked through the overarching argument of *De lib. arbit.*, we can see that the root of the problem is simply an issue of scale. The earlier works each reached a moment of *aporia*, moved forward through a moment of self-reflection and built their plausible account around individual terms drawn from Scripture. *De lib. arbit.*'s three books move through three basic formulations of POE, each book invoking further *aporiai* in the process. Moments of self-reflection figure in all three books, yet 2.7–29 is taken up with nothing but self-reflection. And while all three books present plausible conclusions, book 2 expands on the Cassiciacum form by presenting three plausible conclusions via three little *orationes*, while book 3's encounter with Scripture amounts to the longest, most intricate of all seven dialogues' concluding accounts. Nevertheless, we find the same basic rhetorical shape of the early dialogues, as discussion is followed by *oratio* using the same basic method of aporetic debate and self-reflection to set the stage for a plausible conclusion.

While *De lib. arbit.* develops this rhetorical form and philosophical method in various ways, the work sits on a trajectory established by *Sol.* + *De imm. an.* and *De Mus.* Both works build on *De ord.* 2.47's definition of philosophy as a twofold inquiry into God and the soul, as each work presents a threefold structure as two rounds of ARP devoted to the soul and its cause (God) set the stage for an extended scriptural account. This basic structure spans the three books of *De lib. arbit.*: book 1's account of temporal and eternal law is ultimately about the soul; book 2's account of God as the source of all goods is about the soul's cause, while book 3 works both into a larger scriptural account. In short, the methods, formal divisions and preoccupations of Augustine's earlier dialogues present useful models with which to analyze *De lib. arbit.*

Over and above these technical considerations, the more basic and perhaps most useful contribution of this study to readings of *De lib. arbit.* is to recognize that Augustine uses the dialogue genre as a way of cultivating particular virtues. While the progression through three formulations of POE shows, at a minimal level, how book 3 completes the project begun in book 1, we get a much more robust sense of the work's unity if we recognize that its first two books are meant to instill the pious attitude that Augustine sees as necessary for the scriptural explorations of book 3. Piety allows us to see that the answer to the theoretical POE is pride, while the same piety provides a practical solution to the problem that evil creates in the lives of the faithful. Piety thus ties together in a single project two approaches that we often separate today into theoretical and pastoral issues.[179] Even after the ample attention Augustine's "free will defense" received during the twentieth-century debate over the problem of evil, its rich scriptural explorations and emphasis on explanatory power have yet more to offer this new century. Beyond the debate over evil, the work provides a model for how to be religious, as it embraces the richness of a lived tradition structured through critical thought and self-reflection in a project of faith seeking understanding.

---

[179] Harrison 2006 traces many of these same connections, although when it comes to setting them within a single project, he looks to "Augustine's way into the will," i.e. a gradual process of self-reflection and articulation through which Augustine sets out his doctrine of the will. I would argue that piety provides a single thread that runs just as deep as this theoretical exposition of the will. If anything, piety runs deeper insofar as it embraces both the work's theoretical and practical projects.

Conclusion
Augustine and the Academy Today

To borrow a phrase from Plato, I have attempted to "cut" each of Augustine's dialogues "along its natural joints."[1] My readers may judge the success of the endeavor. The goal of this study from the outset was to bring scholarship on Augustine's dialogues back to the drawing board. The payoff is a reading that motivates the dialogues' failed arguments and seeming lack of focus, by setting them within a larger project devoted to a certain kind of teaching. This more holistic approach has allowed us to read the dialogues with fresh eyes. In the preceding chapters, I used this approach to draw out the relevance of individual works to contemporary debates on a variety of issues, while Chapters 4–6 looked at the uses of the Cassiciacum dialogues as a set. I would like to close by offering my own provisional conclusions about this study's contribution to Augustine scholarship and broader debates about the nature and value of liberal education.

Reading Augustine

I claimed at the outset that twentieth-century scholarship on the dialogues has backed us into a corner, inadvertently creating obstacles to a holistic reading. Problems started with the debate over whether or not the scenic dialogues from Cassiciacum – *C. Acad., De beata v., De ord.* – were transcripts of actual conversations. While the question is harmless in itself, it built on and reinforced the impression that these works were not terribly well organized. If the present study contributes anything to this debate, it is to show each dialogue to be carefully planned and skillfully crafted. The loose ends of actual conversations generally do not come neatly together around terms drawn from Wisdom 11:20, particularly when these conversations explore multiple topics over the span of a couple weeks. One hundred and twenty years after Hirzel challenged the dialogues' historicity,

[1] Plato, *Phdr.* 265e.

230

though, the question is perhaps not whether Augustine had a hand in structuring them but to what extent. My reading might advance this discussion – if it is actually worth perpetuating – by changing the question from *how much* Augustine structured them to *how* he structured them. Augustine's Platonic pedagogical method, ARP, starts by sorting out basic questions, using students' current opinions to generate puzzles and then letting students work through them. For any given question, there are only so many ways a conversation will likely go. If we grant that the young Augustine was rhetorically skilled and dialectically savvy, then it strikes me as entirely plausible that the opinions, questions and confusions expressed by his companions in the dialogues correspond more-or-less to those expressed by his flesh-and-blood companions at Cassiciacum. For all we know, they might even have had a notetaker present. That is not to suggest that the dialogues are simply transcripts presenting conversations in the order that they actually occurred. Augustine's role as author, rather, is akin to a French organist of the grand old days – a Cochereau or Dupré – who would accept themes from audience members and improvise canons, symphonies or fugues on the spot. To see how the dialogues may be both transcripts and literary works we must simply recognize that Augustine's companions supplied the content while Augustine supplied the structure, using the philosophical method and rhetorical form, which we have explored, to develop and arrange his companions' thoughts – likely taking liberties at points – into the dialogues we now have.

Our second obstacle was the debate over the status of Augustine's conversion. Developmentalists argue for a sea change as his views at Cassiciacum (386CE), which are more Platonist than Christian, give way to the mature Christianity expressed in *Conf.* (397–401CE). Unitarians, in turn, argue for consistency throughout. My more basic problem with this debate is that it imposes on the dialogues a set of concerns out of sync with their own central project. This, too, would be fine so far as it goes. Over time, though, it has blinded scholars to the fact that the dialogues, in fact, have a central project, one centrally concerned with Christian Scripture. While Plato occasionally deals with matters of traditional religion and Cicero even more so, Augustine's works are unique in the body of ancient dialogues for their systematic and sustained project of developing philosophical and religious outlooks in tandem. They merely do not follow the agenda that *Conf.* has led scholars to look for in them. Rather than engage *Conf.*'s thinking about sin, grace and Christ's role as Mediator, the earliest dialogues ask more basic questions about human nature, the virtues and the providential structure of creation. *De lib. arbit.* straddles the gap between the two projects, with its exploration of piety and pride, which is in keeping at once with the Cassiciacum dialogues' exploration of the virtues and with the particular theological concerns of *Conf.* In terms of chronology, *De lib. arbit.* 1 was written in 388CE, and books 2 and 3 were completed in 395 or 396CE.[2] While many view this text, too, as loosely structured, I have argued that a concern for piety drives the work from the very beginning. With this, we can identify a degree of continuity in Augustine's writings. While scholars typically approach such questions in terms of Augustine's doctrinal commitments, I suggest reframing the discussion around issues of philosophical method and rhetorical strategy. In this we find a new kind of progression. *C. Acad.* establishes a method, ARP, and associated rhetorical form – dedication, debate, *oratio* – which structure the three scenic dialogues (386CE). *De ord.* 2.47 refines this project with its depiction of philosophy as a twofold inquiry into God and the soul. *Sol.* (386CE) + *De imm. an.* (387CE) presents a first, albeit abandoned, attempt at this more daring structure. *De Mus.* 6 (387CE) follows through, as its two rounds of ARP dedicated to the soul and God set the stage for the elaboration of a plausible, scriptural account of creation. Yet it is not until the three books of *De lib. arbit.* that this structure is brought to its fullest fruition. If we are to extend this methodological history beyond the dialogues, it is worth noting that *Conf.* also ends with an extended reading of Genesis. The unity of *Conf.*'s narrative and nonnarrative halves – books 1–9 and 10–13, respectively – is itself a matter of huge dispute. Yet the work's strings upon strings of puzzles, its shift from nine books of remembering to book 10's discussion of memory and its closing exploration of Scripture suggest that something akin to ARP is still at play.

Our final obstacle stemmed from the habit of philosophers, particularly analytic philosophers, to focus on individual arguments in isolation from their original contexts. Yet even analytic philosophers can recognize that context matters. We find this in the problem of evil debate, as Adams looks to the particulars of religious traditions for conceptual enrichments, and Stump augments argument with narrative. In Chapter 7, I argued that *De lib. arbit.* has as much to offer these twenty-first-century concerns as it did the logically oriented debates of the twentieth. Yet all the dialogues have something to tell us about the nature of the philosophical undertaking. The dialogues' account of philosophy as purification and their pursuit of the various kathartic virtues show us the potential for dialectical argument to change individuals' character. Meanwhile, their willingness to embrace perplexity and trade in provisional solutions brings out the skeptical side of a Father of the Church. Many now take skepticism and faith to be

---

[2] See Harrison, *Augustine's Way into the Will*, 17–21 for discussion of this chronology.

mutually opposed and will likely find the idea of Christian skepticism to be mildly contradictory if not simply offensive. I find it to be quite attractive, not only for Roman Catholics and other Christians who typically look to Augustine for a model, but for anyone looking to adhere to a particular tradition, whether religious or intellectual, without ignoring the ambiguities and tensions of our larger society. Like us, Augustine lived at a time of religious pluralism and cultural upheaval. Constantine had converted earlier in the same century, and Augustine was 7 years old when the Emperor Julian "the Apostate" (361–363CE) attempted to undermine Christianity and restore the old religion. As Augustine grew, he was presented with multiple competing philosophical schools and multiple competing versions of Christianity, including the Manicheism he came to see as mere superstition. This is precisely the kind of pluralistic mess that Augustine developed ARP to help navigate. I would like to close by speaking to teachers in particular and to suggest ways that Augustine's dialogues and their characteristic method may prove useful in addressing the demands of a twenty-first-century classroom.

Augustine and the Liberal Academy Today

"Faith seeking understanding" has been a favorite motto among Christian educators for centuries.[3] There is a growing scholarly literature relating Augustine's pedagogical thought to contemporary Catholic institutions[4] and a somewhat newer literature presenting his contribution to the liberal arts tradition more generally.[5] Rather than reiterate what these scholars have said, I will turn to what is unique to this study and draw out some implications for today's liberal academy at large. It will suit this purpose to focus, in turn, on each element of the dialogues' three-part method, ARP.

The picture that emerges is of human beings who are natural philosophers and a world that offers continual opportunities for engaging in a process of reflection through which we may draw closer to characteristically human goods. Each individual has within himself everything needed to make this journey, yet the pursuit of sensual pleasures, the demands of everyday life and the opinions of human society present obstacles along the way. At the most basic level, a teacher's task is to remove these obstacles and support students as they embrace and develop their natural curiosity.

---

[3] Anselm, who uses the phrase as the original title to his *Proslogion*, provides an early example.
[4] See Topping, *Happiness and Wisdom* and *St. Augustine*.
[5] See Pollmann & Vessey, *Augustine and the Disciplines*.

When viewed in these most basic terms, the dialogues share the mindset of the emerging Philosophy for Kids movement.[6] Children are inquisitive, imaginative, easily moved by wonder and willing to run with ideas far beyond the point at which most adults grow tired. These are all characteristics of an excellent philosopher. In my own experience working with children, people are ready to engage in philosophical discussions as soon as they can speak in complete sentences, i.e. somewhere around age four.[7] Yet in the United States, at least, these philosophical qualities tend to get snuffed out by the time students reach Junior High, as a growing vocationalism and test-taking culture trains them to answer questions but not to ask them. A good deal of "un-learning" is often needed to get college students back to the level of the children they once were. College students in one of my own Philosophy for Kids courses have noted that they were more prone to fall back on bad habits of thought than the fourth- and fifth-graders with whom they worked.[8] Augustine expresses a similar perspective when he holds up Licentius for his father to imitate as he calls Romanianus back to the "breasts of philosophy" (*philosophia . . . cuius uberibus*).[9] We would do well to take Augustine's love of puzzles seriously. In practical terms, this means encouraging students to admit confusion and helping them develop skills in framing questions. The Cassiciacum dialogues model such training, as the defensive, competitive stance that Licentius and Trygetius take in *C. Acad.* 1 gradually gives way to their willingness in *De ord.* 2 to embrace *aporia* and even anticipate problems with their own positions. Philosophers are uniquely well equipped to rekindle this love of inquiry, which is in many ways a prerequisite to engaging in any field of study.

Removing obstacles is merely the first step, however. Augustine's method proceeds by calling students to "know themselves" via reflection on their own rational activities. I invoked this call to self-reflection in Chapter 4 to explain *De ord.*'s attitude toward the liberal disciplines as useful yet ultimately unnecessary starting points for philosophical inquiry into the soul and God. Even those of us who are suspicious of Augustine's theological conclusions can benefit from taking seriously the process of

---

[6] While the literature connected with this movement is growing rapidly, Gareth Matthews, *The Philosophy of Childhood* (Cambridge, MA: Harvard University Press, 1994), and Thomas Wartenberg, *Big Ideas for Little Kids* (New York: Rowman & Littlefield, 2014), provide useful theoretical and practical introductions, respectively.

[7] See my "Art & Dialogue: An Experiment in Pre-K Philosophy," *Analytic Teaching and Philosophical Praxis*, Diane Terorde-Doyle, co-author 37:2 (2017) 26–35.

[8] The college students in question were first-years at Rollins College. The fourth- and fifth-graders were members of the gifted class at Fern Creek Elementary School in Orlando, Florida.

[9] *C. Acad.* 1.4. Cf. philosophy's "bosom" (*gremium*) at *De beata v.* 1.4.

self-reflection through which he arrives at them. Over the centuries, the humanities have developed in close conjunction with a body of literature we have come to think of as the Western Canon. While this body of literature has, in fact, been changing all the while, the culture wars of recent decades have driven an unusually large wedge between the humanities and their traditional content. Add to this a growing concern for acquiring marketable skills, and the result is general confusion about what content, if any, must be learned if one is to be liberally educated. If the study of comic books and the study of Shakespeare are held to be of equal value, why bother with either? The project of thinking about thinking, announced in *De ord.* and pursued in *De Mus.* provides a framework for addressing this question. Humanistic inquiry is, at bottom, an expression of what we are as human beings. We may thus come to know ourselves better by engaging in such inquiry in a self-reflective way. In this respect, Augustine is in line with contemporary educational theories that stress the importance of metacognition.[10] Not all literature will be as useful for moving all audiences to inquiry. As Plato put it in a somewhat different context, some perceptions are "summoners" to rational inquiry (*parakalounta*),[11] others are not. In practical terms, this means choosing readings not on the basis of what they have to say but on the kind of response they might elicit.[12] Whatever else we might say about Plato, students either love his Socrates or hate him. Either way, they are engaged. As teachers we must orchestrate such opportunities, encourage students to follow their initial responses with further exploration and see to it that they take seriously what they find out about themselves in the process. The ultimate point of all this un-learning and self-reflection is to improve how we think about ourselves and our place in the world.

Descartes engaged in a similar project and attempted to rebuild all human knowledge upon the foundation of indubitable first principles. From today's perspective, his attempt was simply naive. Augustine took a

---

[10] See, for instance, Derek Cabrera & Laura Colosi, *Thinking at Every Desk: Four Simple Skills to Transform Your Classroom* (New York: W. W. Norton & Company, 2012).

[11] Plato, *R.* 523c.

[12] This is somewhat easier to see if we focus on children's literature. For every book such as Shel Silverstein's *The Giving Tree*, which raises puzzles, embraces ambiguity and invites thoughtful response, there are dozens in which the "moral of the story" is obvious to anyone paying attention. Such stories leave little room for discussion. One of the challenges in teaching children philosophy from story books is finding stories that are aporetic in a way that is useful for engaging children in a fruitful discussion. The works of Leo Lionni, Arthur Lobel and William Steig stand out as particularly useful. Thomas Wartenberg, *A Sneetch Is a Sneetch and Other Philosophical Discoveries* (Oxford: Wiley-Blackwell, 2013), presents an introduction to Philosophy for adults through a collection of sixteen story books written for children.

humbler approach, embracing ideas as plausible in those instances when there is no clearly right answer, yet some position must be taken. This is the heritage of skepticism. The next thousand years of religious politics and changes in philosophical fashion put a premium on demonstrative proof and led medieval thinkers down a path that eventually arrived at Descartes, for whom an argument for a plausible conclusion is simply a failed argument.[13] Further changes in politics and philosophical fashions since then have left members of today's liberal academy wary of absolutes, as large portions of the broader culture descend into various forms of fundamentalism. While there is no easy solution to this problem, Augustine's dialogues provide at least one model for how the liberal academy might prepare its students for the challenges of twenty-first-century life. In practical terms, this means changing how we frame our discussions. The propositions P and not-P cannot both be true, and the attempt to prove one at the expense of the other is a quick way to create factions. The twentieth-century debate over the problem of evil is a case in point. In some cases, there is nothing wrong with factions. They can often be quite useful. Yet when it comes to those issues in ethics and religion for which no clearly right answer is forthcoming, a black-or-white attitude can lead to intellectual stagnation and potentially dangerous conflict in the greater world. Augustine's search for explanatory power offers a different way forward. We may come to see, for instance, that Christianity and Islam both offer rich explanations for a wide range of questions about human life, recognizing all the while our uncertainty as to what extent the claims of either are actually correct. By embracing this approach, an individual may wholeheartedly commit to the one tradition while just as wholeheartedly respecting other individuals' commitment to the other. This is not a failure of religious conviction. It is a mature approach to it. As it happens, each of Augustine's dialogues ends by embracing some form of Christianity as the most plausible way forward. Yet they are honest about the kinds of argument that back those conclusions, and they remain open to alternatives. In this the dialogues model a form of flexibility and tolerance that would serve students well in our own pluralistic world.

---

[13] In "Augustine to the Carolingian Renaissance," I argue for the merits of the early medieval period. Before the reintroduction of Aristotle to the West, philosophy proceeded via something more like the skeptical-Platonist mindset described in the present study's Chapter 2. The emphasis was on first-person spiritual exercises and conceptual development rather than third-person proofs and arguments from first principles.

Bibliography

Texts, Commentaries, Translations

Armstrong, Arthur Hilary. *Plotinus: Enneads.* Cambridge, MA: Harvard University Press, 1988.

Bostock, David. *Plato's* Phaedo. Oxford, 1986.

Bouton-Touboulic, Anne-Isabelle. *L'ordre caché.* Paris: Institut d'Études Augustiniennes, 2004.

Brisson, Luc. *Porphyre: Sentences.* Paris: Libraire Philosophique J. Vrin, 2005.

Brittain, Charles. *Cicero: On Academic Skepticism.* Indianapolis, IN: Hackett Publishing Company, Inc., 2006.

Catapano, Giovanni. *Aurelio Agostino: Tutti i dialoghi.* Milan: Il Pensiero Occidentale, 2006.

Dolbeau, François. "Sermon inédit de saint Augustin sur la providence divine." *Revue des Études Augustiniennes* 41 (1995): 267–289.

Doignon, Jean. *Œuvres de Saint Augustin: Dialogues philosophiques:* La Vie heureuse. Paris: Bibliothèque Augustinienne, 1986.

   Œuvres de Saint Augustin: Dialogues philosophiques: L'Ordre. Paris: Bibliothèque Augustinienne, 1997.

Foley, Helene. *The Homeric Hymn to Demeter.* Princeton, NJ: Princeton University Press, 1994, esp. 65–75.

Foley, Michael. *The* De Ordine *of St. Augustine.* Dissertation. Boston College, 1999.

Fuhrer, Therese. *Augustin:* Contra Academicos *Bücher 2 und 3.* Berlin: Walter de Gruyter & Co., 1997.

Green, W. M., ed. *Corpus Christianorum Series Latina* 29/2 (1970).

Jackson, Belford Darrell, ed. *Augustine: De Dialectica.* Synthese Historical Library 16. Dordrecht: Synthese Historical Library, 1975.

King, Peter, trans. *Augustine: Against the Academicians and the Teacher.* Indianapolis, IN: Hackett Publishing Company, Inc., 1995.

Korsgaard, Christine. "Introduction." In *Kant: Groundwork of the Metaphysics of Morals,* edited by Mary Gregor and Jens Timmermann, ix–xxxvi. Cambridge: Cambridge University Press, 2012.

Long, Anthony and David Sedley, eds. *Hellenistic Philosophers.* Cambridge: Cambridge University Press, 1987.

Nehamas, Alexander and Paul Woodruff. *Plato: Symposium*. Indianapolis, IN: Hackett Publishing Company, Inc., 1989.

O'Donnell, James. *Augustine* Confessions*: Volume 2: Commentary, Books 1–7*. Oxford: Oxford University Press, 1992.

O'Meara, John, trans. *Against the Academics*. Westminster: Ancient Christian Writers 12, 1950.

Reynolds, L. D., ed. *L. Annaei Senecae ad Lucilium Epistulae Morales*. Oxford: Oxford University Press, 1965.

——— ed. *M. Tulli Ciceronis De Finibus Bonorum et Malorum Libri Quinque*. Oxford: Oxford University Press, 1998.

Russel, Robert, trans. *Divine Providence and the Problem of Evil: A Translation of St. Augustine's De Ordine*. New York, NY: Cosmopolitan Science & Art Service Co., Inc., 1942.

Schäublin, Christoph. *Marcus Tullius Cicero: Über die Wahrsagung/ De Divinatione*. Düsseldorf: Artemis & Winkler, 2002.

Schlapbach, Karin. *Augustin* Contra Academicos (vel De Academicis) *Buch 1 Einleitung und Kommentar*. Berlin: De Gruyter, 2003.

Trelenberg, Jörg. *Augustins Schrift* De ordine. Tübingen: Mohr Siebeck, 2009.

Watson, Gerard. *Saint Augustine: Soliloquies and Immortality of the Soul*. Warminster: Aris & Phillips, 1986.

General Bibliography

Adams, Marilyn McCord. *Horrendous Evils and the Goodness of God*. Ithaca, NY: Cornell University Press, 1999.

Adams, Marilyn McCord and Robert Merrihew Adams, eds. *The Problem of Evil*. Oxford: Oxford University Press, 1990.

Alfaric, Prosper. *L'évolution intellectuelle de saint Augustin*. Paris: Émile Nourry, 1918.

Algra, Keimpe. "Chrysippus, Carneades, Cicero: The Ethical *Divisiones* in Cicero's *Lucullus*." In *Assent and Argument*, edited by Brad Inwood and Jaap Mansfeld, 107–139. Leiden: Brill, 1997.

Allen, James. "Academic Probabilism and Stoic Epistemology." *Classical Quarterly* 44 (1994): 85–113.

Asiedu, F. "The Wise Man and the Limits of Virtue in *De Beata Vita*: Stoic Self-Sufficiency or Augustinian Irony?" *Augustiniana* 49 (1999): 215–234.

Ayres, Lewis. "'Giving Wings to Nicaea': Reconceiving Augustine's Earliest Trinitarian Theology." *Augustinian Studies* 38/1 (2007): 21–40.

BeDuhn, Jason. *Augustine's Manichaean Dilemma, 1: Conversion and Apostasy, 373–388 C.E.* Philadelphia, PA: University of Pennsylvania Press, 2009.

Benson, Hugh. *Socratic Wisdom: The Model of Knowledge in Plato's Early Dialogues*. Oxford: Oxford University Press, 2000.

——— *Clitophon's Challenge: Dialectic in Plato's* Meno, Phaedo, *and* Republic. Oxford: Oxford University Press, 2015.

Bermon, Emmanuel. "'*Contra Academicos vel De Academicis*' (*Retract.* I, 1): Saint Augustin et les *Academica* de Cicéron." *Revue des Études Anciennes* 111/1 (2009): 75–93.

Betegh, Gábor. "Tale, Theology and Teleology in *Phaedo*." In *Plato's Myths*, edited by Catalin Partenie, 77–100. Cambridge: Cambridge University Press, 2009.

Bett, Richard. "Carneades' Distinction between Assent and Approval." *Monist* 73/1 (1990): 3–20.

Bouton-Touboulic, Anne-Isabelle. "Les valeurs d'*ordo* et leur réception chez saint Augustin." *Revue des Études Augustiniennes* 45 (1999): 295–334.

"Dire l'ordre caché: Les discours sur l'ordre chez saint Augustin." *Revue des Études Augustiniennes* 52 (2006): 143–166.

Boyer, Charles. *Christianisme et néo-platonisme dans la formation de saint Augustin*. Paris: G. Beauchesne, 1920.

Boys-Stones, George. *Post-Hellenistic Philosophy*. Oxford: Oxford University Press, 2001.

Brittain, Charles. *Philo of Larissa: The Last of the Academic Skeptics*. Oxford: Oxford University Press, 2001.

"Attention Deficit in Plotinus and Augustine: Psychological Problems in Christian and Platonist Theories of the Grades of Virtue." *Proceedings of the Boston Area Colloquium in Ancient Philosophy* 28 (2003): 223–263.

"Common Sense: Concepts, Definitions and Meaning In and Out of the Stoa." In *Language and Learning*, edited by Dorothea Frede and Brad Inwood, 165–209. Cambridge: Cambridge University Press, 2005.

"Augustine as a Reader of Cicero." In *Tolle Lege: Essays on Augustine and Medieval Philosophy*, edited by Richard Taylor, David Twetten and Michael Wren, 81–114. Milwaukee, WI: Marquette University Press, 2011.

"Self-knowledge in Cicero and Augustine (*De Trinitate*, X, 5,7–10, 16)." *Medioevo* 37 (2012): 107–136.

Brown, Peter. *Augustine of Hippo: A Biography*. Berkeley, CA: University of California Press, 2000.

Burnyeat, Miles. "Carneades Was No Probablist." Unpublished.

Cabrera, Derek and Laura Colosi. *Thinking at Every Desk: Four Simple Skills to Transform Your Classroom*. New York, NY: W. W. Norton & Company, 2012.

Cary, Phillip. "An Abandoned Proof." In *Augustine's Invention of the Inner Self: The Legacy of a Christian Platonist*. Oxford: Oxford University Press, 2000, 95–104.

Cary, Phillip S. "What Licentius Learned." *Augustinian Studies* 29/1 (1998): 141–163.

Catapano, Giovanni. "Augustine's Treatise *De Immortalitate Animae* and the Proof of the Soul's Immortality in *Soliloquia*." *Documenti e studi sulla tradizione filosofica medievale* 25 (2014): 67–84.

"*In philosophiae gremium confugere*: Augustine's View of Philosophy in the First Book of his *Contra Academicos*." *Dionysius* 18 (2000): 45–68.

"Quale scetticismo viene criticato de Agostino nel *Contra Academicos?*" *Quaestio* 6 (2006): 1–13.

"The Development of Augustine's Metaphilosophy: Col 2:8 and the 'Philosophers of This World'." *Augustinian Studies* 38/1 (2007): 233–254.

Chisholm, Roderick. "The Defeat of Good and Evil." In *The Problem of Evil*, edited by Marilyn McCord Adams and Robert Merrihew Adams, 53–68. Oxford: Oxford University Press, 1990.

Claes, Martin. "Limitations to the *exercitatio mentis*: Changes in Rhetorical Style in Augustine's Dialogues." *Augustiniana* 57 (2007): 387–398.

Clark, Gillian. "Can We Talk? Augustine and the Possibility of Dialogue." In *The End of Dialogue in Antiquity*, edited by Simon Goldhill, 117–134. Oxford: Oxford University Press, 2008.

Cloeren, Herman J. "St. Augustine's *De Magistro*, a Transcendental Investigation." *Augustinian Studies* 16 (1985): 21–27.

Conybeare, Catherine. *The Irrational Augustine*. Oxford: Oxford University Press, 2006.

Couissin, Pierre. "The Stoicism of the New Academy." In *The Skeptical Tradition*, edited by M. Burnyeat, 31–63. Berkeley, CA: University of California Press, 1983.

Courcelle, Pierre. *Les lettres grecques en Occident, de Macrobe à Cassiodore*. Paris: Bibliothèque des Écoles françaises et de Rome, 1943.

Recherches sur les Confessions *de saint Augustin*. Paris: de Boccard, 1968.

Curley, Augustine. *Augustine's Critique of Skepticism*. New York, NY: Studies in the Humanities Literature – Politics – Society, 1996.

Cutino, Michele. "I *Dialogi* di Agostino dinanzi al *De regressu animae* di Porfirio." *Recherches Augustiniennes* 27 (1994): 41–74.

Diggs, Bernard J. "St. Augustine against the Academicians." *Traditio* 7 (1951): 73–93.

Dobell, Brian. *Augustine's Intellectual Conversion*. Cambridge: Cambridge University Press, 2009.

Dodaro, Robert. "Augustine on the Statesman and the Two Cities." In *A Companion to Augustine*, edited by Mark Vessey, 386–397, Oxford: Blackwell Publishing, 2012, esp. 393–397.

Doignon, Jean. "La *praxis* de l'*admonitio* dans les Dialogues de Cassiciacum de saint Augustin." *Vetera Christianorum* 23 (1986): 21–37.

"Saint Augustin et sa culture philosophique face au problème du bonheur." *Freiburger Zeitschrift für Philosophie und Theologie* 34/3 (1987): 339–359.

"Développements stoïcisants d'Augustin autour de l'"*exemplum*" cicéronien d'Orata." *Signum Pietatis* 60 (1989): 53–61.

Dubreucq, Eric. "Augustin et le scepticisme académicien." *Recherches de Science Religieuse* 86/3 (1998): 335–365.

Dutton, Blake. "Augustine, Academic Skepticism, and Zeno's Definition." *Augustiniana* 53 (2003): 7–30.

Augustine and Academic Skepticism: A Philosophical Study. Ithaca, NY: Cornell University Press, 2016.

Emilsson, Eyjólfur Kjalar. "Cognition and Its Object." In *Cambridge Companion to Plotinus*, edited by Lloyd Gerson, 217–249. Cambridge: Cambridge University Press, 1996.

Plotinus on Intellect. Oxford: Oxford University Press, 2007.

Fine, Gail. "Knowledge and Belief in *Republic* 5–7." In *Plato*, vol. 1, pp. 215–246. Oxford: Oxford University Press, 1999.

"Inquiry in the *Meno*." In *Plato on Knowledge and Forms*, 200–226. Oxford: Oxford University Press, 2003.

Foley, Michael. "Cicero, Augustine, and the Philosophical Roots of the Cassiciacum Dialogues." *Revue des Études Augustiniennes* 45 (1999): 51–77.

Frede, Michael. "Stoics and Skeptics on Clear and Distinct Impressions." In *Essays in Ancient Philosophy*, 151–176. Minneapolis, MN: University of Minnesota Press, 1987.

"The Sceptic's Beliefs." In *Essays in Ancient Philosophy*, 179–200. Minneapolis, MN: University of Minnesota Press, 1987.

"The Sceptic's Two Kinds of Assent." In *Essays in Ancient Philosophy*, 201–222. Minneapolis, MN: University of Minnesota Press, 1987.

"The Stoic Notion of a *Lekton*." In *Language*, edited by Steven Everson, 109–128. Cambridge: Cambridge University Press, 1994.

"Stoic Epistemology." In *The Cambridge History of Hellenistic Philosophy*, edited by Keimpe Algra, Jonathan Barnes, Jaap Mansfeld and Malcolm Schofield, 295–322. Cambridge: Cambridge University Press, 1999.

Fredriksen, Paula. "Paul and Augustine: Conversion Narratives, Orthodox Traditions and the Retrospective Self." *Journal of Theological Studies* 37 (1986): 3–34.

Fuhrer, Therese. "Das Kriterium der Wahrheit in Augustins *Contra Academicos*." *Vigiliae Christianae* 46 (1992): 257–275.

"Der Begriff *veri simile* bei Cicero und Augustin." *Museum Helveticum* 50/2 (1993): 107–125.

"Skeptizismus und Subjektivität: Augustins antiskeptische Argumentation und das Konzept der Verinnerlichung." In *Geschichte und Vorgeschichte der modernen Subjektivität*, edited by Reto Luzius Fetz, Roland Hagenbüchle and Peter Schulz, 319–339. Berlin: Walter de Gruyter, 1998.

"Augustins Frühdialoge als Inszenierung der Einheit von religiöser Praxis und philosophischem Dialog." In *Metaphysik und Religion*, edited by Theo Kobusch and Michael Erler, 309–322. Munich: K. G. Saur, 2002.

"Zum erkenntnistheoretischen Hintergrund von Augustins Glaubensbegriff." In *Die christlich-philosophischen Diskurse der Spätantike: Texte, Personen, Institutionen*, edited by Therese Fuhrer, 191–210. Stuttgart, 2008.

Gilligan, Carol. *In a Different Voice: Psychological Theory and Women's Development*. Cambridge, MA: Harvard University Press, 1982.

Glucker, John. *Antiochus and the Late Academy*. Göttingen: Vandenhoeck & Ruprecht, 1978.

Goldhill, Simon, ed. *The End of Dialogue in Antiquity*. Oxford: Oxford University Press, 2008.

Hadot, Ilsetraut. *Arts libéraux et philosophie dans la pensée antique.* Paris: *Études Augustiniennes,* 1948.

Hadot, Pierre. "Le *Contra Academicos* de saint Augustin et l'histoire de l'Académie." *École Pratique des Hautes Études, section 5: Sciences religieuses* 77 (1969): 291–295.

"La présentation du platonisme par Augustin." In Kerygma *und* Logos, edited by A. M. Ritter, 272–279. Göttingen: Vandenhoeck & Ruprecht, 1979.

Hagendahl, Harald. *Augustine and the Latin Classics.* Göteborg: Studia Graeca et Latina Gothoburgensia, 1967.

Halliburton R. J. "The Inclination to Retirement – The Retreat of Cassiciacum and the 'Monastery' of Tagaste." *Studia Patristica* 5 (1962): 329–340.

Harding, Brian. "Skepticism, Illumination and Christianity in Augustine's *Contra Academicos.*" *Augustinian Studies* 34/2 (2003): 197–212.

"Epistemology and Eudaimonism in Augustine's *Contra Academicos.*" *Augustinian Studies* 37/2 (2006): 247–274.

Harrison, Carol. "Augustine of Hippo's Cassiciacum *Confessions*: Towards a Reassessment of the 390s." *Augustinian Studies* 31/2 (2000): 219–224.

Rethinking Augustine's Early Theology. Oxford: Oxford University Press, 2006.

Harrison, Simon. *Augustine's Way into the Will: The Theological and Philosophical Significance of* De Libero Arbitrio. Oxford: Oxford University Press, 2006.

Harwardt, Sabine. "Die Glücksfrage der Stoa in Augustins *De Beata Vita*: Übernahme und Anwendung stoischer Argumentationsmuster." In *Zur Rezeption der hellenistischen Philosophie in der Spätantike,* edited by Theresa Fuhrer and Michael Ehler, 153–171. Stuttgart: Franz Steiner, 1999.

Heath, Malcolm. *Unity in Greek Poetics.* Oxford: Oxford University Press, 1989.

Heil, John. "Augustine's Attack on Skepticism: the *Contra Academicos.*" *Harvard Theological Review* 65/1 (1972): 99–116.

Hick, John. "Soul-Making and Suffering." In *The Problem of Evil,* edited by Marilyn McCord Adams and Robert Merrihew Adams, 168–188. Oxford: Oxford University Press, 1990.

Hirzel, Rudolf. *Der Dialog, ein literarhistorischer Versuch.* Leipzig: S. Hirzel, 1895.

Holt, Laura. "Scripture: Wisdom's Teacher: Augustine at Cassiciacum." *Augustinian Studies* 29 (1998): 47–59.

Holte, Ragnar. *Béatitude et Sagesse: Saint Augustin et le problème de la fin de l'homme dans la philosophie ancienne.* Paris: Études Augustiniennes, 1962.

Howard-Snyder, Daniel. *The Evidential Argument from Evil.* Indianapolis, IN: Indiana University Press, 1996.

Hübner, Wolfgang. "Der *Ordo* der Realien in Augustins Frühdialog *De ordine.*" *Revue des Études Augustiniennes* 33 (1987): 23–48.

Jordan, Mark D. "Ancient Philosophical Protreptic and the Problem of Persuasive Genres." *Rhetorica* 4/4 (1986): 309–333.

Jordan, William. "Augustine on Music." In *Grace, Politics and Desire: Essays on Augustine,* edited by Hugo Anthony Meynell, 123–135. Calgary: University of Calgary Press, 1990.

Kamimura, Naoki. "Self-Knowledge and the Disciplines '*in uita*' in Augustine's *De ordine.*" *Patristica,* Suppl. vol. 2 (2006): 76–96.

Kenyon, Erik. "The Order of Augustine's Cassiciacum Dialogues," *Augustinian Studies* 42/2 (2011): 173–188.

"Augustine and the Liberal Arts," *Arts and Humanities in Higher Education* 21/1 (2012): 105–113.

"Platonic Pedagogy in Augustine's Dialogues," *Ancient Philosophy* 34 (2014): 151–168.

Kenyon, Erik and Diane Terorde-Doyle. "Art & Dialogue: An Experiment in Pre-K Philosophy." *Analytic Teaching and Philosophical Praxis* (2017): 26–35.

"Augustine to the Carolingian Renaissance," In *Cambridge Companion to Medieval Ethics*, edited by Thomas Williams (Cambridge: Cambridge University Press, forthcoming).

Kidd, Erika. "Making Sense of Virgil in *De Magistro*." *Augustinian Studies* 46/2 (2015): 211–224.

King, Peter. "Augustine's Encounter with Neoplatonism." *Modern Schoolman* 82 (2005): 213–233.

Kirwan, Christopher. "Against the Skeptics." In *Augustine*, 15–34. London: Routledge, 1989.

Kolbet, Paul R. *Augustine and the Cure of Souls: Reviving a Classical Ideal*. Notre Dame, IN: University of Notre Dame Press, 2010.

Kraut, Richard. "Introduction to the Study of Plato," In *Cambridge Companion to Plato*. Cambridge: Cambridge University Press, 1992.

Kretzmann, Norman. "Faith Seeks, Understanding Finds: Augustine's Charter for Christian Philosophy." In *Christian Philosophy*, edited by Thomas Flint, 1–36. Notre Dame: University of Notre Dame Press, 1990.

Law, Vivian. "St. Augustine's '*De grammatica*': Lost or Found?" *Recherches Augustiniennes* 19 (1984): 155–183.

Leher, Seth. *Boethius and Dialogue: Literary Method in "The Consolation of Philosophy"* Princeton: Princeton University Press, 1985.

LeMoine, Fannie. "Augustine: On Education and the Liberal Arts." In *Saint Augustine the Bishop: A Book of Essays*, edited by Fannie LeMoine and Christopher Kleinhenz, 179–188. New York: Garland Publishing, 1994.

Levy, Carlos. "Scepticisme et dogmatisme dans l'Académie: 'l'ésotérisme' d'Arcésilas." *Revue des Études Augustiniennes* 56 (1979): 335–348.

Lewis, Charlton T. and Charles Short. *A Latin Dictionary*. Oxford: Oxford University Press, 1963.

Lim, Richard. "Christians, Dialogues and Patterns of Sociability in Late Antiquity." In *The End of Dialogue in Antiquity*, edited by Simon Goldhill, 151–172. Oxford: Oxford University Press, 2008.

Long, Alex. "Plato's Dialogues and a Common Rationale for Dialogue Form." In *The End of Dialogue in Antiquity*, edited by Simon Goldhill, 45–59. Oxford: Oxford University Press, 2008.

MacDonald, Scott. "Augustine." In *A Companion to the Middle Ages*, edited by Jorge Gracia and Timothy Noone, 154–171. Oxford: Blackwell Publishing Ltd, 2003.

Mackie, John L. "Evil and Omnipotence." *Mind* 64 (1955): 200–212.

Madec, Goulven. "L'*Hortensius* de Cicéro dans les livres XIII–XIV de *De Trinitate.*" *Revue des Études Augustiniennes* 15 (1969): 167–173.

"L'historicité des Dialogues de Cassiciacum." *Revue des Études Augustiniennes* 32 (1986): 207–231.

Markus, Robert. *Conversion and Disenchantment in Augustine's Spiritual Career.* Villanova, PA: Villanova University Press, 1989.

Marrou, Henri-Irénée. *Saint Augustin et la fin de la culture antique.* Paris: E. de Boccard, 1938.

Matthews, Gareth. *Thought's Ego in Augustine and Descartes.* Ithaca, NY: Cornell University Press, 1992.

Socratic Perplexity and the Nature of Philosophy. Oxford: Oxford University Press, 1999.

The Philosophy of Childhood. Cambridge, MA: Harvard University Press, 1994.

"Knowledge and Illumination." In *Cambridge Companion to Augustine*, edited by Eleonore Stump and Norman Kretzmann, 171–185. Cambridge: Cambridge University Press, 2001.

Augustine. Oxford: Oxford University Press, 2005.

McWilliam, Joanne. "The Cassiciacum Autobiography." *Studia Patristica* 17 (1990): 14–43.

Meister, Chad. *Evil: A Guide to the Perplexed.* London: Continuum, 2012.

Menn, Stephen. *Descartes and Augustine.* Cambridge: Cambridge University Press, 1998.

Meulenbroek, B. L. "The Historical Character of Augustine's Cassiciacum Dialogues." *Mnemosyne* 13 (1947): 203–229.

Miles, Richard. "'Let's (Not) Talk About It' Augustine and the Control of Epistolary Dialogue." In *The End of Dialogue in Antiquity*, edited by Simon Goldhill, 135–148. Oxford: Oxford University Press, 2008.

Miller, Mitchell. "Beginning the 'Longer Way'." In *Cambridge Companion to Plato's* Republic, edited by G. R. F. Ferrari. Cambridge: Cambridge University Press, 2007, 310–344.

Mosher, David. "The Argument of St. Augustine's *Contra Academicos.*" *Augustinian Studies* 12 (1981): 89–114

Mourant, John. "Augustine and the Academics." *Recherches Augustiniennes* 4 (1966): 67–96.

Neiman, Alven Michael. "The Argument of Augustine's *Contra Academicos.*" *Modern Schoolman* 59 (1982): 255–279.

Newman, Lex. "Descartes' Epistemology." In *Stanford Encyclopedia of Philosophy.* http://plato.stanford.edu/ (2014).

Obbink, Dirk. "'What All Men Believe Must Be True': Common Conceptions and *consensio omnium.*" *Oxford Studies in Ancient Philosophy* 10 (1992): 193–231.

O'Connell, Robert. *St. Augustine's Early Theory of Man.* Cambridge, MA: Harvard University Press, 1968.

Ohlmann, Desiderius. *De Sancti Augustini dialogis in Cassiciaco scriptis.* Strassburg: Argentorati, 1897.

O'Meara, Dominic. J. "Scepticism and Ineffability in Plotinus." *Phronesis* 45/3 (2000): 240–251.

O'Meara, John. "Neo-Platonism in the Conversion of Saint Augustine." *Dominican Studies* 3 (1950): 334–343.

"The Historicity of the Early Dialogues of Saint Augustine." *Vigiliae Christianae* 5 (1951): 150–178.

"Porphyry's *Philosophy from Oracles* in Eusebius' *Praeparatio Evangelica* and Augustine's Dialogues of Cassiciacum." *Recherches Augustiniennes* 6 (1969): 107–138.

Parma, Christian. Pronoia *und* Providentia: *Der Vorsehungsbegriff Plotins und Augustins.* Leiden: Brill, 1971.

Pike, Nelson. "Hume on Evil." *The Philosophical Review* 72 (1963): 180–197.

Plantinga, Alvin. "God, Evil, and the Metaphysics of Freedom." In *The Problem of Evil,* edited by Marilyn McCord Adams and Robert Merrihew Adams, 83–110. Oxford: Clarendon Press, 1990.

Pollmann, Karla and Mark Vessey. *Augustine and the Disciplines.* Oxford: Oxford University Press, 2005.

Powell, J. G. F. *Cicero the Philosopher.* Oxford: Oxford University Press, 1995.

Pucci, Joseph. *Augustine's Virgilian Retreat: Reading the* Auctores *at Cassiciacum.* Toronto: Pontifical Institute of Medieval Studies, 2014.

Rappe, Sara. "Self-Knowledge and Subjectivity in the *Enneads.*" In *Cambridge Companion to Plotinus,* edited by Lloyd Gerson, 250–274. Cambridge: Cambridge University Press, 1996.

Rief, Josef. *Der Ordobegriff des jungen Augustinus.* Paderborn: Abhandlungen zur Moraltheologie, 1962.

Rist, John. "Certainty, Belief and Understanding." In *Augustine: Ancient Thought Baptized,* 41–91. Cambridge: Cambridge University Press, 1994.

"Faith and Reason." In *Cambridge Companion to Augustine,* edited by Eleonore Stump and Norman Kretzmann, 26–39. Cambridge: Cambridge University Press, 2001.

Rowe, William. "The Problem of Evil and Some Varieties of Atheism." *American Philosophical Quarterly* 16 (1979): 335–341.

Schäfer, Christian. "*Aqua haeret:* A View on Augustine's Technique of Biographical Self-Observation in *De Ordine.*" *Index Augustiniana* 51 (2001): 65–75.

Schanzer, Danuta. "Augustine's Disciplines: *Silent diutius Musae Varronis?*" In *Augustine and the Disciplines,* edited by Karla Pollmann and Mark Vessey, 71–112. Oxford: Oxford University Press, 2005.

Schlapbach, Karin. "Ciceronisches und Neoplatonisches in den Proömien von Augustin, *Contra Academicos* 1 und 2." In *Zur Rezeption der hellenistischen Philosophie in der Spätantike,* edited by Theresa Fuhrer and Michael Ehler, 139–151. Stuttgart: Franz Steiner, 1999.

"Divination, Wissen und Autorität in Augustins Cassiciacum-Dialogen." *Museum Helveticum* 62 (2005): 84–98.

Schofield, Malcolm. "Academic Epistemology." In *Cambridge History of Hellenistic Philosophy,* edited by Keimpe Algra, Jonathan Barnes, Jaap

246

Bibliography

Mansfeld and Malcolm Schofield, 323–351. Cambridge: Cambridge University Press, 1999.

"Ciceronian Dialogue." In *The End of Dialogue in Antiquity*, edited by Simon Goldhill, 63–84. Oxford: Oxford University Press, 2008.

Scott, Dominic. *Plato's* Meno. Cambridge: Cambridge University Press, 2006.

Sedley, David. "The Motivation of Greek Scepticism." In *Skeptical Tradition*, edited by Miles Burnyeat, 9–29. Berkeley, CA: University of California Press, 1983.

Smalbrugge, Matthias S. "L'argumentation probabiliste d'Augustin." *Revue des Études Augustiniennes* 32 (1986): 41–55.

Solignac, Aimé. "Doxographies et manuels dans la formation philosophique de saint Augustin." *Recherches Augustiniennes* 1 (1958): 8–148.

Sommer, Andreas Urs. "Weltordnung und geordnetes Leben beim jungen Augustinus: Einige Bemerkungen zu *De ordine*." *Prima Philosophia* 12/3 (1999): 85–107.

Slings, Simon R. "Protreptic in Ancient Theories of Philosophical Literature." In *Greek Literary Theory after Aristotle*, edited by Jelle Abbenes, Simon Slings, Ineke Sluiter and Dirk Schenkeveld, 173–192. Amsterdam: VU University Press, 1995.

Stock, Brian. *Augustine's Inner Dialogue: The Philosophical Soliloquy in Late Antiquity*. Cambridge: Cambridge University Press, 2010.

Striker, Gisela. "On the Difference between the Pyrrhonists and the Academics." In *Essays on Hellenistic Epistemology and Ethics*, 135–149. Cambridge: Cambridge University Press, 1996.

"Sceptical Strategies." In *Essays on Hellenistic Epistemology and Ethics*, 92–115. Cambridge: Cambridge University Press, 1996.

Stump, Eleanore. *Wandering in Darkness*. Oxford: Oxford University Press, 2010.

Tarrant, Harold. "Socratic Method and Socratic Truth." In *A Companion to Socrates*, edited by Sara Ahbel-Rappe and Rachana Kamtekar, 254–272. Oxford: Oxford University Press, 2006.

TeSelle, Eugene. *Augustine the Theologian*. New York, NY: Herder and Herder, 1970.

Theiler, Willy. *Porphyrios und Augustin*. Halle: Niemeyer, 1933.

Topping, Ryan. "The Perils of Skepticism: The Moral and Educational Argument of *Contra Academicos*." *International Philosophical Quarterly* 49/3 (2009): 333–350.

St. Augustine. New York: Continuum International Publishing Group, 2010.

Happiness and Wisdom: Augustine's Early Theology of Education. Washington, DC: Catholic University of America Press, 2012.

Tornau, Christian. "*Ratio in subiecto*? The Sources of Augustine's Proof for the Immortality of the Soul in the *Soliloquia* and its defense in *De immortalitate animae*." *Phronesis* 62 (2017): 319–354.

Trout, Dennis E. "Augustine at Cassiciacum: *Otium honestum* and the Social Dimensions of Conversion." *Vigiliae Christianae* 42/2 (1988): 132–146.

Valentin, Pierre. "Un protreptique conservé de l'antiquité: le '*Contra Academicos*' de Saint Augustin." *Revue des Sciences Religieues* 43/1 (1969): 1–26.

Van der Meeren, Sophie. "La sagesse 'droit chemin de la vie': une métaphore du *Contra Academicos* relue à la lumière du protreptique philosophique." *Revue des Études Augustiniennes* 53 (2007): 81–111.

Van Fleteren, Frederick. "Authority and Reason, Faith and Understanding in the Thought of St. Augustine." *Augustinian Studies* 4 (1973): 33–71.

"The Cassiciacum Dialogues and Augustine's Ascents at Milan." *Mediaevalia* 4 (1978): 59–82.

Van Geest, Paul. "Stoic against His Will? Augustine on the Good Life in *De Beata Vita* and the *Praeceptum*." *Augustiniana* 54 (2004): 533–550.

Van Haeringen, Johann Hendrik. *De Augustini ante baptismum rusticantis operibus*. Groningen: M. de Waal, 1917.

Verhees, Jacques. "Augustins Trinitätsverständnis in den Schriften aus Cassiciacum." *Recherches Augustiniennes* 10 (1975): 45–75.

Vlastos, Gregory. "Socrates' Disavowal of Knowledge." *Philosophical Quarterly* 35 (1985): 1–31.

"The Socratic Elenchus." In *Plato*, vol. 1, edited by Gail Fine. Oxford: Oxford University Press, 1999, 36–63.

"Socrates' Disavowal of Knowledge." In *Plato*, vol. 2, edited by Gail Fine. Oxford: Oxford University Press, 1999, 64–92.

Voss, Bernd Reiner. *Der Dialog in der frühchristlichen Literatur*. Munich: W. Fink, 1970.

Wallis, R. T. "Skepticism and Neoplatonism." *Aufstieg und Niedergang der Römischen Welt* 36/2 (1987): 911–954.

Wartenberg, Thomas. *A Sneetch Is a Sneetch and Other Philosophical Discoveries*. Oxford: Wiley-Blackwell, 2013.

Big Ideas for Little Kids. New York, NY: Rowman & Littlefield, 2014.

Westernik, L., J. Trouillard and A. Segonds, trans. *Prolégomènes à la philosophie de Platon*. Paris: Les Belles Lettres, 1990.

Wetzel, James. *Augustine and the Limits of Virtue*. Cambridge: Cambridge University Press, 1992.

Wolf, Susan. "Two Levels of Pluralism." *Ethics* 102/4 (1992): 785–798,

Index